THE
FIRST
AMENDMENT

THE
FIRST
AMENDMENT

With an Introduction by Kenneth L. Karst

Selections from the
Encyclopedia of the American Constitution
Edited by
Leonard W. Levy, Kenneth L. Karst, and
Dennis J. Mahoney

MACMILLAN PUBLISHING COMPANY
NEW YORK

Collier Macmillan Canada
TORONTO

Maxwell Macmillan International
NEW YORK   OXFORD   SINGAPORE   SYDNEY

Copyright © 1986, 1990 by Macmillan Publishing Company
A Division of Macmillan, Inc.

Macmillan Publishing Company
866 Third Avenue, New York, NY 10022

Collier Macmillan Canada, Inc.
1200 Eglinton Avenue East, Suite 200, Don Mills, Ontario M3C 3N1

Library of Congress Catalog Card Number: 90–36087

Printed in the United States of America

printing number
1 2 3 4 5 6 7 8 9 10

Library of Congress Cataloging-in-Publication Data

Encyclopedia of the American Constitution. Selections
    First amendment : selections from the Encyclopedia of the American
Constitution / edited by Leonard W. Levy, Kenneth L. Karst, and
Dennis J. Mahoney.
        p.   cm.
    Includes bibliographical references.
    ISBN 0–02–917065–6
    1. Freedom of speech—United States—Dictionaries.   2. United
States—Constitution—Amendments—1st—Dictionaries.   I. Levy,
Leonard Williams, 1923–   .   II. Karst, Kenneth L.   III. Mahoney,
Dennis J.   IV. Title.   V. Title: 1st amendment.
KF4770.A68E5325   1990
342.73′023′03—dc20
[347.3022303]   90–36087
                                                                    CIP

CONTENTS

Regulation of Speech Content

Prior Restraint

Symbolic Expression

Special Problems of the Print and Broadcast Media

Freedom of Association; Rights of Government Employees

Political Parties and Elections

Religion: The Establishment Clause

Religion: The Free Exercise Clause

INTRODUCTION

On its face the First Amendment proclaims two different kinds of rights. First, the amendment prohibits any "law respecting an establishment of religion" and guarantees the free exercise of religion; second, it protects the freedoms of speech, press, assembly, and petition. Although modern commentary on the amendment customarily treats these two clusters of rights separately, the framers had sound instincts in linking them. The various clauses overlap in ways both trivial and profound.

At the simplest level of analysis of constitutional doctrine, it is a commonplace that many "free speech" cases involve religious speakers. Decisions protecting these speakers might just as well be rested on the freedom of religion. The Supreme Court's opinion in *Cantwell v. Connecticut* (1940), for example, invoked the free exercise clause as well as the freedom of speech. The advantage to liberty in resting a religious freedom decision like *Cantwell* on a free speech ground is that the case can serve as a precedent in future cases involving nonreligious speakers. Surely this awareness informed the Court's opinions in *Lovell v. Griffin* (1938) and *Cox v. New Hampshire* (1941). Both cases involved expressive activity by Jehovah's Witnesses, both decisions were rested broadly on free speech grounds, and both opinions became landmarks of the constitutional law governing "prior restraints" on speech. A more recent example is *Widmar v. Vincent* (1981), in which a student religious group successfully claimed a right of equal access to a state university's facilities. The Court's opinion, grounded on the freedom of speech, is a leading modern precedent on the rights of would-be speakers in government-controlled institutions.

To make this doctrinal point is not to say very much; any two constitutional guarantees can overlap in support of a particular litigant's claim. The important connection between the First Amendment's religion clauses and its more general freedoms of expression is functional. In protecting the expression of outsiders—especially cultural outsiders—all these guarantees serve to widen the circle of effective citizenship. This contribution is easy to see in the religion clauses, which protect not only the liberty but also the civic status of Americans who are not followers of the dominant religions. But the freedoms of speech and press also play a crucial role in promoting equal citizenship in our multi-cultural society. Persistently, throughout the nation's history, groups of people have found themselves excluded from full partici-pation on the basis of traits other than religion: race, ethnicity, sex, sexual orientation—the list need not be prolonged for the point to be clear. Part of this exclusion is the silencing of outsiders' voices.

The story is almost as old as the First Amendment itself. When the nation was still new, Congress embarked on its first major experiment in safety through repression: the Alien and Sedition Acts of 1798. It was natural for the Sedition Act, which essentially made strong criticism of the government a crime, to be packaged with the Alien Acts. The Federalists feared that aliens were engaging in "treasonable or secret machinations against the government,"[1] and sedition was seen as treasonable: "those who corrupt our opinions . . . are the most dangerous of all enemies."[2] The main victims of the Sedition Act's enforcement were foreign-born critics of the government.[3]

The 1798 laws provoked scathing criticism. Their definitive rejection by the political majority that came to power in 1800 was part of a larger political change that shaped the nation's understanding of the First Amendment. As Leonard W. Levy has shown, the freedom of the press came to be seen as forbidding a national law of seditious libel, largely through the efforts of newspaper editors who claimed the freedom of the press in their daily activities.[4] With the Sedition Act repealed, and a more liber-tarian view of press freedoms in place, few occasions arose for judicial pronouncements on the reach of the First Amendment.

The nineteenth century was a time of constitutional ferment and judicial activism, but neither the religion clauses nor the speech and press clauses received serious attention from the Supreme

---

1. J. Carey, Deportation of Aliens from the United States to Europe 37 (1931).
2. W. Preston, Aliens and Dissenters 22 (1963). The Federalists' rhetoric linked atheism with sedition, thus providing an early example of the functional overlap of the religion clauses and the freedoms of speech and press. L. Levy, The Emergence of a Free Press 288–89 (1985).
3. M. Jones, American Immigration 88 (1960).
4. L. Levy, note 2 *supra*, passim.

Court. Religious strife agitated the politics of the great cities of the North during the antebellum period, but the Bill of Rights was still interpreted to limit only Congress, not the states. During the Civil War the national government did suppress dissent that seemed to threaten its military mission, but the Union's mode of repression kept constitutional questions about speech and press freedoms out of court. The army locked the most inflammatory dissenters in stockades, Lincoln suspended the writ of habeas corpus, and that was that.

The treatment of dissenters during World War I was another matter. Congress adopted laws designed to punish interference with the war effort, and federal prosecutors brought those laws to bear on dissidents who expressed antiwar sentiments in speeches, leaflets, and newspapers. Virtually all the people prosecuted were socialists or anarchists, and many were aliens who had arrived in America just in time to encounter a particularly virulent form of xenophobia. In 1919 these cases produced the Supreme Court's first serious consideration of the First Amendment's freedoms of speech and press. With the Red Scare at its climax, the Supreme Court's affirmance of all these convictions came as no surprise. In the last of the 1919 cases, *Abrams v. United States,* Justice Holmes transformed his "clear and present danger" formula into a doctrinal test protecting the speech of political dissenters—but the test had no immediate application, for Holmes himself was writing in dissent.

From the Sedition Act to the Red Scare to the treatment of black critics of the Vietnam War, the distrust of cultural outsiders periodically has led large numbers of citizens who think of themselves as the "true" Americans to equate the outsiders' dissenting views with disloyalty. Predictably, politicians have responded to these fears by seeking to suppress the expression of dissent. A measure of a nation's self-confidence and stability is its willingness to tolerate strong criticism of what a majority may see as the very foundations of government. The toleration of this kind of expression lies at the core of the First Amendment's guarantees of speech and press freedoms.[5] Half a century after the World War I cases, when most Americans were less nervous about internal

---

5. S. Shiffrin, The First Amendment, Democracy, and Romance (forthcoming 1990).

security, the Supreme Court could express a more confident view of the First Amendment. In *Brandenburg v. Ohio* (1969) a unanimous Court reworked "clear and present danger" into a doctrine that protects the speech of political dissidents so long as they stop short of inciting imminent unlawful conduct.

One of *Brandenburg's* many ironies was that the speakers, associated with the Ku Klux Klan, benefited from the Supreme Court's new hospitality to First Amendment claims, a hospitality that owed much to the civil rights movement.[6] Above all, that movement was a stream of expressions countering Jim Crow's systematic group defamation with new self-defining messages of freedom and equal citizenship. From the sit-in demonstrations to the freedom marches, the movement's messages of liberation often took nontraditional forms, some of which fell outside the boundaries of "speech" as conventional constitutional doctrine defined it. In defending the movement's expressive freedom against political attack, the Supreme Court widened the reach of the First Amendment not just for cultural minorities but for would-be speakers generally.

Consider, for example, what the law of defamation might be without *New York Times v. Sullivan* (1964); what the freedom of association might be without *NAACP v. Alabama* (1958); what the law of legislative investigations might be without *Gibson v. Florida Legislative Investigation Committee* (1963); what the "hostile audience" doctrine might be without *Edwards v. South Carolina* (1963); or what the public forum doctrine might be without *Cox v. Louisiana* (1965).[7] In expanding the boundaries of the First Amendment's protection, the civil rights movement was carrying forward a process begun by other cultural outsiders, mainly religious minorities and foreign-born radicals. In 1965 Harry Kalven captured this historical sequence in an epigram, remarking that the preceding three decades of First Amendment issues could be summed up just by saying, "Jehovah Witnesses, Communists, Negroes."[8]

In its substantive messages, the civil rights movement chal-

---

6. H. Kalven, The Negro and the First Amendment (1965).

7. In establishing the public forum doctrine, the *Cox* decision had a mighty assist from Harry Kalven's article, The Concept of the Public Forum: Cox v. Louisiana, 1965 Supreme Court Review 1.

8. Kalven, note 6 *supra*, at 136.

lenged a pattern of group subordination. The movement's modes of expression offered a different kind of challenge, contesting the prevailing model of the freedom of expression. In that model the speech most deserving of protection was civic deliberation: citizens sitting around a table, deliberating with civility, reasoning together toward civic truth.

The civic deliberation model seems apt for a polity in which nearly all major values are shared and disagreements mainly concern ways and means. If the model has plausibility, the reason is that most Americans are members of at least some such communities, and have witnessed civic discussions in the deliberative mode. But another persistent theme in the American polity is deep cultural division. At the cultural boundaries, expression typically is not deliberative, and often is not civil. A model of the First Amendment focused on the speech of Reason is bad news for cultural outsiders.

One who assumes that the freedom of speech is designed for reasoned deliberation may find it easy to conclude that little is lost when Unreason is suppressed. And what kinds of speech are consigned to the category of Unreason? Speech that rejects the common sense of what "we all know" (where "we" are those who share the prevailing conventional wisdom), and modes of expression that go against the dominant cultural grain. For America's cultural minorities the greatest danger in a model of the freedom of expression centered on civic deliberation is that the definition of Reason—and of what counts as a reason—is largely in the hands of culturally dominant groups.

The era of the civil rights movement also saw the intensification of cultural conflict on another front. By the late 1960s the air was filled with messages challenging both traditional sexual morality and traditional views of the role of women—and the two challenges were interrelated. The birth control pill had not only weakened the grip of conventional morality but also offered women a new control over their intimate lives, a control that was already beginning to produce important changes in the status of women in American society. Cultural dominance means control over the meanings assigned to behavior. Thus, the messages of sexual freedom and women's liberation were not merely instruments in the clash of cultures but central objects of the struggle. It was a cultural revolution, and the revolutionaries had seized the transmitters.

As the cultural insurgents were mobilizing the freedoms of speech and the press, religious minorities were mobilizing the establishment clause against state-sponsored religion in the public schools and state funding of religious schools. In the 1960s the Supreme Court held unconstitutional the use of prayers or readings from the Bible as part of the public schools' classroom instruction. By 1985 the Court had applied these rulings in *Wallace v. Jaffree* to forbid an official classroom "moment of silence for meditation or voluntary prayer." During the same era the Court at first interpreted the establishment clause to forbid virtually all forms of state financial aid to religious elementary and secondary schools. Then, as the Court's personnel changed, the new majority softened those restrictions, increasingly permitting state and local governments to provide substantial aid to religious schools, particularly when the aid was channeled, as in *Mueller v. Allen* (1983), through the parents of those schools' pupils.

Throughout the past several decades the free exercise clause has been seen, both by the Justices and by the Court's commentators, as a strong protection of the freedom of religious outsiders. The doctrinal pattern was set in *Sherbert v. Verner* (1963) and *Wisconsin v. Yoder* (1971), in which the Court demanded compelling justification for laws that commanded people to engage in conduct forbidden by their religion or that conditioned state benefits on such conduct. Those decisions retain most of their doctrinal vigor today. Recently, however, the Court has been less zealous in using the establishment clause to protect religious outsiders against state sponsorship of religion. A leading case is *Lynch v. Donnelly* (1984), in which a 5–4 majority upheld the constitutionality of the City of Pawtucket's official sponsorship of a Christmas Nativity display celebrating the birth of Jesus. Ignoring the display's clear (though implicit) message of religious dominance, the majority sent its own chilling message to all Americans who are members of the hundreds of religions in this country that are not Christian.

Soon after the Supreme Court's school prayer decision, the new sexual freedoms that had come to the fore in the same decade were reflected in the Court's narrowing of the category of obscenity subject to state control. If the expansion of the First Amendment troubled religious conservatives in the 1960s, the Court's abortion decisions in the next decade galvanized them into a political movement. Among today's cultural confrontations, none is more in-flamed than the abortion controversy, a dispute inextricably con-nected with the status of women in society. Plainly, any description of the role of the Constitution in today's clashes of cultures will be incomplete without a recognition that the First Amendment is only part of the story.

Expression can be a means of cultural domination, and it can be a means of liberation. In each of these uses, often the expression that matters is not the speech of Reason; indeed, it may not be speech at all. The system of racial domination called Jim Crow was maintained in part by explicit speech but in far greater part by the messages contained in everyday behavior. More recently, the movements for women's liberation and gay liberation have been promoted by speech but even more by the behavior of individuals claiming their equal citizenship in actions that speak louder than words.[9] If anything has become clear in the quarter-century since Harry Kalven wrote of the civil rights movement's contributions to the growth of First Amendment freedoms, it is this: Our speech and press freedoms, like our freedoms of religion, must be seen in their larger social contexts if they are to be under-stood. Lee Bollinger has argued that the freedom of speech, by training us to accept "freedom for the thought we hate," serves to produce a society that is generally more tolerant of people who live on the other side of social boundaries.[10] Some may be skeptical about the power of the freedom of speech to perform this salutary function. Yet even the skeptic must agree that the speech protected by the First Amendment interacts constantly with all the assignments of meaning to behavior that add up to culture itself.

Not all expression, then, lies in the province of the First Amendment. Neither in its terms nor in its predictable judicial elaboration does the amendment protect the freedom to marry, or the freedom of access to the abortion clinic. Yet marriage, especially in today's world, is preeminently a statement about two people's self-identification and identification with each other. And

---

9. Karst, Boundaries and Reasons: Freedom of Expression and the Subordina-tion of Groups, 1990 University of Illinois Law Review 101.
10. L. Bollinger, The Tolerant Society: Freedom of Speech and Extremist Speech in America (1986).

the abortion clinic not only symbolizes women's new control over their own lives but also gives visibility to sex outside traditional marriage.[11] Both of these forms of expression threaten further erosion of a once-dominant worldview emphasizing women's domestic role. The First Amendment can be stretched into protecting some of the expressive values in activities like these, but surely their main constitutional protections lie elsewhere. Telling that story, however, would require still another collection of articles.[12]

Although the readings in this volume explore the First Amendment from its historical and doctrinal beginnings, they also highlight the explosive expansion of the amendment's reach since the 1960s. In elaborating the two religion clauses and the freedoms of speech and press, the Supreme Court in the last quarter-century has contributed to a redefinition of the polity of our multicultural society. Here, as in its more celebrated expansions of the Constitution's guarantees of liberty and equality, the Court has helped to reshape the meanings of America.

KENNETH L. KARST

---

11. R. Petchesky, Abortion and Woman's Choice: The State, Sexuality, and Reproductive Freedom 209 (1984).
12. Indeed, such a volume exists: Civil Rights and Equality: Selections from the Encyclopedia of the American Constitution (L. Levy, K. Karst, and D. Mahoney eds., 1989).

PUBLISHER'S NOTE

The essays in this volume form an overview of the history of the First Amendment, from its framing up to and including the Burger Court. They are chosen from the four-volume set of the *Encyclopedia of the American Constitution*, which Macmillan published in 1986.

In these articles the reader will find certain words, names, and court cases set in small capital letters. This cross-referencing system was used in the *Encyclopedia* to refer to separate entries on those subjects. Readers of this volume who want to find out more about these topics will want to consult the *Encyclopedia of the American Constitution* for further information. In addition, each essay has a bibliography that will aid the reader in pursuing his or her own study of the subject.

This volume is the third in a series on topics of constitutional interest. We are publishing the series to make the contents of the *Encyclopedia of the American Constitution* more readily accessible to students. Other volumes in this series treat the subjects of American constitutional history, civil rights and equality, criminal justice, and the judicial power.

ABOUT THE EDITOR

Kenneth L. Karst has been professor of law at the University of California, Los Angeles, since 1965. Mr. Karst is Associate Editor of the *Encyclopedia of the American Constitution* (Macmillan, 1986). Among his many books and articles is the recently published *Belonging to America: Equal Citizenship and the Constitution* (1989).

Overviews

FIRST AMENDMENT

Archibald Cox

The First Amendment today protects the overlapping realms of the spirit—of belief, emotion, and reason—and of political activity against intrusion by government. The amendment directly forbids federal violation of the individual's RELIGIOUS LIBERTY, freedom of expression, FREEDOM OF ASSEMBLY, and associated political liberties. The amendment indirectly forbids state violation because it is held to be incorporated into the FOURTEENTH AMENDMENT's restrictions upon the powers of the states. The body of law presently defining First Amendment liberties has been shaped not so much by the words or intent of the original sponsors as by the actors and events of much later history. The story is one of the continual expansion of individual freedom of expression, of the FREEDOM OF THE PRESS, and, until 1980, of widening SEPARATION OF CHURCH AND STATE.

The CONSTITUTIONAL CONVENTION OF 1787 saw no need to include guarantees of religious liberty, FREEDOM OF SPEECH, or other human rights. Most of the Framers believed in some such rights but supposed that the powers proposed for the new federal government were so severely limited by specific enumeration as to leave scant opportunity for either Congress or President to threaten individual liberty. The threats would come from state law and state governments. For protection against these, the Framers looked to the constitutions of the individual states. In the struggle for RATIFICATION OF THE CONSTITUTION, however, those who feared abuse of federal power exacted an undertaking that if the proposed Constitution were ratified by the states, the first Congress would be asked to propose amendments constituting a BILL OF RIGHTS. The First Amendment is thus the first and most far-reaching of the ten articles of amendment submitted by JAMES MADISON, proposed by Congress, and ratified by three-quarters of the states in 1791 solely as restrictions upon the new federal government, the powers of which were already severely limited.

The assumption that the amendment would have only a narrow function made it possible to ignore fundamental differences that would produce deep divisions more than a century later, after the amendment had been extended to the several states. The colonists held a variety of religious beliefs, though nearly all were Christian and a majority were Protestant. Whatever the limits of their tolerance back home in their respective states where one church was often dominant, they had reason to understand that the coherence of the federal union could be fixed only if the new federal government were required to respect the free exercise of religion. The men of South Carolina with their state-established religion and of Massachusetts with religion appurtenant to their state government could therefore support a prohibition against any *federal* ESTABLISHMENT OF RELIGION shoulder to shoulder with the deist THOMAS JEFFERSON and other eighteenth-century rationalists who opposed any link between church and state. Similarly, in applying ROGER WILLIAMS's vision of "the hedge or wall of separation between the garden of the church and the wilderness of the world," there was originally no need to choose between his concept of protection for the church against the encroachments of worldly society and Jefferson's concept of protection for the state against the encroachments of religion.

The conditions and political assumptions of 1791 also made it easy to guarantee "the freedom of speech or of the press" without accepting or rejecting the Blackstonian view that these guarantees bar only licensing and other previous restraints upon publication, leaving the government free to punish SEDITIOUS LIBELS and like unlawful utterances. Because the original amendment left the states unhampered in making and applying the general body of civil and criminal law, except as the people of each state might put restrictions into its own constitution, there was no need to consider how the First Amendment would affect the law of LIBEL and slander, the power of the judges to punish CONTEMPT of court, or the operation of laws punishing words and demonstrations carrying a threat to the public peace, order, or morality. Such questions could and would arise only after the First Amendment was extended to the states.

The fulcrum for extending the First Amendment to the states was set in place in 1868 by the adoption of the Fourteenth Amendment, which provides in part: ". . . nor shall any State deprive any person of life, liberty or property without DUE PROCESS OF LAW."

The effects of the new amendment upon religious and political liberty and upon freedom of expression were slow to develop. As late as 1922 the Court declared in *Prudential Insurance Co. v. Cheek* that "neither the Fourteenth Amendment nor any other provision of the Constitution of the United States imposes upon the States any restrictions about 'freedom of speech.'" Within another decade, however, the First Amendment's guarantee of freedom of expression had been incorporated into the Fourteenth by judicial interpretation. INCORPORATION of the other clauses, including the prohibition against laws "respecting an establishment of religion," followed somewhat later. Today the First Amendment restricts both state and federal governments to the same extent and in the same fashion.

Yet the historic sequence is important. Many questions of First Amendment law cannot be resolved truly in terms of the original intention because the questions could not arise while the original assumption held. Resolution of the issues was thus postponed until the middle decades of the twentieth century, an era in which liberalism, secularism, and individualism dominated American jurisprudence.

Disparate strains of thought were merged even in the writing of the First Amendment. Subsequent events, including current controversies, have poured new meaning into the words, yet the juxtaposition of the key phrases still tells a good deal about the chief strains in the philosophy underpinning and binding together guarantees of several particular rights.

The Framers put first the prohibition against any law "respecting an establishment of religion or prohibiting the free exercise thereof." The sequence attests the primacy ascribed to religion. The colonists belonged to diverse churches. Many had fled to the New World to escape religious oppression. Rigid though some might be in their own orthodoxy, probably a majority rejected the imposition of belief or the use of government to stamp out heresy. Certainly, they rejected use of federal power.

It was natural for the authors of the amendment to link "the freedom of speech, or of the press" with freedom of religious belief and worship. The one church was breaking up in late sixteenth- and seventeenth-century Britain. New faiths were emerging based upon individual study of the Holy Word. The man or woman who has discovered the road to salvation has a need, even feels a duty, to bring the gospel to others. Liberty of expression benefits more than the speaker. Suppression would deny the opportunity to hear and read the word of God, and thus to discover the road to salvation. Modern legal analysis recognizes the importance of the hearers' and readers' access to information and ideas in cases in which the author's interest lacks constitutional standing or would, if alone involved, be subject to regulation. (See LISTENERS' RIGHTS.)

Concern for a broader spiritual liberty expanded from the religious core. The thinking man or woman, the man or woman of feeling, the novelist, the poet or dramatist, and the artist, like the evangelist, can experience no greater affront to his or her humanity than denial of freedom of expression. The hearer and reader suffer violation of their spiritual liberty if they are denied access to the ideas of others. The denial thwarts the development of the human potential, the power and responsibility of choice. Although concerned chiefly with religion, John Milton stated the broader concern in *Areopagitica* (1644), the single most influential plea, known to the Framers, for unlicensed access to the printing press.

The Enlightenment gave the argument a broader, more rationalistic flavor. Thomas Jefferson and other children of the Enlightenment believed above all else in the power of reason, in the search for truth, in progress, and in the ultimate perfectibility of man. Freedom of inquiry and liberty of expression were deemed essential to the discovery and spread of truth, for only by the endless testing of debate could error be exposed, truth emerge, and men enjoy the opportunities for human progress.

After John Stuart Mill one should perhaps speak only of the ability to progress *toward truth,* and of the value of the process of searching. The compleat liberal posits that he has not reached, and probably can never reach, the ultimate truth. He hopes by constant search—by constant open debate, by trial and error—to do a little better. Meanwhile he supposes that the process of searching has inestimable value because the lessons of the search—the readiness to learn, the striving to understand the minds and hearts and needs of other men, the effort to weigh their interests with his own—exemplify the only foundation upon which men can live and grow together.

It was not chance that America's most eloquent spokesman for freedom of speech, OLIVER WENDELL HOLMES, was also a profound skeptic. Dissenting in ABRAMS V. UNITED STATES (1919), he wrote:

When men have realized that time has upset many fighting faiths, they may come to believe even more than they believe the very foundations of their own conduct that the ultimate good desired is better reached by free trade in ideas—that the best test of truth is the power of the thought to get itself accepted in the competition of the market, and that truth is the only ground upon which their wishes safely can be carried out. That at any rate is the theory of our Constitution.

On the far side of the First Amendment's guarantee of freedom of speech and of the press one finds the political rights "peaceably to assemble, and to petition the Government for a redress of grievances." (See FREEDOM OF PETITION; FREEDOM OF ASSEMBLY AND ASSOCIATION.) The juxtaposition recalls that freedom of speech and of the press have a political as well as a spiritual foundation; and that the First Amendment protects political activity as part of and in addition to the world of the spirit. American thought, especially in Supreme Court opinions, puts the greater emphasis on the political function of free expression. In GARRISON V. LOUISIANA (1964), for example, the Court explained that "speech is more than self-expression; it is the essence of self-government." ALEXANDER MEIKLEJOHN, perhaps the foremost American philosopher of freedom of expression, argued that whereas other constitutional guarantees are restrictions protecting the citizens against abuse of the powers delegated to government, the guarantees of freedom of speech and of the press hold an absolute, preferred position because they are measures adopted by the people as the ultimate rulers in order to retain control over the government, the people's legislative and executive agents. James Madison, the author of the First Amendment, expressed a similar thought in a speech in 1794. "If we advert to the nature of Republican Government, we shall find that the censorial power is in the people over the Government, and not in the Government over the people."

Despite the eloquence of Justice Holmes, most of us reject the notion that the ability of an idea to get itself accepted in free competition is the best test of its truth. Some propositions seem true or false beyond rational debate. Some false and harmful, political and religious doctrines gain wide public acceptance. Adolf Hitler's brutal theory of a "master race" is sufficient example. We tolerate such foolish and sometimes dangerous appeals not because they may prove true but because freedom of speech is indivisible. The liberty cannot be denied to some persons and extended to others. It cannot be denied to some ideas and saved for others. The reason is plain enough: no man, no committee, and surely no government, has the infinite wisdom and disinterestedness accurately and unselfishly to separate what is true from what is debatable, and both from what is false. To license one to impose his truth upon dissenters is to give the same license to all others who have, but fear to lose, power. The judgment that the risks of suppression are greater than the harm done by bad ideas rests upon faith in the ultimate good sense and decency of free people.

Constitutional law has been remarkably faithful to this philosophy in dealing with both religious and political ideas. In the prosecution of the leader of a strange religious cult for obtaining money by false pretenses, as in UNITED STATES V. BALLARD (1963), the truth or falsity of the leader's claims of miraculous religious experiences is legally irrelevant; conviction depends upon proof that the defendant did not believe his own pretenses. Similarly, although distaste for political ideology may have influenced some of the decisions in the 1920s affirming the convictions of anarchists and communists for advocacy of the overthrow of the government by force and violence, the social, political, or religious activists seeking changes that frighten or annoy all "right-minded" people receive wide protection in their resort to the SIT-INS, PICKETING, marches, mass demonstrations, coarse expletives, affronts to personal and public sensibilities, and other unorthodox vehicles that are so often their most effective means of expression. Such methods of expression may prejudice opposing public and private interests because of the time, place, or manner of communication, regardless of the content of the message; therefore, the amendment allows regulation of particular forms of expression, or of expression at a particular time or place, regardless of content, provided that the restriction protects important interests that cannot be secured by less restrictive means. The courts have typically scrutinized such restrictions, however, with an eye zealous to condemn as unconstitutional any statute or ordinance ostensibly designed to protect the public peace and order but phrased in such loose words as either to deter constitutionally protected expression or to invite discrimination by police, public prosecutors, or judges against radical "troublemakers" and other unpopular minorities. Thus, the American Nazis were secured the right to parade in uniform with swastikas in an overwhelmingly Jewish community many of whose residents had fled the Holocaust.

Distrust of official evaluation of the worth of ideas may also lie behind the decisions barring regulation of political debate in the interest of "fairness" or equality of opportunity. In BUCKLEY v. VALEO (1976), holding that the freedom of speech clause bars laws restricting the dollars that may be spent in a political campaign, the Court observed: "The concept that government may restrict the speech of some elements of our society in order to enhance the relative voice of others is wholly foreign to the First Amendment." Similarly, in MIAMI HERALD v. TOR-NILLO (1974) the Court held a state law granting a political candidate a right of space in which to reply to a newspaper's attacks upon his or her record to be unconstitutional interference with the editorial freedom of the newspaper. Only in the area of BROADCASTING has the Court thus far recognized that realization of the ideal of free competition of ideas may be irreconcilable with total freedom from regulation in an era in which the public's chief sources of ideas and information are expensive media of mass communication, which are often under monopolistic control. Federal statutes and regulations subject radio and television broadcasters to loosely defined duties to present public issues fairly and to give a degree of access to political candidates and parties.

Although only deliberately false religious or political representations fall wholly outside the First Amendment, the law is more willing to try to separate the worthless from the valuable in the field of literature and the arts. The amendment gives no protection to "obscene" publications. For many years the definition of OBSCENITY was broad enough to cover works containing individual words or short passages that would tend to excite lustful thoughts in a particularly susceptible person. This standard condemned *Lady Chatterley's Lover, An American Tragedy,* and *Black Boy.* From 1930 to 1973 the legal definition of obscenity was gradually narrowed so tightly that many jurists concluded that the First Amendment would protect the most prurient of matter unless it was "utterly without redeeming social value." After 1973 changes in the composition of the Court led to a somewhat less permissive formulation. A work is obscene if a person applying contemporary community standards would find that it appeals to the prurient interest; if it represents or describes ultimate sexual acts, excretory functions, or the genitals in a patently lewd or offensive manner; and if it lacks serious literary, artistic, political, or scientific value. YOUNG v. AMERICAN MINI THEATRES (1976) suggests that explicity sexual books and motion pictures, even when not obscene, may be regulated as to the places and perhaps the time and manner of their distribution in ways that are forbidden for other materials.

These exceptions from the principle that bars any branch of government, including the judiciary, from judging the value of ideas and sensations seem attributable partly to the emphasis that American law puts upon the political values of the First Amendment, partly to the diminishing but still traditional concern of government for public morals, and partly to the actual or supposed links between producers and distributors of commercial pornography and the criminal underworld.

So long as one is dealing with beliefs and expressions separable from conduct harmful to other individuals or the community, the essential unity of the philosophical core of the First Amendment makes it unnecessary to distinguish for legal purposes among religious beliefs, political ideologies, and other equally sincere convictions. In upholding the First Amendment privilege of Jehovah's Witnesses to refuse to join other school children in a daily salute to the United States flag, the Court pointedly refrained from specifying whether the privilege arose under the free exercise clause or the guarantee of freedom of speech: ". . . compelling the flag salute and pledge . . . invades the sphere of intellect and spirit which it is the purpose of the First Amendment to reserve from all official control." (See FLAG SALUTE CASES, 1940, 1943.) Test oaths, like particular beliefs, cannot be required for holding public office or receiving public grants. In upholding the conviction of a Mormon for POLYGAMY in REYNOLDS v. UNITED STATES (1879), despite his plea that the free exercise clause protected him in obeying his religious duty, the Supreme Court sought to erect this distinction between the realm of ideas and the world of material action into a constitutional principle: "Congress was deprived of all legislative power over mere opinion, but was left free to reach actions which were in violation of social duties or subversive of good order."

As the guarantees of the freedoms of speech and press and of free exercise of religion seek to bar hostile governmental intrusion from the realm of the spirit, so do modern interpretations of the establishment clause bar state sponsorship of, or material assistance to, religion. In the beginning religion and established churches were dominant forces in American life. Nearly all men and women were Christians; Protestants were predominant. In South Carolina the Constitution of 1778 declared the "Protestant religion to be the established religion of this State." Church and state were intertwined in Massachusetts. Where there was no official connection, both the laws and practices of government bore evidence of benevolent cooperation with the prevailing creeds. SUNDAY CLOSING LAWS were universal. Oaths were often required of state officials. Legislative sessions began with prayer. The crier in the United States

Supreme Court still begins each session by invoking divine blessing. The coinage states, "In God We Trust." Church property was and remains exempt from taxation. As public education spread, prayers and Bible-reading became the first order of each school day.

These traditional links between church and state were challenged after incorporation of the First Amendment into the Fourteenth Amendment, not only by anticlerical secularists but also by religious minorities whose members were set apart by official involvement in religious practices and who were fearful that their isolation would hamper full assimilation into all aspects of American life and might stimulate INVIDIOUS DISCRIMINATION. The Supreme Court was then forced to choose among the competing strains of religious and political philosophy whose adherents had agreed only that the federal government, but not the States, should be barred from "an establishment of religion." The majority's inclination during the years 1945–1980 toward Jefferson's strongly secular, anticlerical view of the wall of separation between church and state led to two important lines of decision.

One line bars both state and federal governments from giving direct financial aid to sectarian primary and secondary schools even though the same or greater aid is given to the public schools maintained by government. The decisions leave somewhat greater latitude not only for aid to parents but also to include religious institutions in making grants for higher education. (See GOVERNMENT AID TO SECTARIAN INSTITUTIONS.)

The second important line of decisions required discontinuance of the widespread and traditional practice of starting each day in the public schools with some form of religious exercise, such as saying an ecumenical prayer or reading from the Bible. The latter decisions provoked such emotional controversy that in the 1980s, more than two decades after the decisions were rendered, fundamentalist groups were actively pressing for legislation abolishing the Supreme Court's JURISDICTION to enforce the establishment clause in cases involving school prayer, thus leaving interpretation of the clause to the vagaries of judges in individual states. (See RELIGION IN PUBLIC SCHOOLS.)

Even though the line between the realm of the spirit and the world of material conduct subject to government regulation is fundamental to the jurisprudence of the First Amendment, the simple line between belief and conduct drawn in the polygamy cases was too inflexible to survive as a complete constitutional formula. Religious duties too often conflict with the commands of civil authority. Conversely, the public has compelling interests in the world of conduct that sometimes cannot be secured without interference with the expression of ideas.

Two cases suggest the line limiting constitutional protection for religious disobedience to the commands of the state. In WISCONSIN V.

YODER (1972) the Supreme Court held that the free exercise clause secured Amish parents the privilege of holding fourteen- and fifteen-year-old children out of high school contrary to a state compulsory attendance law but pursuant to their religious conviction that salvation requires simple life in a church community apart from the world and worldly influence. The Court's constitutional, judicial duty—the Court said—required balancing the importance of the interests served by the state law against the importance to believers of adherence to the religious practice in question. Striking such a balance, the Court held in NEGRE v. LARSEN (1971) that a faithful Roman Catholic's belief that the "unjust" nature of the war in Vietnam required him to refuse to participate did not excuse his refusal to be inducted into the armed forces.

When belief is invoked to justify otherwise unlawful conduct, it may become significant that the First Amendment speaks of the free exercise of "religion," but not of other kinds of belief held with equal sincerity. In UNITED STATES v. SEEGER (1965) the Court skirted establishment clause questions by refusing to make any distinction between the teachings of religion and other moral convictions for the purposes of the Selective Service Act. That act exempted from military service CONSCIENTIOUS OBJECTORS opposed to war in any form by reason of their "religious training and belief" and defined such belief as one "in relation to a Supreme Being involving duties superior to those arising from any human relation." A majority held that, despite the references to religion and a belief in a Supreme Being, the exemption extended "to any belief that occupies a place in the life of its possessor parallel to that filled by the orthodox belief in God of one who clearly qualifies for the exemption." In the *Yoder* case, on the other hand, the opinion of the Court by Chief Justice WARREN E. BURGER, calling upon the example of Henry D. Thoreau, stated that a "philosophical and personal" belief "does not rise to the demands of the Religion Clauses." Perhaps this declaration of orthodoxy puts an end to the question, but in an age of subjectivism it is likely to press for fuller debate and deliberation.

Where religious objectors seek exemption from laws of general application, both federal and state governments must walk a narrow line. On the one hand, the free execise clause may require exception. On the other hand, excepting religious groups from laws of general application may be an unconstitutional "establishment of religion." Here again the decisions call for ad hoc balancing of the individual and public interests affected by the particular legislative act.

The requirement of self-preservation exerts the strongest pressures upon government to violate the realm of the spirit by suppressing the publication of ideas and information. Here, as in other areas, judicial elaboration of the First Amendment has been increasingly favorable to freedom of expression.

The expansion of the freedom by interpretation began within a decade from ratification. WILLIAM BLACKSTONE had taught that the freedoms of speech and press were freedoms from PRIOR RESTRAINTS, such as licensing, and did not bar subsequent liability or punishment for unlawful words, including seditious libels. Dispute arose when Congress enacted a Sedition Act and the Federalist party then in office prosecuted the editors of journals supporting their political opponents, the Jeffersonian Republicans, for publishing false, scandalous, and malicious writings exciting the hatred of the people. (See ALIEN AND SEDITION ACTS.) Thomas Jefferson and James Madison led the attack upon the constitutionality of the Sedition Act by drafting the VIRGINIA AND KENTUCKY RESOLUTIONS declaring that the act violated the First Amendment. The lower federal courts followed the orthodox teaching of Blackstone, upheld the act, and convicted the Republican editors. Jefferson pardoned them after his election to the presidency. Still later, Congress appropriated funds to repay their fines. Events thus gave the speech and press clauses an interpretation extending the guarantees beyond mere prohibition of previous restraints. The Supreme Court subsequently ratified the teaching of history.

The modern law defining freedom of expression began to develop shortly after World War I when pacifists and socialists who made speeches and published pamphlets urging refusal to submit to conscription for the armed forces were prosecuted for such offenses as willfully obstructing the recruiting or enlistment service of the United States. In affirming the conviction in SCHENCK V. UNITED STATES (1919), Justice Holmes coined the famous CLEAR AND PRESENT DANGER test: "The question in every case is whether the words used are of such a nature as to create a clear and present danger that they will bring about the substantive evils that Congress has a right to prevent." When Justice Holmes wrote these words, they gave little protection to propaganda held subversive by dominant opinion. Speaking or circulating a paper, the Justice held, is not protected by the First Amendment if the "tendency" of the words and the intent with which they are uttered are to produce an unlawful act. Later, after Justice Holmes's sensitivity to the dangers of prosecution for words alone had been increased by the prosecution of tiny groups of anarchists and communists for holding meetings and distributing political pamphlets in time of peace, criticizing the government, and preaching its overthrow by force and violence, he and Justice LOUIS D. BRANDEIS in a series of dissenting opinions tightened their definition of "clear and present danger" and laid the emotional and philosophical foundation for the next generation's expansion of the First Amendment guarantees. Justice Brandeis's eloquent opinion in WHITNEY V. CALIFORNIA (1927) is illustrative:

Those who won our independence by revolution were not cowards. They did not fear political liberty. To courageous, self-reliant men, with confidence in the power of free and fearless reasoning applied through the processes of popular government, no danger flowing from speech can be deemed clear and present, unless the incidence of the evil apprehended is so imminent that it may befall before there is opportunity for full discussion. If there be time to expose through discussion the falsehood and fallacies, to avert the evil by the processes of education, the remedy to be applied is more speech, not enforced silence. Only an emergency can justify repression. Such must be the rule if authority is to be reconciled with freedom. Such, in my opinion, is the command of the Constitution. It is, therefore, always open to Americans to challenge a law abridging free speech and assembly by showing that there was no emergency justifying it.

Moreover, even imminent danger cannot justify resort to prohibition of these functions essential to effective democracy, unless the evil apprehended is relatively serious. . . . There must be the probability of serious injury to the state. Among freemen, the deterrents ordinarily to be applied to prevent crime are education and punishment for violations of the law, not abridgement of the rights of free speech and assembly.

In the 1920s a majority of the Justices consistently rejected the views expressed by Justices Holmes and Brandeis. GITLOW v. NEW YORK (1925) held that (1) a state, despite the First Amendment, may punish utterances inimical to the public welfare; (2) a legislative finding that a class of utterances is inimical to the public welfare will be accepted by the Court unless the finding is arbitrary or capricious; (3) the Court could not set aside as arbitrary or capricious a legislative finding that teaching the overthrow of the government by force or violence involves danger to the peace and security of the State because the spark of the utterance "may kindle a fire that, smoldering for a time, may burst into a sweeping and destructive conflagration"; and (4) the Court would not consider the kind or degree of evil threatened by a particular utterance if it fell within a class of utterances found by the legislature to be dangerous to the state.

Ironically, in the very years in which the Court was deferential to legislative restrictions upon radical political expression, the Court was going behind legislative judgment to invalidate minimum wage laws, the regulation of prices and other restrictions upon FREEDOM OF CONTRACT. Beginning in 1937, however, a philosophy of judicial self-restraint became dominant among the Justices. "We have returned to the original proposition that courts do not substitute their social and economic beliefs for the judgment of legislative bodies, who are elected to pass laws," the Court declared in FERGUSON v. SKRUPA (1963). (See JUDICIAL ACTIVISM AND JUDICIAL RESTRAINT.)

Such sweeping denigration of JUDICIAL REVIEW put civil libertarians in a dilemma. On the one hand, the need for consistency of institutional theory cautioned against activist judicial ventures even under the First Amendment. On the other hand, self-restraint would leave much CIVIL LIBERTY at the mercy of executive or legislative oppression. The only logical escape was to elevate civil liberties to a "preferred position" justifying standards of judicial review stricter than those used in judging economic regulations. The dissenting opinions by Justices Holmes and Brandeis seemed to point the way. Three rationales were offered:

(i) In a famous footnote in UNITED STATES V. CAROLENE PRODUCTS COMPANY (1938), Justice HARLAN FISKE STONE suggested that legislation restricting the dissemination of information or interfering with political activity "may be subject to more exacting judicial scrutiny . . . than most other types of legislation" where the legislation "restricts those political processes which can ordinarily be expected to bring about the repeal of undesirable legislation." The rationale fails to justify STRICT SCRUTINY in cases involving religious liberty, freedom of expression in literature, entertainment, and the arts, and other nonpolitical, personal liberties.

(ii) "Personal liberties" deserve more stringent protection than "property rights." The rationale does not explain why holding property is not a preferred "personal" liberty.

(iii) Stricter review is appropriate in applying the First Amendment, and the First when incorporated into the Fourteenth, because the guarantees of the First Amendment are more specific than the general constitutional prohibitions against deprivation of life, liberty, or property without due process of law. The difference in specificity is considerable, but its relevance is less obvious. Justice HUGO L. BLACK stood almost alone in the supposition that the language of the First Amendment could be read literally. (See ABSOLUTISM.) Perhaps the most that can be said is that the Bill of Rights marks particular spheres of human activity for which the Framers deemed it essential to provide judicially enforced protection against legislative and executive oppression. During the debate in Congress, James Madison observed: "If they [the Amendments] are incorporated into the Constitution, independent tribunals of justice will consider themselves in a peculiar manner the guardian of those rights; they will be an impenetrable bulwark against every assumption of power in the Legislative or Executive. . . ."

At bottom all the rationales assert that the ultimate protection for minorities, for spiritual liberty, and for freedom of expression, political activity, and other personal liberties comes rightfully from the judiciary. In this realm the political process, filled with arbitrary compromises and responsive, as in some degree it must be, to short-run pressures, is deemed inadequate to enforce the long-range enduring values that often bespeak a people's aspirations instead of merely reflecting their practices.

Propelled by this judicial philosophy, the Court greatly expanded the First Amendment guarantees of freedom of expression. The Court avowedly adopted the strict Holmes-Brandeis "clear and present danger" test for judging whether prosecution for a subversive utterance is justified by its proximity to activities the government has a right to prevent. The amendment bars restrictions upon the publication of information or ideas relating to public affairs because of harm which the government asserts will result from the impact of the message unless the government shows pressing necessity to avoid an immediate public disaster. The case of the Pentagon Papers (1971) illustrates the principle. (See NEW YORK TIMES v. UNITED STATES.) A consultant to the Department of Defense, cleared for access to classified information, gave copies of highly secret papers describing military operations and decision making to newspapers for publication. The Department of Justice upon instructions from the President asked the courts to enjoin publication, making strong representations that the risks of injury to national interests included "the death of the soldiers, the destruction of alliances, the greatly increased difficulty of negotiation with our enemies, the inability of our diplomats to negotiate . . . and the prolongation of the war." All the weight of these executive representations was insufficient to induce the Court to bar disclosure.

After 1940 the PREFERRED FREEDOMS theory coupled with the incorporation of the First Amendment into the Fourteenth led to Supreme Court review and invalidation or modification of many familiar state statutes and well-established COMMON LAW doctrines restricting or penalizing sundry forms of expression: libel and slander, contempt of court, obscenity, BREACH OF THE PEACE, and laws limiting access to the streets, parks, or other public places for the purposes of expression. A short reference to the law of contempt will illustrate the trend.

The interest in the impartial disposition of judicial business solely upon the evidence and arguments presented in court often conflicts with the interest in free discussion of public affairs. Newspaper editorials and like public pressures upon a judge may improperly influence or seem to influence the disposition of a pending judicial proceeding. In English and early American law such publications were enjoinable and punishable as contempt of court. Today the First Amendment is held to protect such expression. Similarly, the English law and some American decisions treated the pretrial publication of EVIDENCE as contempt of court where, as in a notorious criminal case, the publicity might reach actual or prospective jurors and serve to make it difficult to assure the accused a FAIR TRIAL and a jury verdict based solely upon the evidence presented in the court room. The Supreme Court has now set its face firmly against GAG ORDERS forbidding newspapers to print or broadcast or publicize confessions or other damaging evidence before their admissibility has been determined and they have been received in court.

The heavy emphasis that constitutional law puts upon the role of the First Amendment in the operation of representative government has led some commentators to ascribe special significance to the amendment's particular mention of "the freedom of the press" in addition to the more general guarantee of "the freedom of speech." In a crowded society, newspapers, radio, and television not only are the most effective vehicles for disseminating ideas and information but also have by far the best, if not the only, adequate resources for gathering information concerning the conduct of public affairs by the vast and omnipresent agencies of government. Starting from this premise, proponents of a "structural view" of the First Amendment argue that the special functions of the "fourth estate" entitle its members to special protection. Some of the claims to exemption from laws of general applicability have been patently excessive, such as the claims to exemption from antitrust laws, labor relations laws, and wage and hour regulation. With much greater force but scarcely greater success, the media have claimed that the First Amendment protects reporters in refusal to disclose their sources or give unpublished information to a court or GRAND JURY in compliance with the general testimonial obligation of all citizens. (See REPORTER'S PRIVILEGE.) On the other hand, the near-immunity from liability for libels upon public figures which the Court has granted to the press under the First Amendment has not yet been extended by that Court to other writers and publishers.

The words of the First Amendment move from religion to speech and press and then to the purely political rights of free assembly and petition for redress of grievances. Denials of the rights of assembly and petition have been infrequent. The express mention of a "right of the people peaceably to assemble" is also taken, however, to symbolize the much broader freedom of association that the amendment is held to secure.

The freedom of association thus far held to be protected by the First Amendment, while broad, is narrower than the freedom of individuals to associate themselves for all purposes in which they may be interested, the right debated by Thomas Hobbes and Jean-Jacques Rousseau, on one side, and, on the other side, by JOHN LOCKE. The enactment of labor relations acts securing employees the right to form, join, and assist labor unions made it unnecessary for workers to appeal to a constitutional right of freedom of association. Only the antitrust laws barring unreasonable restraints on competition impose substantial restrictions upon business combinations. In consequence, the decisional law treats association as a necessary and therefore protected incident of other First Amendment liberties: speech, political action, and religious purposes. Associations formed to provide legal services in litigation have been treated as "political" not only in the plausible instances of suits to establish civil liberties and CIVIL RIGHTS but also in the incongruous instances of actions for damages for personal injuries.

Legislative efforts to outlaw associations formed for religious or political purposes have been infrequent, except in the case of the Communist party. A decision in 1961 sustained the power of Congress to require the party to register and disclose its membership as a foreign-dominated organization dedicated to subversion of the government, but the sanctions directed at members, for example, denial of passports and employment in defense facilities, were held unconstitutional. Associations and their members have had more occasion to complain of coerced disclosure under disclosure laws and in LEGISLATIVE INVESTIGATIONS. Prima facie the First Amendment protects privacy of association. Governmentally compelled disclosure must be justified by a showing of important public purpose. Where the unpopularity of the association makes it likely that disclosure will result in reprisals, an even stronger justification may be required. Similarly, a state must justify by a strong public purpose any interference with the conduct of a religious organization's or political party's internal affairs.

Any pressure for substantial new growth in First Amendment interpretation will probably come in three areas. First, the amendment was intended and has nearly always been construed as a prohibition against active government interference. Today government has a near-monopoly upon much information essential to informed self-government. Although FREEDOM OF INFORMATION ACTS may at least partially satisfy the need, there is likely to be pressure to read into the First Amendment's explicit verbal barrier to abridgment affirmative governmental duties to provide access to official proceedings and even to supply otherwise inaccessible information in the government's possession.

Second, in the crowded modern world broadcasters, newspapers, and other media of mass communication dominate the dissemination of information and formation of public opinion. New technologies make prediction hazardous, but the concentration of control over the most influential media appears to be increasing. In this context the old assumption, that the widest dissemination of information and freest competition of ideas can be secured by forcing government to keep hands off, is open to doubt. Such questions as whether the First Amendment permits government regulation to secure fair access to the mass media and whether the amendment itself secures a right of access to media licensed by government may well multiply and intensify.

Third, the electoral influence of political advertising through the mass media, coupled with its high cost, gives great political power to the individuals and organizations that can raise and spend the largest sums of money in political campaigns. Even though decisions already rendered tend to accord political expenditures the same protection as speech, important future litigation over legislative power to limit the use and power of money in elections seems assured. (See CAMPAIGN FINANCING.)

The First Amendment secures the people of the United States greater freedom against governmental interference in the realms of the spirit, intellect, and political activity than exists in any other country. The future may bring shifts of boundary lines and emphasis. A threat to national survival could revive earlier restrictions. Generally speaking, however, the modern First Amendment appears to meet the nation's needs.

Bibliography

ABERNATHY, GLENN 1961 *The Right of Assembly and Association.* Columbia: University of South Carolina Press.

CHAFEE, ZECHARIAH, JR. 1948 *Free Speech in the United States.* Cambridge, Mass.: Harvard University Press.

COX, ARCHIBALD 1981 *Freedom of Speech in the Burger Court.* Cambridge, Mass.: Harvard University Press.

EMERSON, THOMAS I. 1970 *The System of Freedom of Expression.* New York: Random House.

HOWE, MARK DeWOLFE 1965 *The Garden and the Wilderness.* Chicago: University of Chicago Press.

KONVITZ, MILTON 1957 *Fundamental Liberties of a Free People: Religion, Speech, Press, Assembly.* Ithaca, N.Y.: Cornell University Press.

LEVY, LEONARD W. 1963 *Freedom of Speech and Press in Early American History: Legacy of Suppression.* New York: Harper & Row.

——— 1972 "No Establishment of Religion: The Original Understanding." Pages 169–224 in *Judgments: Essays in American Constitutional History.* Chicago: Quadrangle.

MEIKLEJOHN, ALEXANDER 1960 *Political Freedom: The Constitutional Powers of the People.* New York: Harper & Bros.

PFEFFER, LEO 1967 *Church, State, and Freedom.* Rev. ed. Boston: Beacon Press.

STOKES, ANSON PHELPS 1950 *Church and State in the United States.* 3 Vols. New York: Harper & Bros.

——— 1964 *Church and State in the United States.* Rev. ed., with Leo Pfeffer. New York: Harper & Row.

FREEDOM OF SPEECH

Thomas I. Emerson

Freedom of speech is guaranteed in the American Constitution by the FIRST AMENDMENT. Adopted in 1791 as the first provision of the BILL OF RIGHTS, the First Amendment reads (excluding the clauses on religion): "Congress shall make no law . . . abridging the freedom of speech, or of the press, or the right of the people peaceably to assemble, and to petition the Government for a redress of grievances." Although the provision names four specific rights—freedom of speech, FREEDOM OF THE PRESS, FREEDOM OF ASSEMBLY, and FREEDOM OF PETITION—the several guarantees have never been clearly differentiated; rather the First Amendment has been construed as guaranteeing a composite right to freedom of expression. The term "freedom of speech," therefore, in popular usuage as well as in legal doctrine, has been considered roughly coextensive with the whole of the First Amendment.

The precise intentions of the framers of the First Amendment have never been entirely clear. The debates in Congress when the amendment was proposed do not throw much light upon the subject. The right to freedom of speech derives from English law and tradition. And it is agreed that the English law of the time, following the lapse of the censorship laws at the end of the seventeenth century, did not authorize advance censorship of publication. The English law of SEDITIOUS LIBEL, however, did provide punishment, after publication, for speech that criticized the government, its policies or its officials, or tended to bring them into contempt or disrepute. These features of English law were under severe attack, both in England and in the American colonies, but whether the First Amendment was meant to abolish or change them has been a matter of dispute. Similarly, the application of the First Amendment to other aspects of free speech, such as civil libel, BLASPHEMY, OBSCENITY, and the like, remained obscure.

Passage of the ALIEN AND SEDITION ACTS in 1798, which incorporated much of the English law of seditious libel, stimulated public discussion of the meaning of the First Amendment. The constitutional issues, however, never reached the Supreme Court. Nor, despite widespread suppression of speech at certain times in our history, such as took place during the abolitionist movement, the Civil War, and the beginnings of the labor movement, did the Supreme Court have or take the occasion to address in any major way the development of First Amendment doctrine. The reason for this failure of the constitutional guarantee to be translated into legal action seems to lie partly in the fact that the Bill of Rights had been construed by the Court to apply only to action of the federal government, not to state or local governments; partly in the fact that, insofar as suppression emanated from federal sources, it was the executive not the legislature that was involved; and partly in the fact that the role of the courts in protecting CIVIL LIBERTIES had not matured to the point it has reached today.

In any event this state of affairs ended at the time of World War I. Legislation enacted by Congress in 1917 and 1918, designed to prohibit interference with the war effort, raised clear-cut issues under the First Amendment. Beginning in 1919, a series of cases challenging the wartime legislation came before the Supreme Court. These were followed by cases arising out of the Red scare of the early 1920s. In 1925, in GITLOW v. UNITED STATES, the Court accepted the argument that the First Amendment was applicable to the state and local governments as a "liberty" that could not be denied without DUE PROCESS OF LAW under the FOURTEENTH AMENDMENT. It also became clear that, while the First Amendment literally refers only to "Congress," its provisions extend not only to the legislature but to the executive and judicial branches of government as well. As the First Amendment has come to be applied to more and newer problems growing out of the operation of a modern technological society, there has developed an extensive network of principles, legal rules, implementing decisions, and institutional practices which expand and refine the constitutional guarantee.

The fundamental values underlying the concept of freedom of speech, and the functions that principle serves in a democratic society, are widely accepted. They have been summarized in the following form:

First, freedom of speech is essential to the development of the individual personality. The right to express oneself and to communicate with others is central to the realization of one's character and potentiality as a human being. Conversely, suppression of thought or opinion is an affront to a person's dignity and integrity. In this respect freedom of speech is an end in itself, not simply an instrument to attain other ends. As such it is not necessarily subordinate to other goals of the society.

Second, freedom of speech is vital to the attainment and advancement of knowledge. As John Stuart Mill pointed out, an enlightened judgment is possible only if one is willing to consider all facts and ideas, from whatever source, and to test one's conclusion against opposing views. Even speech that conveys false information or maligns ideas has value, for it compels us to retest and rethink accepted positions and thereby promotes greater understanding. From this function of free speech it follows that the right to express oneself does not depend upon whether society judges the communication to be true or false, good or bad, socially useful or harmful. All points of view, even a minority of one, are entitled to be heard. The MARKETPLACE OF IDEAS should be open to all sellers and all buyers.

Third, freedom of speech is a necessary part of our system of self-government. ALEXANDER MEIKLEJOHN, the leading exponent of this view of the First Amendment, stressed that under our Constitution, sovereignty resides in the people; in other words, the people are the masters and the government is their servant. If the people are to perform their role as sovereign and instruct their government, they must have access to all information, ideas, and points of view. This right of free speech is crucial not only in determining policy but in checking the government in its implementation of policy. The implication of this position is that the government has no authority to determine what may be said or heard by the citizens of the community. The servant cannot tell the master how to make up its mind.

Fourth, freedom of speech is vital to the process of peaceful social change. It allows ideas to be tested in advance before action is taken, it legitimizes the decision reached, and it permits adaptation to new conditions without the use of force. It does not eliminate conflict in a society, but it does direct conflict into more rational, less violent, channels. From this it follows, in the words of Justice WILLIAM J. BRENNAN in NEW YORK TIMES v. SULLIVAN (1964), that speech will often be "uninhibited, robust, and wide-open."

There is also general agreement that speech is entitled to special protection against abridgment by the state. Freedom of thought and communication are central to any system of individual rights. Most other rights of the person against the collective flow from and are dependent upon that source. Moreover, speech is considered to have less harmful effects upon the community—to be less coercive—than other forms of conduct. And, as a general proposition, the state possesses sufficient power to achieve social goals without suppressing beliefs, opinions, or communication of ideas. Hence, in constitutional terms, freedom of speech occupies a "preferred position."

One further background factor should be noted. Toleration of the speech of others does not come easily to many people, especially those in positions of power. As Justice OLIVER WENDELL HOLMES remarked in ABRAMS v. UNITED STATES (1919), "If you have no doubt of your premises or your powers and want a certain result with all your heart you naturally express your wishes in law and sweep away all opposition." Hence the pressures leading to suppression of speech are widespread and powerful in our society. The mechanisms for protecting freedom of speech, therefore, must rely heavily upon an independent judiciary, standing somewhat outside the fray, and upon the creation of legal DOCTRINES that are precise and realistic.

The principal controversies that have engaged our system of freedom of speech have concerned the formulation of these implementing rules. In general the issues have centered on two basic questions. The first is what kind of conduct is to be considered "speech" entitled to special protection under the First Amendment. The second concerns what degree of protection, or encouragement, must be given that speech under the constitutional mandate.

As to the first question—the issue of coverage—it has been argued from time to time that certain categories of speech are totally outside the purview of the First Amendment. Thus it has been contended that totalitarian and racist groups should not be permitted to advance anti-democratic ideas. The argument has been that political groups that would destroy democratic institutions if they came to power should not be entitled to take advantage of these institutions in order to promote their cause; only those who adhere to the rules of the game should be allowed to participate. Similarly it has been urged that racist speech violates the dignity and integrity of fellow persons in the community, performs no social function, and should not be tolerated in a civilized society dedicated to human rights.

While this position has been strongly urged it has not prevailed in the United States. For both theoretical and practical reasons the concept of freedom of speech has been interpreted to mean that all persons should be allowed to express their beliefs and opinions regardless of how obnoxious or "fraught with death" those ideas may be. As a matter of principle, all ideas must be open to challenge; even totalitarian and racist speech serves a useful purpose in forcing a society to defend and thereby better comprehend its own basic values. Moreover, groups that promote totalitarian or racist ideas do not operate in a political vacuum. Their speech reflects fears, grievances, or other conditions which society should be aware of and in some cases take action to deal with. Suppression of such speech simply increases hostility, diverts attention from underlying problems, and ultimately weakens the society.

In practical terms, experience has shown that it is difficult or impossible to suppress any set of ideas without endangering the whole fabric of free speech. The dividing line between totalitarian and racist speech, on the one hand, and "acceptable" speech, on the other, cannot be clearly drawn and thus is open to manipulation. The apparatus necessary to suppress a political movement—involving government investigation into beliefs and opinions, the compiling of dossiers, the employment of agents and informers—inevitably creates an atmosphere damaging freedom of all speech. Frequently actions ostensibly directed against the outlawed group are merely a pretext for harassment of unwanted political opposition. Most important, once the dike has been broken all unorthodox or minority opinion is in danger. The only safe course is to afford protection to all who wish to speak.

The Supreme Court, accepting the prevailing view, has consistently taken the position that antidemocratic forms of speech are within the coverage of the First Amendment. Thus, while upholding the conviction of the Communist party leaders under the Smith Act for advocating overthrow of the government by force and violence in DENNIS V. UNITED STATES (1951), the Court never suggested that the defendants were not entitled to the protection of the First Amendment. Likewise in BRANDEN-BURG V. OHIO (1969) racist speech by members of the Ku Klux Klan was given full First Amendment protection. The viewpoint taken by the Court was perhaps most dramatically formulated by Justice Holmes when he said in *Gitlow v. New York:* "If in the long run the beliefs expressed in proletarian dictatorship are destined to be accepted by the dominant forces of the country, the only meaning of free speech is that they should be given their chance and have their way."

It has also been contended that the coverage of the First Amendment should be limited to speech that relates to "political issues." Meiklejohn, who emphasized the role of the First Amendment in the process of self-government, advocated this interpretation, although he ultimately reached a broad definition of "political speech." Other commentators, arguing for a similar limitation, have adopted a far more restrictive concept of "political speech." The position has not, however, been accepted. For one thing, the proposed restriction has no inner logic; virtually all speech has political overtones or ramifications. In any event, there is no convincing reason for restricting the coverage of the First Amendment in this way. Speech concerned with literature, music, art, science, entertainment, ethics, and a host of other matters serves the functions sought by the First Amendment and should be equally entitled to its protection. The Supreme Court has consistently so held.

Other, narrower, categories of speech have also been said to be excluded from First Amendment coverage. In CHAPLINSKY V. NEW HAMP-SHIRE (1942) the Supreme Court observed that restrictions on speech that was obscene, profane, libelous, or involved FIGHTING WORDS had "never been thought to raise any Constitutional problem." But this OBITER DICTUM has been eroded in the course of time. Obscenity is still, in theory, excluded from First Amendment protection; but in formulating the definition of "obscenity" the Court has brought constitutional considerations back into the decision. The exception for profanity has been disregarded. The dictum concerning libel has been expressly overruled. And the "fighting words" exemption, which has been narrowly construed to apply only to face-to-face encounters, turns more on the proposition that "fighting words" are not really speech at all than upon a concept of exclusion from First Amendment protection. Thus virtually all conduct that can be considered "speech" falls within the coverage of the First Amendment.

There are certain areas of speech where, although the First Amendment is applicable, the governing rules afford somewhat less protection than in the case of speech generally. These areas include speech in military institutions, which are not structured according to democratic principles, and speech by or addressed to children, who are "not possessed of that full capacity for individual choice which is the presupposition of First Amendment guarantees." COMMERCIAL SPEECH, that is, speech concerned solely with buying or selling goods or services for a profit, was at one time excluded from First Amendment protection. It is now covered by the First Amendment but is entitled to less stringent safeguards than noncommercial speech.

The most controversial aspect of the coverage question concerns not whether conduct that is recognized as speech is exempted from First Amendment protection but what conduct is to be considered speech and what is to be held non-speech, or "action," and hence not protected by the First Amendment. The resolution of this problem poses obvious difficulties. Clearly some verbal conduct, such as words exchanged in planning a CRIMINAL CONSPIRACY, does not constitute "speech" within the intention of the First Amendment. Likewise some nonverbal conduct, such as operating a printing press, is an integral part of the speech which it is the purpose of the First Amendment to protect. Some conduct, such as PICKETING, combines elements of speech and action.

Two approaches to this dilemma are possible. One is to attempt to define "speech" or "action" in light of the values and functions served by the First Amendment. The other is to abandon any effort at a sharp definition of "speech" and to hold that any conduct containing an "expressive element" is within the coverage of the First Amendment. The advantage of the first approach is that it allows the development of more clear-cut rules for protecting conduct found to be "speech," that is, all "speech" or most "speech" could be fully protected without the need for devising elaborate qualifications difficult to apply. The advantage of the second approach is that it avoids the necessity of making refined, and in some cases unpersuasive, distinctions between "speech" and "action." The Supreme Court has, on the whole, tended to follow the second path of analysis. However, in the overwhelming majority of cases where First Amendment protection is invoked, there is no serious question but that the conduct involved is properly classified as "speech."

The second major problem in interpreting and applying the First Amendment is the determination of what degree of protection from government interference, or encouragement by government, is to be afforded "speech." Most of the controversy over the meaning of the First Amendment has involved this issue. The Supreme Court has varied its approach from time to time and no consistent or comprehensive theory has emerged. The question arises in a great variety of situations, and only a brief summary of some of the principal results is possible.

The starting point is that, as a general proposition, the government cannot prohibit or interfere with speech because it objects to the content of the communication. Legitimate government interests must be achieved by methods other than the control of speech. Thus speech that is critical of the government or its officials, that interferes with government efficiency, that makes the attainment of consensus in the society more difficult, that urges radical change, or that affects similar societal interests cannot be abridged.

Somewhat less stringent rules have been applied where the speech is of such a character as to lead to concern that it will provoke violence or other violation of a valid law. Many of the Supreme Court decisions have involved issues of this nature, and a series of legal doctrines emerged. In the earlier cases, mostly growing out of legislation designed to prevent interference with the conduct of World War I or to suppress emerging radical political parties, the Court adopted a BAD TENDENCY TEST under which any speech that had a tendency to cause a violation of law could be punished. Such a test, of course, gives very little protection to nonconforming speech. Subsequently, on the initiative of Justices Holmes and LOUIS D. BRANDEIS, the Court accepted the CLEAR AND PRESENT DANGER TEST. Under this doctrine speech could be penalized only when it created a clear and present danger of some significant evil that the government had a right to prevent. In some cases the Court has used an ad hoc BALANCING TEST, by which the interest in freedom of speech is balanced against the social interest in maintaining order. Ultimately the Court appears to have settled upon the so-called *Brandenburg* test. "[T]he constitutional guarantees of free speech and free press," the Court said in *Brandenburg v. Ohio,* "do not permit a State to forbid or proscribe advocacy of the use of force or of law violation except where such advocacy is directed to inciting or producing imminent lawless action and is likely to incite or produce such action." An approach which attempts to separate "speech" from "action" and gives full protection to speech has never appealed to a majority of the Justices. But the Court has progressively tightened the originally loose restrictions on the government's power to punish militant political rhetoric.

In recent years the question has been posed in various forms whether or not speech can be curtailed where it may cause injury to NATIONAL SECURITY. The term "national security" has never been precisely defined and could of course include virtually every aspect of national life. Generally speaking it is clear that the usual First Amendment principles apply in national security cases; the society must seek to achieve national security by methods that do not abridge freedom of speech. Nevertheless, qualifications of the general rule have been urged with increasing vigor. The chief issues have involved publication of information alleged to jeopardize national security and the conduct of intelligence agencies seeking to acquire information relating to national security matters.

The Supreme Court in NEW YORK TIMES v. UNITED STATES (1971) (the Pentagon Papers case), a landmark decision in this area, rejected attempts by the government to enjoin the *New York Times* and the *Washington Post* from publishing a secret classified history of the VIETNAM WAR obtained illicitly by a former government employee, despite government claims that publication would cause "grave and irreparable injury" to the national security. The decision rested on the ground that the government had not met the "heavy burden of showing justification for the imposition of [a PRIOR] RESTRAINT." The majority were unable to agree, however, upon a single theory of the case. Three Justices thought that an INJUNCTION against publication of information should never, or virtually never, be allowed, but others, including the dissenters, would have accepted less rigorous standards. In UNITED STATES v. UNITED STATES DISTRICT COURT (1972), another critical decision in the national security area, the Court ruled that government intelligence agencies were bound to adhere to constitutional limitations (in that case the FOURTH AMENDMENT) in gathering information pertaining to national security, but it expressed no opinion as to "the issues which may be involved with respect to activities of foreign powers or their agents." The degree to which the Supreme Court will accept claims to national security as ground for qualifying First Amendment rights thus remains uncertain.

Cases where the exercise of free-speech rights runs into conflict with other social or individual interests frequently come before the Supreme Court. Interests invoked as ground for limiting speech have included the right of an accused person to obtain a FAIR TRIAL free from prejudice caused by adverse newspaper publicity; the interest of society in assuring fair elections through regulation of contributions and expenditures in political campaigns; the patriotic interest of the community in protecting the American flag against desecration by political dissenters; the aesthetic interests of the public in maintaining certain areas free from unsightly billboards; and many others. Where the countervailing interest is an appealing one the Court has tended to apply a balancing test: individual and social interests in freedom of speech are balanced against the opposing interests at stake. Likewise, where a government regulation is ostensibly directed at some other objective but has the effect of restricting speech, as in the case of government LOYALTY-

SECURITY PROGRAMS or LEGISLATIVE INVESTIGATIONS, the balancing test is usually employed.

The balancing test has come to assume various forms. When most protective of free speech it requires that the government (1) has the burden of justifying any restriction on speech (2) by demonstrating "compelling" reasons and (3) showing that less intrusive means for advancing the government interest are not available. On the other hand, in some cases the balancing test is applied without giving any special weight to First Amendment considerations. The consequence of using a balancing test is that the outcome in any particular case is difficult to predict. Thus in BUCKLEY V. VALEO (1976) the Supreme Court held, in substance, that limitations on the amount of funds that can be contributed to a candidate in a political campaign are permissible but limitations on expenditures are not. Moreover, the balancing test is such a loose standard that, in times of stress, it might afford very little protection to freedom of speech. Thus far, however, the balances struck by the Court have given a substantial degree of support to free-speech rights.

Special rules for measuring the protection accorded speech have evolved in several areas. With respect to laws punishing obscene publications the Supreme Court, as noted above, still adheres to the theoretical position that obscenity is not covered by the First Amendment but it does take constitutional factors into account in determining whether or not a particular publication is obscene. As set forth in MILLER V. CALIFORNIA (1972), the current definition of obscenity is "(a) whether the average person, applying contemporary community standards, would find that the work, taken as a whole, appeals to the prurient interest; (b) whether the work depicts or describes, in a patently offensive way, sexual conduct specifically defined by the applicable state law; and (c) whether the work, taken as a whole, lacks serious literary, artistic, political, or scientific value." In practical application, as nearly as it can be articulated, the *Miller* test allows regulation only of "hard-core pornography."

The Supreme Court has also imposed substantive limitations upon actions for libel. Criminal libel laws have been narrowly construed and, although a GROUP LIBEL law was upheld in BEAUHARNAIS V. ILLINOIS (1952), subsequent developments have cast doubt upon the present validity of that decision. In the field of civil libel the Supreme Court held, in *New York Times v. Sullivan,* that public officials could maintain a suit for libel only when they can establish that a damaging statement about them was not only false but was made with "actual malice," that is, "with knowledge that it was false or with reckless disregard of whether it was false or not." Later the "actual malice" rule was extended to "public figures." As to others, namely "private individuals," the Court has held that the state or federal government could adopt any rule respecting libel so long as it required at least a showing of negligence on the part of the defendant. Although the Court in recent years has tended to take a narrow view of who is a "public figure," and the costs of defending libel actions frequently operate as a restraint upon speech, the curtailment of public discussion through libel laws has been somewhat held in check.

Constitutional doctrine for reconciling the right to freedom of speech with the RIGHT OF PRIVACY remains unformed. In most respects the two constitutional rights do not clash but rather supplement each other. Conflict may arise, however, at several points, such as where a communication contains information that is true, and hence is not covered by the libel laws, but relates to the intimate details of an individual's personal life that are not relevant to any issue of public concern. The scope of the constitutional right of privacy has never been clearly delineated. Nor has the Supreme Court ever held that the right of privacy prevails over the right to freedom of speech. Nevertheless the issue is a recurring one and sooner or later an accommodation between the two constitutional rights will have to be formulated.

The degree of protection afforded speech under the First Amendment may also hinge on various other factors. Where the physical facilities for communication are limited, and the government is therefore forced to allocate available facilities among those seeking to use them, the government has the power, indeed the obligation, to lay down certain conditions in order to assure that the scarce facilities will be used in the public interest. This is the situation with respect to radio and television BROADCASTING where, at least at the present time, the number of broadcast channels is limited. On this theory, government regulations such as the FAIRNESS DOCTRINE, requiring that broadcasting stations give adequate coverage to public issues and that such coverage be fair in accurately reflecting opposing views, have been upheld by the Supreme Court. Such regulatory powers, however, extend only to what might be termed a "macro level" of intervention. The government may require that a broadcasting station devote a certain proportion of its time to public interest programs, but it may not censor or determine the content of particular programs, that is, it may not exercise control at the "micro level."

Likewise special considerations enter when a person seeking to exercise rights to freedom of speech is an employee of the government or is confined in a government institution such as a mental hospital or a prison. Here the relationship of the individual to the government is somewhat different from the relationship of the ordinary citizen to the general community; the goals and interests of the particular institution involved are entitled to more immediate recognition. The Supreme Court has dealt with these issues by applying a balancing test, but the weights have been cast largely on the government side of the scales.

One further aspect of government attempts to regulate the content of speech should be noted. The letter and spirit of the EQUAL PROTECTION clause have had an important bearing upon the right to freedom of speech. The equal protection element guarantees the universality of the rules protecting the right to speak. It means that the government cannot differentiate, at least without a compelling reason, between speakers on the basis of the content of their communications. Hence if the government allows a patriotic organization to march down the main street of town it must grant equal opportunity to unpopular or radical organizations. If it grants the use of a public building for a meeting to a group of one political persuasion it must grant the same use to all political groups. This combination of the First Amendment and the equal protection clause thus helps to assure that unorthodox speech will receive the same treatment as conventional speech.

Apart from attempts to control the content of speech, government regulation has also dealt with various issues in the administration of the free speech system. Thus the requirement of a permit to hold a meeting in a public building, or to conduct a demonstration that may interfere with traffic, clearly constitutes a justifiable regulation. Likewise, a municipal ordinance may legitimately keep soundtrucks from operating in a residential area during certain hours of the night. It is frequently said that "time, place, and manner" restrictions on speech are permissible so long as they are "reasonable." Such generalizations, however, are overbroad. In many situations, "time, place, and manner" restrictions can be used to curtail freedom of speech to the same degree as content regulations. And to accord them all validity would be inconsistent with the basic premise that the right of free speech is entitled to a preferential position among competing interests. A more precise statement of the applicable legal doctrine would be to say that administrative regulations dealing with physical incompatibilities between the exercise of free speech rights and other interests are permissible. Thus government could validly allocate use of the streets between those seeking to hold a demonstration and those using the streets for passage. And the physical intrusion of noises from soundtrucks would also be subject to control. The principle for resolving such physical conflicts is not mere "reasonableness" but a fair accommodation between the competing interests.

Other legal doctrines play an important role in maintaining the system of freedom of speech. Thus the courts have held that the rules against undue VAGUENESS or OVERBREADTH in legislation or administrative regulation will be applied with special rigor where First Amendment rights are affected. And the prohibition in the Fourth Amendment against

UNREASONABLE SEARCHES and seizures is given added force when invoked
to protect freedom of speech. Perhaps the most significant supportive
doctrine of this nature is the rule against prior restraint. Attempts by
the government to prevent publication in advance, through a system
of censorship, an injunction, or similar measures, are presumptively
invalid and rarely allowed. Thus the silencing of speech before it is
uttered—a particularly effective form of suppression—is normally not
available as a method of control.

The constitutional doctrines thus far discussed have been of a negative character in that they have been directed against government interference with freedom of speech. In recent years, however, increasing
attention has been given to questions relating to the affirmative side of
the constitutional guarantee: to what extent does the First Amendment
allow or require the government to encourage or promote a more effective system of free speech? These issues are important because of growing
distortions within the system. More and more, as the mass media have
become concentrated in fewer hands and have tended to express a single
economic, social, and political point of view, the concept of a marketplace
of diverse ideas has failed to conform to original expectations. The
problems are difficult to solve because they involve using the government
to expand freedom of speech while at the same time continuing to
prohibit the government from controlling or inhibiting speech.

Not only does government itself engage in speech, for example,
through schools and libraries and the statements of officials (see GOVERN-
MENT SPEECH), but government also promotes the freedom of speech
in many ways. One of the most significant involves assuring access to
the means of communication. The courts have gone some distance in
recognizing the obligation of government to make facilities for communication available. Thus the courts have held that the streets, parks, and
other public places must be open for meetings, parades, demonstrations,
canvassing, and similar activities. Other public facilities have likewise
been considered PUBLIC FORUMS and available, to the extent compatible
with other uses, for free speech purposes. At one time the Supreme
Court ruled that SHOPPING CENTERS and malls, privately owned but open
to the public, could not exclude persons seeking to engage in speech
activities. However, the Court later withdrew from this position. A very
limited right of access to radio and television, justified by the scarcity
principle, has been upheld. On the other hand, the Court has refused
to allow a right of access to the columns of privately owned newspapers,
on the grounds that intervention of this nature would destroy the independence of the publisher. Expansion of a right of access, without jeop-
ardizing the rights of those already using the facilities of communication,
remains a critical problem, the solution to which appears to depend
more upon legislative than judicial action.

Affirmative governmental promotion of speech also takes the form of subsidies. Government contributions to educational, cultural, research, and other speech activities are widespread. Most of these subsidies have gone unchallenged in the courts. In *Buckley v. Valeo,* however, the Supreme Court did consider the constitutionality of legislation providing for the public financing of presidential election campaigns, upholding that measure upon the grounds that the use of "public money to facilitate and enlarge public discussion . . . furthers, not abridges, pertinent First Amendment values." The decision apparently accepts the basic validity of all government funding that can be found to promote public discussion. Nevertheless certain limitations on the power of government to finance nongovernment speech would seem to be clear. Thus government subsidy of religious speech would certainly be prohibited under the religion clauses of the First Amendment. And although the government would be free to choose at the "macro" level of intervention, that is, to determine the nature of the speech activity to be subsidized, it would have no power to intervene at the "micro" level, that is, to control the content of a particular communication. Likewise some rules against IN-VIDIOUS DISCRIMINATION, though giving government more leeway than when it is undertaking to regulate speech, would certainly apply. Development of these and other limiting principles, however, remains for the future.

Further support for affirmative promotion of speech rests on the constitutional doctrine of the RIGHT TO KNOW. The concept of a right to know includes not only the right of listeners and viewers to receive communications but also the right of those wishing to communicate to obtain information from the government. In earlier decisions the Supreme Court rejected right-to-know arguments that news reporters had a constitutional right to be admitted to prisons in order to observe conditions and interview inmates. But in RICHMOND NEWSPAPERS V. VIRGINIA (1980) the Court, changing directions, ruled that the public and the press could not be excluded from criminal trials, thereby holding for the first time that some right to obtain information from the government existed. How much further the Court will go in compelling the government to disclose information remains to be seen. Most likely the right of would-be speakers to obtain information from the government will continue to rest primarily upon FREEDOM OF INFORMATION and sunshine laws.

Efforts to expand and improve the system of free speech by affirmative governmental action, although they incur serious risks, remain essential to the continued vitality of the system. Major progress in this area will probably depend, however, more on legislative than judicial action.

The right to freedom of speech embodied in the First Amendment has expanded into an elaborate constitutional structure. This theoretical framework has some weaknesses. At some points it does not extend sufficient protection to speech, and at other places loosely formulated doctrine may not stand up in a crisis. On the whole, however, the legal structure provides the foundation for a workable system. The extent to which freedom of speech is actually realized in practice depends, of course, upon additional factors. The underlying political, economic, and social conditions must be favorable. Above all, freedom of speech, a sophisticated concept, must rest on public interest and understanding.

Bibliography

CHAFEE, ZECHARIAH, JR. (1920)1941 *Free Speech in the United States.* Cambridge, Mass.: Harvard University Press.

DORSEN, NORMAN; BENDER, PAUL; and NEUBORNE, BURT 1976 Emerson, Haber and Dorsen's *Political and Civil Rights in the United States,* 4th ed. Vol. 1. Boston: Little, Brown.

EMERSON, THOMAS I. 1970 *The System of Freedom of Expression.* New York: Random House.

HAIMAN, FRANKLYN S. 1981 *Speech and Law in a Free Society.* Chicago: University of Chicago Press.

HUDON, EDWARD G. 1963 *Freedom of Speech and Press in America.* Washington, D.C.: Public Affairs Press.

LEVY, LEONARD W. 1960 *Legacy of Suppression.* Cambridge, Mass.: Harvard University Press.

MEIKLEJOHN, ALEXANDER (1948)1960 *Political Freedom.* New York: Harper.

MILL, JOHN STUART 1859 *On Liberty,* R. B. McCallum, ed., London: Oxford University Press.

NIMMER, MELVILLE B. 1984 *Nimmer on Freedom of Speech.* New York: Mathew Bender.

REDISH, MARTIN H. 1984 *Freedom of Expression: A Critical Analysis.* Charlottesville, Va.: Michie Co.

FREEDOM OF THE PRESS

Thomas I. Emerson

The constitutional basis for freedom of the press in the United States is the FIRST AMENDMENT, which provides: "Congress shall make no law . . . abridging the FREEDOM OF SPEECH, or of the press, or the right of the people peaceably to assemble, and to petition the Government for a redress of grievances." In a constitutional interpretation the separate rights enumerated in the First Amendment are merged into a composite right to freedom of expression. Within this general system freedom of the press focuses on the right to publish. Originally concerned with the product of printing presses—newspapers, periodicals, books, pamphlets, and broadsides—the term "press" now includes the electronic media. In general the constitutional issues involving freedom of the press are similar to those pertaining to other aspects of freedom of expression. However, certain areas are of special interest to the press, particularly to the mass media.

Freedom of the press has its roots in English history. When printing presses were introduced into England at the end of the fifteenth century they were quickly brought under total official control. Through a series of royal proclamations, Parliamentary enactments, and Star Chamber decrees a rigid system of censorship was established. No material could be printed unless it was first approved by a state or ecclesiastical official. Further, no book could be imported or sold without a license; all printing presses were required to be registered; the number of master printers was limited; and sweeping powers to search for contraband printed matter were exercised. (See PRIOR RESTRAINT AND CENSORSHIP.)

In 1695, when the then current licensing law expired, it was not renewed and the system of advance censorship was abandoned. The laws against SEDITIOUS LIBEL remained in effect, however. Under the libel law any criticism of the government or its officials, or circulation of information that reflected adversely upon the government, regardless of truth or falsity, was punishable by severe criminal penalties. Sir WILLIAM BLACKSTONE, summarizing the English law as it existed when he published his *Commentaries* in 1769, put it in these terms: "The liberty of the press is indeed essential to the nature of a free state; but this consists in laying no *previous* restraints upon public actions, and not in freedom from censure for criminal matter when published. Every free man has an undoubted right to lay what sentiments he pleases before the public; to forbid this, is to destroy the freedom of the press; but if he publishes what is improper, mischievous or illegal, he must take the consequences of his own temerity."

Developments in the American colonies followed those in England. Censorship laws existed in some of the colonies well into the eighteenth century. Likewise, prosecutions for seditious libel were not uncommon. in both England and America, however, there was strong opposition to the seditious libel laws. Thus in the famous ZENGER'S CASE, where the publisher of a newspaper was prosecuted for printing satirical ballads reflecting upon the governor of New York and his council, the defense argued vigorously (but unsuccessfully) that truth should be a defense, and urged the jury (successfully) to give a general verdict of not guilty.

The law was in this state of flux when the First Amendment, with its guarantee of freedom of the press, was added to the Constitution in 1791. The specific intention of the Framers was never made explicit. It is generally agreed that the First Amendment was designed to make unconstitutional any system of advance censorship of the press, or "prior restraint," but its impact upon the law of seditious libel has been the subject of controversy. The latter issue was brought into sharp focus when the ALIEN AND SEDITION ACTS, which did include a modified seditious libel law, were enacted by Congress in 1798. Prosecutions under the Sedition Act were directed largely at editors of the press. The constitutionality was upheld by a number of trial judges, including some members of the Supreme Court sitting on circuit, but the issues never reached the Supreme Court. The lapse of the Alien and Sedition Acts after two years ended public attention to the problem for the time being.

For well over a century, although freedom of the press was at times not realized in practice, the constitutional issues did not come before the Supreme Court in any major decision. This situation changed abruptly after World War I as the Court confronted a series of First Amendment problems. Two of these early cases were of paramount importance for freedom of the press. In NEAR v. MINNESOTA (1931) the Court considered the validity of the so-called Minnesota Gag Law. This statute provided that any person "engaged in the business" of regularly publishing or circulating an "obscene, lewd and lascivious" or a "malicious, scandalous and defamatory" newspaper or periodical was "guilty of a nuisance," and could be enjoined from further committing or maintaining such a nuisance. The Court held that the statutory scheme constituted a "prior restraint" and hence was invalid under the First Amendment. The Court thus established as a constitutional principle the doctrine that, with some narrow exceptions, the government could not censor or otherwise prohibit a publication in advance, even though the communication might be punishable after publication in a criminal or other proceeding. In a second decision, GROSJEAN v. AMERICAN PRESS

Co. (1936), the Court struck down a Louisiana statute, passed to advance the political interest of Senator Huey Long, that imposed a two percent tax on the gross receipts of newspapers and periodicals with circulations in excess of 20,000 a week. The *Grosjean* decision assured the press that it could not be subjected to any burden, in the guise of ECONOMIC REGULATION, that was not imposed generally upon other enterprises.

In the years since *Near* and *Grosjean* an elaborate body of legal doctrine, interpreting and applying the First Amendment right to freedom of the press in a variety of situations, has emerged. Before we turn to a survey of this constitutional structure, two preliminary matters need to be considered.

First, the functions that freedom of the press performs in a democratic society are, in general, the same as those served by the system of freedom of expression as a whole. Freedom of the press enhances the opportunity to achieve individual fulfillment, advances knowledge and the search for understanding, is vital to the process of self-government, and facilitates social change by the peaceful interchange of ideas. More particularly the press has been conceived as playing a special role in informing the public and in monitoring the performance of government. Often referred to as the "fourth estate," or the fourth branch of government, an independent press is one of the principal institutions in our society that possesses the resources and the capacity to confront the government and other centers of established authority. This concept of a free press was forcefully set forth by Justice HUGO L. BLACK in his opinion in NEW YORK TIMES CO. V. UNITED STATES (1971) (the Pentagon Papers case): "In the First Amendment the Founding Fathers gave the free press the protection it must have to fulfill its essential role in our democracy. The press was to serve the governed, not the governors. The Government's power to censor the press was abolished so that the press would remain forever free to censure the Government. The press was protected so that it could bare the secrets of government and inform the people. Only a free and unrestrained press can effectively expose deception in government."

A second preliminary issue is whether the fact that the First Amendment specifically refers to freedom "of the press," in addition to "freedom of speech," means that the press is entitled to a special status, or special protection, different from that accorded other speakers. It has been suggested that the First Amendment should be so construed. Thus Justice POTTER STEWART has argued that the Framers of the Constitution intended to recognize "the organized press," that is, "the daily newspapers and other established news media," as "a fourth institution outside the Government," serving as "an additional check on the three official branches." As such an institution, he suggested, the press was entitled to enjoy not only "freedom of speech," available to all, but an additional right to "freedom of the press." Some commentators have echoed Justice Stewart's argument.

There are obvious drawbacks to according a special status to the "organized press." It is difficult to draw a line between "the press" and others seeking to communicate through the written or spoken word, such as scholars, pamphleteers, or publishers of "underground" newspapers. Nor are there persuasive reasons for affording the one greater advantages than the other. Any attempt to differentiate would merely tend to reduce the protection given the "nonorganized" publisher. In any event the Supreme Court has never accepted the distinction.

However, there are some situations where the capacities and functions of the "organized press" are taken into account. Thus where there are physical limitations on access to the sources of information, as where a courtroom has only a limited number of seats, or only a limited number of reporters can ride on the President's airplane, representatives of the "organized press" may legitimately be chosen to convey the news to the general public. Beyond this point, however, the rights of the "organized press" to freedom of expression are the same as those of any writer or speaker.

The constitutional issues that have been of most concern to the press fall into two major categories. One involves the constraints that may be placed upon the publication of material by the press. The other relates to the rights of the press in gathering information.

On the whole the press has won its battle against the law of seditious libel. The Sedition Act of 1798 has never been revived. In NEW YORK TIMES CO. V. SULLIVAN (1964) the Supreme Court, declaring that the Sedition Act violated the central meaning of the First Amendment, said: "Although the Sedition Act was never tested in this Court, the attack upon its validity has carried the day in the court of history." Many states still retain criminal libel laws upon the books, but they have been so limited by the Supreme Court as to be largely inoperative. Even vigorous attacks upon the courts for their conduct in pending cases, traditionally a sensitive matter, are not punishable unless they present a CLEAR AND PRESENT DANGER to the administration of justice. (See CONTEMPT POWER.) Only the civil libel laws impose restrictions. The result is that the press is free to criticize the government, its policies, and its officials, no matter how harsh, vituperative, or unfair such criticism may be. Likewise it is free to publish information about governmental matters, even though incorrect, subject only to civil liability for false statements knowingly or recklessly made.

The extent to which the press can be prevented from publishing material claimed to be injurious to NATIONAL SECURITY has become a matter of controversy in recent years. The issues are crucial to the operation of a democratic system. Clearly there are some areas, particularly those relating to tactical military operations, where government secrecy is justified. On the other hand, the process of self-government cannot go on unless the public is fully informed about matters pending decision. Moreover, the very concept of "national security," or "national defense," is virtually open-ended, capable of covering a vast area of crucial information. Hence any constitutional doctrine allowing the government to restrict the flow of information alleged to harm national security would be virtually without limits. In addition, claims of danger to national security can be, and have been, employed to hide incompetence, mistaken judgments, and even corruption on the part of government officials in power.

For these reasons no general statutory ban on the publication of material deemed to have an adverse effect upon national security has ever been enacted by Congress. Laws directed at traditional espionage do, of course, exist. And Congress has passed legislation, thus far untested, instituting controls in certain very narrow areas. Thus the Intelligence Identities Protection Act (1982) forbids disclosure of any information that identifies an individual as the covert agent of an agency engaged in foreign intelligence. Beyond this, however, statutory controls on freedom of the press in the national security area have never been attempted. Even during wartime, censorship of press reporting on information pertaining to military operations has taken place only on a voluntary basis.

The constitutional authority of the government to restrict the publication of national security information was considered by the Supreme Court in the Pentagon Papers case. There the government sought an INJUNCTION against the *New York Times* and the *Washington Post* to prevent the publication of a government-prepared history of United States involvement in the Vietnam War. The documents had been classified as secret but were furnished to the newspapers by a former government employee who had copied them. The government contended that publication of the Pentagon Papers would result in "grave and irreparable injury" to the United States.

The Supreme Court ruled, 6–3, that the attempt at prior restraint could not stand, concluding that the government had not met "the heavy burden of showing justification for the imposition of such a restraint." Several theories of the right of the government to prohibit the publication of national security information emerged, none of which commanded a majority of the Court. At one end of the spectrum Justices Black and WILLIAM O. DOUGLAS thought that the government possessed no power to "make laws enjoining publication of current news and abridging freedom of the press in the name of 'national security.' " Justice WILLIAM J. BRENNAN held the same view, except that he would have allowed the government to stop publication of information that "must inevitably, directly and immediately cause the occurrence of an event kindred to imperiling the safety of a transport already at sea." Justices Stewart and BYRON WHITE believed that a prior restraint was permissible if the government could demonstrate "direct, immediate, and irreparable damage to our Nation or its people," a showing they concluded had not been made in the case before them. Justice THURGOOD MARSHALL, not passing on the First Amendment issues, took the position that, in the absence of express statutory authority, the government had no power to invoke the JURISDICTION OF THE FEDERAL COURTS to prevent the publication of national security information. At the other end of the spectrum Chief Justice WARREN E. BURGER and Justices JOHN M. HARLAN and HARRY L. BLACKMUN, the dissenters, urged that the function of the judiciary in reviewing the actions of the executive branch in the area of FOREIGN AFFAIRS should be narrowly restricted and that in such situations the Court should not attempt "to redetermine for itself the probable impact of disclosure on national security."

The result in the Pentagon Papers case was a significant victory for the press. Had the decision gone the other way the road would have been open for the government to prevent publication of any material when it could plausibly assert that national security was significantly injured. Yet the failure of the Court to agree upon a constitutional doctrine to govern in national security cases left the press vulnerable in future situations. Moreover, the issues were limited to an effort by the government to impose a prior restraint. The Justices did not address the question whether, if appropriate legislation were enacted, a criminal penalty or other subsequent punishment for publication of national security information would be valid.

In two subsequent cases the Supreme Court revealed some reluctance to restrict the executive branch in its efforts to control the publication of information relating to foreign intelligence. In SNEPP v. UNITED STATES (1980) the Court upheld an injunction to enforce an agreement, which the Central Intelligence Agency required each of its employees to sign, that the employee would not publish any information or material relating to the agency, either during or after employment, without the advance approval of the agency. The Court treated the issue primarily as one of private contract law; it dealt with First Amendment questions only in a footnote, saying that the government has "a compelling interest in protecting both the secrecy of information important to our national security and the appearance of confidentiality so essential to effective operation of our foreign intelligence service." Likewise in HAIG v. AGEE (1981) the Court upheld the action of the secretary of state in revoking the passport of a former CIA employee traveling abroad, on the grounds that he was causing "serious damage to the national security [and] foreign policy of the United States" by exposing the names of undercover CIA officers and agents. The constitutional RIGHT TO TRAVEL abroad, said the majority opinion, is "subordinate to national security and foreign policy considerations," adding that [m]atters intimately related to foreign policy and national security are rarely proper subjects for judicial intervention." Unless these later decisions are limited to their somewhat unusual facts, the right of the press to publish national security information that the government wishes to keep secret could be sharply curtailed.

Civil libel laws have also been a matter of paramount concern to the press. For many years it was assumed that the First Amendment was not intended to restrict the right of any person, under COMMON LAW or statute, to bring a suit for damages to reputation arising out of false and defamatory statements. In its well-known OBITER DICTUM in CHAPLINSKY V. NEW HAMPSHIRE (1942) the Supreme Court had declared that there were "certain well-defined and narrowly limited classes of speech," including the "libelous," which had never been thought to raise any constitutional problem.

In time it became clear, however, that libel laws could be used to impair freedom of the press and other First Amendment rights. In 1964 the issue came before the Supreme Court in *New York Times Co. v. Sullivan.* In that case the commissioner of public affairs in Montgomery, Alabama, sued the *New York Times* for publication of an advertisement, paid for by a New York group called the Committee to Defend Martin Luther King, which criticized certain actions of the police in dealing with CIVIL RIGHTS activity in Montgomery. Some of the statements in the advertisement were not factually correct. The Alabama state courts, after a jury trial, awarded the police commissioner $500,000 in damages. The majority opinion of the Court, stating that "libel can claim no talismanic immunity from constitutional limitations," went on to say: "Thus we consider this case against the background of a profound national commitment to the principle that debate on public issues should be uninhibited, robust, and wide-open, and that it may well include vehement, caustic, and sometimes unpleasantly sharp attacks on government and public officials." The Court ruled that public officials could recover damages in a libel action only if they could prove that a false and defamatory statement was made with "actual malice," that is, "with knowledge that it was false or with reckless disregard of whether it was false or not." Three Justices would have gone further and given the press full protection against libel suits regardless of proof of actual malice.

The "actual malice" rule for reconciling First Amendment rights with the libel laws was extended in 1967 to suits brought by "public figures," and in 1971 to all suits involving matters "of public or general interest." At this point it appeared that, although a majority of the Supreme Court had not gone the full distance, the press did have substantial protection against harassing libel suits. Weaknesses in the press position, however, soon developed. In 1974 the Court, changing directions, held that, apart from cases involving "public officials" and "public figures," libel laws would be deemed to conform to First Amendment standards so long as they did not impose liability in the absence of negligence. Moreover, the Court greatly narrowed the definition of "public figure," holding in one case that a person convicted of contempt of court for refusing to appear before a GRAND JURY investigating espionage was not a "public figure." In addition, juries in some cases began to award large sums in damages, legal expenses skyrocketed, and the costs in time and money of defending libel suits, even where the defense was successful, often became a heavy burden. By the same token, persons or organizations without substantial resources found it difficult to finance libel actions.

Efforts to dispose of unjustified libel suits at an early stage by motions to dismiss received a setback from the Supreme Court in HERBERT V. LANDO (1979). Lieutenant Colonel Anthony Herbert brought a libel suit against Columbia Broadcasting System because of a program on "60 Minutes" which suggested that Herbert had falsely accused his superior officers of covering up war crimes. Conceding he was a "public figure" and had to show "actual malice," Herbert sought in DISCOVERY proceedings to inquire into the mental states and editorial processes of the CBS officials who were responsible for the program. The Court held that, despite the CHILLING EFFECT of such probing and the resulting protraction of libel proceedings, the right to make such inquiries was inherent in the "actual malice" rule. The result of the *Herbert* case has been to diminish substantially the value to the press of the "actual malice" doctrine.

Because of these considerations, sections of the press as well as some commentators have urged that libel laws are incompatible with the First Amendment and should be abolished, at least where matters of public interest are under discussion. The courts, however, have shown no disposition to follow this course. The solution most in accord with First Amendment principles would be to provide for a right of reply by the person aggrieved. Yet this poses other difficulties. The press argues, with considerable justification, that it would be impossible for the government to supervise and enforce an effective right of reply system without sacrificing the independence of the media in the process. Federal Communication Commission regulations now grant a limited right of reply where "personal attacks" are made over radio or television and, because of the pervasive governmental controls already in place, such regulation probably does not appreciably reduce existing freedoms of the electronic media. But any broad extension to the printed press or to other forms of communication would almost certainly be seriously inhibiting. Indeed in MIAMI HERALD PUBLISHING CO. V. TORNILLO (1974) the Supreme Court unanimously invalidated a state statute requiring a newspaper to grant equal space for a political candidate attacked in its columns to reply. Moreover, practical difficulties, such as finding a suitable forum, would greatly limit the effectiveness of any attempt to substitute a right of reply for an action for damages. Thus the tension between the libel laws and freedom of the press is likely to continue.

A similar tension exists between freedom of the press and the RIGHT OF PRIVACY. Common law and statutory actions for invasion of privacy are permitted in most states. Moreover, the Supreme Court has recognized a constitutional right of privacy, running against the government, which would seem to impose restrictions upon disclosure to the press of certain information in the government's possession. The Supreme Court has held that the publication of material already in the public domain, such as the name of a rape victim which is available from public records, cannot be prohibited. However, it has never ruled upon the broad issue whether publication of information that is true but is alleged to invade the privacy of an individual can under some circumstances be restricted. The press has expressed concern over the possibility that the right of privacy might be used to curtail its freedom to publish. If the right of privacy is not narrowly limited—and there is presently no agreement upon the scope of the right—the chilling effect upon the press could be substantial. Nevertheless, in view of the current power of the press and the relative weakness of persons seeking to preserve privacy, any danger to the independence of the press from recognition of the right of privacy would seem to be remote.

Another conflict between freedom of the press and rights of the individual arises over the publication of news relating to criminal proceedings. The administration of justice is, of course, a matter of great public concern, and the role of the press in informing the public about such matters is crucial to the maintenance of a fair and effective system of justice. In most cases no conflict arises. On the other hand press reporting of occasional sensational crimes can be of such a nature as to prejudice the right of an accused to a FAIR TRIAL guaranteed by the DUE PROCESS clause and the Sixth Amendment. (See FREE PRESS/FAIR TRIAL.)

A number of remedies are available to the courts by which fairness in criminal proceedings can be assured without imposing restrictions upon the conduct of the press. These include change of VENUE, postponement of the trial, careful selection of jurors to weed out those likely to be prejudiced by the publicity, warning instructions to the jury, sequestration of witnesses and jurors, and, as a last resort, reversing a conviction and ordering a new trial. By and large the courts have found the use of these devices adequate. In some cases, however, trial courts have issued "gag" orders prohibiting the press from printing news about crimes or excluding the press from courtrooms.

In NEBRASKA PRESS ASSOCIATION v. STUART (1976) the Supreme

Court dealt at some length with the "gag order" device. The majority opinion pointed out that the trial judge's order constituted a prior restraint, "the most serious and least tolerable infringement on First Amendment rights," but declined to hold that the press was entitled to absolute protection against all restrictive orders. The issue, the Court ruled, was whether in each case the newspaper publicity created a serious and likely danger to the fairness of the trial. And that issue in turn depended upon what was shown with respect to "(a) the nature and extent of pretrial news coverage; (b) whether other measures would be likely to mitigate the effects of unrestrained pretrial publicity; and (c) how effectively a restraining order would operate to prevent the threatened danger." The Court's ruling thus left the issue open to separate decision in each instance. The conditions laid down by the Court for issuance of a restrictive order, however, afford little room for use of that device except under rare circumstances. Three Justices urged that a prior restraint upon publication in this situation should never be allowed.

The exclusion of the press from courtrooms in criminal cases has also received the attention of the Supreme Court. Initially the Court rejected the contention that the Sixth Amendment's guarantee of a PUBLIC TRIAL entitled the press and the public to attend criminal trials, holding that the right involved was meant for the benefit of the defendant alone. Subsequently, however, in RICHMOND NEWSPAPERS, INC. v. VIRGINIA (1980) the Court recognized that the First Amendment extended some protection against exclusion from criminal trials. The Court again refused to hold that the First Amendment right was absolute, but it did not spell out the nature of any exceptions. Because it is always possible in a criminal trial for the judge to sequester the jury, few occasions for closing trials are likely to arise. On the other hand, the right of the press to attend pretrial hearings, where opportunity for sequestration does not exist, was left uncertain.

For many years the press has urged the courts to permit the use of radio, television, and photographic equipment in courtrooms. The courts have been reluctant to allow such forms of reporting. And in 1964 the Supreme Court overturned the conviction of Billie Sol Estes, accused of a notorious swindle, on the grounds that the broadcasting of parts of the trial by radio and television had been conducted in such a manner as to deprive him of a fair trial. Recently the courts have been more willing to open the courtroom to the electronic media and many of them have done so. The movement received the sanction of the Supreme Court in CHANDLER v. FLORIDA (1981) when an experimental program in Florida, which allowed broadcast and photographic coverage of trials subject to certain guidelines and under the control of the trial judge, was upheld by a unanimous vote.

The right of the press to gather news, as distinct from its right to publish the news, raises somewhat different issues. Freedom of the press implies in some degree a right to obtain information free of governmental interference. Indeed the Supreme Court in BRANZBURG v. HAYES (1972) expressly recognized that news-gathering did "qualify for First Amendment protection," saying that "without some protection for seeking out the news, freedom of the press could be eviscerated." But the limits of the constitutional right are difficult to define and remain undeveloped. The issue has arisen in three principal areas: REPORTER'S PRIVILEGE, the application of the FOURTH AMENDMENT to the press, and the right of the press to obtain information from the government.

The press has consistently asserted a right to refuse to disclose the sources of information obtained under a pledge of confidentiality—a claim known as "reporters' privilege." From the point of view of the press the right to honor a commitment to secrecy is essential to much reporting, particularly investigative reporting into organized crime, government corruption, and similar sensitive areas. On the other hand, under certain circumstances the need to obtain evidence in the possession of a reporter is also pressing, particularly where the information is necessary for defense in a criminal prosecution or to prove malice in a libel suit. Over the years the courts have generally refused to recognize the reporters' privilege, but they have attempted to avoid open conflict with the press. Reporters nevertheless continued to urge their claim, often to the point of going to jail for CONTEMPT OF COURT. A number of states have passed legislation recognizing the privilege in whole or in part, but the courts have tended to construe such statutes in a grudging manner, sometimes invoking constitutional objections.

The question whether reporters could invoke the privilege as a constitutional right under the First Amendment came before the Supreme Court in the *Branzburg* case. The reporters, who had refused to appear before grand juries, did not assert an absolute privilege but claimed they should not be compelled to give testimony unless the government demonstrated substantial grounds for believing they possessed essential information not available from other sources. The Court, in a 5–4 decision, rejected their claims. The majority opinion said that reporters had no greater claims to refuse testimony than other citizens. However, Justice LEWIS F. POWELL, whose vote was necessary to make the majority, expressed a more qualified position in a CONCURRING OPINION: "if the newsman . . . has reason to believe that his testimony implicates confidential source relationships without a legitimate need of law enforcement," the court should strike the "balance of these vital constitutional and societal interests on a case-by-case basis." In practice the courts appear to have accepted the Powell formula. Thus, although reporters cannot count on substantial constitutional protection the courts still prefer to avoid direct confrontation with the press tradition that reporters will not reveal confidential sources.

The First Amendment right to freedom of the press and the Fourth Amendment right to be secure from unreasonable SEARCHES AND SEIZURES have historically been closely linked. It was the GENERAL WARRANTS, used in America to obtain evidence of customs violations (and in England to find seditious publications), that in large part prompted the framing of the Fourth Amendment. At times the Supreme Court has recognized that Fourth Amendment protection extends with particular rigor to governmental intrusions affecting First Amendment rights. In the much discussed case of ZURCHER V. STANFORD DAILY (1978), however, the Court displayed less sympathy for the traditional position. The issue was whether the police could search the offices of a student newspaper for evidence of criminal offenses growing out of a student demonstration, or whether they should be confined to the issuance of a SUBPOENA requiring the newspaper to produce what evidence it had. Despite the vulnerability of the press to police searches tht could result in the ransacking of their news rooms, the Court by a 5–3 vote approved the warrant procedure. The press greeted the decision with strong criticism, mixed with alarm.

The third major issue with respect to operations of the press relates to the right of the press to obtain information from the government. The constitutional basis for such a claim grows out of the broader doctrine of the RIGHT TO KNOW. For many years the Supreme Court has recognized that the First Amendment embraces not only a right to communicate but also a right to receive communications. (See LISTENERS' RIGHTS.) The press has insisted that this feature of the First Amendment includes a right to have access to information in the possession of the government. Because a major purpose of the First Amendment is to facilitate the process of self-government, a strong constitutional argument can be advanced that, apart from a limited area of necessary secrecy, all material relating to operations of the government should be made available to the public. The press urged this position in a series of cases where it sought access to prisons in order to interview inmates and report on conditions inside. The Supreme Court, however, was not receptive. In rejecting the press proposals four of the Justices expressly declared in *Houchins v. KQED* (1978) that "the First and Fourteenth Amendments do not guarantee the public a right of access to informa..ion generated or controlled by government."

In 1980, in the Richmond Newspapers case, the Supreme Court shifted its position. In ruling that the press had a First Amendment right to attend criminal trials the majority relied heavily upon the right-to-know doctrine. Moreover, the concurring Justices were plainly willing to carry the right-to-know concept beyond the confines of the particular case before them. As Justice JOHN PAUL STEVENS correctly observed, the decision constituted "a watershed case": "never before has [the Court] squarely held that the acquisition of newsworthy material is entitled to any constitutional protection whatsoever." The full scope of the right to obtain information from the government remains to be seen. The development, however, is potentially one of great significance for the press.

Taken as a whole, freedom of the press in the United States rests upon a relatively firm constitutional footing. The press has not been granted any special status in the First Amendment's structure, but its general right to publish material, regardless of potential impacts on government operations or other features of the national life, has been accepted. There are some weaknesses in the position of the press. The law with respect to publication of national security information is obscure and, in its present form, poses some threat to press freedoms. The press is also vulnerable to libel suits, as the protections thought to have been afforded by the "actual malice" rule have not been altogether realized. Likewise the courts have been reluctant to assist the press in its news-gathering activities. From an overall view, however, constitutional developments have left the press in a position where it is largely free to carry out the functions and promote the values sought by the Framers of the First Amendment.

Bibliography

ANDERSON, DAVID A.   1983   The Origins of the Press Clause. *University of California at Los Angeles Law Review* 30:455–537.

BARRON, JEROME A.   1973   *Freedom of the Press for Whom?* Bloomington: Indiana University Press.

LEVY, LEONARD W., ED.   1966   *Freedom of the Press from Zenger to Jefferson.* Indianapolis: Bobbs-Merrill.

LOFTON, JOHN   1980   *The Press as Guardian of the First Amendment.* Columbia: University of South Carolina Press.

NELSON, HAROLD L., ED.   1967   *Freedom of the Press from Hamilton to the Warren Court.* Indianapolis: Bobbs-Merrill.

SCHMIDT, BENNO C., JR.   1976   *Freedom of the Press vs. Public Access.* New York: Praeger.

SIEBERT, FREDRICK SEATON   1952   *Freedom of the Press in England 1476–1776.* Urbana: University of Illinois Press.

SYMPOSIUM   1975   First Amendment and the Media. *Hastings Law Journal* 26:631–821.

FREEDOM OF ASSEMBLY AND ASSOCIATION

David Fellman

The FIRST AMENDMENT's "right of the people peaceably to assemble" and the FOURTEENTH AMENDMENT have supplied a basis for federal protection of undefined FUNDAMENTAL RIGHTS from violation by the states. In the landmark case of UNITED STATES v. CRUIKSHANK (1876), the Supreme Court, in the course of allowing some lynchers to escape federal prosecution, said by way of OBITER DICTUM that the right peaceably to assemble was an attribute of CITIZENSHIP under a free government that antedated the Constitution, and that it was a privilege of national citizenship provided that the assembly in question concerned matters relating to the national government. (See PRIVILEGES AND IMMUNITIES.)

With respect to STATE ACTION, the right of peaceable assembly is now regarded as a Fourteenth Amendment DUE PROCESS right. Thus, in DE JONGE v. OREGON (1937), the Supreme Court reversed a conviction for CRIMINAL SYNDICALISM under an Oregon statute of a man who had participated in a peaceful meeting called by the Communist party for a lawful purpose, on the grounds that the due process clause of the Fourteenth Amendment had been violated. Chief Justice CHARLES EVANS HUGHES wrote for a unanimous Court: "The right of peaceable assembly is a right cognate to those of free speech and free press and is equally fundamental," and "peaceable assembly for lawful discussion cannot be made a crime," no matter under whose auspices the meeting is held.

In addition, the rights of assembly and petition are mentioned in rather standardized language in all but two of the fifty state CONSTITUTIONS. The first such statement appeared in the North Carolina constitution of 1776, and the New Hampshire constitution of 1784 began the practice of adding the word "peaceable" to the right of assembly guarantee. Furthermore, the constitutions of Missouri, New Jersey, and New York specifically guarantee a particular form of association, the right of employees to bargain collectively through representatives of their own choosing; the North Carolina constitution forbids "secret political societies" as being "dangerous to the liberties of a free people"; and there is a declaration in the Georgia constitution, of dubious validity, that "freedom from compulsory association at all levels of public education shall be preserved inviolate."

The right of assembly, like nearly all other rights, is not and cannot be regarded as without limit. As Justice Louis D. Brandeis wrote in 1927, concurring in Whitney v. California, "although the rights of free speech and assembly are fundamental, they are not in their nature absolute. Their exercise is subject to restriction, if the particular restriction proposed is required in order to protect the State from destruction or from serious injury, political, economic or moral." The right of assembly does not protect an unlawful assembly, usually defined in American law as a gathering of three or more people for the purpose of committing acts that will give firm and courageous people in the neighborhood grounds to apprehend a breach of the peace. It must be shown that those who assembled intended to do an unlawful act or a lawful act in a violent, boisterous, or tumultuous manner. Thus the right to engage in peaceful picketing is protected by the Constitution, but picketing in a context of violence or having the purpose of achieving unlawful objectives, may be forbidden.

In American law the right of assembly extends to meetings held in such public forums as the streets and parks. This point was first spelled out in Hague v. C.I.O. (1939), extending constitutional protection to street meetings since, in the words of Justice Owen J. Roberts, streets "have immemorially been held in trust for the use of the public and, time out of mind, have been used for purposes of assembly, communicating thoughts between citizens, and discussing public questions." Public authorities may be given the power to license parades or processions on the public streets as to time, place, and manner, provided that the licensing law does not confer an arbitrary or unbridled administrative discretion upon them. (See Prior Restraint.) In addition, Justice Roberts wrote in Cantwell v. Connecticut (1940) that "When a clear and present danger of riot, disorder, interference with traffic upon the public streets, or other immediate threat to public safety, peace, or order, appears, the power of the State to prevent or punish is obvious." Thus, a leading decision has upheld the right to assemble on the grounds of a state house, but the Court has drawn the line at the picketing of a courthouse or holding a demonstration on jail grounds. The Court extended the concept of the right of assembly in Richmond Newspapers, Inc. v. Virginia (1980) by ruling invalid a state judge's order barring all members of the public and the press from the courtroom where a murder case was being tried, on the grounds that the First Amendment rights of speech, press, and assembly were violated.

Although the right of association is not mentioned specifically either in the United States Constitution or in the state constitutions, it is now recognized through judicial interpretation of various constitutional clauses, particularly those dealing with the rights of assembly and petition, the right of free press, and the privileges and immunities of citizens.

The first forthright recognition by a majority of the Supreme Court that due process embraces the right to freedom of association, as distinguished from the more limited concept of assembly, came in NAACP v. ALABAMA (1958), although the idea had been advanced in several earlier minority opinions. In the *Alabama* case, the Court unanimously held unconstitutional a statute that required the NAACP to give to the state's attorney general the names and addresses of all its members, reasoning that such compelled disclosure of affiliation could constitute an effective restraint on freedom of association. Justice JOHN MARSHALL HARLAN wrote: "Effective advocacy of both public and private points of view, particularly controversial ones, is undeniably enhanced by group association, as this Court has more than once recognized by remarking upon the close nexus between the freedoms of speech and assembly. . . . Of course, it is immaterial whether the beliefs sought to be advanced by association pertain to political, economic, religious or cultural matters, and state action which may have the effect of curtailing the freedom to associate is subject to the closest scrutiny." In later years the Supreme Court, in a series of decisions, protected the NAACP's associational rights from various forms of harassment, subtle as well as heavy-handed, by local authorities.

A leading case involving education was SHELTON v. TUCKER (1960), where the Supreme Court, by a 5–4 vote, declared unconstitutional an Arkansas statute requiring every teacher in the public schools to file annually an affidavit listing all organizations to which the teacher belonged or contributed money during the preceding five years, because disclosure of every associational tie undoubtedly impaired the teacher's right of free association. Furthermore, in HEALY v. JAMES (1972), the Court upheld the right of a student association to receive university recognition, including access to various campus facilities, even though the president of the college regarded the group's philosophy as abhorrent; the Court added that the university might lawfully require the group to agree to obey reasonable rules relating to student conduct.

The Court took an even more generous view of the right of association in GRISWOLD v. CONNECTICUT (1965), in which a state anticontraceptive statute was held unconstitutional. Justice WILLIAM O. DOUGLAS reasoned that the statute operated directly on the intimate relationship of husband and wife, thus invading the right of association broadly construed. In his opinion there was a first suggestion that although the right of association grows out of the PENUMBRA of the First Amendment, its scope is larger and extends to the marriage relationship. (See FREEDOM OF INTIMATE ASSOCIATION.)

The right of association, however vital it may be in a society committed to maximum freedom of speech and action, is not absolute but is subject to reasonable limitations required by substantial public interests.

For example, the right of workers to organize and bargain collectively through representatives of their own choosing is firmly established in statute and judge-made law. But trade unions are not free to organize or participate in SECONDARY BOYCOTTS, since Congress did not intend "to immunize labor unions who aid and abet manufacturers and traders in violating the SHERMAN ACT. . . ." (See ALLEN BRADLEY CO. v. LOCAL UNION #3, 1945.) On the other hand, the Court has ruled that a labor leader cannot be required to secure a license to give a speech soliciting new members.

The right to form or engage in the activities of POLITICAL PARTIES is protected by the constitutional right of association. "The First Amendment," the Supreme Court said in BUCKLEY v. VALEO (1976), "protects political association as well as political expression." In that case the Court upheld a federal statute imposing limitations on contributions to political parties, on the theory that the limitations were designed to prevent corruption and the appearance of corruption, and to open up the political system to candidates who lacked access to large amounts of money. In addition, the right of political association extends to members of minor parties as well as to the two major parties. Many cases hold that government may protect the right to vote in party primaries, and ensure that voters cast ballots of approximately equal weight, but the two large parties are not obliged to apportion national convention delegates among the states according to the ONE-PERSON, ONE-VOTE concept, because party strength varies from state to state, and the parties must have the freedom to operate effectively. Similarly, the Supreme Court has ruled that a national party convention is not bound by state law and state judicial power in deciding which of two slates of delegates from a state should be seated. A state does have the power to decide upon the strength a party must demonstrate in order to get a place on the election ballot, but such a statute may not impose a rigid and arbitrary formula that applies equally to sparsely settled and populous counties, and unreasonably large signature requirements will not be permitted. Furthermore, the Supreme Court has conceded that, in order to protect the integrity of the electoral process, states may require some sort of party registration during a reasonable period before a primary election is held. Similarly, a state may require that candidates for party nominations pay filing fees, but the fees must not be so excessive as to be patently exclusionary.

Finally, in the unusual case of ELROD v. BURNS (1976), a bare majority of the Court read something new into party membership by holding that in discharging persons in non-civil service positions because they were Republicans, the newly elected Democratic sheriff of Cook County was placing an unconstitutional restraint on freedom of belief and association. This ruling does not apply, however, to persons holding policymaking positions involving broad functions and goals.

Membership in the Communist party or subversive organizations has for some years posed complex issues of constitutional law. (See SUB-VERSIVE ACTIVITIES AND THE CONSTITUTION.) In AMERICAN COMMUNICA-TIONS ASSOCIATION V. DOUDS (1950), the Court upheld a section of the TAFT-HARTLEY ACT of 1947 which denied access to the facilities of the National Labor Relations Board to any union whose officers were members of the Communist party. The Court reasoned that the act validly protected INTERSTATE COMMERCE from the obstruction caused by political strikes and applied only to those who believed in the violent overthrow of the government as a concrete objective and not merely as a prophecy. Similarly, in SCALES V. UNITED STATES (1961), the Court upheld the clause in the SMITH ACT of 1940 making membership in any organization advocating the overthrow of government by force or violence (in that instance, membership in the Communist party) a criminal offense. But the Court stressed that it was reading the statute to mean that the Smith Act did not proscribe mere membership in the Communist party as such but only membership of an individual who knew of the party's unlawful purposes and specifically intended to further those purposes; the proscribed membership must be active and not nominal, passive, or merely theoretical. This construction of the Smith Act was fully consistent with the position the Court had taken in YATES V. UNITED STATES (1957). The distinction between INCITEMENT and abstract teaching was underscored by the Court in the important case of BRANDENBURG V. OHIO (1969), which held the Ohio Criminal Syndicalism Act unconstitutional. Thus, mere membership in the Communist party, without more, cannot be made a predicate for the denial of a passport, or a job in a defense facility, or of public employment. The Court has recognized that membership may be innocent, and that groups may change their positions from time to time.

Whether unions or other associations may engage the services of such regulated professionals as doctors and lawyers has been the subject of much recent litigation. Because the practice of medicine is subject to comprehensive and detailed regulation by the state under its POLICE POWER for compelling reasons, a state statute prohibiting laymen from forming CORPORATIONS for the delivery of medical care has been upheld on the theory that limiting the formation of such corporations to licensed physicians tends to preserve important doctor–patient relationships and prevents possible abuses which may result from lay control.

The constitutionality of regulation of lawyers presents more complex issues. The Supreme Court has ruled that a state may lawfully compel all lawyers in the state to belong to an integrated bar, and a state bar association may be authorized to discipline a lawyer for personally soliciting clients for pecuniary gain, although the Court ruled in BATES V. STATE BAR OF ARIZONA (1977) that a state, through its bar association, may not forbid lawyers to engage in truthful advertising of routine legal services. Furthermore, the Court held in KONIGSBERG V. STATE BAR OF CALIFORNIA (1961) that a state may refuse to admit to the practice of law a candidate who refuses to reply to questions regarding membership in the Communist party, although the Court has also ruled that there must be a showing of knowing, active membership before an applicant can be excluded on this ground.

The Supreme Court has decided that such associations as trade unions, the NAACP, and the AMERICAN CIVIL LIBERTIES UNION may employ lawyers to provide legal services for their members. In BROTHERHOOD OF RAILROAD TRAINMEN V. VIRGINIA EX REL. VIRGINIA STATE BAR (1964), the Court held that a union has an associational right to advise injured members to use the services of specific approved lawyers. Moreover, a labor union is constitutionally entitled to employ a licensed attorney on a salary basis to represent any of its members who desire his services in prosecuting workers' compensation claims. In NAACP V. BUTTON (1963), the Court upheld the right of this association to finance certain types of litigation through its own staff of lawyers. The Court noted that NAACP litigation is not a mere technique for resolving private differences but a means of achieving the lawful objective of legal equality. Similarly, the Court has affirmed the right of the American Civil Liberties Union to employ attorneys in the pursuit of its objectives.

The right of association has been explored in a wide variety of other situations. Many years ago, in WAUGH V. BOARD OF TRUSTEES OF THE UNIVERSITY OF MISSISSIPPI (1915), the Supreme Court held constitutional a Mississippi statute prohibiting Greek-letter fraternities and other secret societies in all public educational institutions of the state, on the theory that this was a reasonable moral and disciplinary regulation which the legislature might believe would save the students from harmful distraction. Several state appellate courts have sustained the validity of such regulations as applied to high schools. In NEW YORK EX REL. BRYANT V. ZIMMERMAN (1928), the Supreme Court upheld a state statute, aimed at the Ku Klux Klan, which required all secret oath-bound organizations having over twenty members to supply to a designated public official a roster of its members and a list of its officers. In NAACP V. ALABAMA (1958), holding unconstitutional a similar disclosure requirement of the NAACP, the Court noted that the *Zimmerman* decision "was based on the particular character of the Klan's activities, involving acts of unlawful intimidation and violence, which the Court assumed was before the state legislature when it enacted the statute, and of which the Court itself took judicial notice." (See COMMUNIST PARTY V. SUBVERSIVE ACTIVITIES CONTROL BOARD, 1961.) On the other hand, in LANZETTA V. NEW JERSEY (1939), the Court ruled unconstitutional a state statute that purported to make it illegal to associate with gangsters, on the ground that the key words in the statute were so vague, indefinite, and uncertain that it lacked the specificity required of penal enactments.

Although the right of association as such is not mentioned in the Constitution, it holds a firm, indeed expanding, place in American constitutional law. This right is partly an emanation from the First Amendment's cognate guarantees of freedom of speech and assembly, partly a privilege or immunity of citizenship, and partly a by-product of democratic voting and representative government. However the right of association is tied to the text of the Constitution, it is regarded by the judges as such a fundamental right that doubts are resolved in favor of protecting the right of association from governmental restraints.

Bibliography

ABERNATHY, GLEN 1961 *The Right of Assembly and Association.* Columbia: University of South Carolina Press.

FELLMAN, DAVID 1963 *The Constitutional Right of Association.* Chicago: University of Chicago Press.

HORN, ROBERT A. 1956 *Groups and the Constitution.* Stanford, Calif.: Stanford University Press.

KALVEN, HARRY, JR. 1965 The Concept of the Public Forum. *Supreme Court Review* 1965:1–32.

RAGGI, REENA 1977 An Independent Right to Freedom of Association. *Harvard Civil Rights-Civil Liberties Law Review* 12:1–30.

MARKETPLACE OF IDEAS

Steven Shiffrin

The "marketplace of ideas" argument in FIRST AMENDMENT jurisprudence was first enunciated in Justice OLIVER WENDELL HOLMES's dissenting opinion in ABRAMS v. UNITED STATES (1919):

But when men have realized that time has upset many fighting faiths, they may come to believe even more than they believe the very foundations of their own conduct that the ultimate good desired is better reached by free trade in ideas—that the best test of truth is the power of thought to get itself accepted in the competition of the market, and that truth is the only ground upon which their wishes safely can be carried out. That at any rate is the theory of our Constitution. It is an experiment, as all life is an experiment. . . . While that experiment is part of our system I think that we should be eternally vigilant against attempts to check the expression of opinions that we loathe and believe to be fraught with death, unless they so imminently threaten immediate interference with the lawful and pressing purpose of the law that an immediate check is required to save the country.

Holmes's stirring words recall similar but distinct passages from John Milton and John Stuart Mill. Extravagant as Holmes's passage is, it is in significant respects more careful than the implications of Milton's rhetorical question: "[W]ho ever knew truth put to the worse, in a free and open encounter?" Holmes did not claim that truth always or even usually emerges in the marketplace of ideas. Holmes's claim was more confined—that the best test of truth is the competition of the marketplace.

On the other hand, Milton spoke of a free and open encounter; Holmes spoke of the competition of the marketplace. A recurrent problem in First Amendment cases is that these two notions are not the same. Those who seek access to the broadcast media, as in RED LION BROADCASTING v. FCC (1969), or to powerful newspapers, as in MIAMI HERALD PUBLISHING CO. v. TORNILLO (1974), argue that the competition of the marketplace is not free and open. They urge that truth cannot emerge in the market if the gatekeepers do not let it in. A more general criticism of the Holmes position is that the claim that the marketplace is the best test of truth cannot itself be tested without an independent test of truth, yet the argument by its terms denies any superior test of truth that is independent of the marketplace.

These criticisms aside, the question arises whether the marketplace argument overvalues truth. Holmes's view that the expression of opinion should be free until an immediate check is needed to "save the country" has never been adopted by the Supreme Court. Advocacy of illegal action, for example, may be restricted when it is directed to and likely to incite or produce imminent lawless action, whether or not the country itself is endangered. Indeed, if the marketplace argument extends to facts as well as opinions, it is clear that showings far more pedestrian than Holmes's proposed requirements are sufficient to justify repression. The expression of factual beliefs can be restricted in order to protect reputation or privacy, and, in the commercial sphere, to further any substantial government interest.

Nonetheless, the marketplace argument has been a powerful theme in First Amendment law. For example, some defamatory facts and all defamatory opinion are protected in order to guarantee the breathing space we need for robust, uninhibited, and wide-open debate. Ironically, however, the marketplace argument serves to restrict speech as well as to protect it. "Under our Constitution," said the Court in GERTZ v. ROBERT WELCH, INC. (1974), "there is no such thing as a false idea," yet obscenity is divorced from speech protection because it is thought to be unnecessary for the expression of any idea. At bottom, First Amendment methodology is grounded in a paradox. Government must be restrained from imposing its views of truth. But government itself determines when this principle has been abandoned.

Bibliography

SCHAUER, FREDERICK   1978   Language, Truth and the First Amendment: An Essay in Memory of Harry Canter. *Virginia Law Review* 64:263, 268–272.

ACADEMIC FREEDOM

David M. Rabban

Although academic freedom has become a First Amendment principle of special importance, its content and theoretical underpinnings have barely been defined. Most alleged violations of academic freedom can be sorted into three catagories: claims of individual professors against the state, claims of individual professors against the university administration or governing board, and claims of universities against the state. Judicial decisions have upheld claims in all three contexts.

The Supreme Court, however, has not developed a comprehensive theory of academic freedom comparable to its recent elaboration of freedom of association as a distinctive First Amendment doctrine. The relationship between "individual" and "institutional" academic freedom has not been clarified. Nor has the Supreme Court decided whether academic freedom is a separate principle, with its own constitutional contours justified by the unique roles of professors and universities in society, or whether it highlights but is essentially coextensive with the general First Amendment rights of all citizens. Similarly unsettled is the applicability, if any, of academic freedom in primary and secondary schools. While acknowledging that teachers, unlike university professors, are expected to inculcate societal values in their students, the Supreme Court in Board of Education v. Pico (1982) expressed concern about laws that "cast a pall of orthodoxy" over school as well as university classrooms. Student claims of academic freedom also remain unresolved.

This uncertainty about the constitutional definition of academic freedom contrasts with the internal understanding of the university community, which had elaborated its meaning before any court addressed its legal or constitutional significance. The modern American conception of academic freedom arose during the late nineteenth and early twentieth centuries, when the emerging research university eclipsed the religious college as the model institution of higher education. This structural change reflected an equally profound transformation of educational goals from conserving to searching for truth.

Academic freedom became associated with the search for truth and began to define the very idea of the university. Its content developed under the influence of Darwinism and the German university. The followers of Charles Darwin maintained that all beliefs are subject to the tests of inquiry and that apparent errors must be tolerated, and even expected, in the continuous search for truth. The German academic influence reinforced the growing secular tendencies in the United States. Many attributed the international preeminence of German universities to their traditions of academic freedom. As universities in the United States strove for similar excellence, they adapted these traditions.

This adaptation produced several major changes. The clear German differentiation between great freedom for faculty members within the university and little protection for any citizen outside it did not take hold in America. The ideal of FREEDOM OF SPEECH, including its constitutional expression in the First Amendment, and the philosophy of pragmatism, which encouraged the participation of all citizens in social and political life, prompted American professors to view academic freedom as an aspect of more general CIVIL LIBERTIES. The traditions of powerful administrators and lay boards of governors in American universities posed threats to academic freedom that did not exist in Germany, where universities were largely governed by their faculties. As a result, American professors sought freedom from university authorities as well as from external interference. And academic freedom, which in Germany encompassed freedom for both students and professors, became limited to professors in the United States.

The first major codification of the American conception of academic freedom was produced in 1915 by a committee of the nascent American Association of University Professors (AAUP). Subsequent revisions culminated in the 1940 *Statement of Principles on Academic Freedom and Tenure,* jointly sponsored by the AAUP and the Association of American Colleges, and currently endorsed by over 100 educational organizations. The 1940 *Statement* defines three aspects of academic freedom: freedom in research and publication, freedom in the classroom, and freedom from institutional censorship or discipline when a professor speaks or writes as a citizen. Many colleges and universities have incorporated the 1940 *Statement* into their governing documents. In cases involving the contractual relationship between professors and universities, courts have recently begun to cite it as the COMMON LAW of the academic profession. This contractual theory has provided substantial legal protection for academic freedom without the support of the First Amendment, whose applicability to private universities is limited by the doctrine of STATE ACTION.

The emergence of academic freedom as a constitutional principle did not begin until the McCarthy era of the 1950s, when public and university officials throughout the country challenged and investigated the loyalty of professors. Although earlier decisions had imposed some limitations on governmental intrusions into universities and schools, no Supreme Court opinion explicitly referred to academic freedom until Justice WILLIAM O. DOUGLAS, dissenting in ADLER v. BOARD OF EDUCATION (1952), claimed that it is contained within the First Amendment.

The Supreme Court endorsed this identification of academic freedom with the First Amendment in SWEEZY v. NEW HAMPSHIRE (1957), which reversed the contempt conviction of a Marxist scholar who had refused to answer questions from the state attorney general regarding his political opinions and the contents of his university lecture. A plurality of the Justices concluded that the state had invaded the lecturer's "liberties in the areas of academic freedom and political expression." Both the plurality and concurring opinions in *Sweezy* emphasized the importance to a free society of the search for knowledge within free universities and warned against governmental interference in university life. Justice FELIX FRANKFURTER's concurrence included a particularly influential reference to academic freedom that has often been cited in subsequent decisions. Quoting from a plea by South African scholars for open universities, Frankfurter identified " 'the four essential freedoms of a university'—to determine for itself on academic grounds who may teach, what may be taught, how it shall be taught, and who may be admitted to study."

The opinions in *Sweezy* indicated that academic freedom and political expression are distinct yet related liberties, and that society benefits from the academic freedom of professors as individuals and of universities as institutions. Yet neither in *Sweezy* nor in subsequent decisions did the Supreme Court untangle and clarify these complex relationships. Throughout the 1950s, it alluded only intermittently to academic freedom in cases involving investigations of university professors, and reference to this term did not necessarily lead to protective results. Even the votes and reasoning of individual Justices fluctuated unpredictably. During this period, many within the academic community resisted the advocacy of academic freedom as a constitutional principle, fearing that a judicial definition might both weaken and preempt the one contained in the 1940 *Statement* and widely accepted throughout American universities.

Supreme Court opinions since the 1950s have emphasized that academic freedom is a "transcendent value" and "a special concern of the First Amendment," as the majority observed in KEYISHIAN v. BOARD OF REGENTS (1967). Justice LEWIS F. POWELL's opinion in REGENTS OF THE UNIVERSITY OF CALIFORNIA v. BAKKE (1978) reiterated the university's academic freedom to select its student body, but the Court has held in MINNESOTA STATE BOARD FOR COMMUNITY COLLEGES v. KNIGHT (1984) that academic freedom does not include the right of individual faculty members to participate in institutional governance. By eliminating the RIGHT-PRIVILEGE DISTINCTION, which had allowed dismissal of PUBLIC EMPLOYEES for speech otherwise protected by the First Amendment, the Supreme Court during the 1960s and 1970s dramatically expanded the rights of all public employees, including university professors, to speak in ways that criticize or offend their employers. Yet none of these decisions has refined the relationships between "individual" and "institutional" academic freedom or between "academic freedom" and "political expression," issues posed but not resolved in *Sweezy*. The Supreme Court's continuing reluctance even to recognize issues of academic freedom in cases decided on other grounds underlines the primitive constitutional definition of this term.

Cases since the early 1970s have raised novel issues of academic freedom. University administrators and governing boards have asserted the academic freedom of the university as an institution to resist JUDICIAL REVIEW of their internal policies and practices, which have been challenged by government agencies seeking to enforce CIVIL RIGHTS laws and other statutes of general applicability, by citizens claiming rights to freedom of expression on university property, and by professors maintaining that the university violated their own academic freedom or their statutory protection against employment discrimination. Faculty members have even begun to make contradictory claims of academic freedom against each other. Professors have relied on academic freedom to seek a constitutionally based privilege against compelled disclosure of their deliberations and votes on faculty committees to junior colleagues who want this information to determine whether they were denied reappointment or tenure for impermissible reasons, including reasons that might violate their academic freedom. These difficult issues may force the courts to address more directly the meaning and scope of academic freedom and to resolve many of the lingering ambiguities of previous decisions.

Bibliography

HOFSTADTER, RICHARD and METZGER, WALTER   1955 *The Development of Academic Freedom in theUnited States.* New York: Columbia University Press.

LOVEJOY, ARTHUR   1937   Academic Freedom. In E. Seligman, ed., *Encyclopedia of the Social Sciences,* Vol. 1, pages 384–388. New York: Macmillan.

SYMPOSIUM   1963   Academic Freedom. *Law & Contemporary Problems* 28:429–671.

VAN ALSTYNE, WILLIAM   1972   The Specific Theory of Academic Freedom and the General Issue of Civil Liberty, In E. Pincoffs, ed., *The Concept of Academic Freedom,* pages 59–85. Austin: University of Texas Press.

GOVERNMENT SPEECH

Steven Shiffrin

FIRST AMENDMENT commentary has emphasized the danger of government as censor; thus lavish attention has been given to whether government can prevent Nazis from marching in Skokie, Illinois, Communists from advocating revolution, pornographers from selling their wares, or eccentrics from yelling fire in crowded theaters. Much less attention has been paid to the role of government as speaker; yet, one need only notice the ready access of government officials to the mass media, the constant stream of legislative and executive reports and publications, and the massive system of direct grants and indirect subsidies to the communications process (including federal financing of elections) to recognize that speech financed or controlled by government plays an enormous role in the marketplace of ideas. Sometimes the government speaks as government; sometimes it subsidizes speech without purporting to claim that the resulting message is its own. The term "government speech," therefore, includes all forms of state-supported communications: official government messages; statements of public officials at publicly subsidized press conferences; artistic, scientific, or political subsidies; even the classroom communications of public school teachers.

Basic assumptions of First Amendment law are sharply modified when governments speak. A basic canon of First Amendment law is that content distinctions are suspect. Indeed, in POLICE DEPARTMENT OF CHICAGO v. MOSLEY (1972) the Court insisted that government could not deviate " 'from the neutrality of time, place and circumstances into a concern about content.' This is never permitted." When governments speak, however, content distinctions are the norm. Government does not speak at random; it makes editorial judgments; it decides that some content is appropriate for the occasion and other content is not. The public museum curator makes content distinctions in selecting exhibits; the librarian, in selecting books; the public official, in composing press releases. If government could not make content distinctions, it could not speak effectively.

The government speech problem is to determine the constitutional limits, if any, on the editorial decisions of government. BUCKLEY v. VALEO (1976) squarely presented the issue. Certain minor party candidates argued that their exclusion from the system of public financing of presidential elections violated the First Amendment and the DUE PROCESS

CLAUSE of the Fifth Amendment. The Court briskly dismissed the relevance of the First Amendment challenge on the ground that a subsidy "furthers, not abridges, pertinent First Amendment values." This cryptic response has prompted criticism on the ground that it ignores the equality values in the First Amendment. One wonders, for example, how the Court would have reacted if the Congress had funded Democrats but not Republicans. Nonetheless, the Court did consider an equality claim grounded in Fifth Amendment due process, and concluded that the financing scheme was in "furtherance of sufficiently important government interests and has not unfairly or unnecessarily burdened the political opportunity of any party or candidate."

Buckley is important for two reasons. First, it affirms that government subsidies for speech enhance First Amendment values, recognizing that our "statute books are replete with laws providing financial assistance to the exercise of free speech, such as aid to public broadcasting and other forms of educational media . . . and preferential postal rates and antitrust exceptions for newspapers." Second, it seems to recognize that political subsidies are subject to constitutional limits under the equality principle, if not under the principle of free speech.

The First Amendment issues given short shrift in *Buckley* were fully aired in BOARD OF EDUCATION V. PICO (1982). Students alleged that the school board had removed nine books from school libraries because "particular passages in the books offended their social, political and moral tastes and not because the books, taken as a whole, were lacking educational value." The case produced seven different opinions and no clear resolution of the First Amendment issues. Over the dissent of four Justices, the Court ruled that the students' complaint could survive a summary judgment motion. Four of the Justices in the majority stated that if the allegations of the complaint were vindicated, the First Amendment barred the board's action. The fifth Justice, BYRON R. WHITE, thought that because of unresolved questions of fact the case should proceed to trial; he maintained, however, that discussion of the First Amendment issues was premature.

Most of the eight Justices who did discuss the issues expressed three important notes of agreement. First, they agreed that a major and appropriate purpose of government speech in the public schools is to transmit community values "promoting respect for authority and traditional values be they social, moral, or political." There was substantial disagreement, however, about the relevance of this purpose to book selections for a school library. Second, the Justices agreed that local authorities had wide latitude in making content decisions about library materials. Finally, most agreed that discretion could not be employed in a "narrowly partisan or political manner," such as removing all books written by Republicans. Beyond these agreements, however, the Justices struggled over differences between libraries and classrooms, between lower and higher levels of education, between acquiring books and removing books. *Pico* stands for little more than the proposition that government's broad discretion in subsidizing speech is not entirely unfettered by the First Amendment.

Perhaps the most serious challenges of government speech have surrounded government spending to influence the outcome of election campaigns. In many lower court cases, taxpayers have challenged the constitutionality of spending by cities or administrative agencies to influence the outcome of initiative campaigns. Lower courts have frequently avoided constitutional issues, concluding that state law does not authorize the city or administrative agency to spend the money. At least one question is implicitly resolved by these decisions, however, namely, that cities and administrative agencies do not have First Amendment rights against the state, at least none comparable to the rights of individuals or business corporations. The decisions have left open the question of the extent to which the Constitution permits governments to use their treasuries to help one side in an election campaign.

The establishment clause unquestionably prohibits some forms of religious government speech, and the EQUAL PROTECTION clause presumably prohibits some forms of racially discriminatory government speech. It remains to be seen what other limits the First Amendment or the equal protection clause may place on government's massive role in subsidizing speech.

Bibliography

SHIFFRIN, STEVEN   1983   Government Speech. *UCLA Law Review* 27:565–655.
YUDOF, MARK   1983   *When Government Speaks: Politics, Law, and Government Expression in America.* Berkeley and Los Angeles: University of California Press.

PREFERRED FREEDOMS

Leonard W. Levy

Because FIRST AMENDMENT freedoms rank at the top of the hierarchy of constitutional values, any legislation that explicitly limits those freedoms must be denied the usual presumption of constitutionality and be subjected to STRICT SCRUTINY by the judiciary. So went the earliest version of the preferred freedoms doctrine, sometimes called the preferred position or preferred status doctrine. It probably originated in the opinions of Justice OLIVER WENDELL HOLMES, at least implicitly. He believed that a presumption of constitutionality attached to ECONOMIC REGULATION, which needed to meet merely a RATIONAL BASIS test, as he explained dissenting in LOCHNER V. NEW YORK (1905). By contrast, in ABRAMS V. UNITED STATES (1919) he adopted the CLEAR AND PRESENT DANGER test as a constitutional yardstick for legislation such as the ESPIONAGE ACT OF 1917 or state CRIMINAL SYNDICALISM statutes, which limited FREEDOM OF SPEECH.

Justice BENJAMIN N. CARDOZO first suggested a more general hierarchy of constitutional rights in PALKO V. CONNECTICUT (1937), in a major opinion on the INCORPORATION DOCTRINE. He ranked at the top those "fundamental principles of liberty and justice which lie at the base of all our civil and political institutions." He tried to distinguish rights that might be lost without risking the essentials of liberty and justice from rights which he called "the matrix, the indispensable condition, of nearly every other form of freedom." These FUNDAMENTAL RIGHTS came to be regarded as the preferred freedoms. A year later Justice HARLAN F. STONE, in footnote four of his opinion in UNITED STATES V. CAROLENE PRODUCTS (1938), observed that "legislation which restricts the political processes" might "be subjected to more exacting judicial scrutiny" than other legislation. He suggested, too, that the judiciary might accord particularly searching examination of statutes reflecting "prejudice against DISCRETE AND INSULAR MINORITIES."

The First Amendment freedoms initially enjoyed a primacy above all others. Justice WILLIAM O. DOUGLAS for the Court in MURDOCK V. PENNSYLVANIA (1943) expressly stated: "FREEDOM OF THE PRESS, freedom of speech, FREEDOM OF RELIGION are in a preferred position." In the 1940s, despite bitter divisions on the Court over the question whether constitutional rights should be ranked, as well as the question whether the Court should ever deny the presumption of constitutionality, a majority of Justices continued to endorse the doctrine. Justice WILEY B. RUT-LEDGE for the Court gave it its fullest exposition in *Thomas v. Collins* (1945). Justice FELIX FRANKFURTER, who led the opposition to the doctrine, called it "mischievous" in KOVACS v. COOPER (1949); he especially disliked the implication that "any law touching communication" might be "infected with presumptive invalidity." Yet even Frankfurter, in his *Kovacs* opinion, acknowledged that "those liberties . . . which history has established as the indispensable conditions of an open as against a closed society come to the Court with a momentum for respect lacking when appeal is made to liberties which derive merely from shifting economic arrangements."

The deaths of Murphy and Rutledge in 1949 and their replacement by TOM C. CLARK and SHERMAN MINTON shifted the balance of judicial power to the Frankfurter viewpoint. Thereafter little was heard about the doctrine. The WARREN COURT vigorously defended not only CIVIL LIBERTIES but CIVIL RIGHTS and the rights of the criminally accused. The expansion of the incorporation doctrine and of the concept of EQUAL PROTECTION OF THE LAWS in the 1960s produced a new spectrum of FUNDAMENTAL INTERESTS demanding special judicial protection. Free speech, press, and religion continued, nevertheless, to be ranked, at least implicitly, as very special in character and possessing a symbolic "firstness," to use EDMOND CAHN's apt term. Although the Court rarely speaks of a preferred freedoms doctrine today, the substance of the doctrine has been absorbed in the concepts of strict scrutiny, fundamental rights, and selective incorporation.

Bibliography

McKAY, ROBERT B. 1959 The Preference for Freedom. *New York University Law Review* 34:1184–1227.

ABSOLUTISM (Freedom of Speech and Press)

Kenneth L. Karst

In the 1950s and 1960s, some Justices of the Supreme Court and some commentators on the Court's work debated an abstract issue of constitutional theory pressed on it by Justice HUGO L. BLACK: Is the FIRST AMENDMENT an "absolute," totally forbidding government restrictions on speech and the press that fall within the Amendment's scope, or is the FREEDOM OF SPEECH properly subject to BALANCING TESTS that weigh restrictions on speech against governmental interests asserted to justify them? With Black's retirement in 1971, the whole airy question simply collapsed.

The argument that the First Amendment "absolutely" guaranteed speech and press freedoms was first raised in the debate over the Sedition Act (1798) but did not become the focus of debate in Supreme Court opinions for another century and a half. The occasion was presented when the Court confronted a series of cases involving governmental restrictions on SUBVERSIVE ACTIVITIES. For ALEXANDER MEIKLEJOHN, First Amendment absolutism was built into the structure of a self-governing democracy. For Justice Black, it was grounded in the constitutional text.

Black argued that "the Constitution guarantees absolute freedom of speech"—he used the modern locution, including the press when he said "speech"—and, characteristically, he drew support from the First Amendment's words: "Congress shall make no law . . . abridging the freedom of speech, or of the press." He viewed all OBSCENITY and libel laws as unconstitutional; he argued, often supported by Justice WILLIAM O. DOUGLAS, that government could not constitutionally punish discussions of public affairs, even if they incited to illegal action. But Black never claimed that the First Amendment protected all communications, irrespective of context. He distinguished between speech, which was absolutely protected, and conduct, which was subject to reasonable regulation. So it was that the First Amendment absolutist, toward the end of his life, often voted to send marchers and other demonstrators to jail for expressing themselves in places where he said they had no right to be.

First Amendment absolutism fails more fundamentally, on its own terms. A witness who lies under oath surely has no constitutional immunity from prosecution, and yet her perjury is pure speech. Most observers, conceding the force of similar examples, have concluded that even Justice Black, a sophisticated analyst, must have viewed his absolutism as a debating point, not a rigid rule for decision. In the Cold War atmosphere of the 1950s, a debating point was sorely needed; there was truth to Black's charge that the Court was "balancing away the First Amendment." As Judge LEARNED HAND had argued many years previously, in times of stress judges need "a qualitative formula, hard, conventional, difficult to evade," if they are to protect unpopular political expression against hostile majorities. A "definitional" technique has its libertarian advantages. Yet it is also possible to "define away" the First Amendment, as the Court has demonstrated in its dealings with obscenity, FIGHTING WORDS, and some forms of libel and COMMERCIAL SPEECH.

Even when the Court is defining a category of speech out of the First Amendment's scope, it states its reasons. Thus, just as "balancers" must define what it is that they are balancing, "definers" must weigh interests in order to define the boundaries of protected speech. Since Justice Black's departure from the Court, First Amendment inquiry has blended definitional and interest-balancing techniques, focusing—as virtually all constitutional inquiry must ultimately focus—on the justifications asserted for governmental restrictions. Justice Black's enduring legacy to this process is not the theory of First Amendment absolutes, but his lively concern for the values of an open society.

Bibliography

KALVEN, HARRY, JR. 1967 Upon Rereading Mr. Justice Black on the First Amendment. *UCLA Law Review* 14:422–453.

BALANCING TEST

Martin Shapiro

Although the intellectual origins of the balancing of interests formula lie in ROSCOE POUND's sociological jurisprudence, the formula was introduced into constitutional law as a means of implementing the Supreme Court's oft-repeated announcement that FIRST AMENDMENT rights are not absolute. In determining when infringement on speech may be justified constitutionally, the Court may balance the interest in FREEDOM OF SPEECH against the interest that the infringing statute seeks to protect. Thus the Court may conclude that the interests in NATIONAL SECURITY protected by the Smith Act outweigh the interests in speech of those who advocate forcible overthrow of the government, or that the free speech interests of pamphleteers outweigh the interest in clean streets protected by an antilittering ordinance forbidding the distribution of handbills.

The 1950s campaign against alleged subversives brought two interlocking problems to the Supreme Court. The dominant free speech DOCTRINES of the Court were PREFERRED FREEDOMS and the CLEAR AND PRESENT DANGER TEST. Because alleged subversives were exercising preferred speech rights and the government was unprepared to offer evidence that their speech did constitute a present danger of violent overthrow of the government, the Court found it difficult under the existing formulas to uphold government anticommunist action. Because established First Amendment doctrine appeared to be on a collision course with an anticommunist crusade that appeared to enjoy overwhelming popular support, free speech provided the crucial arena for the penultimate crisis of the judicial self-restraint movement. (The ultimate crisis came in BROWN v. BOARD OF EDUCATION, 1954.) Although the logical implication of that movement suggested that the Court ought never declare an act of Congress unconstitutional as a violation of the BILL OF RIGHTS, the Court was not prepared to go so far. The Justices' dilemma was that they were the inheritors of pro-freedom of speech doctrines but wished to uphold infringements upon speech without openly abdicating their constitutional authority.

The way out of this dilemma was the balancing formula. It allowed the Court to vindicate legislative and executive anticommunist measures case by case without ever flatly announcing that the Court had gone out of the business of enforcing the First Amendment. LEARNED HAND's "clear and probable" or "discounting" formula adopted by the Supreme Court in DENNIS V. UNITED STATES (1951) was the vital bridge in moving from a clear and present danger test that impels judicial action to a balancing test that veils judicial withdrawal. For Hand's test permits conversion of the danger test from an exception to freedom of speech invoked when speech creates an immediate danger of violent crime to a general formula for outweighing speech claims whenever the goals espoused in the speech are sufficiently antithetical to those of the majority. Justice FELIX FRANKFURTER's concurrence in *Dennis* and the majority opinion in BARENBLATT V. UNITED STATES (1959) not only made the antispeech potential of the balancing doctrine clear but also exhibited its great potential for absolute judicial deference to coordinate branches. For if constitutional judgments are ultimately a matter of balancing interests, in a democratic society who is the ultimate balancer? Necessarily, it is the Congress in which all the competing interests are represented. Thus the Court deferred to Congress's judgment that the needs of national security outweighed the speech rights of the enemies of that security.

Proponents of the balancing doctrine argue that no one is really willing to give any constitutional right absolute sway and that the act of judging always involves a weighing of competing claims. Certainly when constitutional rights such as free speech and FAIR TRIAL come into conflict, balancing of the two appears inevitable. The opponents of balancing argue for "principled" versus "ad hoc" or case-by-case balancing. If judges are left free to balance the particular interests in each particular case, they are always free to decide any case for or against the rights claimed by the way they state the interests. Opponents of ad hoc balancing insist that whatever balancing must be done should be done in the course of creating constitutional rules that will then be applied even-handedly in all cases. Thus, if fair trial and free speech values conflict, we may want a rule that upholds the constitutionality of banning prosecutors from pretrial release of confessions, but we do not want the kind of ad hoc balancing in which judges are free to find that in some cases such bans are constitutional and in others they are not.

Balancing has remained a principal doctrine in the freedom of speech area and has spread to other constitutional areas such as PRIVACY. Its capacity as a vehicle for judicial discretion is illustrated by BUCKLEY V. VALEO (1976), in which the Court used the balancing doctrine to march through the complex CAMPAIGN FINANCE ACT, striking down some provisions and upholding others in what was effectively a total legislative redrafting, and by the ABORTION cases (see ROE V. WADE, 1973) in which the Court used the balancing doctrine to invest with constitutional authority the "trimester" scheme it invented.

In GIBSON V. FLORIDA LEGISLATIVE INVESTIGATING COMMITTEE (1963) the Court held that government might infringe upon a First Amendment right only when it could show a COMPELLING STATE INTEREST. This formula may be viewed as weighting the balance of interests in favor of constitutional rights, but any government interests can be stated in such a way as to appear compelling. The Court's employment of the balancing test always leaves us uncertain whether any legislative infringement of free speech or other rights, no matter how direct or how open, will be declared unconstitutional, for the Court may always be prepared to find some state interest sufficiently weighty to justify the infringement.

(SEE ALSO: Absolutism; Judicial Activism and Restraint.)

Bibliography

FRANTZ, LAURENT B.   1963   Is the First Amendment Law? California Law Review 51:729–754.
HAND, LEARNED   1958   The Bill of Rights. Cambridge, Mass.: Harvard University Press.
MENDELSON, WALLACE   1962   On the Meaning of the First Amendment: Absolutes in the Balance. California Law Review 50:821–828.

INVALID ON ITS FACE

Jonathan D. Varat

Legislation may be unconstitutional as applied to all, some, or none of the behavior it addresses. Usually, affected parties challenge a law's constitutionality only as applied to their own behavior. Occasionally, they claim a law is constitutionally invalid on its face—and therefore unenforceable against anyone, including them—because it would be unconstitutional ever to apply it. A penal law is invalid on its face, for example, when it so vaguely describes the conduct outlawed that it cannot give fair warning to anyone, or when every act the law prohibits is constitutionally protected. A challenge to such a law would present no STANDING problem. Sometimes, however, a litigant will assert that, regardless of whether a law is constitutional as applied to him it should be held invalid on its face because its coverage includes unconstitutional regulation of others.

Normally a federal court will deny standing to raise such a facial challenge when the law constitutionally regulates the would-be challenger, for the court perceives the claim as a request to go beyond the case before it. Responding to the request would require the court to decide what other situations the law governs—frequently an unresolved question of statutory interpretation—and then to decide whether some of the law's unapplied coverage would be unconstitutional. If the court should conclude that part of the law is invalid and part valid, it would have to decide whether the legislative framers would want the valid part to stand separately or the whole law to fall. Finally, if the law is constitutional as applied to the litigant, but would be unconstitutional in hypothetical application to others, the court may still have to decide whether to hold the law facially invalid despite a legislative desire to have the law's valid applications stand.

Formidable considerations militate against judicial rulings that laws are facially invalid. JUDICIAL REVIEW originates in the need to apply constitutional law to decide the case before the court, and a corollary principle requires courts to refrain from deciding hypothetical questions. When a court focuses only on the situation before it, it minimizes the need for unnecessary decisions of issues of both statutory and constitutional interpretation, and avoids considering other possible applications of the law in a factual vacuum. Finally, a conclusion of facial invalidity would prevent the valid enforcement of the law against a party whom the legislature intended to regulate. Normally, then, the Supreme Court denies a litigant STANDING to assert the unconstitutionality of legislation as it would be applied to others, except when the most compelling reasons are present.

The reason most often found compelling is the need to protect the freedom of expression of persons not before the court whom the law might inhibit. That was the rationale, for example, of THORNHILL v. ALABAMA (1940). Specifically, the FIRST AMENDMENT doctrines of OVER-BREADTH and VAGUENESS sometimes permit one whose conduct the law constitutionally could reach to escape punishment, arguing that the law is invalid on its face because its seeming application to others discourages their protected expression. Intense controversy surrounds these facial challenges, however, largely because of differing perceptions of how inhibiting such laws really are. In areas involving other fundamental freedoms, such as the RIGHT TO TRAVEL, facial challenges have occasionally been successful, as in APTHEKER v. SECRETARY OF STATE (1964), again to protect persons who are never likely to be before a court from having their liberty circumscribed by the seeming applicability of an unconstitutional regulation.

A court will hold a law invalid on its face only in a case of necessity: where the law's very existence may affect the exercise of cherished liberties by nonparties lacking opportunity or willingness to challenge them, and where the inhibiting feature of the law cannot easily be cured by statutory interpretation. Absent such conditions federal courts will not, at the request of one whose behavior may constitutionally be regulated, decide how a law might apply and whether the law's potential application to other situations warrants holding it invalid on its face. The degree to which the Supreme Court permits facial challenges to legislation directly reflects the Justices' collective perception of the Court's institutional role in enforcing the Constitution. Narrow views of that role incline the Court to restrict facial challenges; a broader view commends it to entertain and encourage such a challenge in the interest of assuring the constitutional governance of society beyond the immediate case.

OVERBREADTH

Jonathan D. Varat

Judges frequently encounter the claim that a law, as drafted or interpreted, should be invalidated as overbroad because its regulatory scope addresses not only behavior that constitutionally may be punished but also constitutionally protected behavior. The normal judicial response is confined to ruling on the law's constitutionality as applied to the litigant's behavior, leaving the validity of its application to other people and situations to subsequent adjudication. Since THORNHILL v. ALABAMA (1940), however, the Supreme Court has made an exception, most frequently in FIRST AMENDMENT cases but applicable to other precious freedoms, when it is convinced that the very existence of an overbroad law may cause knowledgeable people to refrain from freely exercising constitutional liberties because they fear punishment and are unwilling to litigate their rights. In such cases, the aggregate inhibition of guaranteed freedom in the regulated community is thought to justify both holding the overbroad law INVALID ON ITS FACE and allowing one to whom a narrower law could be applied constitutionally to assert the overbreadth claim. Unlike the alternative of narrowing the unconstitutional portions of an overbroad statute case by case, facial invalidation prevents delay in curing the improper deterrence. Moreover, courts most effectively can address the inhibition of those who neither act nor sue by allowing those who do to raise the overbreadth challenge.

Like a VAGUENESS challenge, an overbreadth challenge implicates judicial governance in two controversial ways. First, if successful, the challenge completely prohibits the law's enforcement, even its constitutional applications, until it is narrowed through reenactment or authoritative interpretation. Second, the challenge requires a court to gauge the law's applications to unidentified people in circumstances that must be imagined, often ignoring the facts of the situation before them—a practice of hypothesizing that is at odds with the court's usual application of law to the facts of concrete CASES OR CONTROVERSIES.

Overbreadth differs from vagueness in that the constitutional defect is a law's excessive reach, not its lack of clarity; yet the defects are related. A law that punished "all speech that is not constitutionally protected" would, by definition, not be overbroad, but it would be unduly vague because people would have to speculate about what it outlawed. A law that prohibited "all speaking" would be unconstitutionally overbroad, but it also might be vague. Although clear enough if taken literally, it might be understood that the legislature did not intend the full reach of its broadly drafted law, and the public would have to speculate about what the contours of the intended lesser reach might be. A law that banned "all harmful speech" would be both overbroad and vague on its face. The key connection, however, is the improper inhibiting effect of the broad or vague law.

As with vagueness, the federal courts approach overbreadth challenges to state and federal laws differently. A federal court must interpret a federal law before judging its constitutionality. In doing so, the court may reduce the law's scope, if it can do so consistently with Congress's intent, a course that may minimize constitutional problems of overbreadth. Only state courts may authoritatively determine the reach of state laws, however. Consequently, when the Supreme Court reviews an overbreadth challenge to a state law on appeal from a state court—which review usually occurs because the challenger raised the claim in defense of state court proceedings against him—the Court must accept the state court's determination of the law's scope and apply its own constitutional judgment to the law as so construed. By contrast, if parties threatened with enforcement of a state statute sue in federal court to have the law declared unconstitutionally overbroad before they are prosecuted or sued in state court, the federal court faces the additional complication of determining the overbreadth question without the guidance of any state court interpretation of the law in this case. If past interpretations of the law's terms make its breadth clear, there is no more difficulty than in Supreme Court review of a state court case. But if there is some question whether a state court might have narrowed the state law, especially in light of constitutional doubts about it, the federal court faces the possibility of making its own incorrect interpretation and basing an overbreadth judgment on that unstable premise.

With other constitutional claims involving uncertain state laws, a federal court normally will abstain from deciding the constitutional question until clarification is sought in state court. However, because the prolongation of CHILLING EFFECTS on constitutionally protected conduct is the basis of the vagueness of overbreadth doctrines, the Supreme Court indicated in DOMBROWSKI v. PFISTER (1965) and *Baggett v. Bullitt* (1964) that abstention is generally inappropriate if the problem would take multiple instances of adjudication to cure. *Babbitt v. United Farm Workers* (1979) followed the implicit corollary, requiring abstention where a single state proceeding might have obviated the need to reach difficult constitutional issues. But BROCKETT v. SPOKANE ARCADES, INC. (1985) shunned abstention in a case where state court clarification was feasible in an expeditious single proceeding, but where the litigants objecting to overbreadth were not people to whom the law could be validly applied but people who desired to engage in constitutionally protected speech. In that circumstance, at least where the unconstitutional portion of the statute was readily identifiable and severable from the remainder, the Court chose to strike that portion rather than abstain to see if the state court would remove it by interpretation.

Brockett also expressed a preference for partial over facial invalidation whenever challengers assert that application of a statute to them would be unconstitutional. The Court's ultimate objective is to invalidate only a statute's overbroad features, not the parts that legitimately penalize undesirable behavior. It permits those who are properly subject to regulation to mount facial overbreadth attacks only to provide an opportunity for courts to eliminate the illegitimate deterrent impact on others. Partial invalidation would do such people no good, and those who are illegitimately deterred from speaking may never sue. In order to throw out the tainted bathwater, the baby temporarily must go too, until the statute is reenacted or reinterpreted with its flaws omitted. Where, as in *Brockett,* one asserts his own right to pursue protected activity, however, no special incentive to litigate is needed. The Court can limit a statute's improper reach through partial invalidation and still benefit the challenger. *Brockett*'s assumption that the tainted part of the statute does not spoil the whole also undercuts Henry Monaghan's important argument that allowing the unprotected to argue overbreadth does not depart from normal STANDING rules because they always assert their own right not to be judged under an invalid statute. The part applied to them is valid, and they are granted standing to attack the whole only to protect others from the invalid part. Finally, the claim that a law is invalid in all applications because based on an illegitimate premise has elements of both partial and facial invalidation. As the invalid premise affects the challenger as well as everyone else, there is no need to provide a special incentive to litigate, but because the whole law is defective, total invalidation is appropriate.

The seriousness of striking the whole of a partially invalid law at the urging of one to whom it validly applies, together with doubts about standing and the reliability of constitutional adjudication in the context of imagined applications, renders overbreadth an exceptional and controversial DOCTRINE. The determination of what circumstances are sufficiently compelling to warrant the doctrine's use has varied from time to time and among judges. The WARREN COURT focused mainly on the scope of the laws' coverage, the chilling effect on protected expression, and the ability of the legislature to draw legitimate regulatory boundaries more narrowly. The Court seemed convinced that overbroad laws inhibited freedom substantially, and thus made that inhibition the basis of invalidation, especially when the laws were aimed at dissidents and the risk of deliberate deterrence was high, as in APTHEKER V. SECRETARY

OF STATE (1964), *United States v. Robel* (1967), and *Dombrowski v. Pfister* (1965). The BURGER COURT has continued to employ the overbreadth doctrine when deterrence of valued expression seems likely, as in *Lewis v. New Orleans* (1974), which struck down a law penalizing abusive language directed at police, and in SCHAD V. MT. EPHRAIM (1981), which struck down an extremely broad law banning live entertainment.

Justice BYRON R. WHITE has led that Court, however, in curtailing overbreadth adjudication. As all laws occasionally may be applied unconstitutionally, there is always a quantitative dimension of overbreadth. White's majority opinion in BROADRICK V. OKLAHOMA (1973) held that the overbroad portion of a law must be "real and substantial" before it will be invalidated. That standard highlights the magnitude of deterrent impact, which depends as much on the motivations of those regulated as on the reach of the law. *Broadrick* also emphasized the need to compare and offset the ranges of a statute's valid and invalid applications, rather than simply assess the dimensions of the invalid range. This substituted a judgment balancing a statute's legitimate regulation against its illegitimate deterrence of protected conduct for a judgment focused predominantly on the improper inhibition.

Broadrick initially limited the "substantial overbreadth" approach to laws seemingly addressed to conduct, leaving laws explicitly regulating expression, especially those directed at particular viewpoints, to the more generous approach. In *Ferber v. New York* (1982) and *Brockett*, however, substantial overbreadth was extended to pure speech cases as well. That these cases involved laws regulating OBSCENITY might suggest that some Justices find the overbreadth doctrine an improper means to counter deterrence of marginally valued expression. More likely, however, the Court generally is abandoning its focus on the subject of a law's facial coverage in favor of a comparative judgment of the qualitative and quantitative dimensions of a law's legitimate and illegitimate scope, whatever speech or conduct be regulated.

Still, the reality of deterrence and the value of the liberty deterred probably remain major factors in overbreadth judgments, even if more must be considered. For example, the Court's pronouncement in BATES V. STATE BAR OF ARIZONA (1977) that overbreadth analysis generally is inappropriate for profit-motivated advertising rested explicitly on a judgment that advertising is not easily inhibited and implicitly on the historic perception of COMMERCIAL SPEECH as less worthy of protection.

Overbreadth controversies nearly always reflect different sensitivities to the worth of lost expression and of lost regulation of unprotected behavior, or different perceptions of the legitimacy and reliability of judicial nullification of laws that are only partially unconstitutional, or different assessments of how much inhibition is really likely, how easy it would be to redraft a law to avoid overbreadth, and how important broad regulation is to the effective control of harmful behavior. Despite controversy and variations in zeal for application of the overbreadth doctrine, however, its utility in checking repression that too sweepingly inhibits guaranteed liberty should assure its preservation in some form.

Bibliography

ALEXANDER, LAWRENCE A.   1985   Is There an Overbreadth Doctrine? *San Diego Law Review* 22:541–554.

MONAGHAN, HENRY P.   1981   Overbreadth. *Supreme Court Review* 1981:1–39.

NOTE   1970   The First Amendment Overbreadth Doctrine. *Harvard Law Review* 83:844–927.

VAGUENESS

Jonathan D. Varat

The Fifth Amendment and FOURTEENTH AMENDMENT respectively prohibit the federal and state governments from taking life, liberty, or property without DUE PROCESS OF LAW. These provisions forbid the enforcement of any law that, in the classic words of *Connally v. General Construction
Co.* (1926), "either forbids or requires the doing of an act in terms so
vague that men of common intelligence must necessarily guess at its
meaning and differ as to its application." Vagueness imperils the fair
administration of legal sanctions in several ways. First, it threatens punishment of people who had no fair warning of what conduct to avoid.
Second, by creating interpretive latitude for those who apply the law—
police, prosecutors, judges, juries, and others—vagueness permits punishment to be inflicted selectively for arbitrary or improper reasons.
Third, a law's vagueness hinders the efforts of reviewing courts to control
such abuses in the law's enforcement; the less clear the law is, the less
visible—and correspondingly more difficult to detect and correct—are
irregular instances of its administration.

To minimize these dangers, the due process requirement of reasonable clarity forbids enforcement even if the legislature constitutionally
could have prohibited, through a clearer law than it did enact, all the
behavior its vague law might have been intended to reach. When the
uncertain coverage of a vague law might extend into areas of behavior
that are constitutionally protected from regulation, however, the ordinary
dangers of arbitrary enforcement are heightened, and two additional
concerns emerge: the risk that a vague law, which inevitably poses an
uncertain risk of prosecution, will inhibit people from exercising precious
liberties that the government has no right to outlaw, and the possibility
that the legislature did not explicitly focus on the liberty interest and
thus did not actually decide that there was compelling reason to regulate
it.

The deterrence of constitutionally guaranteed activity that vagueness
may produce is akin to the deterrence produced by overbroad laws
that encompass both behavior that legitimately may be regulated and
behavior that is constitutionally protected. Vagueness differs from overbreadth in that the source of potential inhibition is the law's lack of
clarity, not its excessive reach. Yet in both cases the ultimate threat is
that those who wish to exercise constitutional rights will refrain from

doing so for fear of being penalized. That vagueness may have the practical effect of overbroad regulation explains the common doctrinal confusion between the two concepts. Vagueness also differs from OVER-BREADTH in another way: an uncertain law that addresses, even in its most expansive interpretation, only behavior that constitutionally may be regulated may still be void for vagueness, but, by definition, cannot be void for overbreadth.

Two questions dominate the law of vagueness: how much vagueness is tolerable before the law violates due process, and who may raise the vagueness objection. The Supreme Court appears to give different answers to each question, depending on whether or not the vagueness implicates constitutionally protected activity. Still, the constitutional issue of vagueness is always a question of degree, of how much interpretive uncertainty is tolerable before the legitimate regulatory interests of government must yield to the perils of vagueness. If the constitutional definition of vagueness is itself uncertain, the reason is that language is inherently imprecise. The public interest in regulating antisocial behavior would be sacrificed if due process mandated impossible standards of clarity before laws validly could be enforced.

The starting point for vagueness analysis is to ascertain the nature of the standard that the law sets. This inquiry requires judges to consider not only the statutory language but also all interpretive aids that may add to the law's precision, such as accepted meanings in the relevant community (or in other areas of law) for terms contained in the statute, implementing regulations, past judicial interpretations that have clarified uncertain terms, and even judicial clarification in the very case raising the vagueness objection—if this after-the-fact clarification does not disregard the legislature's intent and if the challenger reasonably could have anticipated that the law could be construed to cover his conduct. The interpretive option often allows the Supreme Court and lower federal courts to avoid invalidating vague federal laws. When federal courts confront state laws, however, they are limited to determining whether state court clarification has cured any constitutional problems of vagueness. This difference largely explains why state laws are stricken for vagueness more often than are federal laws.

Once a law has received the benefit of all available clarification, a wide range of factors affects a court's judgment whether the law's remaining vagueness renders it unconstitutional. In a case in which the vagueness does not bear on constitutionally shielded behavior, only two vagueness objections are permitted: that the law is vague as applied to the particular behavior of the individual challenger, or that the law is INVALID ON ITS FACE for being unduly vague as applied to anyone, including the challenger, because no one who consulted it could derive fair warning of what conduct was prohibited or could determine whether the legislature meant one thing rather than another. In *Hoffman Estates v. Flipside* (1982) the Supreme Court confirmed that in deciding cases in which the latter objection is raised, greater uncertainty is constitutionally permissible when the law regulates a relatively narrow subject matter; when the law regulates economic behavior (because businesses more reasonably can be expected to consult laws in advance of acting than can individuals); when the law imposes civil rather than criminal penalties (because the consequences of noncompliance are less severe); and when the law applies only to those who intentionally or knowingly violate it (because there is less risk of unfair surprise). Historically, once the Supreme Court determined that ECONOMIC REGULATION posed no significant threat to constitutional freedoms, it became more tolerant of the imprecision in laws banning "unreasonable," "unjust," or "unfair" prices or business practices, as *United States v. National Dairy Products Corp.* (1963) illustrates. Moreover, the Court permits more uncertainty when it perceives the government's regulatory objective to be especially important—as SCREWS v. UNITED STATES (1945) demonstrated in upholding a rather vague CIVIL RIGHTS law protecting individuals—and also when it would be difficult for the legislature to delineate more precisely the penalized behavior.

The Court is especially receptive to a challenge based on vagueness when a law's uncertain coverage risks inhibiting constitutionally safeguarded freedoms. In the last half-century this receptivity has been manifested primarily in FIRST AMENDMENT cases. One indicator of the Court's increased sensitivity is the wide range of people who may now raise the vagueness objection. In cases implicating constitutionally protected activity, the Court not only entertains complaints that a law is vague as applied to the individual litigant or vague in all applications, but it sometimes permits those to whom a law clearly applies to object that it is facially invalid because it is unduly vague as to others. Despite Supreme Court rulings to the contrary both in earlier periods and in cases as recent as PARKER V. LEVY (1974) and BROADRICK V. OKLAHOMA (1973), and despite continuing voices of dissent that this practice allows one as to whom enforcement is fair to assert the hypothetical rights of others and confuses vagueness and overbreadth, the Court currently maintains, in such cases as YOUNG V. AMERICAN MINI THEATRES (1976) and KOLENDER V. LAWSON (1983), that such a person may have the whole law invalidated if the deterrent effect of its vagueness on others is real and substantial.

All of the factors that bear on the acceptable degree of vagueness in laws encompassing only unprotected conduct still apply, some more heavily, to laws that potentially reach constitutionally protected conduct. In addition, the Supreme Court seems to be concerned with other factors: how much protected freedom the vagueness might deter; how important the asserted freedom is; the judges' capacity to preserve the freedom through case-by-case application; the legislature's ability to reformulate the law in less inhibiting fashion; and the extent and importance of legitimate regulation that must be foregone if the law is voided for vagueness.

Although the Court does not always articulate these considerations, they appear to underlie many decisions. In *Baggett v. Bullitt* (1964) and *Cramp v. Board of Public Instruction* (1961), for example, the invalidation of LOYALTY OATH requirements for undue vagueness arrayed important freedoms of association against dubious government needs for assurance. More generally, when the enactment's vagueness risks suppression of unpopular expression or criticism of government, the Court's tolerance level is low. Thus in *Coates v. Cincinnati* (1971) an ordinance barring assembly of three or more persons "annoying" passers-by was held void, as was a law prohibiting "contemptuous treatment" of the American flag in *Smith v. Goguen* (1974).

On the other hand, even vagueness that inhibits valued expression is sometimes indulged if regulatory interests are perceived as powerful. Good examples are the extreme vagueness *Parker v. Levy* permitted the military in punishing "conduct unbecoming an officer and a gentleman" and the lesser, yet undoubted, uncertainty of laws prohibiting partisan political activity by PUBLIC EMPLOYEES that the Court upheld in *Broadrick v. Oklahoma*.

Similarly divergent assessments of the acceptable level of indefiniteness in statutes defining and proscribing OBSCENITY reflect conflict within the Court over the value of sexually explicit, but constitutionally protected, materials. The judgment that deterrence of some sexually explicit adult movies was no cause for alarm led a plurality in *Young v. American Mini Theatres* to uphold a ZONING ordinance restricting the concentration of adult theaters and bookstores in downtown Detroit. A similar judgment underlies the Court's willingness to permit inevitably vague definitions of obscenity to serve as the basis for criminal punishment. By contrast, Justice WILLIAM J. BRENNAN, who is more concerned about the potentially protected sexual expression that might be lost, declared in his important dissent in *Paris Adult Theatre I v. Slaton* (1973) his firm, if belated, conviction that vagueness in defining obscenity is virtually an insuperable problem. Even he, however, did not conclude that the distribution of obscene materials must consequently remain unregulated; rather, he suggested that the protection of juveniles and the privacy of unconsenting adults might render vagueness tolerable, though protection of consenting adults and community mores and aesthetics would not.

The complexity of the vagueness doctrine stems, then, from the dual nature of the constitutional protection that it offers. Individuals are protected in any case from arbitrary enforcement without a fair opportunity to conform their conduct to legitimate law, and the social interest in maximizing constitutional freedoms is central to judgments about vagueness when the law's indefiniteness threatens to inhibit those freedoms.

Bibliography

AMSTERDAM, ANTHONY B.   1960   The Void-for-Vagueness Doctrine in the Supreme Court. *University of Pennsylvania Law Review* 109:67–116.

BOGEN, DAVID S.   1978   First Amendment Ancillary Doctrines. *Maryland Law Review* 37:679, 714–726.

SCHAUER, FREDERICK   1978   Fear, Risk and the First Amendment: Unravelling the "Chilling Effect." *Boston University Law Review* 58:685.

CHILLING EFFECT

Kenneth L. Karst

Law is carried forward on a stream of language. Metaphor not only reflects the growth of constitutional law but nourishes it as well. Since the 1960s, when the WARREN COURT widened the domain of the FIRST AMENDMENT, Justices have frequently remarked on laws' "chilling effects" on the FREEDOM OF SPEECH. A statute tainted by VAGUENESS or OVERBREADTH, for example, restricts the freedom of expression not only by directly subjecting people to the laws' sanctions but also by threatening others. Because the very existence of such a law may induce self-censorship when the reach of the law is uncertain, the law may be held INVALID ON ITS FACE. The assumed causal connection between vague legislation and self-censorship was made by the Supreme Court as early as HERNDON V. LOWRY (1937); half a century later, circulating the coinage of Justice FELIX FRANKFURTER, lawyers and judges express similar assumptions in the language of chilling effects.

The assumption plainly makes more sense in some cases than it does in others. For a law's uncertainty actually to chill speech, the would-be speaker must be conscious of the uncertainty. Yet few of us go about our day-to-day business with the statute book in hand. A statute forbidding insulting language may be vague, but its uncertainty is unlikely to have any actual chilling effect on speech in face-to-face street encounters. Yet a court striking that law down—even in application to one whose insults fit the Supreme Court's narrow definition of FIGHTING WORDS—is apt to speak of the law's chilling effects.

For chilling effects that are real rather than assumed, we must look to institutional speakers—publishers, broadcasters, advertisers, political parties, groups promoting causes—who regularly inquire into the letter of the law and its interpretation by the courts. Magazine editors, for example, routinely seek legal counsel about defamation. Here the uncertainty of the law's reach does not lie in any statutory language, for the law of libel and slander is largely the product of COMMON LAW judges. It was a concern for chilling effects, however, that led three concurring Justices in NEW YORK TIMES V. SULLIVAN (1964) to advocate an absolute rule protecting the press against damages for the libel of a public official. The majority's principle in the case, which would allow damages when a newspaper defames an official knowing that its statement is false, or in reckless disregard of its truth or falsity, may, indeed, chill the press.

Even slight doubt about information may make an editor hesitate to publish it, for fear that it may turn out to be false—and that a jury years later will decide it was published recklessly. The concern is not to protect false information, but that doubtful editors will play it safe, suppressing information that is true.

Conversely, when the Justices are persuaded that the law's threat will not have the effect of chilling speech, they are disinclined to use the overbreadth doctrine. A prominent modern example is the treatment of COMMERCIAL SPEECH. Because advertising is profitable, and advertisers seem unlikely to be chilled by laws regulating advertising, such laws are not subject to challenge for overbreadth.

The worry, when a court discusses chilling effects, is that a law's uncertainty will cause potential speakers to censor themselves. Thus, an overly broad law is subject to constitutional challenge even by one whose own speech would be punishable under a law focused narrowly on speech lying outside First Amendment protection. The defendant in court stands as a surrogate for others whose speech would be constitutionally protected—but who have been afraid to speak, and thus have not been prosecuted, and cannot themselves challenge the law. Whether or not this technique amounts to a dilution of the jurisdictional requirements of STANDING or RIPENESS, it allows courts to defend against the chilling effects of unconstitutional statutes that would otherwise elude their scrutiny.

Bibliography

AMSTERDAM, ANTHONY G.   1960   The Void-for-Vagueness Doctrine in the Supreme Court. *University of Pennsylvania Law Review* 109:67–116.

NOTE   1970   The First Amendment Overbreadth Doctrine. *Harvard Law Review* 83:844–927.

SCHAUER, FREDERICK   1978   Fear, Risk and the First Amendment: Unraveling the "Chilling Effect." *Boston University Law Review* 5:685–732.

LISTENERS' RIGHTS

Steven Shiffrin

The constitutional commitment to FREEDOM OF SPEECH is in part based on the simple idea that people have a right to say what they want to say without government interference. That is, freedom of speech protects the speaker. Yet the FIRST AMENDMENT themes of self-expression and speaker liberty have been recognized only sporadically in Supreme Court opinions. The more prevalent themes in First Amendment jurisprudence have been audience-oriented, albeit implicitly.

One classic justification of freedom of speech has been based on optimistic assessments about the capacity of the marketplace of ideas to distinguish between the false and the true. The emphasis of this justification is not that speakers have a right to say what they want to say, but that speakers must be free to speak so that the society can find truth, that is, so that listeners can hear and evaluate what is said. Listeners' rights are also strongly implicated by the notion that freedom of speech reflects a commitment to democratic self-government. If citizens are to decide how to respond to public issues, they must hear what others have to say. The listeners' rights emphasis of the self-government perspective is best illustrated by ALEXANDER MEIKLEJOHN's observation, approvingly cited by the Supreme Court in COLUMBIA BROADCASTING SYSTEM V. DEMOCRATIC NATIONAL COMMITTEE (1981): "What is essential is not that everyone shall speak, but that everything worth saying shall be said."

For many years, listeners' rights were protected with nary a listener before the Court. In routine cases, the aggrieved speaker invoked the rights of the listeners. In *Thomas v. Collins* (1945), for example, the Court invalidated an attempted prior restraint at the behest of the speaker, in part because of the rights of others "to hear what he had to say."

Ultimately, listeners were permitted to invoke their own rights without any speakers before the Court. In VIRGINIA STATE BOARD OF PHARMACY V. VIRGINIA CITIZENS CONSUMER COUNCIL, for example, consumers challenged a statute that prohibited pharmacists from advertising the prices of prescription drugs. No pharmacist was before the Court, only potential members of the audience for drug price advertising. The Court recognized the rights of "listener" plaintiffs to sue on their own behalf, observing that the First Amendment gives protection "to the communication, to its source and its recipients both."

LAMONT V. POSTMASTER GENERAL (1965) stands for an even broader principle. There the Court struck down a statute directing the postmaster general not to deliver certain "communist political propaganda" unless the addressee, upon notification, requested its delivery. The Court found this to be "an unconstitutional abridgment of the addressee's rights." Many of the potential senders of this "propaganda" were aliens outside the country who had no First Amendment rights of their own. The Court made this distinction explicit in *Kleindeist v. Mandel* (1972). Thus recipients of messages have a First Amendment right to hear that does not depend upon corresponding rights in the speaker. Such rights may extend to situations where the speaker is unwilling to speak; they are then usually referred to as the RIGHT TO KNOW. On the other hand, an unwilling recipient of a message may have a right not to hear, deriving from notions such as a right of privacy.

Bibliography

BEVIER, LILLIAN   1980   An Informed Public, an Informing Press: The Search for a Constitutional Principle. *Stanford Law Review* 68:482–517.

EMERSON, THOMAS I.   1976   Legal Foundations of the Right to Know. *Washington University Law Quarterly* 1976:1–24.

TWO-LEVEL THEORY

Steven Shiffrin

In an important 1960 article, Harry Kalven, Jr., coined the phrase "two-level theory." As he described it, FIRST AMENDMENT methodology classified speech at two levels. Some speech was so unworthy as to be beneath First Amendment protection: no First Amendment review was necessary. Thus the Court in CHAPLINSKY V. NEW HAMPSHIRE (1942) had referred to "certain well-defined and narrowly limited classes of speech, the prevention and punishment of which has never been thought to raise any constitutional problem. These include the lewd and obscene, the profane, the libelous, and the insulting or fighting words." At the second level, speech of constitutional value was protected unless it presented a CLEAR AND PRESENT DANGER of a substantive evil.

In a subsequent article Kalven observed that in NEW YORK TIMES V. SULLIVAN (1964) neither the two-level approach nor the clear and present danger test was an organizing strategy or guiding methodology. He expressed the hope that the *Sullivan* Court's unwillingness to employ the two-level theory presaged the theory's demise along with the clear and present danger test. Kalven's hopes have been only partially realized. Perhaps partly as a result of his persuasive efforts, the Court has been willing to scrutinize state justifications for regulating some types of speech previously thought to raise no constitutional problem. *Chaplinsky*'s offhand assumption that each class of speech in its litany raises no constitutional problem is no longer credible. Nonetheless, the Court continues to be impressed by *Chaplinsky*'s famous OBITER DICTUM that speech beneath the protection of the First Amendment occupies that status because its slight contribution to truth is outweighed by the state interests in order and morality.

Kalven's hope for the complete repudiation of the clear and present danger doctrine also remains unfulfilled. A variation of the doctrine occupies a secure doctrinal place in the context of INCITEMENT TO UNLAWFUL CONDUCT, and the DENNIS V. UNITED STATES (1951) version of the test has been employed by the Court in other contexts, as in *Landmark Communications, Inc. v. Virginia* (1978) and NEBRASKA PRESS ASSOCIATION V. STUART (1976).

If doctrine were described today in terms of levels, many levels would be necessary. At one level, there is the question whether a First Amendment problem is presented: an effort to communicate a message by assassination presumably raises no First Amendment problem. If cognizable First Amendment values are present, there remains the question whether any legal protection is appropriate: advocacy of illegal action often is unprotected despite the existence of cognizable First Amendment interests. If some protection is appropriate, further questions remain: what protection in what contexts, at what times, in what places, and concerning what modes of expression? A multitude of doctrinal tests now govern a multitude of contexts. Harry Kalven would appreciate the Court's sensitivity to the vicissitudes of human conduct, but likely would regret the absence of an overall vision.

Bibliography
KALVEN, HARRY, JR.   1960   The Metaphysics of the Law of Obscenity. *Supreme Court Review* 1960:1–45.
———   1964   The New York Times Case: A Note on "The Central Meaning of the First Amendment." *Supreme Court Review* 1964:191–221.

Regulation of
Speech Content

SEDITION

Dennis J. Mahoney

Sedition is a comprehensive term for offenses against the authority of the government not amounting to TREASON. Such offenses might include the spreading of disaffection or disloyalty, conspiracy to commit insurrection, or any SUBVERSIVE ACTIVITY. Sedition tends toward treason, but does not reach the constitutionally defined offense of "levying war against the United States or adhering to their enemies, giving them aid and comfort."

Historically, the broad category of "sedition" has comprised several kinds of activity, although there has not always been consistency about which constituted criminal offenses. SEDITIOUS LIBEL, the uttering of words bringing the government or its officers into ridicule or disrepute, was an offense at COMMON LAW and under the ALIEN AND SEDITION ACTS of 1798. Seditious membership, that is, active, knowing, and purposeful membership in an organization committed to the overthrow of the government by unlawful means, is an offense under the Smith Act. Seditious advocacy, the public promotion of insurrection or rebellion, and seditious conspiracy, combining with others to subvert the government, violate several statutory provisions; but those offenses must be very carefully defined lest the statutes exert a CHILLING EFFECT on legitimate criticism of government.

The possibility of sedition poses a particular problem for constitutional democracy. Democratic governments, no less than any other kind, need to protect themselves against seditious activity. But measures taken in self-defense must not be so broad in their scope as themselves to become a threat to individual liberty. In the United States, the FIRST AMENDMENT to the Constitution protects FREEDOM OF SPEECH, FREEDOM OF THE PRESS, and FREEDOM OF ASSEMBLY AND ASSOCIATION; these specific constitutional guarantees limit the power of Congress and of the states to legislate against sedition.

For most of American history, the national and state governments exercised a CONCURRENT POWER to define and punish sedition. The power of Congress to legislate against sedition does not derive from any of the specific ENUMERATED POWERS, but is NECESSARY AND PROPER for the carrying out of several of them. In PENNSYLVANIA v. NELSON (1956) the Supreme Court held that Congress, by enacting a pervasive scheme of regulation, had preempted the field of legislation concerning sedition against the United States.

SEDITIOUS LIBEL

David A. Anderson

Though its scope has varied greatly with time and place, the heart of the doctrine of seditious libel is the proposition that government may punish its critics for words it perceives as a threat to its survival. The offending words may be criticism of the government itself, or, more often, of its leaders. What constitutes seditious libel tends to be whatever the government fears most at the time. In fifteenth-century England, where reverence for the crown was considered essential to the safety of the realm, it was a crime to call the king a fool or to predict his death. In colonial America the most frequent offense was criticizing local representatives of the crown. In 1798, the Federalist party feared that Jeffersonian attacks would so undermine public confidence that the fledgling Republic would fall—or at least that the Federalists would lose the election of 1800. They therefore made it a crime to publish any false, scandalous, and malicious writing about either house of Congress or the President of the United States.

In England, seditious libels were once prosecuted as treason, punishable by death. Thus in 1663 William Twyn, who printed a book endorsing the right of revolution, was hanged, emasculated, disemboweled, quartered, and beheaded. Not until the eighteenth century did the law clearly distinguish seditious libel from treason; the latter then was confined to cases in which the seditious words were accompanied by some overt act. Seditious libel became a misdemeanor, punishable by fines, imprisonment, and the pillory. Prosecutions were common in England until the mid-nineteenth century.

Seditious libel was part of the received law in the American colonies, but it was received unenthusiastically. There probably were no more than a dozen seditious libel prosecutions in the entire colonial period, and few were successful. Although no one seems to have doubted that government should have some power to protect itself from verbal attacks, many complained that the doctrine as it had evolved in England allowed legitimate criticism to be swept within the ambit of the seditious libel proscription. The law allowed no defense of truth; the objective was to preserve respect for government, to which truthful criticism was an even greater threat than falsehood. And because the interests to be protected were the government's, it would hardly do to let a jury decide whether the words were actionable. The judges therefore kept for themselves the power to determine whether the speaker's intent was seditious; the jury was only allowed to decide whether he had uttered the words charged.

As ideas of POPULAR SOVEREIGNTY grew, critics on both sides of the Atlantic attacked these rules. In America the issue jelled in the 1735 trial of John Peter Zenger, a New York printer who had criticized the royal governor. Zenger's lawyer, Andrew Hamilton, argued that he should be allowed to defend Zenger by proving the truth of the publication, and that the jury should be allowed to decide whether the words were libelous. The judge rejected both arguments, but the jury acquitted Zenger anyway, even though he had admitted publishing the words. (See ZENGER'S CASE.)

The case made popular heroes of Zenger and Hamilton and destroyed the effectiveness of seditious libel law as a tool for English control of American dissent. There were few, if any, successful common law prosecutions in the colonies after *Zenger*. Colonial legislatures sometimes punished their critics for breaches of "parliamentary privilege," but public resentment eventually made this device ineffective, too.

The intended effect of the FIRST AMENDMENT on the law of seditious libel is still in dispute. It is clear that seditious libel was still the law in 1789, and that the Framers expressed no intent to preclude prosecutions for seditious libel. They certainly did not intend to prevent the states from prosecuting seditious libels; all agreed that the First Amendment was a limitation on federal power only. And within a decade, Congress passed the Sedition Act of 1798, under which the Federalists prosecuted a number of prominent Republican editors. Several Justices of the Supreme Court, sitting as circuit judges, enforced the act. This evidence has persuaded some modern scholars that the Framers had no intention of abolishing seditious libel.

Others have argued that the Framers had at least a nascent understanding that some freedom to criticize government was a prerequisite to self-government, and that England's rigorous concept of seditious libel was inconsistent with that need. Their failure explicitly to condemn it might be explained by the fact that seditious libel prosecutions had not been a serious threat in their lifetimes. The Sedition Act may have been an unprincipled effort by desperate Federalist partisans to keep control of the government, rather than a considered affirmation of the constitutionality of seditious libel.

The Supreme Court has never squarely held that the First Amendment forbids punishment of seditious libels. From World War I through the McCarthy era, state and federal governments prosecuted numerous anarchists, socialists, and communists for advocating draft resistance, mass strikes, or overthrow of the government. Although the statutes authorizing these prosecutions were not called seditious libel acts, they had much the same effect. The Court generally upheld these convictions (usually over the dissents of the more libertarian Justices) until the 1960s, when in BRANDENBURG V. OHIO (1969) it adopted the view that punishment of mere advocacy is unconstitutional unless it is intended to produce imminent lawless action and is likely to do so.

Garrison v. Louisiana (1964) closely resembled a traditional seditious libel prosecution. A district attorney had been convicted of criminal libel for accusing local judges of laziness and corruption. The Court reversed his conviction, but implied that the prosecution might have been permissible if the state had proved that the defendant spoke with reckless disregard of the truth or falsity of his statements.

Nevertheless, the judgment of history is that seditious libel laws are inconsistent with FREEDOM OF SPEECH and FREEDOM OF THE PRESS. JAMES MADISON and THOMAS JEFFERSON argued in 1799 that the Sedition Act was unconstitutional. Justice OLIVER WENDELL HOLMES, dissenting in ABRAMS V. UNITED STATES (1919), wrote, "I wholly disagree with the argument of the Government that the First Amendment left the common law as to seditious libel in force. . . . I had conceived that the United States through many years had shown its repentance for the Sedition Act . . . by repaying the fines that it imposed." And in NEW YORK TIMES V. SULLIVAN (1964) the Court said, "Although the Sedition Act was never tested in this Court, the attack upon its validity has carried the day in the court of history."

Bibliography

ANDERSON, DAVID A.   1983   The Origins of the Press Clause. *University of California at Los Angeles Law Review* 30:455–537.

LEVY, LEONARD W.   1984   *Emergence of a Free Press.* New York: Oxford University Press.

NELSON, HAROLD L.   1959   Seditious Libel in Colonial America. *American Journal of Legal History* 3:160–172.

ALIEN AND SEDITION ACTS

Naturalization Act
1 Stat. 566 (1798)
Alien Act
1 Stat. 570 (1798)
Alien Enemies Act
1 Stat. 577 (1798)
Sedition Act
1 Stat. 596 (1798)

Merrill D. Peterson

These acts were provoked by the war crisis with France in 1798. Three of the four acts concerned ALIENS. Federalist leaders feared the French and Irish, in particular, as a potentially subversive force and as an element of strength in the Republican party. The Naturalization Act increased the period of residence required for admission to CITIZENSHIP from five to fourteen years. The Alien Act authorized the President to deport any alien deemed dangerous to the peace and safety of the United States. The Alien Enemies Act authorized incarceration and banishment of aliens in time of war. The Sedition Act, aimed at "domestic traitors," made it a federal crime for anyone to conspire to impede governmental operations or to write or publish "any false, scandalous, and malicious writing" against the government, the Congress, or the President.

While Republicans conceded the constitutionality, though not the necessity, of the Naturalization and Alien Enemies acts, they assailed the others, not only as unnecessary and unconstitutional but as politically designed to cripple or destroy the opposition party under the pretense of foreign menace. The constitutional argument received authoritative statement in the VIRGINIA AND KENTUCKY RESOLUTIONS. In defense of the Alien Act, with its summary procedures, Federalists appealed to the inherent right of the government to protect itself. The same appeal was made for the Sedition Act. Federalists denied, further, that the act violated FIRST AMENDMENT guarantees of FREEDOM OF SPEECH and PRESS, which they interpreted as prohibitions of PRIOR RESTRAINT only. They also claimed that the federal government had JURISDICTION over COMMON

LAW crimes, such as SEDITIOUS LIBEL, and so could prosecute without benefit of statute. The statute, they said, liberalized the common law by admitting truth as a defense and authorizing juries to return a general verdict.

Despite the zeal of President JOHN ADAMS's administration, no one was actually deported under the Alien Act. (War not having been declared, the Alien Enemies Act never came into operation.) The Sedition Act, on the other hand, was widely enforced. Twenty-five persons were arrested, fourteen indicted (plus three under common law), ten tried and convicted, all of them Republican printers and publicists. The most celebrated trials were those of Matthew Lyon, Republican congressman and newspaper editor in Vermont; Dr. Thomas Cooper, an English-born scientist and political refugee, in Philadelphia; and James T. Callender, another English refugee, who possessed a vitriolic pen, in Richmond. All were fined upward to $1,000 and imprisoned for as long as nine months. Before partisan judges and juries, in a climate of fear and suspicion, the boasted safeguards of the law proved of no value to the defendants, and all constitutional safeguards were rejected.

The repressive laws recoiled on their sponsors, contributing to the Republican victory in the election of 1800. The Sedition Act expired the day THOMAS JEFFERSON became President. He immediately voided actions pending under it and pardoned the victims. In 1802 the Alien Act expired and Congress returned the NATURALIZATION law to its old footing. Only the Alien Enemies Act remained on the statute book. Nothing like this legislation would be enacted again until the two world wars of the twentieth century.

Bibliography

SMITH, JAMES MORTON   1956   *Freedom's Fetters: The Alien and Sedition Laws and American Civil Liberties.*   Ithaca, N.Y.: Cornell University Press.

SUBVERSIVE ACTIVITY

Dennis J. Mahoney

Activity is "subversive" if it is directed toward the overthrow of the existing form of government by force or other unlawful means. Subversive activity comprises TREASON, SEDITION, insurrection, and sabotage, as well as other unlawful acts committed with the requisite intent. Although individuals may engage in subversive activity, concerted or organized subversion is more common and excites more public concern. Active, purposive membership in subversive organizations—such as the Communist party, the American Nazi party, or the Ku Klux Klan—is a federal crime, and between 1950 and 1974 the ATTORNEY GENERAL'S LIST was maintained as an official catalog of such groups.

In twentieth-century America, the suppression of subversion has been controversial where the "activity" has seemed to consist primarily of SUBVERSIVE ADVOCACY. But the controversy should not obscure the fact that there is such a thing as subversive activity and that the survival of constitutional government requires that such activity be controlled.

The critical distinction is not between words and deeds, speech and action. Even the staunchest defenders of CIVIL LIBERTIES agree that INCITEMENT TO UNLAWFUL CONDUCT may be punished by law, at least when the speaker has the intention and capability of inducing his hearers to engage in insurrection, riot, or disobedience of law. Some forms of subversive activity—for example, the attack on the House of Representatives by Puerto Rican nationalists in 1954—are extreme forms of SYMBOLIC SPEECH, known in revolutionary jargon as "propaganda of the deed." The political goal toward which it is aimed is precisely what distinguishes subversive activity.

Because the government of the United States is one of limited and ENUMERATED POWERS, its authority to define and punish subversive activities as crimes is not entirely clear. Treason is defined in Article III, section 2, of the Constitution, and as the same section limits the range of punishment for treason, it implies the power of Congress to prescribe punishment within the permitted range. The Constitution does not define any lesser degree of subversive activity, nor does it expressly grant to Congress the power to define and punish such crimes. Instead, the power must be an IMPLIED POWER incidental to the power to punish treason or else NECESSARY AND PROPER for the carrying out of one or more of the enumerated powers.

In the absence of statutes against insurrection or rebellion, the perpe-
trators of FRIES' REBELLION and the WHISKEY REBELLION were tried for
treason. The prosecutors argued that an armed rising to prevent the
execution of federal law—the normal definition of insurrection—was
at least a constructive treason as the COMMON LAW had understood the
term. Similarly, when AARON BURR assembled an armed force in the
Western territories, for purposes that are still not entirely clear, the
only federal offense for which he could be tried was treason. But a
charge of treason seems manifestly to have been inappropriate in each
of these cases.

On the other hand, the ALIEN AND SEDITION ACTS, enacted when
the country was on the brink of war with France, generously defined
offenses against the United States. Although section 2, defining SEDITIOUS
LIBEL, is more famous, section 1 of the Sedition Act proscribed certain
subversive activities: combination or conspiracy to impede the operation
of law or to intimidate government officials, procuring or counseling
riot or insurrection—whether or not the activity was successful. The
ESPIONAGE ACT OF 1917, enacted while the country was fighting World
War I, treated as criminal any attempt to procure draft evasion or to
interfere with military recruitment while the Sedition Act of 1918 proscribed all advocacy of revolution, however remote the prospect of success.

In the latter half of the twentieth century, the phenomenon of
political terrorism raised new problems. Frequently directed from outside
the United States, terrorist activity, like the extreme forms of subversive
activity, employs politically motivated violence. Although the aim of
terrorism may not be the overthrow of the American government, terrorism shares with the more extreme forms of subversive activity the substitu-
tion of violence for public deliberation and constitutional government.

Bibliography

GRODZINS, MORTON   1956   The Loyal and the Disloyal: Social Boundaries of Patrio-
    tism and Treason. Chicago: University of Chicago Press.
HURST, JAMES WILLARD   1971   The Law of Treason in the United States. Westport,
    Conn.: Greenwood Press.

SUBVERSIVE ADVOCACY

Carl A. Auerbach

The quest for NATIONAL SECURITY has placed strains on the FIRST AMEND-MENT when the country has been at war, or threatened by war, or torn by fear of an external enemy or domestic social unrest. Federal and state governments have sought to silence those regarded as "subversives" and internal enemies because they supported a foreign cause or advocated revolutionary change in American institutions.

The ALIEN AND SEDITION ACTS, passed only seven years after ratification of the First Amendment, were the most extreme of these measures in our history. President JOHN ADAMS and the Federalist Congress used them to stifle the opposition Republicans who were accused of being "servile minions" of France, with which war seemed imminent in early 1798. Seventeen prosecutions were instituted against Republican newspaper editors, officeholders, and adherents, with only one acquittal.

The constitutionality of the Sedition Act was never tested in the Supreme Court, which then had no JURISDICTION to review federal criminal convictions. But the act was sustained by the lower federal courts, including three Supreme Court Justices sitting as trial judges. The modern Supreme Court, in NEW YORK TIMES CO. v. SULLIVAN (1964), has stated that the First Amendment bars prosecution for SEDITIOUS LIBEL. Opposition to the government in power, accompanied by criticism of official policy and conduct, cannot constitutionally be proscribed as "seditious" or "subversive."

During the nineteenth century there was no federal legislation limiting FREEDOM OF SPEECH or FREEDOM OF THE PRESS. No official efforts were made to silence the Federalist denunciation of the War of 1812. Abolitionist sentiment did not fare so well in the succeeding decades of bitter controversy over slavery. Southern states passed laws limiting the freedom to criticize slavery. During the Civil War no sedition act was passed to suppress the widespread opposition to the war in the North. But President ABRAHAM LINCOLN suspended the writ of HABEAS CORPUS, controlled the mails, telegraph, and passports, and approved military detention of thousands of persons accused of disloyalty.

The rapid industrialization and urbanization of the country after the Civil War was accompanied by social unrest. The Haymarket Square bombing in Chicago in 1886, the violent Homestead and Pullman strikes in the 1890s, the assassination of President WILLIAM McKINLEY in 1901 by a presumed "anarchist," and the militant tactics of the Industrial Workers of the World led to the passage of the first state Criminal Anarchy Law in New York in 1902. By 1921, thirty-three states had enacted similar laws making it a crime to advocate the overthrow of existing government by force or violence. Unlike the Sedition Act of 1798, these laws forbade only the advocacy of illegal means to effect political change.

Together with the federal ESPIONAGE ACT of 1917, these state laws were used to suppress opposition to World War I voiced by pacifists, sympathizers with Germany, and international socialists. The 1917 act made it criminal to obstruct recruiting, cause insubordination in the armed forces, or interfere with military operations. Amendments to the Espionage Act (the SEDITION ACT of 1918) made it an offense, among other things, to say or do anything that would favor any country at war with the United States, oppose the cause of the United States in the war, or incite contempt for the American form of government or the uniform of the Army or Navy. Under the Espionage Act 877 people were convicted, almost all for expressing opinions about the merits and conduct of the war. The Supreme Court sustained these convictions, rejecting the contention that they violated the First Amendment.

SCHENCK V. UNITED STATES (1919) was the first of the Espionage Act cases to reach the Supreme Court. Justice OLIVER WENDELL HOLMES wrote the Court opinion affirming the conviction and, for the first time, enunciated the CLEAR AND PRESENT DANGER test to determine when advocacy of unlawful conduct is protected by the First Amendment. Holmes also wrote the opinions of the Court in FROHWERK V. UNITED STATES (1919) and DEBS V. UNITED STATES (1919), sustaining the convictions of a newspaper editor for questioning the constitutionality of the draft and charging that Wall Street had dragged the country into the war, and of Eugene V. Debs, the railroad union and Socialist party leader, for denouncing the war as a capitalist plot. Just what the "clear and present danger" was in these cases was doubtful, and Holmes and Brandeis soon began to dissent from the way the majority used the test.

Their first great dissent came in ABRAMS V. UNITED STATES (1919). In his dissenting opinion, which Brandeis joined, Holmes gave new content to the clear and present danger test by emphasizing the immediacy of the danger that must exist. Although Holmes would have softened this requirement, permitting punishment of speech with the specific intent to bring about the danger even if the danger itself was not "immediate," he did not think the necessary intent had been shown in *Abrams*.

The Red Scare of 1919 and 1920 was induced not only by fear of the Bolshevik revolution and the Communist International but also by the economic and social insecurity that accompanied demobilization after World War I. The PALMER RAIDS expressed the federal government's fears and antiradical sentiments. The states resorted to their criminal anarchy laws and the Supreme Court sustained convictions under these laws in GITLOW v. NEW YORK (1925) and WHITNEY v. CALIFORNIA (1927).

In *Gitlow* the Court assumed that freedom of speech and press, protected by the First Amendment from abridgment by Congress, was a "liberty" protected by the DUE PROCESS clause of the FOURTEENTH AMENDMENT against state impairment. In both *Gitlow* and *Whitney* the Court refused to apply the clear and present danger test because the state legislatures had prohibited a particular class of speech—the advocacy of the doctrine that the government should be overthrown by violence. Gitlow's advocacy of violent revolution violated the law even if there were no clear and present danger of revolution. The legislature might reasonably seek "to extinguish the spark without waiting until it has enkindled the flame or blazed into the conflagration."

Dissenting in *Gitlow,* Holmes argued for application of the clear and present danger test, but did not confront the majority's position. But Brandeis, concurring in *Whitney,* insisted that courts and juries must be free to decide whether, under the circumstances of each case, "the evil apprehended is [relatively serious and its incidence] so imminent that it may befall before there is opportunity for full discussion. . . . Only an emergency can justify repression."

From the end of the Red Scare to the outbreak of World War II, federal action against alleged subversives was limited to deportation of alien communists. State prosecutions under criminal anarchy laws were infrequent after the middle 1920s. The Sedition Act of 1918 was repealed in 1921 and has never been revived.

The Smith Act of 1940 was modeled on the New York Criminal Anarchy law. During World War II, twenty-eight pro-Nazi individuals were prosecuted under it for conspiring to cause insubordination in the armed forces, but the judge died and the prosecution was dropped. Eighteen members of the Trotskyist Socialist Workers party, which opposed the war, were convicted of conspiracy to cause insubordination in the armed forces and to advocate violent overthrow of the government.

On the whole, the country supported World War II. After the Nazi invasion of the Soviet Union, in June 1941, communists became the staunchest supporters of the war. But as soon as the war was won, the activities of the international communist movement resumed. In 1949 eleven leaders of the Communist party were convicted under the Smith Act for conspiring to advocate violent overthrow of the United States government and establishment of a dictatorship of the proletariat, and to organize the Communist party to advocate these goals. The Supreme Court affirmed the convictions, 6–2, in DENNIS v. UNITED STATES (1951).

In 1948 the Soviet Union had blockaded Berlin and engineered the communist coup that overthrew the parliamentary regime in Czechoslovakia. By the time the Supreme Court decided *Dennis,* several Soviet spy rings in the West had been exposed, the communists had taken control in China, and Americans were dying in the KOREAN WAR. The domestic and foreign policies of the American Communist party were consistent with Soviet policies and directives. In light of these events, a plurality of four Justices, speaking through Chief Justice FRED M. VINSON, reformulated the clear and present danger test into a BALANCING TEST that weighed the seriousness of the danger, discounted by its improbability, against the degree of invasion of freedom of speech.

Justice FELIX FRANKFURTER concurred, deferring to Congress's judgment regarding the extent of the danger posed by the Communist party and the world communist movement. With the experience of the Nuremberg war crimes trials still fresh in his memory, Justice ROBERT H. JACKSON also concurred, joining Frankfurter in rejecting the appropriateness of the clear and present danger test to the communist conspiracy.

Though not purporting to overrule *Dennis,* the Supreme Court, in YATES v. UNITED STATES (1957), reversed convictions of the officers of the Communist party in California. Justice JOHN MARSHALL HARLAN's plurality opinion read the Smith Act as requiring proof that the defendants had advocated "unlawful action" and not merely "abstract doctrine" that the United States government should be overthrown. *Yates* did not represent a return to the Holmes-Brandeis version of the clear and present danger test. It emphasized the content of the advocacy, not its consequences. On this view, advocacy of unlawful action was punishable, irrespective of the immediacy of the danger.

After *Yates* was decided, the government concluded that it could not satisfy the requirements of proof demanded by the Supreme Court and abandoned all prosecutions under the Smith Act. Altogether twenty-nine communists were convicted under that act, including the leaders involved in *Dennis* and the only person convicted under the provision proscribing membership in the Communist party. His conviction was upheld in SCALES v. UNITED STATES (1961) because he was an "active member" who knew of the Party's unlawful goals and had a "specific intent" to achieve them.

In 1950, shortly after the outbreak of the Korean War, Congress enacted the SUBVERSIVE ACTIVITIES CONTROL ACT, which required communist organizations to register with the ATTORNEY GENERAL. When the Communist party failed to register, the attorney general asked the Subversive Activities Control Board to order it to register and list its members. In COMMUNIST PARTY v. SUBVERSIVE ACTIVITIES CONTROL BOARD (1961) the Court upheld the board's finding that the party was a communist-action organization and its order requiring the party to register. Only Justice HUGO L. BLACK dissented from the majority view that the First

Amendment did not prohibit Congress from removing the party's "mask of anonymity."

The Supreme Court in 1961 did not pass upon the contention that compulsory registration would violate the RIGHT AGAINST SELF-IN-CRIMINATION afforded by the Fifth Amendment because it would subject party members to prosecution under the Smith Act and the 1954 COMMU-NIST CONTROL ACT. This contention was eventually sustained in ALBERT-SON V. SUBVERSIVE ACTIVITIES CONTROL BOARD (1965). As a result, neither the Communist party nor any of its members ever registered under the act, and no organization ever registered as a communist front. In 1968, Congress removed the registration obligation. Instead, the Subver-sive Activities Control Board was authorized to keep records, open to public inspection, of the names and addresses of communist organizations and their members. But in 1969 and 1970 the courts held that mere membership in the party was protected by the First Amendment, and the board was disbanded in 1973.

The Communist Control Act of 1954 purported to deprive the Com-munist party of the "rights, privileges, and immunities attendant upon legal bodies." It was not clear whether Congress intended this provision to dissolve the party as a legal organization or only to bar it from the ballot and benefits such as mailing privileges. Though the Supreme Court has not passed upon its constitutionality, the act has become a dead letter.

Although the Espionage Act and the Smith Act remained in force during the VIETNAM WAR, no prosecutions were brought under either measure. In *Bond v. Floyd* (1966) the Supreme Court assumed that opposition to the war and the draft was protected by the First Amend-ment.

In 1967 a Ku Klux Klan leader was convicted of violating the Ohio CRIMINAL SYNDICALISM LAW by making a speech at a Klan rally to which only television newsmen had been invited. The speech was derogatory of blacks and Jews and proclaimed that if the white race continued to be threatened, "it's possible that there might have to be some revengence [sic] taken." In a PER CURIAM opinion in BRANDENBURG V. OHIO (1969) the Supreme Court reversed the conviction and held the Ohio statute unconstitutional. In so doing, it overruled *Whitney v. California* and again reformulated the clear and present danger doctrine: "constitutional guar-antees of free speech and free press do not permit a State to forbid or proscribe advocacy of the use of force or of law violation except where such advocacy is directed to inciting or producing such action." Although the Court purported to follow *Dennis,* commentators generally conclude that *Brandenburg* overruled *Dennis.* In *Communist Party of Indiana v. Whitcomb* (1974) the Supreme Court held that it was unconstitutional for Indiana to refuse a place on the ballot to the Communist party of Indiana because its officers had refused to submit an oath that the party "does not advocate the overthrow of local, state or national government by force or violence."

The *Brandenburg* formula, the most speech-protective standard yet evolved by the Supreme Court, has been criticized from opposing sides. Concurring in *Brandenburg,* Justices WILLIAM O. DOUGLAS and Black would have abandoned the clear and present danger test in favor of a distinction between ideas and overt acts. Some critics reject even this concession on the ground that an incitement-of-overt-acts test can be manipulated by the courts to cut off speech just when it comes close to being effective.

Others argue that advocacy of the forcible overthrow of the government, or of any unlawful act, is not protected by the First Amendment. Such advocacy is not political speech because it is a call to revoke the results that political speech has produced; violent overthrow destroys the premises of our system. An organization that seeks power through illegal means refuses to abide by the legitimate conditions of party competition in a democracy.

Furthermore, in suppressing totalitarian movements, even if they purport to reject illegal means, a democratic society is not acting to protect the status quo but the very same interest which freedom of speech itself seeks to secure—the possibility of peaceful progress under freedom. In this view, the *Brandenburg* formula would deny our democracy the constitutional right to act until it might be too late to prevent a totalitarian victory.

Although one may disagree with the view that the problem of a totalitarian party's competing for political power in a democracy is solely one of "freedom of expression," the reasons for toleration—to keep even the freedom of expression open to challenge lest it become a "dead dogma," and to allow extremist groups to advocate revolution because they may represent real grievances that deserve to be heard—must be seriously considered by legislators in determining whether suppression is a wise policy. But if wisdom may sometimes dictate toleration, that conclusion does not imply that the Constitution gives the enemies of freedom the right to organize to crush it.

Bibliography

GUNTHER GERALD 1975 Learned Hand and the Origins of Modern First Amendment Doctrine: Some Fragments of History. *Stanford Law Review* 27:719–773.

LEVY, LEONARD W. 1985 *Emergence of a Free Press*. New York: Oxford University Press.

LINDE, HANS A.   1970   "Clear and Present Danger" Reexamined: Dissonants in the Brandenburg Concerto. *Stanford Law Review* 22:1163–1186.

NATHANSON, NATHANIEL L.   1950   The Communist Trial and the Clear-and-Present-Danger Test. *Harvard Law Review* 63:1167–1175.

INCITEMENT TO UNLAWFUL CONDUCT

Kent Greenawalt

Incitement to unlawful conduct raises a central and difficult issue about the proper boundaries of freedom of expression and of the First Amendment. Many of the Supreme Court's most important freedom of speech decisions have involved some form of incitement. Though the term incitement sometimes refers to emotionally charged appeals to immediate action, the word is most often used to cover any urging that others commit illegal acts.

The basic problem about incitement is fairly simple, involving a tension between a criminal law perspective and a free speech perspective. Any society seeks to minimize the number of crimes that are committed. Some people commit crimes because others urge them to do so. Although the person who actually commits a crime may usually seem more to blame than someone who encourages him, on other occasions the inciter, because of greater authority, intelligence, or firmness of purpose, may actually be more responsible for what happens than the person who is the instrument of his designs. In any event, because the person who successfully urges another to commit a crime bears some responsibility and because effective restrictions on incitement are likely to reduce the amount of crime to some degree, sound reasons exist for punishing those who incite.

Anglo-American criminal law, like the law of other traditions, has reflected this view. In 1628, Edward Coke wrote that "all those that incite . . . any other" to commit a felony are guilty of a crime; and, at least by 1801, unsuccessful incitement was recognized as an offense in England. Modern American criminal law generally treats the successful inciter on a par with the person who performs the criminal act; the unsuccessful inciter is guilty of criminal solicitation, treated as a lesser crime than the one he has tried to incite.

From the free speech perspective, the problem of incitement takes on a different appearance. A basic premise of a liberal society is that people should be allowed to express their views, especially their political views. Some important political views support illegal actions against actual or possible governments. Indeed, one aspect of the political tradition of the United States is that revolutionary overthrow of existing political authority is sometimes justified. Other views deem certain illegal acts justified even when the government is acceptable. Were all encouragements of illegal activity suppressed, an important slice of political and social opinions would be silenced. Further, in the practical administration of such suppression some opinions that did not quite amount to encouragement would be proceeded against and persons would be inhibited from saying things that could possibly be construed as encouragements to commit crimes. Thus, wide restrictions on incitement have been thought to imperil free expression, particularly when statutes penalizing incitement have been specifically directed to "subversive" political ideologies.

The tension between criminal law enforcement and freedom of expression is addressed by both legislatures and courts. Legislatures must initially decide what is a reasonable, and constitutionally permissible, accommodation of the conflicting values. When convictions are challenged, courts must decide whether the statutes that legislatures have adopted and their applications to particular situations pass constitutional muster.

Most states have statutes that make solicitation of a crime illegal. These laws are drawn to protect speech interests to a significant extent. To be convicted of solicitation, one must actually encourage the commission of a specific crime. Therefore, many kinds of statements, such as disinterested advice that committing a crime like draft evasion would be morally justified, approval of present lawbreaking in general, or urging people to prepare themselves for unspecified future revolutionary acts, are beyond the reach of ordinary solicitation statutes.

One convenient way to conceptualize the First Amendment problems about incitement is to ask whether any communications that do amount to ordinary criminal solicitation are constitutionally protected and whether other communications that encourage criminal acts but fall short of criminal solicitation lack constitutional protection.

All major Supreme Court cases on the subject have involved political expression of one kind or another and have arisen under statutes directed at specific kinds of speech. Some of the cases have involved CRIMINAL CONSPIRACY charges, but because the conspiracy has been to incite or advocate, the constitutionality of punishing communications has been the crucial issue. In SCHENCK v. UNITED STATES (1919) the Court sustained a conviction under the 1917 ESPIONAGE ACT, which made criminal attempts to obstruct enlistment. The leaflet that Schenck had helped to publish had urged young men to assert their rights to oppose the draft. Writing the majority opinion that found no constitutional bar to the conviction, Justice OLIVER WENDELL HOLMES penned the famous CLEAR AND PRESENT DANGER test: "The question in every case is whether the words used are used in such circumstances and are of such a nature as to create a clear and present danger that they will bring about the substantive evils that Congress has a right to prevent." Much was unclear about this test as originally formulated and as subsequently developed, but the results in *Schenck* and companion cases show that the Court then did not conceive the standard as providing great protection for speech. During the 1920s, while the majority of Justices ceased using the test, eloquent dissents by Holmes and LOUIS D. BRANDEIS forged it into a principle that was protective of speech, requiring a danger that was both substantial and close in time in order to justify suppressing communication. Even these later opinions, however, did not indicate with clarity whether the test applied to ordinary criminal solicitation or whether an intent to create a clear and present danger would be sufficient for criminal punishment.

During the 1920s, the majority of the Supreme Court was willing to affirm convictions for expression, so long as the expression fell within a statutory prohibition and the statutory prohibition was reasonable. Thus, in GITLOW v. NEW YORK (1925) the Court upheld a conviction under a criminal anarchy statute that forbade teaching the propriety of illegally overthrowing organized government. The Court concluded that the legislature could reasonably anticipate that speech of this type carried the danger of a "revolutionary spark" kindling a fire. The standard applied in *Gitlow* and similar cases would permit suppression of virtually any type of speech that a legislature might consider to create a danger of illegal activity, a category far broader than ordinary criminal solicitation.

In the 1930s the Supreme Court began to render decisions more protective of speech, and in HERNDON v. LOWRY (1937) the Court reversed a conviction for attempting to incite insurrection, when the evidence failed to show that the defendant, a Communist party organizer, had actually urged revolutionary violence. The majority in *Herndon* referred to the clear and present danger test with approval. In a series of subsequent decisions, that test was employed as an all-purpose standard for First Amendment cases.

In 1951, the Supreme Court reviewed the convictions of eleven leading communists in DENNIS v. UNITED STATES. The defendants had violated the Smith Act by conspiring to advocate the forcible overthrow of the United States government. As in *Gitlow,* the expressions involved (typical communist rhetoric) fell short of inciting to any specific crime. The plurality opinion, representing the views of four Justices, accepted clear and present danger as the appropriate standard, but interpreted the test so that the gravity of the evil was discounted by its improbability. In practice, this formulation meant that if the evil were very great, such as overthrow of the government, communication creating a danger of that evil might be suppressed even though the evil would not occur in the near future and had only a small likelihood that it would ever occur. The dissenters and civil libertarian observers protested that this interpretation undermined the main point of "clear and present" danger. *Dennis* is now viewed by many as a regrettable product of unwarranted fears of successful communist subversion. In subsequent cases, the Court emphasized that the Smith Act reached only advocacy of illegal action, not advocacy of doctrine. In the years since *Dennis* only one conviction under the act has passed this stringent test.

The modern constitutional standard for incitement cases arose out of the conviction of a Ku Klux Klan leader for violating a broad CRIMINAL SYNDICALISM statute, not unlike the statute involved in *Gitlow*. Unsurprisingly, the Court said in BRANDENBURG v. OHIO (1969) that the broad statute was unconstitutional. But it went on to fashion a highly restrictive version of clear and present danger: that a state may not "forbid or proscribe advocacy of the use of force or of law violation except where such advocacy is directed to inciting or producing imminent lawless action and is likely to incite or produce such action." This test requires lawless action that is likely, imminent, and intended by the speaker. Only rarely could such a test possibly be met by speech that does not amount to criminal solicitation, and under this test both solicitation of crimes in the distant future and solicitation unlikely to be acted upon are constitutionally protected. In *Brandenburg*, however, the Court had directly in mind public advocacy; it is unlikely that this stringent test also applies to private solicitations of crime that are made for personal gain. The present law provides significant constitutional protection for political incitements, but how far beyond political speech this protection may extend remains uncertain.

Bibliography

AMERICAN LAW INSTITUTE 1985 *Model Penal Code,* Section 5.02 and Commentary. St. Paul, Minn.: West Publishing Co.

GREENAWALT, KENT 1980 Speech and Crime. *American Bar Foundation Research Journal* 1980:647–785.

LINDE, HANS A. 1970 "Clear and Present Danger" Reexamined: Dissonance in the Brandenburg Concerto. *Stanford Law Review* 22:1163–1186.

ESPIONAGE ACT

40 Stat. 451 (1917)

Paul L. Murphy

When on April 2, 1917, President WOODROW WILSON asked Congress to recognize a STATE OF WAR, he included in his indictment of Germany the activities of German agents in the United States. Such activity, he said, should be treated with "a firm hand of stern repression." Nine weeks later, a much discussed and much amended Espionage Act was signed into law.

The initial measure, an amalgamation of seventeen bills prepared in the attorney general's office, was intended to "outlaw spies and subversive activities by foreign agents." Critics, particularly in the American press, quickly complained that the measure was far too restrictive and imposed a type of PRIOR RESTRAINT AND CENSORSHIP potentially destructive to basic American liberties. Thus, despite Wilson's contention that the administration must have authority to censor the press since this was "absolutely necessary to the public safety," the most overt censorship provisions were removed. The belief of a majority of national lawmakers that now the bill could not be used to suppress critical opinion overlooked the fact that two of the twelve titles of the act as passed still bore directly on freedom of expression. One provided punishment for (1) making or conveying false reports for the benefit of the enemy; (2) seeking to cause disobedience in the armed forces; and (3) willfully obstructing the recruiting or enlistment service. Another section closed the mails to any item violating any of the act's provisions.

The constitutional basis of these two provisions rested on a broad interpretation of the federal WAR POWERS and upon the argument that a denial of use of the mails did not constitute censorship, since the federal courts had ruled that the mails constituted an optional federal service. Thus, it was argued, refusal to extend the facility did not deprive anyone of a constitutional right. Further, the measure's supporters argued that FREEDOM OF SPEECH was not absolute and could not protect a person who deliberately sought to obstruct the national war effort.

The difficulty of applying the law, however, was clear from the outset, since the statute sought to punish questionable intent, a difficult factor to measure. With punishment set at a $10,000 fine, imprisonment for up to twenty years, or both, and with its interpretation largely in the hands of patriotic enforcers, many suffered under the measure and its subsequent amendments. The Justice Department prosecuted more than 2,000 cases. At least 1,050 citizens were convicted under its terms, including Industrial Workers of the World leaders, Socialists (especially Eugene V. Debs), and a number of suspect hyphenates, particularly German-Americans, whose verbal criticism of aspects of the war were often brutally repressed. The Supreme Court upheld the constitutionality of the act's prohibitions on causing disobedience in the armed forces and obstructing enlistment in a series of postwar decisions: SCHENCK V. UNITED STATES (1919), FROHWERK V. UNITED STATES (1919); DEBS V. UNITED STATES (1919).

Under the mails provisions, the postmaster general exercised virtually dictatorial authority over the effective circulation of the American press, a power which he used capriciously and subjectively for punitive reasons. In an effort to preserve FIRST AMENDMENT values through the process of statutory construction, Judge LEARNED HAND construed the mails provision narrowly to exclude its application to ordinary criticism of government policies, including war policy. Hand's decision, however, was reversed by the court of appeals. (See MASSES PUBLISHING CO. V. PATTEN, 1917.)

The measure remained on the books through the 1920s and 1930s and was reenacted in March 1940, Congress increasing its penalties for peacetime violation. The Supreme Court narrowed its application in *Hartzel v. United States* (1944) by interpreting its provisions through a literal application of Holmes's clear and present danger test. The government again turned to it in 1971, seeking unsuccessfully to prevent the publication by the *New York Times* of the "Pentagon papers," which the government called harmful to the security of the United States. (See NEW YORK TIMES CO. V. UNITED STATES, 1971.)

Bibliography

CHAFEE, ZECHARIAH 1941 *Free Speech in the United States.* Cambridge, Mass.: Harvard University Press.
MURPHY, PAUL 1979 *World War I and the Origin of Civil Liberties in the United States.* New York: Norton.

SEDITION ACT

40 Stat. 553 (1918)

Paul L. Murphy

As World War I progressed, enthusiastic war supporters argued more and more that the Espionage Act of 1917 did not adequately restrict domestic critics of the war effort. Advocates of additional restriction argued that weakness of the existing loyalty legislation forced citizens to take the law into their own hands. If firmer federal policies could be established, such distasteful forms of repression might be averted. Thus a more restrictive amendment to the Espionage Act was proposed and, despite strong congressional protest that the measure virtually terminated freedom of expression, was signed into law on May 16, 1918. The amendment, called the Sedition Act, defined eight offenses punishable by $10,000 fine or more than twenty years in prison, or both. The new offenses included: uttering, printing, writing, or publishing any disloyal, profane, scurrilous, or abusive language intended to cause contempt, scorn, contumely or disrepute as regards the form of government of the United States, or the Constitution, or the flag, or the uniform or the Army or Navy, or any language intended to incite resistance to the United States or to promote the cause of its enemies; urging any curtailment of production or anything necessary to the prosecution of the war with intent to hinder its prosecution; advocating, teaching, defending, or suggesting the doing of any of these acts; and words or acts supporting or favoring the cause of any country at war with the United States, or opposing the cause of the United States therein.

The 1918 act also enlarged the censorship functions of the postmaster general, empowering him to refuse to deliver mail to any individual or business employing the mails in violation of the statute. He was to order a letter that he deemed undeliverable to be returned to the sender with the phrase "Mail to this address undeliverable under the Espionage Act" stamped on the envelope. Thus the postmaster general was empowered to damage or destroy the business or reputation of any American citizen.

Enforced extensively in the period from May to November 1918, the measure virtually terminated wartime criticism until the Armistice. While efforts were made to reenact its provisions in a peace-time sedition statute during the A. Mitchell Palmer "red scare" period, Congress balked and ultimately took the act off the books in March 1921.

The extremely broad language of the act would today make it vulnerable to attack on the grounds of OVERBREADTH. In 1919, however, the Supreme Court upheld the conviction of five anarchists for circulating a leaflet urging curtailment of war production and encouraging resistance to the participation of U.S. forces in opposition to the Russian revolution. Justice OLIVER WENDELL HOLMES wrote a famous dissent, joined by Justice LOUIS D. BRANDEIS, in ABRAMS v. UNITED STATES (1919). (See CLEAR AND PRESENT DANGER.)

Bibliography

MURPHY, PAUL L. 1979 *World War I and the Origin of Civil Liberties in the United States.* New York: Norton.

BAD TENDENCY TEST

Martin Shapiro

In 1920 New York convicted Benjamin Gitlow of violating its statute prohibiting "advocating, advising or teaching the doctrine that organized government should be overthrown by force." Gitlow had published in the journal *Revolutionary Age* a "Left Wing Manifesto," thirty-four pages of Marxist rhetoric calling for class struggle leading to revolution and the dictatorship of the proletariat.

In GITLOW v. NEW YORK (1925) Gitlow's counsel argued in the Supreme Court that since the manifesto contained no direct INCITEMENT to criminal action, Gitlow must have been convicted under the "bad tendency test." That test was borrowed from the eighteenth-century English law of SEDITIOUS LIBEL which made criticism of government criminal because such criticism might tend to contribute to government's eventual collapse.

This bad tendency test ran counter to the CLEAR AND PRESENT DANGER test of SCHENCK v. UNITED STATES (1919). In *Gitlow* Justice EDWARD SANFORD virtually adopted the bad tendency test for instances in which a legislature had decided that a particular variety of speech created a sufficient danger. Even though there was no evidence of any effect resulting from the Manifesto's publication, the Court stressed that its language constituted advocacy of

mass action which shall progressively foment industrial disturbances, and, through . . . mass action, overthrow . . . government. . . . The immediate danger is none the less real and substantial because the effect of a given utterance cannot be accurately foreseen. . . . A single revolutionary spark may kindle a fire that, smoldering for a time, may burst into a sweeping and destructive conflagration. . . . [The State] cannot reasonably be required to defer the adoption of measures for its own peace and safety until the revolutionary utterances lead to . . . imminent and immediate danger of its own destruction.

Justices OLIVER WENDELL HOLMES and LOUIS D. BRANDEIS dissented in *Gitlow,* invoking the clear and present danger test. When that test came to dominate the Court's FIRST AMENDMENT opinions in the 1930s and early 1940s, the bad tendency test seemed to be overthrown.

Nevertheless much of Sanford's approach survived. Judge LEARNED HAND's "discounting formula" as adopted in DENNIS v. UNITED STATES (1951) allows speech to be suppressed "where the gravity of the evil, discounted by its improbability" justifies suppression. As *Dennis* itself illustrates, if the danger is painted as sufficiently grave, speech may be suppressed even if there is a very low probability that the evil will occur or that the particular speech in question will contribute to that occurrence. In *Dennis* the Court replaced the present danger test with the requirement that where an organized subversive group exists, the group intends to bring about overthrow "as speedily as the circumstances would permit." Such an approach echoed Sanford's plea that the government need not wait until the danger of revolution is imminent.

Bibliography

CHAFEE, ZECHARIAH, JR.   (1941)1969   *Free Speech in the United States.* New York: Atheneum.

LINDE, HANS   1970   "Clear and Present Danger" Reexamined: Dissonance in the Brandenburg Concerto. *Stanford Law Review* 22:1163–1186.

CLEAR AND PRESENT DANGER

Martin Shapiro

The clear and present danger rule, announced in SCHENCK V. UNITED STATES (1919), was the earliest FREEDOM OF SPEECH doctrine of the Supreme Court. Affirming Schenck's conviction, Justice OLIVER WENDELL HOLMES concluded that a speaker might be punished only when "the words are used in such circumstances and are of such a nature as to create a clear and present danger that they will bring about the substantive evils that Congress has a right to prevent." Holmes was drawing on his own earlier Massachusetts Supreme Judicial Court opinion on the law of attempts. There he had insisted that the state might punish attempted arson only when the preparations had gone so far that no time was left for the prospective arsonist to change his mind, so that the crime would have been committed but for the intervention of the state. In the free speech context, Holmes and Justice LOUIS D. BRANDEIS assimilated this idea to the MARKETPLACE OF IDEAS rationale, arguing that the best corrective of dangerous speech was more speech rather than criminal punishment; government should intervene only when the speech would do an immediate harm before there was time for other speech to come into play.

In the context of *Schenck,* the danger rule made particular sense; the federal statute under which the defendant was prosecuted made the *act* of espionage a crime, not the speech itself. The danger rule in effect required that before speech might be punished under a statute that forbade action, a close nexus between the speech and the action be shown. The concentration of the rule on the intent of the speaker and the circumstances surrounding the speech also seem most relevant in those contexts in which speech is being punished as if it constituted an attempt at a criminal act. Opponents of the danger rule have often insisted that Holmes initially intended it not as a general FIRST AMENDMENT test but only for cases in which a statute proscribing action was applied to a speaker.

In *Schenck,* Holmes wrote for the Court. The most extended statement of the danger rule came some months later in ABRAMS V. UNITED STATES (1919), but by then it was to be found in a Holmes dissent, joined by Brandeis. In GITLOW V. NEW YORK (1925) the Court used the BAD TENDENCY TEST which openly rejected the imminence or immediacy element of the danger rule—again over dissents by Holmes and Brandeis. Brandeis kept the danger rule alive in a concurrence in WHITNEY V. CALIFORNIA (1927) in which he added to the immediacy requirement that the threatened evil be serious. The danger of minor property damage, for example, would not justify suppression of speech.

In the 1930s and 1940s the Court was confronted with a series of cases involving parades and street corner speakers in which the justification offered for suppressing speech was not concern for the ultimate security of the state but the desire to maintain peaceful, quiet, and orderly streets and parks free of disturbance. Behind the proffered justifications usually lurked a desire to muzzle unpopular speakers while leaving other speakers free. In this context the clear and present danger rule was well designed to protect unpopular speakers from discrimination. It required the community to prove that the particular speaker whom it had punished or denied a license did in fact constitute an immediate threat to peace and good order. In such cases as HERNDON V. LOWRY (1937) (subversion), THORNHILL V. ALABAMA (1941) (labor PICKETING), *Bridges v. California* (1941) (contempt of court), WEST VIRGINIA BOARD OF EDUCATION V. BARNETTE (1943) (compulsory flag salute), and *Taylor v. Mississippi* (1943) (state sedition law), the clear and present danger rule became the majority constitutional test governing a wide range of circumstances, not only for statutes punishing conduct but also those regulating speech itself.

Even while enjoying majority status the rule came under attack from two directions. The "absolutists" led by ALEXANDER MEIKLEJOHN criticized the rule for allowing too broad an exception to First Amendment protections. The rule made the protection of speech dependent on judicial findings whether clear and present danger existed; judges had notoriously broad discretion in making findings of fact, as FEINER V. NEW YORK (1951) and TERMINIELLO V. CHICAGO (1949) illustrated. When applied to radical or subversive speech, the danger test seemed to say that ineffectual speech would be tolerated but that speech might be stifled just when it showed promise of persuading substantial numbers of listeners. On the other hand, those favoring judicial self-restraint, led by Justice FELIX FRANKFURTER, argued that the rule was too rigid in its protection of speech and ought to be replaced by a BALANCING TEST that weighed the interests in speech against various state interests and did so without rendering the immediacy of the threat to state interests decisive.

Later commentators have also argued that the distinction between speech and conduct on which the danger rule ultimately rests is not viable, pointing to picketing and such SYMBOLIC SPEECH as FLAG DESECRATION which intermingle speech and action. The danger rule also engenders logically unresolvable HOSTILE AUDIENCE problems. If Holmes's formula had demanded a showing of the specific intent of the speaker to bring about violence or of specific INCITEMENT to crime in the content of the speech, it might have afforded greater protection to some speakers. The independent weight the danger formula gives to surrounding circumstances may permit the stifling of speakers because of the real or imagined act or threats of others. Yet focusing exclusively upon intent or upon the presence of the language of incitement may lead to the punishment of speakers whose fervently revolutionary utterances in reality have little or no chance of bringing about any violent action at all.

In DENNIS v. UNITED STATES (1951) the clear and *present* danger test was converted overtly into a clear and *probable* danger test and covertly into a balancing test. As its origin in the law of attempts reminds us, the cutting edge of Holmes's test had been the imminence or immediacy requirement. Speech might be punished only if so closely brigaded in time and space with criminal action that no intervening factor might abort the substantive evil. The probable danger test held that if the anticipated evil were serious enough the imminence requirement might be greatly relaxed. In practice this evisceration of the danger test left the Court free to balance the interests to be protected against the degree of infringement on speech, as the proponents of judicial self-restraint argued the Court had always done anyway under the danger standard.

Since *Dennis* the Court has consistently avoided the precise language of the clear and present danger test and with few exceptions commentators announced its demise. In BRANDENBURG v. OHIO (1969), however, the Court announced that "constitutional guarantees of free speech . . . do not permit a State to forbid . . . advocacy of the use of force or of law violation except where such advocacy is directed to inciting or producing imminent lawless action and is likely to incite or produce such action." The text and footnotes surrounding this pronouncement, its careful avoidance of the literal clear and present danger formula itself, plus the separate opinions of several of the Justices indicate that *Brandenburg* did not seek to revive Holmes's danger rule per se. Such earlier proponents of the rule as HUGO L. BLACK and WILLIAM O. DOUGLAS, feeling that it had been too corrupted by its *Dennis* conversion to retain any power to protect speech, had moved to the position of Meiklejohnian absolutism and its rejection of the danger standard. On the other hand, those Justices wishing to preserve low levels of protection for subversive speech and the high levels of judicial self-restraint toward legislative efforts to curb such speech that had been established in *Dennis* and YATES v. UNITED STATES (1957), shied away from the danger test because they knew that, in its Holmesian formulation, it was antithetical to the results that had been achieved in those cases. Apparently, then, Holmes's formula was avoided in *Brandenburg* because some of the participants in the PER CURIAM opinion thought the danger rule protected speech too little and others thought it protected speech too much.

Yet *Brandenburg* did revive the imminence requirement that was the cutting edge of the danger test, and it did so in the context of subversive speech and of OVERRULING *Whitney v. California,* in which the Brandeis and Holmes clear and present danger "concurrence" was in reality a dissent. Even when the danger test was exiled by the Supreme Court it continued to appear in state and lower federal court decisions and in popular discourse. Although the distinction between speech and action—like all distinctions the law seeks to impose—is neither entirely logical nor entirely uncontradicted by real life experience, clear and present danger reasoning survives because most decision makers do believe that the core of the First Amendment is that people may be punished for what they do, not for what they say. Yet even from this basic rule that speech alone must not be punished, we are compelled to make an exception when speech becomes part of the criminal act itself or a direct incitement to the act. Even the most absolute defenders of free speech would not shy from punishing the speaker who shouts at a mob, "I've got the rope and the dynamite. Let's go down to the jail, blow open the cell and lynch the bastard." However imperfectly, the Holmesian formula captures this insight about where the general rule of free speech ends and the exception of punishment begins. It is for this reason that the danger rule keeps reappearing in one form or another even after its reported demise.

The danger rule is most comforting when the speech at issue is an open, particular attack by an individual on some small segment of government or society, such as a street corner speech denouncing the mayor or urging an end to abortion clinics. In such instances the general government and legal system clearly retain the strength to intervene successfully should the danger of a substantive evil actually become clear and present. The emasculation of the danger test came in quite a different context, that of covert speech by an organized group constituting a general attack on the political and legal system as a whole. Unlike the situation in particularized attacks, where the reservoir of systemic power to contain the anticipated danger remains intact, should subversive speech actually create a clear and present danger of revolution the system as a whole might not have the capacity to contain the danger. It is one thing to wait until the arsonist has struck the match and quite another to wait until the revolution is ready to attack the police stations. For this reason the Court in *Dennis* reverted to the *Gitlow*-style reasoning that the government need not wait until the revolutionaries had perfected their campaign of conversion, recruitment, and organization. *Dennis* and *Yates* carve out a Communist party exception to the immediacy requirement of the clear and present danger rule. They say that where the speech is that of a subversive organization, the government need not prove a present danger of revolution but only that the organization intends to bring about the revolution as speedily as circumstances permit. Thus the government is permitted to intervene early enough so that its own strength is still intact and that of the revolutionaries still small. When in defense of the danger rule Holmes argued that time had overthrown many fighting faiths, he did so with a supreme confidence that it was the American, democratic, fighting faith that time favored and that subversive movements would eventually peter out in America's liberal climate. It was a failure of that faith in the face of the communist menace that led to the emasculation of the danger rule during the Cold War of the 1950s. With hindsight we can see that Holmes's confidence remained justified, and that communist subversion could not have created even a probable, let alone a present danger. Nonetheless American self-confidence has eroded sufficiently that the Supreme Court remains careful not to reestablish the full force of the danger rule lest it handicap the political and legal system in dealing with those who organize to destroy it.

Bibliography

ANTIEAU, CHESTER JAMES 1950 "Clear and Present Danger"—Its Meaning and Significance. *Notre Dame Lawyer* 1950:3–45.

——— 1950 The Rule of Clear and Present Danger: Scope of Its Applicability. *Michigan Law Review* 48:811–840.

MENDELSON, WALLACE 1952 Clear and Present Danger—From Schenck to Dennis. *Columbia Law Review* 52:313–333.

——— 1953 The Degradation of the Clear and Present Danger Rule. *Journal of Politics* 15:349–355.

——— 1961 Clear and Present Danger—Another Decade. *Texas Law Review* 39:449–456.

STRONG, FRANK 1969 Fifty Years of "Clear and Present Danger": From Schenck to Brandenburg—And Beyond. *Supreme Court Review* 1969:427–480.

SCHENCK v. UNITED STATES

249 U.S. 47 (1919)

Martin Shapiro

The FREEDOM OF SPEECH provisions of the FIRST AMENDMENT played a singularly retiring role in American constitutional law until the time of World War I or, more precisely, until the Russian Revolution and the Red Scare that it generated in the United States. The Sedition Act of 1798 (see ALIEN AND SEDITION ACTS) obviously posed serious First Amendment questions but was not tested in the Supreme Court and was soon repealed. A scattering of free speech claims and oblique pronouncements by the federal courts occurred after 1900, but speech issues, even when they did arise, typically appeared in state courts in the contexts of OBSCENITY prosecutions and labor disputes. The Court did not declare the First Amendment applicable to the states through the due process clause of the FOURTEENTH AMENDMENT (see INCORPORATION DOCTRINE) until GITLOW v. NEW YORK (1925). Furthermore, in its most direct pronouncement on the freedom of speech provision of the First Amendment, *Patterson v. Colorado* (1907), the Court, speaking through Justice OLIVER WENDELL HOLMES, had suggested that the provision barred only prior restraints, a position that Holmes abandoned in *Schenck*.

In 1917 Congress passed an ESPIONAGE ACT making it a crime to cause or attempt to cause insubordination in the armed forces, obstruct recruitment or enlistment, and otherwise urge, incite, or advocate obstruction or resistance to the war effort. Although there had been much bitter debate about U. S. entry into World War I, the speakers whose prosecutions raised First Amendment issues that ultimately reached the Supreme Court were not German sympathizers. They were left-wing sympathizers with the Russian Revolution who were provoked by the dispatch of Allied expeditionary forces to Russia. If the American war machine was to be turned on the Revolution, it must be stopped.

Prosecutions of such revolutionary sympathizers triggered three important federal court decisions that initiated the jurisprudence of the First Amendment: MASSES PUBLISHING COMPANY v. PATTEN (1917), *Schenck v. United States,* and ABRAMS v. UNITED STATES (1919). *Schenck* was the first major Supreme Court pronouncement on freedom of speech.

Schenck was general secretary of the Socialist Party which distributed to prospective draftees a leaflet denouncing CONSCRIPTION and urging recipients to assert their opposition to it. He was convicted of conspiracy to violate the Espionage Act by attempting to obstruct recruiting. Following his own earlier writing on attempts, Holmes, writing for a unanimous Court, said: It seems to be admitted that if an actual obstruction of the recruiting service were proved, liability for words that produced that effect might be enforced. The statute of 1917 . . . punishes conspiracies to obstruct as well as actual obstruction. If the act (speaking, or circulating a paper), its tendency and the intent with which it is done are the same, we perceive no ground for saying that success alone warrants making the act a crime. In response to Schenck's First Amendment claims, Holmes said:

We admit that in many places and in ordinary times the defendants in saying all that was said in the circular would have been within their constitutional rights. But the character of every act depends upon the circumstances in which it is done. The most stringent protection of free speech would not protect a man in falsely shouting fire in a theatre and causing a panic. . . . The question in every case is whether the words used are used in such circumstances and are of such a nature as to create a CLEAR AND PRESENT DANGER that they will bring about the substantive evils that Congress has a right to prevent. It is a question of proximity and degree.

That the clear and present danger test was first announced in a context in which speech was treated as an attempt to commit an illegal act rather than in a situation in which the statute declared certain speech itself criminal was important for several reasons. First, the attempts context necessarily drew the judicial focus to the nexus between speech and criminal action and thus to the circumstances in which the speech was uttered rather than to the content of the speech itself. Questions of intent and circumstances, crucial to the law of attempts, thus became crucial to the danger test. Second, if the link between speech and illegal act was necessarily a question of degree, then much discretion was necessarily left to the judge. The clear and present danger test has often been criticized for leaving speakers at the mercy of judicial discretion. Having invoked the danger test, the Court affirmed Schenck's conviction. Third, supporters of judicial self-restraint subsequently sought to narrow the scope of the danger test by insisting that it was to be employed only in situations where the government sought to prosecute speech under a statute proscribing only action. In this view, the test was inapplicable when the legislature itself had proscribed speech, having made its own independent, prior judgment that a certain class of speech created a danger warranting suppression.

Although Holmes wrote in Schenck for a unanimous court, he and Justice LOUIS D. BRANDEIS were the danger test's sole supporters in the other leading cases of the 1920s: *Abrams, Gitlow,* and WHITNEY v.

CALIFORNIA (1927). A comparison of these cases indicates that Holmes's "tough guy" pose was deeply implicated in his clear and present danger decisions. In the later cases, Holmes seemed to be saying that a self-confident democracy ought not to descend to the prosecution of fringe-group rantings about socialist revolution. In *Schenck*, however, where the speech was concretely pointed at obstructing war time recruitment, Holmes said: "When a nation is at war, many things that might be said in time of peace are such a hindrance to its effort that their utterance will not be endured so long as men fight and that no Court could regard them as protected by any constitutional right."

Bibliography

CHAFEE, ZECHARIAH   1941   *Free Speech in the United States.* Cambridge, Mass.: Harvard University Press.

FROHWERK *v.* UNITED STATES

249 U.S. 204 (1919)

Michael E. Parrish

In the second major test of the wartime ESPIONAGE ACT to reach the
Supreme Court, the Justices unanimously affirmed the conviction of
the publisher of a pro-German publication for conspiring to obstruct
military recruitment through publication of antidraft articles. Justice
OLIVER WENDELL HOLMES invoked the CLEAR AND PRESENT DANGER test.
"We do not lose our right to condemn either measures or men because
the Country is at war," he wrote, "But . . . it is impossible to say that
it might not have been found that the circulation of the paper was in
quarters where a little breath would be enough to kindle a flame. . . ."
Holmes and his brethren declined to inquire themselves into the degree
or probability of the danger represented by the publication.

DEBS v. UNITED STATES

249 U.S. 211 (1919)

Michael E. Parrish

During his long and controversial career as a labor leader and radical, Eugene V. Debs twice ran afoul of the federal government, which looked upon his activities as a threat to the nation's economic and political orthodoxy. In 1894 he was sentenced to six months' imprisonment for contempt of court as part of the GROVER CLEVELAND administration's efforts to crush the Pullman boycott in Chicago. In IN RE DEBS (1895) the United States Supreme Court affirmed this conviction and upheld the sweeping labor INJUNCTION which Debs and other leaders of the American Railway Union were alleged to have violated. Two decades later, as the leader of the American Socialist Party and one of the most visible critics of the WOODROW WILSON administration's decision to enter World War I, Debs again found himself in federal court, this time charged with violating the ESPIONAGE ACT of 1917.

Debs was tried and convicted on the basis of a speech he delivered at a socialist, antiwar rally in Canton, Ohio, for inciting insubordination, disloyalty, and mutiny in the armed forces and for obstructing military recruitment. In his oration, Debs praised other imprisoned leaders of the party who had been convicted for aiding and abetting resistance to the draft. In the course of his speech Debs also accused the government of using false testimony to convict another antiwar activist and he labeled the war as a plot by "the predatory capitalist in the United States" against the working class, "who furnish the corpses, having never yet had a voice in declaring war and . . . never yet had a voice in declaring peace." He told the audience that "you need to know that you are fit for something better than slavery and cannon fodder," and he ended by noting: "Don't worry about the charge of TREASON to your masters; but be concerned about the treason that involves yourselves." Debs was sentenced to ten years in prison.

When the *Debs* case reached the Supreme Court, a postwar "red scare" had descended on the nation. CRIMINAL CONSPIRACY trials of leaders of the Industrial Workers of the World were still underway. The Department of Justice had embarked on a large-scale program that would culminate in the PALMER RAIDS and the deportation of hundreds of ALIEN radicals.

Without even a reference to the CLEAR AND PRESENT DANGER test enunciated a week earlier, a unanimous Supreme Court affirmed Debs's conviction in an opinion written by Justice OLIVER WENDELL HOLMES. Although Holmes conceded that "the main theme" of Debs's speech had concerned socialism, its growth, and its eventual triumph, he argued that "if a part of the manifest intent of the more general utterance was to encourage those present to obstruct recruiting . . . the immunity of the general theme may not be enough to protect the speech." As Harry Kalven has remarked, "It is somewhat as though George McGovern had been sent to prison for his criticism of the [Vietnam] war." Holmes saw the case as a routine criminal appeal; in a letter to Sir Frederick Pollock, Holmes referred to the *Debs* case, saying, "there was a lot of jaw about free speech."

Debs remained in federal prison long after the armistice. Although a convicted felon, he received the Socialist Party nomination for President in 1920 and nearly a million votes. President Wilson, in failing health and embittered by the war and its critics, refused to pardon Debs before leaving the White House in 1921. His successor, the Republican conservative WARREN G. HARDING, displayed greater compassion by granting the socialist leader a pardon.

Bibliography

FREUND, ERNST   1919   The Debs Case and Freedom of Speech. *The New Republic,* May 3, 1919, p. 13. Reprinted in *University of Chicago Law Review* 40:239–42 (1973).

ABRAMS v. UNITED STATES

250 U.S. 616 (1919)

Martin Shapiro

In SCHENCK V. UNITED STATES (1919) Justice OLIVER WENDELL HOLMES introduced the CLEAR AND PRESENT DANGER test in upholding the conviction under the ESPIONAGE ACT of a defendant who had mailed circulars opposing military CONSCRIPTION. Only nine months later, in very similar circumstances, the Supreme Court upheld an Espionage Act conviction and Holmes and LOUIS D. BRANDEIS offered the danger test in dissent. *Abrams* is famous for Holmes's dissent which became a classic libertarian pronouncement.

Abrams and three others distributed revolutionary circulars that included calls for a general strike, special appeals to workers in ammunitions factories, and language suggesting armed disturbances as the best means of protecting the Russian revolution against American intervention. These circulars had appeared while the United States was still engaged against the Germans in World War I. Their immediate occasion was the dispatch of an American expeditionary force to Russia at the time of the Russian revolution. The majority reasoned that, whatever their particular occasion, the circulars' purpose was that of hampering the general war effort. Having concluded that "the language of these circulars was obviously intended to provoke and to encourage resistance to the United States in the war" and that they urged munitions workers to strike for the purpose of curtailing the production of war materials, the opinion upheld the convictions without actually addressing any constitutional question. The majority obviously believed that the Espionage Act might constitutionally be applied to speech intended to obstruct the war effort.

Justice Holmes mixed a number of elements in his dissent, and the mixture has bedeviled subsequent commentary. Although it is not clear whether Holmes was focusing on the specific language of the Espionage Act or arguing a more general constitutional standard, his central argument was that speech may not be punished unless it constitutes an attempt at some unlawful act; an essential element in such an attempt must be a specific intent on the part of the speaker to bring about the unlawful act. He did not read the circulars in evidence or the actions of their publishers as showing the specific intent to interfere with the war effort against Germany that would be required to constitute a violation of the Espionage Act.

His *Abrams* opinion shows the extent to which Holmes's invention of the danger rule was a derivation of his thinking about the role of specific intent and surrounding circumstances in the law of attempts. For in the midst of his discussion of specific intent he wrote, "I do not doubt . . . that by the same reasoning that would justify punishing persuasion to murder, the United States constitutionally may punish speech that produces or is intended to produce a clear and imminent danger that it will bring about forthwith certain substantive evils that the United States constitutionally may seek to prevent. . . . It is only the present danger of immediate evil or an intent to bring it about that warrants Congress in setting a limit to the expression of opinion . . . ."

Over time, however, what has survived from Holmes's opinion is not so much the specific intent argument as the more general impression that the "poor and puny anonymities" of the circulars could not possibly have constituted a clear and present danger to the war effort. At least in contexts such as that presented in *Abrams*, the clear and present danger test seems to be a good means of unmasking and constitutionally invalidating prosecutions because of the ideas we hate, when the precautions are undertaken not because the ideas constitute any real danger to our security but simply because we hate them. Although the specific intent aspect of the *Abrams* opinion has subsequently been invoked in a number of cases, particularly those involving membership in the Communist party, the *Abrams* dissent has typically been cited along with *Schenck* as the basic authority for the more general version of the clear and present danger standard that became the dominant FREEDOM OF SPEECH doctrine during the 1940s and has since led a checkered career.

Justice Holmes also argued in *Abrams* that the common law of SEDITIOUS LIBEL has not survived in the United States; the Supreme Court finally adopted that position in NEW YORK TIMES v. SULLIVAN (1964).

The concluding paragraph of the *Abrams* dissent has often been invoked by those who wish to make of Holmes a patron saint of the libertarian movement.

Persecution for the expression of opinions seems to me perfectly logical . . . but when men have realized that time has upset many fighting faiths, they may come to believe even more the very foundations of their own conduct that the ultimate good desired is better reached by free trade in ideas—that the best test of truth is the power of the thought to get itself accepted in the competition of the market, and that truth is the only ground upon which their wishes safely can be carried out. That at any rate is the theory of our Constitution. It is an experiment, as all life is an experiment. Every year if not every day we have to wager our salvation upon some prophecy based upon imperfect knowledge. While that experiment is part of our system I think that we should be eternally vigilant against attempts to check the expression of opinions that we loathe and believe to be fraught with death, unless they so imminently threaten immediate interference with the lawful and pressing purposes of the law that an immediate check is required to save the country. . . . Only the emergency that makes it immediately dangerous to leave the correction of evil counsels to time warrants making any exception to the sweeping command, "Congress shall make no law . . . abridging the freedom of speech."

Sensitized by the destructive powers of such "fighting faiths" as Fascism and communism, subsequent commentators have criticized the muscular, relativistic pragmatism of this pronouncement as at best an inadequate philosophic basis for the libertarian position and at worst an invitation to totalitarianism. The ultimate problem is, of course, what is to be done if a political faith that proposes the termination of freedom of speech momentarily wins the competition in the marketplace of ideas and then shuts down the market. Alternatively it has been argued that Holmes's clear and present danger approach in *Abrams* was basically conditioned by his perception of the ineffectualness of leftist revolutionary rhetoric in the American context of his day. In this view, he was saying no more than that deviant ideas must be tolerated until there is a substantial risk that a large number of Americans will listen to them. The clear and present danger test is often criticized for withdrawing protection of political speech at just the point when the speech threatens to become effective. Other commentators have argued that no matter how persuasive Holmes's comments may be in context, the clear and present danger approach ought not to be uncritically accepted as the single freedom of speech test, uniformly applied to speech situations quite different from those in *Abrams*. Perhaps the most telling criticism of the Holmes approach is that it vests enormous discretion in the judge, for ultimately it depends on the judge's prediction of what will happen rather than on findings of what has happened. Subsequent decisions such as that in FEINER v. NEW YORK (1951) showed that judges less brave than Holmes or less contemptuously tolerant of dissident ideas, might be quicker to imagine danger.

Bibliography

CHAFEE, ZECHARIAH 1941 *Free Speech in the United States.* Cambridge, Mass.: Harvard University Press.

MASSES PUBLISHING COMPANY v. PATTEN

244 Fed. 535 (1917)

Martin Shapiro

Judge LEARNED HAND's *Masses* opinion was one of the first federal opinions dealing with free speech. It remains influential even though Hand was reversed by the court of appeals and many years later himself abandoned his initial position. A postmaster had refused to accept the revolutionary monthly *The Masses* for mailing, citing the ESPIONAGE ACT. Hand, sitting in a federal district court, interpreted the act not to apply to the magazine. He noted that any broad criticism of a government or its policies might hinder the war effort. Nevertheless, to suppress such criticism "would contradict the normal assumption of democratic government." Hand advanced a criminal incitement test. He conceded that words can be "the triggers of action" and, if they counseled violation of law, were not constitutionally protected. If, however, the words did not criminally incite and if the words stopped short "of urging upon others that it is their duty or their interest to resist the law . . . one should not be held to have attempted to cause its violation."

Hand's concentration on the advocacy content of the speech itself is thought by some to be more speech-protective than the CLEAR AND PRESENT DANGER rule's emphasis on the surrounding circumstances.

COMMONWEALTH v. SACCO AND VANZETTI

(Massachusetts, 1921)

Michael E. Parrish

On August 23, 1927, the Commonwealth of Massachusetts electrocuted two Italian immigrants, Nicola Sacco and Bartolomeo Vanzetti, for the crimes of armed robbery and murder. The executions stirred angry protest in the United States and throughout the world by millions of people who believed that the two men had been denied a fair trial because of their ethnic background and political opinions.

Sacco and Vanzetti, ALIENS and anarchists who had fled to Mexico to avoid the draft during World War I, were arrested in 1920 and quickly brought to trial in Dedham, Massachusetts, for the murder of a paymaster and a guard during the robbery of a shoe factory. The trial took place at the end of the postwar Red Scare in a political atmosphere charged with hysteria against foreigners and radicals. Although the ballistics evidence was inconclusive and many witnesses, most of them Italian, placed the two men elsewhere at the time of the robbery, the jury returned guilty verdicts after listening to patriotic harangues from the chief prosecutor, Frederick Katzmann, and the trial judge, Webster Bradley Thayer.

During his cross-examination of the two defendants, Katzmann constantly emphasized their unorthodox political views and their flight to Mexico during the war. Thayer tolerated a broad range of political questions, mocked the two men's anarchism, and urged the members of the jury to act as "true soldiers . . . in the spirit of supreme American loyalty."

A diverse coalition of Bay State aristocrats, law professors such as FELIX FRANKFURTER, Italian radicals, and New York intellectuals attempted to secure a new trial for the condemned men during the next seven years. They marshaled an impressive amount of evidence pointing to Thayer's prejudice, the doubts of key prosecution witnesses, and the possibility that the crime had been committed by a gang of professional outlaws. The Massachusetts Supreme Judicial Court, however, relying on principles of trial court discretion that made it virtually impossible to challenge any of Thayer's rulings, spurned these appeals and refused to disturb either the verdict or the death sentences. A similar conclusion was reached by a special commission appointed by Governor Alvan T.

Fuller and headed by Harvard University president A. Lawrence Lowell.

Last-minute efforts to secure a stay of execution from federal judges, including Supreme Court Justices OLIVER WENDELL HOLMES and LOUIS D. BRANDEIS, also proved unavailing. Attorneys for Sacco and Vanzetti argued that because of Thayer's hostility their clients had been denied a FAIR TRIAL guaranteed by the DUE PROCESS clause of the FOURTEENTH AMENDMENT. But with the exception of MOORE v. DEMPSEY (1923), where a state murder trial had been intimidated by a mob, the Supreme Court had shown great reluctance to intervene in local criminal proceedings. "I cannot think that prejudice on the part of a presiding judge however strong would deprive the Court of jurisdiction," wrote Holmes, "and in my opinion nothing short of a want of legal power to decide the case authorizes me to interfere. . . ." Whether Sacco and Vanzetti received a fair trial is questionable; however, Francis Russell has shown how illusory is the old contention that they were wholly innocent.

Bibliography

JOUGHN, G. LOUIS and MORGAN, EDMUND M.   1948   *The Legacy of Sacco and Vanzetti.* New York: Harcourt, Brace.

RUSSELL, FRANCIS   1962   *Tragedy in Dedham: The Story of the Sacco-Vanzetti Case.* New York: Harper & Row.

CRIMINAL SYNDICALISM LAWS

Richard B. Bernstein

Criminal syndicalism statutes were but one of several kinds of statutes punishing manifestations of unpopular thought and expression for their probable bad tendency enacted during and just after World War I by many midwestern and western states. The laws were a response to the economic unrest of the postwar period, specifically to the doctrines and activities of the Industrial Workers of the World (IWW), and to the antiradical hysteria prompted by the Russian Revolution of 1917. Twenty-two states and territories enacted—and eight other states considered but rejected—criminal syndicalism statutes between 1917 and 1920. Attempts to enact a federal criminal syndicalism law in 1919 and 1920 came to nothing, but the Smith Act of 1940 was patterned after the earlier model.

The Idaho statute, the first of its kind and a model for those adopted by other states, defined criminal syndicalism as "the doctrine which advocates crime, sabotage, violence or other unlawful methods of terrorism as a means of accomplishing industrial or political reform." Offenses punished as FELONIES under such statutes included oral or written advocacy of criminal syndicalism; justifying commission of or attempts to commit criminal syndicalism; printing or displaying written or printed matter advocating or advising criminal syndicalism; organizing or being or becoming a member of any organization organized or assembled to teach or advocate criminal syndicalism, or even presence at such an assembly. Though most citizens and state legislators believed that these statutes were directed solely against the use or advocacy of force and violence, in practice they jeopardized FREEDOM OF SPEECH, because they were used to punish those who expressed or even held opinions offensive to the majority of the community.

Criminal syndicalism statutes almost uniformly survived constitutional challenges in the state courts. In WHITNEY V. CALIFORNIA (1927) the United States Supreme Court upheld the California Criminal Syndicalism Act; Justice LOUIS D. BRANDEIS's eloquent opinion, concurring only in the result, set forth the most sophisticated formulation of the theoretical foundations and practical applications of the CLEAR AND PRESENT DANGER test previously formulated in other FIRST AMENDMENT cases.

In *Fiske v. Kansas* (1927), the first decision overturning a conviction under a criminal syndicalism statute, the Supreme Court merely invalidated the statute's application, holding that the state had not shown that the defendant had advocated any but lawful methods to achieve the goals of the IWW. In DE JONGE v. OREGON (1937) a unanimous Court struck down the application of the Oregon Criminal Syndicalism Act to defendants who had merely attended a peaceful meeting of the Communist party; the Oregon legislature later repealed the statute. The labor troubles of the 1930s prompted efforts to strengthen existing criminal syndicalism laws, but these came to nothing, and several states followed Oregon's example in repealing their criminal syndicalism statutes. State criminal syndicalism statutes fell into disuse after the 1930s; in BRANDENBERG v. OHIO (1969) the Supreme Court declared the Ohio Criminal Syndicalism Act unconstitutional on its face, overruling *Whitney*, adopting the principles of Justice Brandeis's concurring opinion, and making successful prosecutions under criminal syndicalism statutes virtually impossible.

Bibliography

CHAFEE, ZECHARIAH, JR.   1941   *Free Speech in the United States.*   Cambridge, Mass.: Harvard University Press.

DOWELL, ELDRIDGE FOSTER   1939   *A History of Criminal Syndicalism Legislation in the United States.*   Baltimore: Johns Hopkins University Studies in Historical and Political Science, Series 57, No. 1.

GITLOW v. NEW YORK

268 U.S. 652 (1925)

Martin Shapiro

Gitlow was convicted under a state statute proscribing advocacy of the overthrow of government by force. In a paper called *The Revolutionary Age,* he had published "The Left Wing Manifesto," denouncing moderate socialism and prescribing "Communist revolution." There was no evidence of any effect resulting from the publication. Rejecting the CLEAR AND PRESENT DANGER test which OLIVER WENDELL HOLMES and LOUIS D. BRANDEIS reasserted in their dissent, Justice EDWARD SANFORD for the Court upheld the statute. Enunciating what subsequently came to be called the remote BAD TENDENCY TEST, Sanford declared that the state might "suppress the threatened danger in its incipiency." "It cannot reasonably be required to defer the adoption of measures for its own . . . safety until the revolutionary utterances lead to actual disturbances of the public peace or imminent and immediate danger of its own destruction."

Unwilling to reverse its decision in SCHENCK V. UNITED STATES (1919), the Court limited the clear and present danger test enunciated there to the situation in which a speaker is prosecuted under a statute prohibiting acts and making no reference to language. Under such a statute the legislature has made no judgment of its own as to the danger of any speech, and the unlawfulness of the speech must necessarily depend on whether "its natural tendency and probable effect was to bring about the substantive evil" that the legislature had proscribed. In short, Sanford sought to confine the danger test to its origin in the law of attempts and to strip it of its imminence aspect. He argued that where a legislature itself had determined that a certain category of speech constituted a danger of substantive evil, "every presumption [was] to be indulged in favor of the validity" of such an exercise of the police power.

The PREFERRED FREEDOMS doctrine that became central to the speech cases of the next two decades was largely directed toward undermining the *Gitlow* position that state statutes regulating speech ought to be subject to no more demanding constitutional standards than the reasonableness test applied to state economic regulation.

The *Gitlow* formula was rejected in the 1930s, but the Court returned to some of its reasoning in the 1950s, particularly to the notion that where revolutionary speech is involved, government need not wait until "the spark . . . has enkindled the flame or blazed into the conflagration." Such reasoning, bolstered by the *Gitlow* distinction between advocacy and abstract, academic teaching informed the DENNIS v. UNITED STATES (1951) and YATES v. UNITED STATES (1951) decisions that upheld the Smith Act, a federal statute in part modeled on the New York criminal anarchy statute sustained in *Gitlow*.

The Court's language in *Gitlow* was equivocal, and it provided no rationale. Indeed, *Gitlow* is most often cited today for its dictum, "incorporating" FIRST AMENDMENT free speech guarantees into the DUE PROCESS clause of the FOURTEENTH AMENDMENT, thus rendering the Amendment applicable to the states as well as to Congress. (See INCORPORATION DOCTRINE.)

Holmes's *Gitlow* dissent did not address the question so troublesome to believers in judicial self-restraint: why should courts not defer to the legislature's judgment that a particular kind of speech is too dangerous to tolerate when, in applying the due process clause, they do defer to other legislative judgments? He did attack the majority's distinction between lawful abstract teaching and unlawful INCITEMENT in language that has become famous:

Every idea is an incitement. It offers itself for belief and if believed it is acted on unless some other belief outweighs it. . . . The only difference between the expression of an opinion and an incitement in the narrower sense is the speaker's enthusiasm for the result. . . . If in the long run the beliefs expressed in proletarian dictatorship are destined to be accepted by the dominant forces of the community, the only meaning of free speech is that they should be given their chance and have their way.

Bibliography

CHAFEE, ZECHARIAH 1941 *Free Speech in the United States.* Cambridge, Mass.: Harvard University Press.

WHITNEY v. CALIFORNIA

274 U.S. 357 (1927)

Martin Shapiro

SCHENCK V. UNITED STATES (1919), ABRAMS V. UNITED STATES (1919), GITLOW V. NEW YORK (1925), and *Whitney* are the four leading FREEDOM OF SPEECH cases of the 1920s in which the CLEAR AND PRESENT DANGER rule was announced but then rejected by the majority in favor of the BAD TENDENCY test announced in *Gitlow*. In *Whitney*, Justice EDWARD SANFORD repeated his *Gitlow* argument that a state law does not violate FIRST AMENDMENT rights by employing the "bad tendency" test as the standard of reasonableness in speech cases. The state may reasonably proscribe "utterances . . . tending to . . . endanger the foundations of organized government." Here Justice Sanford added that "united and joint action involves even greater danger to the public peace and security than the isolated utterances . . . of individuals." Miss Whitney had been convicted of organizing and becoming a member of an organization that advocated and taught CRIMINAL SYNDICALISM in violation of the California Criminal Syndicalism Act of 1919. The Court upheld the act's constitutionality.

After *Schenck,* the clear and present danger position had been reiterated in dissenting opinions by OLIVER WENDELL HOLMES and LOUIS D. BRANDEIS in *Abrams* and *Gitlow*. Brandeis, joined by Holmes, concurred in *Whitney*. Brandeis's reason for concurring rather than dissenting was that Whitney had not properly argued to the California courts that their failure to invoke the danger test was error, and that the Supreme Court might not correct errors by state courts unless those errors were properly raised below.

Brandeis's concurrence was a forceful reiteration of the value to a democracy of freedom of speech for even the most dissident speakers. The framers knew that "fear breeds repression; that repression breeds hate; that hate menaces stable government; that the path of safety lies in the opportunity to discuss freely supposed grievances . . . and that the fitting remedy for evil counsels is good ones." Brandeis reemphasized the imminence requirement of the danger rule. "To courageous, self-reliant men, with confidence in the power of free and fearless reasoning applied through the processes of popular government, no danger flowing from speech can be deemed clear and present, unless the incidence of the evil apprehended is so imminent that it may befall before there is opportunity for full discussion. If there be time . . . to avert the evil by the process of education, the remedy to be applied is more speech, not enforced silence."

Whitney is often cited for an addition by Brandeis to the original clear and present danger formula. The evil anticipated must be not only substantive but also serious. "The fact that speech is likely to result in some violence or in destruction of property is not enough to justify its suppression. There must be the probability of serious injury to the state. . . ."

The Court overruled *Whitney* in BRANDENBURG v. OHIO (1969).

STROMBERG v. CALIFORNIA

283 U.S. 359 (1931)

Michael E. Parrish

A California law made it a crime to display a red flag or banner "as a sign, symbol or emblem of opposition to organized government or as an invitation or stimulus to anarchistic action or as an aid to propaganda that is of a seditious character. . . ." A member of the Young Communist League who ran a summer camp where the daily ritual included the raising of "the workers' red flag" was convicted for violating the statute, although a state appellate court noted that the prohibition contained in the first clause—"opposition to organized government"—was so vague as to be constitutionally questionable. That court nonetheless upheld the conviction on the grounds that the defendant had been found guilty of violating the entire statute and that the other two clauses relating to "anarchistic action" and "seditious character" were sufficiently definite.

Chief Justice CHARLES EVANS HUGHES and six other members of the Supreme Court reversed the conviction. In his opinion, Hughes pointed out that, the jury having rendered a general verdict, it was impossible to know under which clause or clauses the defendant had been convicted. If any of the three clauses were invalid, the conviction could not stand. The Court found the first clause "so vague and indefinite" that it violated the DUE PROCESS clause of the FOURTEENTH AMENDMENT because it prohibited not only violent, illegal opposition to organized government but also "peaceful and orderly opposition to government by legal means. . . ." Justices JAMES C. MCREYNOLDS and PIERCE BUTLER dissented.

HERNDON v. LOWRY

301 U.S. 242 (1937)

Martin Shapiro

Herndon was a black organizer convicted of attempting to incite insurrection in violation of a state law. Herndon had sought to induce others to join the Communist party. At the time the party was seeking to organize southern blacks and calling for separate black states in the South. While only indirectly adopting the CLEAR AND PRESENT DANGER test, the Court refused to apply the BAD TENDENCY TEST of GITLOW v. NEW YORK (1925) and stressed the absence of any immediate threat of insurrection. In an opinion by Justice OWEN ROBERTS, a 5–4 Court held (1) that the evidence presented failed "to establish an attempt to incite others to insurrection" even at some indefinite future time; and (2) that the statute was unconstitutionally vague as applied and contrued because "every person who attacks existing conditions, who agitates for a change in the form of government, must take the risk that if a jury should be of opinion he ought to have foreseen that his utterances might contribute in any measure to some future forcible resistance to the existing government he may be convicted of the offense of inciting insurrection." The VAGUENESS DOCTRINE invoked was not specifically articulated as a FIRST AMENDMENT standard; instead, the general criminal standard of "a sufficiently ascertainable standard of guilt" was applied.

The state supreme court believed that a conviction would be justified if the defendant intended that insurrection "should happen at any time within which he might reasonably expect his influence to continue to be directly operative in causing such action by those whom he sought to induce. . . ." This formula, which the Supreme Court found constitutionally infirm, must be compared with its own of the 1950s upholding convictions for conspiracy to advocate overthrow of the government where the intention was that of an organized group to bring about overthrow "as speedily as circumstances would permit."

ALIEN REGISTRATION ACT

54 Stat. 670 (1940)

Paul L. Murphy

This measure, popularly known as the Smith Act, was destined to become the most famous of the anticommunist measures of the Cold War, McCarthy period. The act required all ALIENS living in the United States to register with the government, be fingerprinted, carry identification cards, and report annually. Persons found to have ties to "subversive organizations" could be deported. The registration requirement was rescinded in 1982.

Such alien registration was only one of the various purposes of the act. It was directed primarily at SUBVERSIVE ACTIVITIES which were causing growing concerns on the eve of war, particularly communist-inspired strikes intended to injure American defense production. As the first federal peacetime SEDITION statute since 1798, the Smith Act in its most significant section made it a crime to "knowingly, or willfully, advocate, abet, advise, or teach the duty, necessity, desirability, or propriety of overthrowing or destroying any government in the United States by force and violence. . . ." Any attempts forcibly to overthrow the government of the United States by publication or display of printed matters, to teach, or to organize any group, or to become a "knowing" member of such an organization were forbidden. Section 3 forbade conspiracy to accomplish any of these ends. The act carried maximum criminal penalties of a $10,000 fine or ten years in prison or both; no one convicted under the law was to be eligible for federal employment during the five years following conviction.

The act, which did not mention the Communist party, attracted little attention at the time of its passage, and initial enforcement was spotty. Although five million aliens were registered and fingerprinted shortly following its passage, its antisubversive sections were not used until 1943, when a small group of Minneapolis Trotskyites were convicted. When the Cold War intensified, following 1947, the HARRY S. TRUMAN administration began a series of dramatic prosecutions of Communist party leaders. These and subsequent prosecutions eventually forced the Supreme Court to clarify the act's terms, starting with DENNIS v. UNITED STATES (1951), and extending through YATES v. UNITED STATES

(1957), SCALES V. UNITED STATES (1961), and *Noto v. United States* (1961). As a result of these rulings, the measure's advocacy, organizing, and membership provisions were limited and made more precise.

Bibliography

BELKNAP, MICHAEL R.   1977   *Cold War Political Justice: The Smith Act, the Communist Party, and American Civil Liberties.*   Westport, Conn.: Greenwood Press.

LOYALTY-SECURITY PROGRAMS

Ralph S. Brown

This hyphenated phrase refers chiefly to the measures that were taken under Presidents HARRY S. TRUMAN and DWIGHT D. EISENHOWER to exclude from public employment, and from defense industries, persons who were believed to pose risks to national security. Because the gravest threat to security was believed to flow from world communism, loyalty and security programs were designed almost entirely to counter communist influence and penetration.

In earlier periods of tension attendant upon wars, LOYALTY OATHS were the preferred device for separating the loyal from the disloyal. If oaths were taken seriously, they were self-enforcing. But when necessity or duplicity led to bales of unreliable oaths, the authorities responded by empowering officials to go behind the oaths with investigations and to make their own judgments. Such procedures, usually under military control and untrammeled by judicial control, were widespread during the Civil War and Reconstruction.

World War I was distinguished by the overzealous prying of the American Protective League and other amateurs who were given extraordinary aid and comfort by the Department of Justice. In World War II the military departments, both determined to avoid the excesses of the crusade against the Kaiser, effectively centralized loyalty screening. They emerged with a minimum of criticism. After the war, the Soviet Union abruptly came to be viewed as enemy rather than ally. The insecurities of the postwar world aroused mistrust and anxiety. President Truman, aiming to forestall harsher congressional action, launched a new kind of program with his EXECUTIVE ORDER 9835 of March 21, 1947.

The Truman loyalty program covered all civilian employees. The Department of Defense had its own program for the armed services. Defense and the Atomic Energy Commission had programs for employees of defense contractors. The Coast Guard screened maritime workers. A few states developed systematic programs of their own. Many millions thus became subject to proceedings that sought to establish whether, in the language of E.O. 9835, there were "reasonable grounds" for a belief that they were disloyal (softened in 1951 to require only a finding of "reasonable doubt" as to loyalty). In 1953 President Eisenhower's

Executive Order 10450 replaced the Truman program. It required employment to be "clearly consistent with the interests of the national security." That standard remains in effect.

All of these programs worked from personal histories supplied by the employee (or applicant) backed up by investigative reports. If "derogatory information" led to a tentative adverse judgment, that was usually the end for an applicant's chances of employment. But an incumbent could have the benefit of formal charges, a hearing, and review. The trouble was that the investigations ranged widely into associations, opinions, and flimsy appraisals. The sources of none of these were accessible to the employee. He could only guess who his detractors were.

These programs were only one array in the frantic mobilization against subversion. They were flanked by oaths and affidavits and questionnaires. To falsify any of these was a criminal offense. In order to establish what associations were forbidden, the 1947 executive order systematized the secret preparation and open use of the ATTORNEY GENERAL'S LIST of Subversive Organizations. Long before and for some years after the heyday of Senator JOSEPH R. MCCARTHY (1950–1954), congressional investigating committees took as their specialty the exposure of groups and individuals with communist ties. Their disclosures encouraged blacklists in private employment, notoriously in films and broadcasting. Senator McCarthy took the lead in stigmatizing the "Fifth-Amendment Communist"—a witness who invoked the RIGHT AGAINST SELF-INCRIMINATION. Senator Patrick A. McCarran initiated the idea that naming names was the only true badge of repentance for those who said they were no longer communists. A mass of legislation sought to expose and condemn the Communist party and its affiliates, while the Department of Justice jailed its leaders for sedition.

All of these measures raised intertwining constitutional problems, so those of loyalty-security programs are not easily isolated. However, two strands can be picked out. First, there were demands for fair process, notably to confront the source of accusations. Second, there were claims for First Amendment rights, set against the supposed necessities of national security. However, the courts often trimmed the reach of the programs without deciding such issues. They would invoke their usual preference for avoiding constitutional collisions, and simply find that executive or legislative authority was lacking.

The position that DUE PROCESS OF LAW was wanting in the rules and administration of employment tests first had to surmount the proposition that employment was not a right but only a privilege that could be summarily withheld. First Amendment claims also encountered this barrier, curtly expressed in Justice OLIVER WENDELL HOLMES'S now battered epigram: "The petitioner may have a constitutional right to talk politics, but he has no constitutional right to be a policeman." After some early hesitation, this dismissive argument was itself dismissed, notably by Justice TOM C. CLARK, who was usually a steadfast supporter of security measures. In an oath case, WIEMAN V. UPDEGRAFF (1952), he wrote for the Court: "We need not pause to consider whether an abstract right to public employment exists. It is sufficient to say that constitutional protection does extend to the public servant whose exclusion . . . is patently arbitrary or discriminatory."

What process is then due? The government perennially opposes the right of confrontation by invoking the need to protect confidential informants. The court came close to requiring a trial-type hearing, with confrontation and cross-examination, in the industrial security case of *Greene v. McElroy* (1959). But it used the avoidance technique. It said that there would have to be, at the threshold, explicit authorization from the President or Congress to conceal sources, and that it could not find such authorization. The decision had little effect. The statute authorizing security removals of government employees still requires only that charges "be stated as specifically as security considerations permit." It is doubtful that, in a time of perceived crisis, and in sensitive employment, the Constitution would be read to compel confrontation.

The Court worked its way to a firmer position on narrowing grounds for removal. It found that First Amendment rights to freedom of association were impaired by a flat proscription of employing communists in a "defense facility." In UNITED STATES V. ROBEL (1967) the employee, a shipyard worker, was an avowed Communist party member. A majority of the Court, declaring that "the statute quite literally establishes guilt by association alone," held that some less restrictive means would have to be employed to guard against disruption or sabotage. If *Robel* and like cases are followed where charges of disloyalty are brought, and where the accusation stems from political associations, the government may be unable to remove an employee except for conduct that would support a criminal prosecution.

This does not mean an end to the reliance on prying and gossiping that made loyalty-security programs disreputable. In satisfying itself of the reliability of applicants for employment, the government (or a private employer) can still probe for flaws of character, so long as standards for expulsion do not invade areas protected by the First Amendment or by ANTIDISCRIMINATION LEGISLATION. Investigators may even demand answers to questions, for example, on communist connections, that come close to protected zones, as long as the ultimate standards are correct, and the questions are helpful in seeing that the standards are satisfied. This seems to be the upshot of a tortuous line of cases involving admission to the practice of law.

From these unavoidable clashes between individual rights and security claims, a remarkable course of events has followed. Once the fevers of the 1950s had subsided, loyalty-security programs simply shrank to very modest levels. It is noteworthy that the VIETNAM WAR did not check the decline. Yet the KOREAN WAR, which broke out in 1950, undoubtedly deepened the fears of that era.

The contraction has been helped along by the courts. Congress and the executive have perhaps done more to limit the scale at which the federal programs have been operating (the last dismissal on loyalty grounds was in 1968). The PRIVACY ACT of 1974 and similar statutes greatly restricted the flow of official information about misbehavior. President RICHARD M. NIXON abolished the Attorney General's List in the same year. Nudged by lower court decisions, the Civil Service Commission first stopped asking applicants for nonsensitive positions about subversive associations, and then in 1977 scrapped the questions for sensitive jobs too. Appropriations for investigative staff both in the Federal Bureau of Investigation and in the Defense Department have declined.

Do recent developments represent a slackening of our defenses? A revulsion against the excesses of McCarthyism? Because the prime mover in all the loyalty-security programs was hostility to communism, the programs may revive if our relations with the Soviet Union worsen. If the programs do revive, it seems unlikely that the courts will check recurrence of past excesses.

Bibliography

BROWN, RALPH S.   1958   *Loyalty and Security: Employment Tests in the United States.* New Haven, Conn.: Yale University Press.

CAUTE, DAVID   1978   *The Great Fear: The Anti-Communist Purge under Truman and Eisenhower.* New York: Simon & Schuster.

DEVELOPMENTS IN THE LAW   1972   The National Security Interest and Civil Liberties. *Harvard Law Review* 85:1130–1326.

LEWY, GUENTER   1983   *The Federal Loyalty-Security Program: The Need for Reform.* Washington and London: American Enterprise Institute.

EXECUTIVE ORDERS 9835 AND 10450 (1947, 1953)

Stanley I. Kutler

As a result of domestic political and security pressures after 1945, Presidents HARRY S. TRUMAN and DWIGHT D. EISENHOWER instituted sweeping loyalty investigations of federal workers. Truman's Executive Order 9835, affecting over two million employees, established loyalty review boards in executive departments to evaluate information provided by Federal Bureau of Investigation or Civil Service Commission investigations and informants. The basic standards for dismissal required "reasonable grounds for belief in disloyalty," which included evidence of affiliation with groups on the ATTORNEY GENERAL'S LIST of subversive organizations. Critics who alleged widespread subversion nevertheless demanded more stringent measures, and Truman's Executive Order 10241 (April 28, 1951) altered the criterion to one of "reasonable doubt" of loyalty. The change effectively shifted the burden of proof to the accused or suspected employee. Eisenhower, however, later complained that the Truman program reflected "a complacency . . . toward security risks," such as homosexuals and alcoholics, and in April 1953, he issued Executive Order 10450 that made security, not loyalty, the primary concern.

The loyalty probes produced new bureaucracies, with agendas of their own and standards and practices that varied widely in different departments. Between 1947 and 1956, approximately 2,700 employees were dismissed and another 12,000 resigned because of the inquiries. After 1953, the security program provided for immediate suspension without pay, and many employees undoubtedly resigned to avoid the stigma of combating the charges, however flimsy. Then, too, the program's shroud of secrecy, including the use of unknown informants, made challenges difficult.

The Supreme Court responded cautiously to the program. In *Bailey v. Richardson* (1951) an evenly divided bench sustained Bailey's dismissal even though she had been denied an opportunity to confront her accusers. The same day, in JOINT ANTI-FASCIST REFUGEE COMMITTEE v. McGRATH, the Court questioned the procedures for compiling the attorney general's list of subversive organizations, yet did not prevent its continued use. Some individuals successfully challenged their dismissals, but courts carefully avoided broader constitutional issues. In *Peters v. Hobby* (1955) the Supreme Court overturned a medical professor's dismissal because his position was nonsensitive, yet the Justices ignored Peters's challenge against secret informers. Similar reasoning was employed in *Cole v. Young* (1956) to reverse the discharge of an employee who had challenged the use of the attorney general's list as a violation of rights of association. The real turning point came in *Service v. Dulles* (1957) when the Court reversed the dismissal of one of the "China Hands" who had been purged from the State Department. Finally, in *Greene v. McElroy* (1959), Chief Justice EARL WARREN condemned the use of "faceless informers," unknown to the accused. Without determining constitutional issues, the Court held that the government's evidence must be disclosed to the individual to give him an opportunity to refute it.

Although the Court's decisions undoubtedly demonstrated that abusive, illegal governmental actions could be brought to account, such challenges required extraordinary individual persistence and courage as well as financial and emotional cost. For all the government's efforts, the results were dubious. Judith Coplon, convicted of passing Justice Department documents to a Soviet agent, had escaped the program's net. And in 1954, the Civil Service Commission acknowledged that no communist or fellow traveler had been uncovered in its probes.

Bibliography

HARPER, ALAN D.   1969   *The Politics of Loyalty.* Greenwich, Conn.: Greenwood Press.

ATTORNEY GENERAL'S LIST

Paul L. Murphy

President HARRY S. TRUMAN's Executive Order 9835 inaugurated a comprehensive investigation of all federal employees and made any negative information a potential basis for a security dismissal. A list of subversive organizations was to be prepared by the attorney general, and membership in any listed group was a ground for REASONABLE DOUBT as to an employee's loyalty. The only guidelines the order provided were that any designated organization must be "totalitarian, Fascist, Communist, or subversive," or one "approving the commission of acts of force or violence to deny to others their constitutional rights." During the first year under the order, the attorney general so designated 123 organizations. Over time, and frequently as a result of protests, certain organizations were deleted; new ones were also added. By November 1950, 197 organizations had been so listed, eleven of which were labeled subversive, twelve as seeking to overthrow the government by unconstitutional means, and 132 as communist or communist front.

Critics questioned the constitutionality of the list's compilation and use, on FIRST AMENDMENT grounds, as an "executive BILL OF ATTAINDER" and as involving unfair procedures violating the DUE PROCESS CLAUSE of the Fifth Amendment. The Supreme Court in JOINT ANTI-FASCIST REFUGEE COMMITTEE v. McGRATH (1951) raised serious questions regarding the fairness of the compilation procedure, and demands grew for suitable hearings to be granted organizations before their inclusion. No procedural changes were instituted in the Truman years, however, and the list continued to be used under the Eisenhower loyalty program. (See LOYALTY-SECURITY PROGRAMS.)

Bibliography

BONTECOU, ELEANOR 1953 *The Federal Loyalty-Security Program.* Ithaca, N.Y.: Cornell University Press.

LOYALTY OATH

Ralph S. Brown

A mild form of loyalty oath is embedded in the Constitution itself. The President must swear (or affirm): "that I will faithfully execute the office of President of the United States, and will to the best of my ability, preserve, protect and defend the constitution of the United States." And Article VI, in conjunction with the supremacy clause, requires that members of Congress, state legislators, and "all executive and judicial officers, both of the United States and of the several states, shall be bound by oath or affirmation, to support this constitution." These are usually called affirmative oaths, in contrast to negative oaths in which oath-takers are required to abjure certain beliefs, words, or acts. In their most searching form, negative oaths probe the past as well as the future.

In Article VI, the constitutional oath of support is immediately followed by the proscription of any religious test for holding office. Loyalty oaths, called test oaths, were rife in an age of warring faiths defended by princes. They tested orthodoxy of belief and thus loyalty to the sovereign. Henry VIII launched Anglo-American constitutional practice on a sea of oaths, whose chief purpose was to root out followers of the pope of Rome. The Stuart kings exacted oaths from the first settlers, and the settlers in turn invoked them against each other. When George Calvert, the Roman Catholic first Lord Baltimore, attempted to settle in Virginia, he was confronted with an oath that he could not take. He perforce made the hard voyage back to England; his successors got their own grant to what became Maryland and promptly imposed an oath pledging fidelity to themselves.

Wary though they became of oaths with a religious content, those who made our Revolution, as well as those who resisted it, routinely exacted political loyalty oaths from military and civilians under their control. When one occupying force displaced the other, it could become a matter of life and liberty to have one's name on the wrong roster. At the same time, there was room for claims of duress and duplicity. BENJAMIN FRANKLIN expressed with his usual pithiness what was doubtless a shared cynicism when he wrote in 1776: "I have never regarded oaths otherwise than as the last recourse of liars."

One might have thought that the Framers, with revolutionary excesses fresh in their memories, meant the constitutional oaths to be exclusive of any others; but when the Civil War came, loyalty oaths again became ubiquitous. In the Confederacy, oaths were linked to the passes routinely required for any travel. Of more gravity, taking an oath was often for captives and hostile civilians the only alternative to rotting in prison or starving. The multiplicity of oaths and the pressure to yield to them resulted in their becoming unreliable indicia of loyalty. Union authorities were impelled to create a bureaucracy to interrogate oath-takers, thus anticipating modern LOYALTY-SECURITY PROGRAMS.

President ABRAHAM LINCOLN favored relatively mild oaths pledging only future loyalty. The sterner Congress fashioned the "ironclad" test oath that required denials of past conduct that secessionists could not possibly make. Those oaths barred even repentant rebels from government and the professions. The Supreme Court plausibly characterized such oaths as legislative punishment, and declared them BILLS OF ATTAINDER, in the TEST OATH CASES (1867).

Little was heard of loyalty oaths in World War I. After that war, many states singled out teachers for loyalty oaths; but they were only affirmative oaths on the constitutional model, repugnant chiefly because of the mistrust implicit in demanding them.

The waves of anticommunist sentiment that subsided only during the World War II alliance with Russia led to a new proliferation of oaths that penalized membership in subversive organizations (sometimes specifying the Communist party) and advocacy or support of violent overthrow of governments.

All this came to a boil in the tormented Cold War-McCarthy era, when oaths old and new, state and federal, were combined with loyalty-security programs to purge communist influences from public employment and licensed occupations.

When oath cases came before the Court in the 1950s, it first sustained the constitutionality of elaborate oaths, requiring only that communist affiliations must be with knowledge of illegal ends (WIEMAN V. UPDEGRAFF, 1952), and suggesting that an employee must have an opportunity for an explanatory hearing (*Nostrand v. Little,* 1960). But in the 1960s, when the tide of public opinion turned against the excesses of the 1950s, the Court turned too. In half a dozen cases, of which the climactic one was KEYISHIAN V. BOARD OF REGENTS (1967), the Court found oaths that were barely distinguishable from those it had upheld in the 1950s to be void for vagueness or overbreadth. The majority opinions paraded an alarming catalog of possible dilemmas that teachers in particular could not escape and overwhelmed the expostulations of dissenters that the Court had created a "whimsical straw man" who was "not only grim but Grimm." For good measure, the Court, in UNITED STATES v. BROWN (1965), unsheathed the bill of attainder weapon of 1867 to strike down an oath that would exclude a former communist from any office in a labor union.

Such successes against negative oaths emboldened teachers and other public servants who resented having essentially affirmative oaths directed at them. But variants of the Article VI oath to support the Constitution were uniformly upheld. The capstone case was *Cole v. Richardson* (1972). There the Court, while reaffirming in generous FIRST AMENDMENT terms the 1960s cases, found no fault in an obligation first to support and defend the constitutions of the United States and the Commonwealth of Massachusetts and, second, to oppose their violent overthrow. The second clause, Chief Justice WARREN E. BURGER wrote, "does not expand the obligation of the first; it simply makes clear the application of the first clause to a particular issue. Such repetition, whether for emphasis or cadence, seems to be the wont of authors of oaths." He added in a footnote that "The time may come when the value of oaths in routine public employment will be thought not 'worth the candle' for all the division of opinion they engender." Justice THURGOOD MARSHALL, arguing in partial dissent that the second clause should be repudiated, reflected the persisting division between willing and unwilling oath-takers when he wrote, understatedly, that "Loyalty oaths do not have a very pleasant history in this country."

The fear that hellfire would follow a false oath must have faded since the seventeenth century. Nowadays public exposure, and a perjury prosecution, are the serious sanctions. Compulsory oath-taking is welcome to some, a matter of indifference to others, an offense to conscience for a few. A notable instance of a loyalty oath that hit the wrong targets occurred at the University of California in 1949–1952. When the university regents, after prolonged and wounding controversy, insisted on their power to impose a noncommunist oath, twenty-six members of the faculty refused to take it and were ejected. They won a pyrrhic victory in the California Supreme Court, which held that the regents' oath had been supplanted by an oath required of all state employees, but that the statewide oath somehow did not contravene a state constitutional prohibition of any test oath beyond the constitutional oath of support. Some of the nonsigners in time returned; one became president of the university and so did the historian of the episode, who called it "a futile interlude."

Bibliography

GARDNER, DAVID P. 1967 *The California Oath Controversy.* Berkeley and Los Angeles: University of California Press.

HYMAN, HAROLD M.   1959   *To Try Men's Souls: Loyalty Tests in American History.*
Berkeley and Los Angeles: University of California Press.

SAGER, ALAN M.   1972   The Impact of Supreme Court Loyalty Oath Decisions.
American University Law Review 22:39–78.

MCCARTHYISM

David M. Oshinsky

On February 9, 1950, Senator Joseph R. McCarthy of Wisconsin claimed that 205 communists were presently "working and shaping the policy of the State Department." Although McCarthy produced no documentation for this preposterous charge, he quickly emerged as the nation's dominant Cold War politician—the yardstick by which citizens measured patriotic or scurrilous behavior. McCarthy's popularity was not difficult to explain. Americans were frightened by Soviet aggression in Europe. The years since World War II had brought a series of shocks—the Hiss trial, the fall of China, the KOREAN WAR—which fueled the Red Scare and kept it alive.

President HARRY S. TRUMAN played a role as well. In trying to defuse the "Communist issue," he established a federal LOYALTY-SECURITY PROGRAM with few procedural safeguards. The program relied on nameless informants; it penalized personal beliefs and associations, not just OVERT ACTS; and it accelerated the Red hunt by conceding the possibility that a serious security problem existed inside the government and elsewhere. Before long, state and local officials were competing to see who could crack down hardest on domestic subversion. Indiana forced professional wrestlers to sign a LOYALTY OATH. Tennessee ordered the death penalty for those seeking to overthrow the *state* government. Congress, not to be outdone, passed the INTERNAL SECURITY ACT of 1950 over Truman's veto, requiring registration of "Communist action groups," whose members could then be placed in internment camps during "national emergencies."

Despite his personal commitment to CIVIL LIBERTIES, President Truman appointed four Supreme Court Justices who opposed the libertarian philosophy of WILLIAM O. DOUGLAS and HUGO L. BLACK. As a result, JUDICIAL REVIEW was all but abandoned in cases involving the rights of alleged subversives. The Court upheld loyalty oaths as a condition of public employment, limited the use of the Fifth Amendment by witnesses before congressional committees, and affirmed the dismissal of a government worker on the unsworn testimony of unnamed informants. As ROBERT G. McCLOSKEY noted, the Court "became so tolerant of governmental restriction on freedom of expression as to suggest it [had] abdicated the field."

By the mid-1950s, the Red Scare had begun to subside. The death of Joseph Stalin, the Korean armistice, and the Senate's censure of Senator McCarthy all contributed to the easing of Cold War fears. There were many signs of this, though none was more dramatic than the Supreme Court's return to libertarian values under Chief Justice EARL WARREN. In *Slochower v. Board of Higher Education* (1956) the Court overturned the discharge of a college teacher who had invoked the Fifth Amendment before a congressional committee. In *Sweezy v. New Hampshire* (1956) it reversed the conviction of a Marxist professor who had refused, on FIRST AMENDMENT grounds, to answer questions about his political associations. In WATKINS V. UNITED STATES (1957) it held that Congress had "no general authority to expose the private affairs of individuals without justification. . . ." "No inquiry is an end in itself," wrote Warren. "It must be related to and in furtherance of a legitimate [legislative] task of Congress."

The reaction in Congress was predictable. A South Carolina representative called the WARREN COURT "a greater threat to this union than the entire confines of Soviet Russia." Bills were introduced to limit the Court's JURISDICTION in national security cases, and legislators both state and federal demanded Warren's IMPEACHMENT. Although this uproar probably caused some judicial retreat in the late 1950s, the Supreme Court played an important role in blunting the worst excesses of the McCarthy era.

Bibliography

OSHINSKY, DAVID M.   1983   *A Conspiracy So Immense: The World of Joe McCarthy.*
New York: Free Press.

GUILT BY ASSOCIATION

Aviam Soifer

The United States Supreme Court frequently proclaims that guilt by association has no place in our constitutional system (for example, *Schneiderman v. United States,* 1943; WIEMAN v. UPDEGRAFF, 1952). Sanctions imposed for membership in a group are said to be characteristic of primitive cultures, or elements of the early COMMON LAW long since eliminated with prohibitions against such punishments as attaint and forfeiture.

In 1920, CHARLES EVANS HUGHES made what is probably still the most famous statement attacking guilt by association as inconsistent with our individualistic legal norms. In protesting the action of the New York Assembly, which had suspended five elected members because they were members of the Socialist Party, Hughes argued: "It is the essence of the institutions of liberty that it be recognized that guilt is personal and cannot be attributed to the holding of opinion or of mere intent in the absence of overt acts."

Other Justices frequently quoted or paraphrased this argument by Hughes, made between the two periods Hughes served on the Court, in decisions invalidating deportations, employment dismissals, and denials of licenses, as well as in criminal prosecutions. It is obvious, however, that frequently ascription of guilt by association is permitted. For example, members of a CRIMINAL CONSPIRACY may be found guilty for actions by their co-conspirators based entirely on their association in the conspiracy. The Supreme Court recognized the potential for abuse in criminal conspiracy in *Krulewitch v. United States* (1949), but convictions of coconspirators still may be upheld without proof of their direct knowledge or participation in the range of crimes committed by other members of the conspiracy.

There are also striking examples of the Court's condoning of government action based on the presumption of guilt by association in constitutional law. These include the JAPANESE AMERICAN CASES (1943–1944), which upheld the internment of West Coast residents of Japanese ancestry during World War II, and numerous decisions during the 1950s, such as AMERICAN COMMUNICATIONS ASSOCIATION v. DOUDS (1950) and BARENBLATT v. UNITED STATES (1959), which allowed sanctions for membership in communist organizations.

Despite reiteration of the unacceptability of punishment premised upon guilt by association, judgments about individuals based upon their membership in groups frequently—perhaps even necessarily—are made in a bureaucratized world in which personal knowledge of others seems increasingly elusive. Nevertheless, the assignment of individual guilt premised on one's associations remains anathema. It is still thought to be an important premise of constitutional law that the government may not use a gross shorthand such as guilt by association to stigmatize or to punish citizens.

Constitutional safeguards derived primarily from the FIRST AMENDMENT and the DUE PROCESS clauses are said to surround FREEDOM OF ASSOCIATION. When the government employs the technique of guilt by association, it endangers this freedom, which the Court proclaimed in DEJONGE V. OREGON (1937) to be among the most fundamental of constitutional protections. Guilt by association also is inconsistent with basic premises of individual responsibility, which lie close to the core of much of America's legal culture.

Bibliography

EMERSON, THOMAS I. 1970 *The System of Freedom of Expression.* Pages 105–110, 126–129, 161–204, 235–241. New York: Random House.
O'BRIAN, JOHN L. 1948 Loyalty Tests and Guilt by Association. *Harvard Law Review* 61:592–611.

DENNIS *v.* UNITED STATES

341 U.S. 494 (1951)

Martin Shapiro

Eugene Dennis and other high officials of the Communist party had been convicted of violating the ALIEN REGISTRATION ACT of 1940 (the Smith Act) by conspiring to advocate overthrow of the government by force and violence. LEARNED HAND, writing the Court of Appeals opinion upholding the constitutionality of the act and of the conviction, was caught in a dilemma. He was bound by the Supreme Court's CLEAR AND PRESENT DANGER rule, and the government had presented no evidence that Dennis's activities had created a present danger of communist revolution in the United States. Hand, however, believed that courts had limited authority to enforce the FIRST AMENDMENT. His solution was to restate the danger test as: "whether the gravity of the evil, discounted by its improbability, justifies such invasion of free speech as is necessary to avoid the danger." Because Dennis's conspiracy to advocate was linked to a grave evil, communist revolution, he could be punished despite the remote danger of communist revolution. Hand's restatement allowed a court to pay lip service to the danger rule while upholding nearly any government infringement on speech. If the ultimate threat posed by the speech is great enough, the speaker may be punished even though there is little or no immediate threat.

The Supreme Court upheld Dennis's conviction with only Justices HUGO L. BLACK and WILLIAM O. DOUGLAS dissenting. Chief Justice FRED M. VINSON's plurality opinion adopted Hand's restatement of the danger rule. At least where an organized subversive group was involved, speakers might be punished so long as they intended to bring about overthrow "as speedily as circumstances would permit."

Justice FELIX FRANKFURTER's concurrence openly substituted a BALANCING TEST for the danger rule, arguing that the constitutionality of speech limitations ultimately depended on whether the government had a weighty enough interest. Congress, he said, surely was entitled to conclude that the interest in national security outweighed the speech interests of those advocating violent overthrow.

Decided at the height of the Cold War campaign against communists, *Dennis* allied the Court with anticommunist sentiment. No statute would seem more flatly violative on its face of the First Amendment than one that made "advocacy" a crime. Indeed, in YATES v. UNITED STATES (1957) the Court later sought to distinguish between active urging or incitement to revolution, which was constitutionally punishable "advocacy," and abstract teaching of Marxist doctrine, which was constitutionally protected speech.

Defenders of the clear and present danger rule criticize *Dennis* for abandoning that rule's essential feature, the immediacy requirement. Such commentators see the Court as correcting its *Dennis* error in BRANDENBURG v. OHIO (1969) in which the Court returned to something like "clear and present danger" and placed heavy emphasis on the immediacy requirement. Justices Black and Douglas subsequently treated *Dennis* as a case applying the clear and present danger rule and thus as an illustration of the failure of the rule to provide sufficient protection for speech and of the need to replace it with the more "absolute" free speech protections urged by ALEXANDER MEIKLE-JOHN. Proponents of balancing applaud Hand's "discounting" formula as one of the roots of the balancing doctrine, although only the most ardent proponents of judicial self-restraint support Frankfurter's conclusion that Congress, not the Court, should do the final balancing.

It is possible to read *Dennis, Yates,* and *Brandenburg* together as supporting the following theory. The clear and present danger rule, including a strong immediacy requirement, applies to street-corner speakers; so long as their speech does not trigger immediate serious harms, others will have the opportunity to respond to it in the marketplace of ideas, and the government will be able to prepare protective measures against violence that may follow. However, where organized, subversive groups engage in covert speech aimed at secret preparations that will suddenly burst forth in revolution, the "as speedily as circumstances will permit" test is substituted for the immediacy requirement. Covert speech cannot easily be rebutted in the marketplace of ideas; by the time underground groups pose a threat of immediate revolution, they may be so strong that a democratic government cannot stop them or can do so only at the cost of many lives.

Whether or not the Communist party of Eugene Dennis constituted such a covert, underground group impervious to the speech of others and posing a real threat of eventual revolution, a theory such as this is probably the reason the Smith Act was never declared unconstitutional and *Dennis* was never overruled although both have been drastically narrowed by subsequent judicial interpretation.

Bibliography

CORWIN, EDWARD S.   1951   Bowing Out Clear and Present Danger. *Notre Dame Lawyer* 27:325–359.

MENDELSON, WALLACE   1952   Clear and Present Danger—From Schenk to Dennis. *Columbia Law Review* 52:313–333.

YATES v. UNITED STATES

354 U.S. 298 (1957)

Paul L. Murphy

Following DENNIS V. UNITED STATES (1951), Smith Act conspiracy prosecutions were brought against all second-rank United States Communist party officials, and convictions were secured in every case brought to trial between 1951 and 1956. In June 1957, however, the Supreme Court, in *Yates,* reversed the convictions of fourteen West Coast party leaders charged with Smith Act violations. The Court, speaking through Justice JOHN MARSHALL HARLAN, declared that the *Dennis* decision had been misunderstood. The Smith Act did not outlaw advocacy of the abstract doctrine of violent overthrow, because such advocacy was too remote from concrete action to be regarded as the kind of indoctrination preparatory to action condemned in *Dennis.* The essential distinction, Harlan argued, was that those to whom the advocacy was addressed had to be urged to *do* something, now or in the future, rather than merely *believe* in something. Without formally repudiating the "sliding scale" reformulation of CLEAR AND PRESENT DANGER set forth in the *Dennis* opinion, the Court erected a stern new standard for evaluating convictions under the Smith Act, making conviction under the measure difficult. As to INDICTMENTS for involvement in organizing the Communist party in the United States, the Court also took a narrow view. Organizing, Harlan maintained, was only the original act of creating such a group, not any continuing process of proselytizing and recruiting. Since the indictments had been made some years following the postwar organizing of their party, the federal three-year statute of limitations had run out. The Court cleared five of the defendants, remanding the case of nine others for retrial. The ruling brought an abrupt end to the main body of Smith Act prosecutions then under way.

SCALES v. UNITED STATES

367 U.S. 203 (1961)

Martin Shapiro

The Supreme Court, always careful to avoid declaring the Smith Act unconstitutional, instead employed statutory interpretation to emasculate its provisions. Here the Court held that the act's clause banning "membership" in certain organizations applied only to members active in the organization's affairs, knowing that its purpose was to bring about the overthrow of the government by force and violence as speedily as circumstances would permit, and with the specific purpose to bring about that overthrow. In the *Scales* case itself, the Court affirmed a conviction under the membership clause. Since that time, however, the act's forbidding BURDEN OF PROOF has discouraged further prosecutions.

KEYISHIAN v. BOARD OF REGENTS

385 U.S. 589 (1967)

Martin Shapiro

ADLER V. BOARD OF EDUCATION (1952) was one of the cases in which the Supreme Court upheld a wide range of regulations barring "subversives" from government employment. *Keyishian* overruled *Adler* and was the culmination of a series of later decisions restricting LOYALTY-SECURITY PROGRAMS, typically by invoking the VAGUENESS and OVERBREADTH doctrines. *Keyishian* struck down some parts of a complex New York law limiting employment in public teaching; the law's use of the term "seditious" was unconstitutionally vague. Other parts of the law were invalid because they prohibited *mere* knowing membership in the Communist party without the specific intent required by ELFBRANDT V. RUSSELL (1966). *Keyishian* confirmed the Court's previous decisions rejecting the doctrine that public employment is a privilege to which government may attach whatever conditions it pleases.

BRANDENBURG v. OHIO

395 U.S. 444 (1969)

Martin Shapiro

Libertarian critics of the CLEAR AND PRESENT DANGER test had always contended that it provided insufficient protection for speech because it depended ultimately on judicial guesses about the consequences of speech. Judges inimical to the content of a particular speech could always foresee the worst. Thus, to the extent that the test did protect speech, its crucial element was the imminence requirement, that speech was punishable only when it was so closely brigaded in time with unlawful action as to constitute an attempt to commit, or incitement of, unlawful action. When the Supreme Court converted clear and present danger to clear and probable danger in DENNIS v. UNITED STATES (1951) it actually converted the clear and present danger test into a BALANCING TEST that allowed judges who believed in judicial self-restraint to avoid enforcing the FIRST AMENDMENT by striking every balance in favor of the nonspeech interest that the government sought to protect by suppressing speech. The *Dennis* conversion, however, was even more damaging to the clear and present danger rule than a flat rejection and open replacement by the balancing standard would have been. A flat rejection would have left clear and present danger as a temporarily defeated libertarian rival to a temporarily triumphant antilibertarian balancing standard. The conversion to probable danger not only defeated the danger test but also discredited it among libertarians by removing the imminence requirement that had been its strongest protection for dissident speakers. Accordingly commentators, both libertarian and advocates of judicial self-restraint, were pleased to announce that *Dennis* had buried the clear and present danger test.

Some critics of the danger test had supported LEARNED HAND's approach in MASSES PUBLISHING CO. v. PATTEN (1917), which had focused on the advocacy content of the speech itself, thus avoiding judicial predictions about what the speech plus the surrounding circumstances would bring. *Masses* left two problems, however: the "Marc Antony" speech which on the surface seems innocuous but in the circumstances really is an incitement, and the speech preaching violence in circumstances in which it is harmless. OLIVER WENDELL HOLMES himself had injected a specific intent standard alongside the danger rule, arguing that govern-

162

ment might punish a speaker only if it could prove his specific intent to bring about an unlawful act.

Eighteen years after *Dennis,* carefully avoiding the words of the clear and present danger test itself, the Supreme Court brought together these various strands of thought in *Brandenburg v. Ohio,* a PER CURIAM holding that "the constitutional guarantees of free speech . . . do not permit a state to forbid or proscribe advocacy of the use of force or law violation except where such advocacy is directed to inciting or producing imminent lawless action and is likely to incite or produce such action." In a footnote the Court interpreted *Dennis* and YATES v. UNITED STATES (1957) as upholding this standard. The decision itself struck down the Ohio Criminal Syndicalism Act which proscribed advocacy of violence as a means of accomplishing social reform. The Court overruled WHITNEY v. CALIFORNIA (1927).

MUNDT-NIXON BILL

(1948–1949)

Paul L. Murphy

Karl Mundt of South Dakota and RICHARD M. NIXON of California, members of the HOUSE COMMITTEE ON UN-AMERICAN ACTIVITIES, sponsored the first anticommunist bill of the Cold War era. They contended that a house-cleaning of the executive department and a full exposure of past derelictions regarding communists would come only from a body in no way corrupted by ties to the administration. The measure (HR 5852) contained antisedition provisions but also reflected the view that the constitutional way to fight communists was by forcing them out into the open. The bill thus would have required the Communist party and "front" organizations to register with the Department of Justice and supply names of officers and members. It would also require that publications of these organizations, when sent through the mails, be labeled "published in compliance with the laws of the United States, governing the activities of agents of foreign principals."

The measure passed the House by a large margin but failed in the Senate after becoming a controversial factor in the presidential campaign of 1948. The bill was denounced by the Republican candidate, Thomas E. Dewey, and numerous respected national publications as a form of unwarranted thought control.

Bibliography

COHEN, MURRAY and FUCHS, ROBERT F. 1948 Communism's Challenge and the Constitution. *Cornell Law Quarterly* 34:182–219, 352–375.

INTERNAL SECURITY ACT

64 Stat. 987 (1950)

Paul L. Murphy

The Internal Security Act, or McCarran Act, of 1950 was a massive and complex conglomeration of varied security measures as well as many features of the MUNDT-NIXON BILL and an Emergency Detention Bill, which had been introduced, unsuccessfully, earlier in 1950. Passed over President HARRY S. TRUMAN's veto in September, shortly after the outbreak of hostilities in Korea, the measure went beyond the Truman loyalty program for government employees and attempted to limit the operation of subversive groups in all areas of American life. It also sought to shift the authority for security matters to congressional leadership.

The measure, the most severe since the SEDITION ACT of 1918, was composed of two parts. Title I, known as the Subversive Activities Control Act, required communist organizations to register with the attorney general and furnish complete membership lists and financial statements. Although membership and office holding in a communist organization was not, by the act, a crime, the measure did make it illegal knowingly to conspire to perform any act that would "substantially contribute" to the establishment of a totalitarian dictatorship in the United States. It also forbade employment of communists in defense plants and granting them passports. Finally it established a bipartisan SUBVERSIVE ACTIVITIES CONTROL BOARD to assist the attorney general in exposing subversive organizations. In ALBERTSON v. SUBVERSIVE ACTIVITIES CONTROL BOARD (1965), the Court held the compulsory registration provisions unconstitutional. (See MARCHETTI v. UNITED STATES, 1968.)

Title II provided that when the President declared an internal security emergency, the attorney general was to apprehend persons who were likely to engage in, or conspire with others to engage in, acts of espionage or sabotage and intern them "in such places of detention as may be prescribing by the Attorney General." Congress subsequently authorized funds for special camps for such purposes. (See PREVENTIVE DETENTION.) Other provisions denied entrance to the country to ALIENS who were members of communist organizations or who "advocate[d] the economic, international, and governmental doctrines of any other form of totalitarianism." Naturalized citizens joining communist organizations within five years of acquiring CITIZENSHIP were liable to have it revoked.

The courts subsequently held invalid the passport, registration, and employment sections of the act. Section 103, establishing detention centers for suspected subversives, was repealed in September 1971.

Bibliography

HARPER, ALAN 1969 *The Politics of Loyalty: The White House and the Communist Issue, 1946–1952*. Westport, Conn.: Greenwood Press.

COMMUNIST CONTROL ACT

68 Stat. 775 (1954)

Paul L. Murphy

This measure marked the culmination of the United States government's program to prevent subversion from within during the loyalty-security years. Conservative senators, eager to facilitate removal of communists from positions of union leadership, and Senator HUBERT H. HUMPHREY, tired of hearing liberals smeared as "soft on communism," pushed the measure through Congress with large majorities in each chamber. Clearly tied to the 1954 elections, the act outlawed the Communist party as an instrumentality conspiring to overthrow the United States government. The bill as initially drafted made party membership a crime. Responding to criticism of the DWIGHT D. EISENHOWER administration that the membership clause would make the provisions of the 1950 INTERNAL SECURITY ACT unconstitutional, because compulsory registration would violate the RIGHT AGAINST SELF-INCRIMINATION, the bill's sponsors removed its membership clause. However, Congress deprived the Communist party of all "rights, privileges, and immunities attendant upon legal bodies created under the jurisdiction of the laws of the United States or any political subdivision thereof." The act added a new category of groups required to register—"communist-infiltrated" organizations. These, like communist and "front" organizations, although outlawed, were expected to register with the SUBVERSIVE ACTIVITIES CONTROL BOARD.

The measure, virtually inoperative from the beginning, raised grave constitutional questions under the FIRST AMENDMENT, the Fifth Amendment, and the ban against BILLS OF ATTAINDER. The Justice Department ignored it and pushed no general test of its provisions in the court. The act summarized well the official policy toward the Communist party at the time—to keep it legal enough for successful prosecution of its illegalities.

Bibliography

AUERBACH, CARL 1956 The Communist Control Act of 1954. *University of Chicago Law Review* 23:173–220.

SUBVERSIVE ACTIVITIES CONTROL BOARD

Paul L. Murphy

The INTERNAL SECURITY ACT of 1950 created the Subversive Activities Control Board (SACB). This agency was to determine, on request of the ATTORNEY GENERAL, whether a particular organization was a communist-action, communist-front, or communist-infiltrated organization. After SACB had issued an order so designating an organization and after the order had been sustained by the courts, various disabilities and sanctions could be imposed on the group and its members. These included being barred from federal jobs, being denied employment in defense-related industries, and being prohibited from using United States passports.

Eleven years after SACB's creation, the Supreme Court sustained its findings that the Communist party was a communist-action organization as defined by the act and upheld an order requiring the party to register. (See COMMUNIST PARTY v. SACB, 1961.) The Court subsequently declared unconstitutional attempts to implement the sanctions of the act, and in 1965 (ALBERTSON v. SACB) it ruled that the forced registration of individual members of the party would violate the RIGHT AGAINST SELF-INCRIMINATION. By the late 1960s, SACB was moribund. Congress, attempting salvage, gave it authority to register with the attorney general the names of persons it had determined were members of communist organizations, and SACB eventually declared seven persons to be in this category. Such limited action, as well as a 1967 decision holding unconstitutional provisions barring members of registered organizations from jobs in defense-related industries, further limited SACB's utility. In 1974, the RICHARD M. NIXON administration, bowing to SACB's critics, requested no further funding, effectively ending its life.

Bibliography

MURPHY, PAUL L. 1972 *The Constitution in Crisis Times, 1918–1969.* New York: Harper & Row.

ROBEL v. UNITED STATES

389 U.S. 258 (1967)

Michael E. Parrish

Over two dissents, the WARREN COURT struck down on FIRST AMENDMENT grounds a section of the SUBVERSIVE ACTIVITIES CONTROL ACT of 1950 that prohibited the employment of members of the Communist party in "defense facilities" designated by the secretary of defense. Because the statute failed to distinguish between those who supported the unlawful goals of the party and those who did not, wrote Chief Justice EARL WARREN, its OVERBREADTH violated the right of association protected by the FIRST AMENDMENT. Warren rejected government arguments seeking to justify the provision by the WAR POWER and national security interests. "It would indeed be ironic if, in the name of national defense, we would sanction the subversion of one of those liberties—the freedom of association—which makes the defense of the Nation worthwhile." Justices BYRON R. WHITE and JOHN MARSHALL HARLAN dissented, observing that the majority "arrogates to itself an independent judgement of the requirements of national security."

LEGISLATIVE INVESTIGATION

Telford Taylor

Although congressional power to conduct investigations and punish re-calcitrant witnesses is nowhere mentioned in the United States Constitution, the inherent investigative power of legislatures was well established, both in the British Parliament and in the American colonial legislatures, more than a century before the Constitution was adopted. Mention of such power in the early state constitutions was generally regarded as unnecessary, but the Massachusetts and Maryland constitutions both gave explicit authorization; the latter, adopted in 1776, empowered the House of Delegates to ". . . inquire on the oath of witnesses, into all complaints, grievances, and offenses, as the grand inquest of this state," and to ". . . call for all public or official papers and records, and send for persons, whom they may judge necessary in the course of inquiries concerning affairs relating to the public interest."

The basic theory of the power was and is that a legislative house needs it in order to obtain information, so that its law-making and other functions may be discharged on an enlightened rather than a benighted basis. Under the Constitution, the power was first exercised by the House of Representatives in 1792, when it appointed a select committee to inquire into the defeat by the Indians suffered the previous year by federal forces commanded by General Arthur St. Clair. The House empowered the committee "to call for such persons, papers and records as may be necessary to assist in their inquiries." After examining the British precedents, President GEORGE WASHINGTON and his cabinet agreed that the House "was an inquest and therefore might institute inquiries" and "call for papers generally," and that although the executive ought to refuse to release documents "the disclosure of which would endanger the public," in the matter at hand "there was not a paper which might not be properly produced," and therefore the committee's requests should be granted.

For nearly a century thereafter, investigations were conducted frequently and without encountering serious challenge, in Congress and the state legislatures alike. They covered a wide range of subjects, and their history is in large part the history of American politics. Among the most interesting state investigations were those conducted in 1855 by the Massachusetts legislature and the New York City Council, under the leadership of the "Know-Nothing" party, in which Irish Roman Catholicism was the target. Inquiries by the New York City Council into alleged Irish domination of the police force were challenged in the New York Court of Common Pleas, and Judge Charles Patrick Daly's opinion in *Briggs v. McKellar* (1855) was the first to hold that, unlike in Britain, in the United States the legislative investigative power is limited by the Constitution.

Fifteen years later, a congressional investigation was for the first time successfully challenged on constitutional grounds, in KILBOURN v. THOMPSON (1881). The House of Representatives had authorized a select committee to investigate the bankruptcy of the Jay Cooke banking firm (which was a depository of federal funds), and when the witness Kilbourn refused to answer questions, the House cited him for contempt and imprisoned him. After his release on HABEAS CORPUS, Kilbourn sued the House sergeant-at-arms for damages from false imprisonment. In an opinion by Justice SAMUEL F. MILLER, the Supreme Court sustained his claim on the grounds of constitutional SEPARATION OF POWERS, declaring that the Jay Cooke bankruptcy presented no legislative grounds for inquiry and that "the investigation . . . could only be properly and successfully made by a court of justice." The Court has never since invalidated a legislative inquiry on that particular basis, and it is probable that today, under comparable circumstances, a sufficient legislative purpose would be found. But the Court's ruling, that Congress's investigative and contempt powers are subject to JUDICIAL REVIEW and must conform to constitutional limitations, has not since been seriously questioned.

Exclusively until 1857, and commonly until 1935, Congress enforced its investigative power against recalcitrant witnesses by its own contempt proceedings: a congressional citation for contempt, and its execution through arrest and confinement of the witness by the sergeant-at-arms. (See LEGISLATIVE CONTEMPT POWER.) Judicial review of the contempt was usually obtained by habeas corpus. But the system was cumbersome, and effective only when Congress was in session. To remedy these shortcomings, Congress in 1857 enacted a statute making it a federal offense to refuse to produce documents demanded, or to answer questions put, by a duly authorized congressional investigatory committee. For some years both the contempt and the statutory criminal procedures were used, but since 1935 the contempt procedure has fallen into disuse. Challenges to congressional investigative authority are currently dealt with by INDICTMENT and trial under the criminal statute, now found in section 192, Title 2, United States Code, the constitutionality of which was upheld by the Supreme Court in *In re Chapman* (1897).

The tone of Justice Miller's opinion in the *Kilbourn* case raised doubts about the scope and even the existence of the congressional contempt power, which were repeatedly voiced during the early years of the twentieth century, when Congress conducted investigations damaging to powerful business and financial institutions. In 1912 the House Committee on Banking and Currency launched what became known as the "Money Trust Investigation," in which practically all the leading financiers of the time—J. P. Morgan the elder, George F. Baker, James J. Hill, and others—were called to answer charges of undue concentration of control of railroads and heavy industries in the hands of a few New York bankers. In 1924, Senate committees probed allegations of corruption and maladministration in the Justice, Interior, and Navy departments.

The legality and propriety of these inquiries aroused vigorous public debate. The famous jurist JOHN HENRY WIGMORE wrote of a "debauch of investigations" which raised a "stench" and caused the Senate to fall "in popular esteem to the level of professional searchers of the municipal dunghills," while then Professor FELIX FRANKFURTER accused the critics of seeking to "divert attention and shackle the future," and argued that the investigative power should be left "untrammeled." The doubters and critics were encouraged when a federal district judge, relying on the *Kilbourn* case, quashed a Senate contempt citation against Attorney General Harry M. Daugherty's brother, but the investigative and contempt powers were vindicated when the Supreme Court reversed that decision and ruled in McGRAIN v. DAUGHERTY (1927) that the investigation was proper as an aid to legislation, and that Mally Daugherty could be required to testify on pain of imprisonment. Consequently, there were no serious or successful legal challenges to the many congressional investigations born of the Great Depression and the "New Deal" period of President FRANKLIN D. ROOSEVELT's administration. (See CONSTITUTIONAL HISTORY, 1933–1945.)

Until this time the main subjects of legislative investigations had been the civil and military operations of the executive branch, industrial and financial problems, and the operation of social forces such as the labor movement. Except for state investigations in the middle years of the nineteenth century directed at Masons and Roman Catholics, ideological matters had not been much involved.

The Russian Revolution of 1917, the spread of communist doctrine, and the Nazi seizure of dictatorial power in Germany soon emerged as major subjects of congressional concern. There were short-lived congressional investigations of communist propaganda in 1919 and 1930, and of Nazi propaganda in 1934. With the establishment of the HOUSE COMMITTEE OF UN-AMERICAN ACTIVITIES in May 1938, SUBVERSIVE ACTIVITIES emerged as the most publicized subject of congressional investigation.

During World War II, in which the United States and the Soviet Union were allies, there was a lull in these inquiries, but the "Iron

Curtain" and "Cold War" revived them, and by 1947 they were again front-page news. Soon, names of prosecutors and witnesses—for example, MARTIN DIES, RICHARD M. NIXON, Alger Hiss, Whittaker Chambers, JOSEPH R. McCARTHY, and Patrick McCarran—became household words. The Senate authorized two bodies to join in the hunt for subversion: the Judiciary Committee's Subcommittee on Internal Security headed by Senator McCarran, and the Government Operations Committee's Subcommittee on Investigations under Senator McCarthy, respectively established in 1946 and 1950.

The principal activity of these agencies was summoning individuals to testify about the communist connections of themselves or others, and their proceedings contributed mightily to a period of public recrimination and bitter controversy that lasted for more than a decade. It was also a period of frequent criminal litigation involving congressional investigative power, as numerous witnesses were indicted for refusing to answer such questions. Some witnesses invoked the Fifth Amendment RIGHT AGAINST SELF INCRIMINATION, and the Supreme Court, in three cases decided in 1955, was unanimously of the opinion that the right is available to witnesses before legislative committees, though three of the Justices thought that the witnesses had not clearly invoked it. Writing for the majority, Chief Justice EARL WARREN confirmed the congressional investigative power and stated further (*Quinn v. United States*):

But the power to investigate, broad as it may be, is also subject to recognized limitations. It cannot be used to inquire into private affairs unrelated to a valid legislative purpose. Nor does it extend to an area in which Congress is forbidden to legislate. Similarly, the power to investigate must not be confused with any of the powers of law enforcement; these powers are assigned under our Constitution to the Executive and Judiciary. Still further limitations on the power to investigate are found in the specific individual guarantees of the BILL OF RIGHTS, such as the Fifth Amendment's privilege against self-incrimination which is in issue here.

Other witnesses, however, invoked the FIRST AMENDMENT's guarantee of FREEDOM OF SPEECH as justification for their refusal to answer, and in 1956 and 1957 two such cases, SWEEZY V. NEW HAMPSHIRE and WATKINS V. UNITED STATES, the first involving a congressional and the second a state investigation, reached the Court. With only Justice TOM C. CLARK dissenting, the Court held that, as a general proposition, First Amendment rights are enjoyed by witnesses in legislative investigations.

But did the First Amendment protect these witnesses from the obligation to answer questions about individual connections with communism? The Court did not meet that issue and based its reversal of both convictions on nonconstitutional grounds. Watkins had not been told that the questions put to him were (as the federal statute requires) "pertinent to the question under inquiry," while in Sweezy's case it was not shown that the state legislature had authorized the investigative agency to ask the questions he declined to answer.

Three years later, however, by a 5–4 vote, the Court held that the First Amendment did not bar requiring a witness to answer questions regarding his own or others' communist connections. (See BARENBLATT v. UNITED STATES; UPHAUS v. WYMAN, 1959.) In his opinion for the Court in the former case, Justice JOHN MARSHALL HARLAN undertook a "balancing . . . of the private and public interests at stake," and concluded that since the Communist party was not "an ordinary political party" and sought overthrow of the government "by force and violence," Congress had "the right to identify a witness as a member of the Communist Party." (See BALANCING TESTS.)

The authority of these two cases was somewhat tarnished in 1963 after Justice ARTHUR J. GOLDBERG had replaced Justice Frankfurter, who had been in the five-member majority. A Florida court authorized a state investigatory committee to require a local branch of the NAACP to produce its membership lists so that the committee could determine whether certain individuals suspected of communist connections were members of the NAACP. Once again the Court divided 5–4, and Justice Goldberg, writing for the majority in GIBSON v. FLORIDA LEGISLATIVE COMMITTEE, ruled that, in the absence of any prior showing of connection between the NAACP and communist activities, such required disclosure was barred by the First Amendment. Three years later, in another New Hampshire investigations case, *DeGregory v. New Hampshire Attorney General*, the Court ruled, 6–3, that the state's interest was "too remote and conjectural" to justify compelling a witness in 1964 to testify about communist activities in 1957.

Since then there have been no Supreme Court and no important state or lower federal court decisions on the constitutional aspects of legislative investigative power. The *Barenblatt* case has not been overruled, and it is perhaps noteworthy that both the *Gibson* and *DeGregory* cases involved state rather than congressional investigations. The attitudes of the Justices who have joined the Court since 1966 remain untested.

It may be surmised, for the future, that if a plausible relation between a legislative inquiry and a valid legislative purpose can be shown, and there are no procedural flaws or manifestations of gross abuse, the Court will be reluctant to deny, on constitutional grounds, the power of a legislative investigating committee to require witnesses to answer questions or produce records.

A different situation might well obtain if a congressional investigating committee should seek to enforce the production of government documents involving NATIONAL SECURITY or for some other reason inappropriate for public disclosure. Presidents have on numerous occasions exercised the right first asserted by George Washington in 1792, to withhold documents "the disclosure of which would endanger the public" or otherwise contravene the public interest. (See EXECUTIVE PRIVILEGE.) Congressional committee efforts to force the production of records of judicial conferences, or other confidential court papers, might likewise encounter constitutional objections based on the separation of powers. Up to the present time, these issues have not confronted the Supreme Court, and the political wisdom of avoiding such confrontations is manifest.

Bibliography

CARR, ROBERT K.   1952   *The House Committee on Un-American Activities*. Ithaca, N.Y.: Cornell University Press.

GOODMAN, WALTER   1968   *The Committee*. New York: Farrar, Straus & Giroux.

LANDIS, JAMES M.   1926   Constitutional Limits on the Congressional Power of Investigation. *Harvard Law Review* 40:153–226.

OGDEN, AUGUST RAYMOND   1945   *The Dies Committee*. Washington, D.C.: Catholic University of America Press.

POTTS, CHARLES S.   1926   Power of Legislative Bodies to Punish for Contempt. *University of Pennsylvania Law Review* 74:691–780.

TAYLOR, TELFORD   1955   *Grand Inquest: The Story of Congressional Investigations*. New York: Simon & Schuster.

HOUSE COMMITTEE ON UN-AMERICAN ACTIVITIES

Paul L. Murphy

In 1938, because of a growing fear of Nazi and communist activity in the United States, conservative congressmen secured passage of a House Resolution creating a Special Committee on Un-American Activities (HUAC). Under publicity-conscious Texas congressman MARTIN DIES, the Committee set out to expose left-wing groups and individuals whom it considered security risks. After five renewals, by overwhelming votes, the group was made into an unprecedented standing committee of the House in 1945. From then until the mid-1950s, the Committee became a sounding board for ex-radicals, publicity seekers, and critics of the New Deal and the Truman administration. It identified the following tasks for itself: to expose and ferret out communists and their sympathizers in the federal government; to show how communists had won control over vital trade unions; and to investigate communist influences in the press, religious and educational organizations, and the movie industry. The sensational Alger Hiss-Whittaker Chambers hearings, in connection with turning over security information, and the resultant perjury conviction of Hiss, a former New Deal official, added to the Committee's prestige. By 1948, the Committee sponsored legislation against the Communist party, pushing the MUNDT-NIXON BILL.

The activities of HUAC, however, raised important constitutional questions. The Committee's constant probing into political behavior and belief led critics to charge that such forced exposure abridged FREEDOM OF SPEECH and association, and punished citizens for their opinions. Also questioned was the legitimacy of its "exposure for its own sake" approach, when action did not seem to relate to legitimate legislative purpose, and when legislative "trials" violated many aspects of DUE PROCESS including the right to be tried in a court under the protection of constitutional guarantees.

The Supreme Court ultimately dealt with both questions, with contradictory and changing results. In three cases (*Emspack v. United States*, 1955; *Quinn v. United States*, 1955; and WATKINS V. UNITED STATES, 1957) the Court narrowly interpreted the statutory authority for punishing recalcitrant witnesses, and questioned forced exposure of views and activities in light of the FIRST AMENDMENT. Facing sharp criticism, the Court retreated in the cases of BARENBLATT V. UNITED STATES (1958), *Wilkinson v. United States* (1961), and *Braden v. United States* (1961), only to move back again to a more critical position as the 1960s progressed—from 1961 to 1966 reversing almost every contempt conviction which came to it from the Committee. By mid-1966, conservative legislators were condemning the "unseemly spectacles" HUAC chronically elicited. Thus, in 1969, it was rechristened the Internal Security Committee, and although its procedures were modified somewhat in this new form, the committee was eventually abolished by the House in 1975.

Bibliography

GOODMAN, WALTER   1968   *The Committee: The Extraordinary Career of the House Committee on Un-American Activities.* New York: Farrar, Straus.

WATKINS v. UNITED STATES

354 U.S. 178 (1957)

SWEEZY v. NEW HAMPSHIRE

354 U.S. 234 (1957)

Kenneth L. Karst

Watkins, a labor leader called to testify before the House Committee on Un-American Activities, had been told by the union president that he would lose his position if he claimed his RIGHT AGAINST SELF-INCRIMINATION. He thus claimed a FIRST AMENDMENT privilege when he declined to answer the committee's questions about the membership of other people in the Communist party. He also objected that these questions were beyond the scope of the committee's activities. For his refusal to answer, Watkins was convicted of contempt of Congress. The Supreme Court reversed his conviction, 8–1.

Writing for the Court, Chief Justice EARL WARREN rested decision on a narrow point: Watkins had been denied PROCEDURAL DUE PROCESS, for he had not been given a sufficient explanation of the subject of inquiry, and thus could not know whether the committee's questions were "pertinent to the questions under inquiry," as the contempt statute specified. Warren's opinion, however, strongly suggested that the Court would be prepared to confront the whole issue of LEGISLATIVE INVESTIGATIONS into political association. He remarked on the use of such investigations to subject people to public stigma, and the absence in such proceedings of effective protection of procedural fairness. "We have no doubt that there is no congressional power to expose for the sake of exposure," Warren wrote. "Who can define the meaning of 'un-American'?" Justice TOM C. CLARK, the sole dissenter, appeared to object as much to these broad OBITER DICTA as to the actual decision. He complained of the Court's "mischievous curbing of the informing function of Congress."

In *Sweezy,* a COMPANION CASE to *Watkins,* the Court held, 6–2, that a state legislative investigation could not constitutionally compel Sweezy to answer questions about the Progressive party and about a lecture he had given at the University of New Hampshire. Chief Justice Warren wrote a PLURALITY OPINION for four Justices, concluding that Sweezy's contempt conviction violated procedural due process because the state legislature had not clearly authorized the attorney general, who conducted the investigation, to inquire into those subjects. Justice FELIX FRANKFURTER, joined by Justice JOHN MARSHALL HARLAN, concurred, arguing that the state had unconstitutionally invaded Sweezy's FOURTEENTH AMENDMENT liberty—here, his "political autonomy," a plain reference to the First Amendment. Justice Frankfurter used a (for him) familiar BALANCING TEST, but articulated a COMPELLING STATE INTEREST standard for cases of invasions of political privacy. The Frankfurter opinion is notable for its early articulation of the constitutional dimension of ACADEMIC FREEDOM. It also led, the following year, to the Court's explicit recognition of the FREEDOM OF ASSOCIATION in NAACP v. ALABAMA (1958). Justice Clark again dissented, now joined by Justice HAROLD H. BURTON.

A number of members of Congress reacted angrily to these opinions and others decided the same year, such as YATES v. UNITED STATES (1957) and *Jencks v. United States* (1957). (See JENCKS ACT.) Bills were proposed in Congress to limit the Supreme Court's jurisdiction over cases involving controls of subversive activities. In the event, not much "curbing" was done, and in retrospect *Watkins* and *Sweezy* appeared to be no more than trial balloons. Two years later, in BARENBLATT v. UNITED STATES (1959), a majority of the Court backed away from the expected confrontation with Congress.

BARENBLATT v. UNITED STATES

STATES

360 U.S. 109 (1959)

Martin Shapiro

In a 5–4 decision, Justice JOHN MARSHALL HARLAN writing for the majority, the Supreme Court upheld Barenblatt's conviction for contempt of Congress based on his refusal to answer questions of the House Committee on Un-American Activities about his membership in the Communist party. He argued that such questions violated his rights of FREEDOM OF SPEECH and association by publically exposing his political beliefs. In an earlier decision, WATKINS v. UNITED STATES (1957), the Court had offered some procedural protections to witnesses before such committees and held out hope that it would offer even greater protections in the future. *Barenblatt* ended that hope.

The Court did follow the *Watkins* approach of denouncing "exposure for the exposure's sake" and requiring that Congress have a legislative purpose for its investigations. But it presumed that Congress did have such a purpose, refusing to look at the actual congressional motives behind the investigation.

Barenblatt is the classic case of a FIRST AMENDMENT ad hoc BALANCING TEST. The Court held that the First Amendment protected individuals from compelled disclosure of their political associations. But Justice Harlan went on to say, "Where First Amendment rights are asserted to bar governmental interrogation, resolution of the issue always involved a balancing by the Courts of the competing private and public interest at stake in the circumstances shown." Then he balanced Barenblatt's interest in not answering questions about his communist associations against Congress's interest in frustrating the international communist conspiracy to overthrow the United States government. The interests thus defined, the Court had no trouble striking the balance in favor of the government. More than any other decision, *Barenblatt* establishes that the freedom of speech may be restricted by government if, in the Court's view, the government's interest in committing the infringement is sufficiently compelling.

GIBSON v. FLORIDA LEGISLATIVE INVESTIGATION COMMITTEE

372 U.S. 539 (1963)

Martin Shapiro

The committee ordered the president of the Miami branch of the NAACP to produce his membership records and refer to them when the committee asked whether specific individuals, suspected of being communists, were NAACP members. Earlier committee attempts to expose the NAACP's entire membership list showed that the communist issue was a screen behind which the state sought to use publicity to weaken a group engaged in activities aimed at racial equality and DESEGREGATION.

The Supreme Court, 5–4, held that Gibson's conviction for contempt for refusal to produce the records infringed the FREEDOM OF ASSOCIATION, which protected associational privacy. The Court, in an opinion by Justice ARTHUR GOLDBERG, was prepared to balance the state interest in legislative investigation against this FIRST AMENDMENT interest, but it held that such an infringement could be constitutional only if "the state convincingly show[s] a substantial relation between the information sought and a subject of overriding and COMPELLING STATE INTEREST," and that Florida had not done so in this instance. Accordingly Gibson's conviction was invalidated.

Gibson and its predecessor, *Bates v. Little Rock* (1960), must be read in conjunction with the BALANCING TEST applied to a congressional investigation into communist activity in BARENBLATT v. UNITED STATES (1959). The later cases may be read narrowly to distinguish *Barenblatt* and provide greater constitutional protection from investigative exposure only for "groups which themselves are neither engaged in subversive or other illegal . . . activities nor demonstrated to have any substantial connections with such activities." Alternatively, *Bates* and *Gibson* can be seen to modify the balancing test of *Barenblatt* to a "preferred position" balancing in which the government must show a compelling interest before it can invade associational privacy.

FIGHTING WORDS

Martin Shapiro

In CHAPLINSKY V. NEW HAMPSHIRE (1942) the Supreme Court upheld the conviction of a Jehovah's Witness who called a policeman "a God damned racketeer" and "a damned Fascist," holding that "fighting words"—face-to-face words plainly likely to provoke the average addressee to fight—were not protected by constitutional free speech guarantees. Viewed narrowly, the fighting words doctrine can be seen as a per se rule effectuating the CLEAR AND PRESENT DANGER principle, relieving the government of proving an actual INCITEMENT by taking the words themselves as decisive. Taken broadly, *Chaplinsky* strips "four-letter words" of free speech protection. "It has been well observed," Justice FRANK MURPHY said, "that such utterances are no essential part of any exposition of ideas, and are of such slight social value as a step to the truth that any benefit that may be derived from them is clearly outweighed by the social interest in order and morality."

The modern tendency of the Court has been to extend partial FIRST AMENDMENT protection to even the "excluded" areas of speech. To the extent that *Chaplinsky* refuses protection to four-letter words because they offend against taste or morality, it has been limited by recent decisions such as COHEN V. CALIFORNIA (1971), *Gooding v. Wilson* (1972), and *Rosenfeld v. New Jersey* (1972). The Justices appear to have been engaging in ad hoc analysis of what persons in what situations are entitled to a measure of protection from the shock to their sensibilities generated by words that, in the language of *Chaplinsky*, "by their very utterances inflict injury."

The shock aspect of four-letter words is obviously related to the shock element in OBSCENITY. In FCC V. PACIFICA FOUNDATION (1978) the Court upheld FCC regulation of "indecent" broadcasting that involved "patently offensive" four-letter words but was not obscene. While admitting that the words in question would warrant constitutional protection under certain circumstances, the Court held that in view of their capacity to offend, their slight social value in the conveying of ideas, and the intrusive character of speech broadcast into the home, their repeated use might constitutionally be banned at least in time slots and programming contexts when children might be listening.

The recent decisions suggest that outside the direct incitement to violence context the Court is prepared to balance PRIVACY against speech interests where four-letter words are at issue. Where statutes go beyond prohibiting incitement to violence, and also bar cursing or reviling, or using opprobrious, indecent, lascivious, or offensive language, they are likely to be held unconstitutionally vague or overbroad. (See *Lewis v. New Orleans*, 1974.)

Bibliography

KONVITZ, MILTON   1978   *Fundamental Liberties of a Free People.* Chap. 17. Westport, Conn.: Greenwood Press.

SHEA, THOMAS   1975   Fighting Words and the First Amendment. *Kentucky Law Journal* 63:1–22.

CHAPLINSKY v. NEW HAMPSHIRE

315 U.S. 568 (1941)

Martin Shapiro

In *Chaplinsky*, Justice FRANK MURPHY, writing for a unanimous Supreme Court, introduced into FIRST AMENDMENT jurisprudence the TWO-LEVEL THEORY that "There are certain well-defined and narrowly limited classes of speech, the prevention and punishment of which have never been thought to raise any constitutional problem. These include the lewd and obscene, the profane, the libelous, and the insulting or 'FIGHTING' WORDS—those which by their very utterance inflict injury or tend to incite an immediate breach of the peace." *Chaplinsky* itself arose under a "fighting words" statute, which the state court had interpreted to punish "words likely to cause an average addressee to fight." In this narrow context the decision can be seen as an application of the CLEAR AND PRESENT DANGER test. COHEN V. CALIFORNIA (1971), emphasizing this rationale, offered protection to an OBSCENITY that created no danger of violence.

In its broader conception of categories of speech excluded from First Amendment protection, the case served as an important doctrinal source for many later obscenity and libel decisions.

LIBEL AND THE FIRST AMENDMENT

Benno C. Schmidt, Jr.

A central historical question about the FIRST AMENDMENT is to what extent it embodied the received eighteenth-century legal traditions of English law and governmental practice as they were reshaped and renewed in the colonial, revolutionary, and formative periods in America. Or was the amendment a break from these traditions? This issue can be stated either as a question of the intent of the Framers and ratifiers or as a matter of the normative impact of an authoritative text, elaborated in our century within an institutional matrix of JUDICIAL REVIEW radically different from that of the eighteenth century on either side of the Atlantic. However the question be stated, the historical problem is in essence whether the First Amendment is to be regarded as expressing a principle of continuity with the received legal tradition or as constituting a declaration of independence from English law, thereby projecting the American law of freedom of expression on a path of autonomous development.

The general view emphasizes continuity, both as a matter of the original understanding of the Framers of the First Amendment and as a matter of the amendment's later—much later—doctrinal elaborations. Indeed, we conventionally measure continuity or discontinuity by reference to the basic conceptual dichotomy of the English legal tradition, as formulated by WILLIAM BLACKSTONE, the oracle of the COMMON LAW for the framing generation:

where blasphemous, immoral, treasonable, schismatical, seditious, or scandalous libels are punished by the English law . . . the liberty of the press, properly understood, is by no means infringed or violated. The *liberty of the press* is indeed essential to the nature of a free state, but this consists in laying no previous restraints upon publications, and not in freedom from censure for criminal matter when published. Every freeman has an undoubted right to lay what sentiments he pleases before the public: to forbid this is to destroy the freedom of the press: but if he publishes what is improper, mischievous, or illegal, he must take the consequences of his own temerity [*Commentaries on the Laws of England*, 1765, Bk. 4, chap. II, pp. 151–52].

The issue whether the First Amendment embraced or departed from the English legal tradition with respect to subsequent punishment tends to be fixed on the treatment of SEDITIOUS LIBEL. The historical argument for the law of seditious libel has been that government ought to have power to punish its most abusive or subversive critics because criticism of government contains the seeds of a variety of evils—disobedience to government, public disorder, even violence—and that no government can subsist if people have the right to criticize it or to call its agents corrupt or incompetent. This is seen in the work of Leonard W. Levy, ZECHARIAH CHAFEE, and others who have lately examined the First Amendment's historical foundations by looking at seditious libel as the exclusive focus for probing the question of continuity and discontinuity with respect to subsequent punishments. Having narrowed the issue to seditious libel, the scholarly tradition put the question of continuity and discontinuity in all-or-nothing terms: Does the First Amendment as a matter of original understanding, or as a matter of latter doctrinal connotation, repudiate or embrace the concept of seditious libel?

When a question about the relationship of a controversial legal tradition to a broadly phrased constitutional text is put in such terms, the answers are likely to fall out along dialectical lines. So it has been with the rejection-or-reception issue concerning seditious libel. The heated debate on the question by the Federalists and Republicans in connection with the passage of the ALIEN AND SEDITION ACTS of 1798 has been echoed through our history. In modern scholarship, the dialectic begins in 1919 when Zechariah Chafee, troubled deeply by the World War I ESPIONAGE ACT prosecutions, wrote in the *Harvard Law Review* that the Framers of the First Amendment "intended to wipe out the common law of SEDITION, and to make further prosecutions for criticism of the government, without any incitement to law-breaking, forever impossible in the United States of America." Six months later, and plainly in emulation, Justice OLIVER WENDELL HOLMES added the weight of his and LOUIS D. BRANDEIS's authority to the Chafee thesis, when he declared in his great dissent in the *Abrams* case: "I wholly disagree with the argument . . . that the first Amendment left the common law as to seditious libel in force. History seems to me against the notion." But the Chafee position never won the broad adherence that most modern scholars seem to think it had. In the World War I free speech cases before the Supreme court, John Lord O'Brien, who briefed the cases for the Justice Department, stated as the official view of the government that seditious libel prosecutions were not rendered invalid by the First Amendment, either as a matter of original intent or as correctly understood in 1919. And others, including EDWARD S. CORWIN, dissented from the Chafee position. Indeed, Chafee himself seems to have changed his tune by 1949, at least on the issue of the Framers' original intent: "The truth is, I think, that the framers had no very clear idea as to what they meant by 'the freedom of speech or the press.' " The dialectic about seditious libel and the First Amendment entered a new phase with the publication of Leonard W. Levy's seminal work, *Legacy of Suppression,* in 1960. This book argued that with respect to the general conceptions of FREEDOM OF THE PRESS prevalent at the time of the framing and ratification of the First Amendment, there was no solid evidence of a consensus to move away from a purely Blackstonian conception of freedom, that is, a conception limited to protecting only against previous restraints. In particular, Levy found considerable evidence that supported the continuing validity of seditious libel prosecutions, and no clear evidence that any lawyer, pamphleteer, philosopher, or statesman repudiated the concept of seditious libel. There was, Levy recognized, a growing sense of the necessity of the defense of truth, although far from a clear consensus even on that. And there was also a growing insistence on the independent power of the jury in a seditious libel prosecution to determine the issue of truth and the question of the seditious quality of any publication, as well as the other factual issues in the case.

Levy's account of the relationship of the First Amendment as a formal constitutional limitation on the power of Congress and his overall conception of intellectual and legal history respecting freedom of expression has from the beginning been confused by the problem of FEDERALISM. At the same time that he has insisted that the conception of freedom of the press guarded against abridgment by the First Amendment does not invalidate seditious libel, he has described the amendment as denying any power whatever by Congress to legislate with respect to the press, except to protect COPYRIGHT. Thus, he concluded that Congress had no power to pass the Sedition Act of 1798, but on federalism grounds, not because the Sedition Act violated any understandings about press freedom embodied in the First Amendment. The states and the federal courts remained empowered to try seditious libel prosecutions.

But Levy's interpretation of the "Congress shall make no law" language in the First Amendment has taken a distant backseat, in his own writing and in that of others, to his overriding emphasis that "the freedom of speech or of the press" was not understood to repudiate the concept of seditious libel. In other words, the First Amendment was understood to embody a Blackstonian conception of freedom of expression as a matter of original intent.

In NEW YORK TIMES CO. v. SULLIVAN (1964) the Supreme Court gave an authoritative modern answer to the question whether prosecution of seditious libel would survive the First Amendment. An advertisement in March 1960, placed by supporters of MARTIN LUTHER KING, JR., in the *New York Times;* recited the repressive activities of Alabama police with several minor inaccuracies and exaggerations. An Alabama jury awarded a local official $500,000 damages against the *New York Times.* The Supreme Court reacted with sweeping changes in the constitutional status of defamation law. Libel would no longer be viewed as a category of expression beneath First Amendment protection. Instead, the Court found that the political repudiation of the Sedition Act of 1798 had revealed the "central meaning" of the First Amendment: a right to criticize government and public officials. As the Court put it, "[A] rule compelling the critic of official conduct to guarantee the truth of all his factual assertions . . . leads to . . . 'self-censorship.' " The Alabama act, "because of the restraint it imposed upon criticism of government and public officials, was inconsistent with the First Amendment.

In place of actual falsity as a basis for liability, the Court imposed a new standard to govern defamation actions brought by public officials. Now, a public official could recover damages for a defamatory falsehood relating to his official conduct only upon a showing "that the statement was made with 'actual malice'—that is, with knowledge that it was false or with reckless disregard of whether it was false or not."

Sullivan effected important changes in constitutional law and practice. Defamation law previously had been left to the states, subject to gradual common law evolution in state courts not often exposed to First Amendment issues. *Sullivan* federalized this diversity of local rules into a single national body of doctrine overseen by a Court peculiarly sensitive to First Amendment problems. Furthermore, the intangibility of defamation law had left wide discretion in trial court juries; *Sullivan* imposed independent appellate court review of the facts in defamation actions as a First Amendment guarantee. And, in place of the complexity of overlapping liabilities, offsetting privileges, and jurisdictional diversity, *Sullivan* instituted a simple national rule that put a stringent burden of proof on plaintiffs.

Decisions following *Sullivan* extended the "actual malice" limitation on the law of defamation beyond the case of criticism of high public officials. The rule was expanded to apply to PUBLIC FIGURES in *Curtis Publishing Co. v. Butts* and *Associated Press v. Walker* (1967). A plurality of the Court even stretched the rule to cover private figures, if the matter was "a subject of public or general interest," in *Rosenbloom v. Metromedia, Inc.* (1971). But the Court retreated from *Rosenbloom* three years later in GERTZ V. ROBERT WELCH, INC. (1974). *Gertz* held that a private person may recover without meeting the actual malice standard. Because private figures have only limited access to the media to correct misstatements of others, and because they have not assumed the risk of injury due to defamatory falsehoods against them, the Court found the interests of private figures to weigh more heavily than those of public figures. The states were left free to establish an appropriate standard of liability, provided they do not impose liability without fault. Moreover, the states were forbidden from awarding presumed or punitive DAMAGES absent a showing of actual malice. More recently, in DUN &

BRADSTREET, INC. v. GREENMOSS BUILDERS, INC. (1985), the Court re-treated still further, permitting recovery of presumed and punitive dam-ages by a private plaintiff without a showing of actual malice, because the defamatory statements did not involve a matter of public concern.

The defamation decisions beginning with *New York Times Co. v. Sullivan* have had the twofold effect of highlighting the core purpose of the First Amendment and constitutionalizing the law of defamation. By invalidating the law of seditious libel, the Court recognized that criticism of government is the type of speech most deserving of First Amendment protection. By establishing minimum standards of liability and limitations on damages for public figures and some private plaintiffs, the Court federalized the law of defamation.

Bibliography

KALVEN, HARRY JR.   1964   The New York Times Case: A Note on "The Central Meaning of the First Amendment." *Supreme Court Review* 1964:191.

LEVY, LEONARD W.   1984   *Emergence of a Free Press.* New York: Oxford University Press.

_____   1960   *Legacy of Suppression: Freedom of Speech and Press in Early American History.* Cambridge, Mass.: Harvard University Press.

GROUP LIBEL

Steven Shiffrin

Group libel statutes pose uniquely difficult issues, for they produce a clash between two constitutional commitments: to equality and to FREE-DOM OF SPEECH. Such laws impose punishments on the defamation of racial, ethnic, or religious groups. Group libel statutes were first enacted following World War II. It was widely believed that the Nazis had come to power in Germany by means of systematic calumny of their opponents and of Jews and other groups that might serve as scapegoats. Group libel statutes were enacted to afford remedies for defamation, to prevent breaches of the peace, and ultimately to protect democracy against totalitarianism. On the other hand, as the Supreme Court stated in NEW YORK TIMES CO. V. SULLIVAN (1964), the FIRST AMENDMENT manifests "a profound national commitment to the principle that debate on public issues should be uninhibited, robust and wide-open." Group libel statutes test that commitment.

The Court purported to settle the question in BEAUHARNAIS V. ILLI-NOIS (1952). A deeply divided Court upheld an Illinois group libel statute by resort to constitutional premises that have been substantially eroded by subsequent decisions. Although the continuing force of *Beauharnais* as a precedent is subject to serious doubt, it has not been overruled and was cited by the Court with seeming approval in *New York v. Ferber* (1982).

Beauharnais had been convicted for circulating a leaflet calling on officials in Chicago "to halt the further encroachment, harassment and invasion of white people, their property, neighborhoods, and persons, by the Negro." Calling upon white people to unite, Beauharnais's leaflet counseled that "if persuasion and the need to prevent the white race from becoming mongrelized by the Negro will not unite us, then the . . . rapes, robberies, knives, guns and marijuana of the Negro surely will."

One of the dissenting Justices, WILLIAM O. DOUGLAS, found it an easy case. In his view, if the "plain command of the First Amendment was to be overridden, the state was required to show that "the peril of speech" was "clear and present."

Justice FELIX FRANKFURTER, writing for the Court's majority, found it unnecessary to consider any CLEAR AND PRESENT DANGER test; libel, he said, is beneath First Amendment protection. Given the history of racial violence in Illinois, he argued, the legislature was not "without reason" in concluding that expressions like Beauharnais's had contributed to the violence and should be curbed.

In dissent, Justice HUGO L. BLACK challenged the Court's equation of group libel and ordinary libel. He suggested that the limited scope of libel assured that it applied to "nothing more than purely private feuds." The move from libel to group libel, he declared, was a move "to punish discussion of matters of public concern" and "a corresponding invasion of the area dedicated to free expression by the First Amendment."

Although Justice Black's characterization of the law of libel exaggerated its limits, constitutional developments since *Beauharnais* strongly support his general perspective. In *New York Times Co. v. Sullivan* the Court ruled that despite prior history, fresh assessment of the First Amendment yielded the conclusion that some libel was indeed within the scope of First Amendment protection. In a trail of decisions from *Sullivan* to GERTZ v. ROBERT WELCH, INC. (1974), the Court concluded that the First Amendment afforded some protection for a broad range of defamatory material. The driving force behind this constitutionalization of the tort of defamation was *Sullivan's* recognition of the First Amendment's commitment to uninhibited debate; moreover, the profound First Amendment importance of expression on public issues has been echoed in many subsequent opinions.

Sullivan and its successor decisions undermine the premises of *Beauharnais*. No Justice today could write an opinion saying that because libel is beneath First Amendment protection, so is group libel. First, most libel is clearly entitled to some measure of First Amendment protection. Second, putting group libel aside, if some libel remains entirely outside the First Amendment's scope, it would be speech of a private or commercial character. Justice Black's point that the move from libel to group libel is a move from the private sphere to the public sphere describes today's doctrine more accurately than it described the doctrine of 1952.

Another reason to doubt *Beauharnais's* continuing vitality is the Court's statement in *Gertz v. Robert Welch, Inc.* that "under our Constitution, there is no such thing as a false idea." That expression has generally been interpreted to mean that opinions are immune from any imposition of liability based on their asserted falsity. Although the line between fact and opinion is hard to draw, and although some group libel contains false assertions of fact, the sting of most group libel comes from unverifiable opinions. For example, what evidence could have proved the "truth" of Beauharnais's pejorative comments about black Americans? A separate issue is whether it is desirable for American trials to be conducted about the truth or falsity of various pejorative statements about ethnic groups.

In the case of religious groups, the legal resolution of such questions could pose serious issues under the religion clauses of the First Amendment.

If group libel statutes are to find constitutional refuge, the necessary constitutional principles will have to be found beyond the defamation decisions. A growing body of opinions resonate with the theme of *Paris Adult Theatre v. Slaton* (1973) pronouncing the right to maintain "a decent society." From *Young v. American-Mini Theatres, Inc.* (1976) to FEDERAL COMMUNICATIONS COMMISSION v. PACIFICA FOUNDATION (1978) and a series of dissents in decisions involving FIGHTING WORDS, there is support for arguments based on concepts of civility, decency, and dignity. Whether or not these arguments succeed in validating group libel statutes, the conflict between public morality and freedom of speech will persist as an abiding theme of constitutional law.

Bibliography

ARKES, HADLEY   1974   Civility and the Restriction of Speech: Rediscovering the Defamation of Groups. *Supreme Court Review* 1974:281–335.

KALVEN, HARRY, JR.   1965   *The Negro and the First Amendment.* Columbus: Ohio State University Press.

BEAUHARNAIS v. ILLINOIS

343 U.S. 250 (1952)

Martin Shapiro

The Supreme Court upheld, 5–4, an Illinois GROUP LIBEL statute that forbade publications depicting a racial or religious group as depraved or lacking in virtue. Justice FELIX FRANKFURTER first argued that certain categories of speech including LIBEL had traditionally been excluded from FIRST AMENDMENT protection, and he then deferred to the legislative judgment redefining libel to include defamation of groups as well as individuals. By mixing excluded-categories arguments with arguments for judicial deference to legislative judgments for which there is a RATIONAL BASIS, the opinion moves toward a position in which the relative merits of a particular speech are weighed against the social interests protected by the statute, with the ultimate constitutional balance heavily weighted in favor of whatever balance the legislature has struck. Although *Beauharnais* has not been overruled, its continued validity is doubtful after NEW YORK TIMES v. SULLIVAN (1964).

SPEECH OR DEBATE CLAUSE

Theodore Eisenberg

The Constitution's speech or debate clause provides that "for any Speech or Debate in either House, [members of Congress] shall not be questioned in any other Place." Despite its narrow phrasing, the clause was read in GRAVEL V. UNITED STATES (1972) and other cases as protecting all integral parts "of the deliberative and communicative process by which Members participate in committee and House proceedings with respect to the consideration and passage or rejection of proposed legislation." The clause also protects members' aides in performing tasks that would be protected if performed by members. An act protected by the clause may not be the basis of a civil or criminal judgment against a member of Congress. Under *Doe v. McMillan* (1973), actions by private citizens are barred even though the English PARLIAMENTARY PRIVILEGE from which the clause derives was concerned with executive encroachments on legislative prerogatives.

There are three inroads upon the speech or debate clause's protection. First, criminal prosecutions for corrupt behavior, such as accepting a bribe to influence legislation, may go forward, as in BREWSTER V. UNITED STATES (1972), on the theory that even if legislative acts were performed in exchange for payment, accepting a bribe is not a legislative act. But this area is not without difficulty, as was evidenced by the Court's refusal in *United States v. Johnson* (1966) and *United States v. Helstoski* (1979) to allow the use of legislative acts as evidence in corruption cases.

Second, in *Gravel v. United States* and HUTCHINSON V. PROXMIRE (1979), the Court implicitly held that communications with a member's constituents are not legislative functions and expressly held that members of Congress could be made to answer for words, written or spoken, or deeds done, outside formal congressional communications channels. Thus Senator Mike Gravel (or his aide) could be interrogated about republishing the Pentagon Papers with a private publisher, even though he could not be asked about reading the papers into the record of a committee hearing (see NEW YORK TIMES CO. V. UNITED STATES, 1971). And Senator William Proxmire could be held liable for defamatory communications.

Third, a citizen aggrieved by a subpoena to appear before, or furnish

194

documentary evidence to, a congressional committee may challenge the subpoena by refusing to comply and defending any resulting contempt citation on the ground that the subpoena was unconstitutional or otherwise defective.

The speech or debate clause also plays a central but somewhat confusing role in delineating state legislators' immunity from suit under SECTION 1983, TITLE 42, UNITED STATES CODE. (See LEGISLATIVE IMMUNITY.) In TENNEY V. BRANDHOVE (1951) the Court relied in part on the speech or debate clause, which by its terms applies only to members of Congress, to find state legislators absolutely immune from damages actions under section 1983. In *United States v. Gillock* (1980), however, the Court held that in a federal criminal prosecution of a state legislator, the speech or debate privilege does not bar using legislative acts as evidence.

Bibliography

REINSTEIN, ROBERT J. and SILVERGATE, HARVEY A. 1973   LEGISLATIVE PRIVILEGE AND THE SEPARATION OF POWERS. *Harvard Law Review* 86:1113–1182.
YANKWICH, LEON R.   1951   The Immunity of Congressional Speech—Its Origin, Meaning and Scope. *University of Pennsylvania Law Review* 99:960–977.

NEW YORK TIMES CO. v. SULLIVAN

376 U.S. 254 (1964)

David A. Anderson

MARTIN LUTHER KING, JR., was arrested in Alabama in 1960 on a perjury charge. In New York a group of entertainers and civil rights activists formed a committee to help finance King's defense. They placed a full-page advertisement in the *New York Times* appealing for contributions. The ad charged that King's arrest was part of a campaign to destroy King's leadership of the movement to integrate public facilities and encourage blacks in the South to vote. It asserted that "Southern violators" in Montgomery had expelled King's student followers from college, ringed the campus with armed police, padlocked the dining hall to starve them into submission, bombed King's home, assaulted his person, and arrested him seven times for speeding, loitering, and other dubious offenses.

L. B. Sullivan, a city commissioner of Montgomery, filed a libel action in state court against the *Times* and four black Alabama ministers whose names had appeared as endorsers of the ad. He claimed that because his duties included supervision of the Montgomery police, the allegations against the police defamed him personally.

Under the common law as it existed in Alabama and most other states, the *Times* had little chance of winning. Whether the statements referred to Sullivan was a fact issue; if the jury found that readers would identify him, it was immaterial that the ad did not name him. Because the statements reflected adversely on Sullivan's professional reputation they were "libelous per se"; that meant he need not prove that he actually had been harmed. The defense of truth was not available because the ad contained factual errors (for example, police had not "ringed the campus," though they had been deployed nearby; King had been arrested four times, not seven). A few states recognized a privilege for good faith errors in criticism of public officials, but Alabama was among the majority that did not.

The jury awarded Sullivan $500,000. In the Alabama Supreme Court, the *Times* argued such a judgment was inconsistent with FREEDOM OF THE PRESS, but that court merely repeated what the United States

Supreme Court had often said: "The First Amendment of the United States Constitution does not protect libelous publications."

When the case reached the Supreme Court in 1964, it was one of eleven libel claims, totaling $5,600,000, pending against the *Times* in Alabama. It was obvious that libel suits were being used to discourage the press from supporting the CIVIL RIGHTS movement in the South. The *Times* urged the Court to equate these uses of libel law with the discredited doctrine of SEDITIOUS LIBEL and to hold that criticism of public officials could never be actionable.

Only three Justices were willing to go that far. The majority adopted a more limited rule, holding that public officials could recover for defamatory falsehoods about their official conduct or fitness for office only if they could prove that the defendant had published with "actual malice." This was defined as "knowledge that [the statement] was false or with reckless disregard of whether it was false or not." The Court further held that this element had to be established by "clear and convincing proof," and that, unlike most factual issues, it was subject to independent review by appellate courts. The Court then reviewed Sullivan's evidence and determined that it did not meet the new standard.

The decision was an important breakthrough, not only for the press and the civil rights movement but also in FIRST AMENDMENT theory. Until then, vast areas of expression, including libel and commercial speech, had been categorically excluded from First Amendment protection. Also, the decision finally repudiated the darkest blot on freedom of expression in the history of the United States, the Sedition Act of 1798.

Over the next few years, the Court went out of its way to make the new rule effective. It defined "reckless disregard" narrowly (*St. Amant v. Thompson,* 1967). It extended the *Sullivan* rule to lesser public officials (*Rosenblatt v. Baer,* 1966), to candidates for public office (*Monitor Patriot Co. v. Roy,* 1971), to PUBLIC FIGURES (*Associated Press v. Walker,* 1967), and to criminal libel (*Garrison v. Louisiana,* 1964). After 1971 the Court retreated somewhat, declining to extend the *Sullivan* rule to private plaintiffs and permitting a de facto narrowing of the public figure category.

From its birth the rule has been criticized, by public officials and celebrities who believe it makes recovery too difficult, and by the news media, which argue that the rule still exposes them to long and expensive litigation, even though ultimately they usually win. The Court, however, has shown no inclination to revise the rule. In *Bose Corp. v. Consumers Union* (1984), the Court was invited to dilute it by abandoning independent appellate review of findings of "actual malice." The Court refused, holding such review essential "to preserve the precious liberties established and ordained by the Constitution."

Bibliography

KALVEN, HARRY, JR.   1964   The New York Times Case: A Note on "The Central Meaning of the First Amendment." *Supreme Court Review* 1964:191–221.
PIERCE, SAMUEL R., JR.   1965   The Anatomy of an Historic Decision: *New York Times Co. v. Sullivan. North Carolina Law Review* 43:315–363.

PUBLIC FIGURE

Leonard W. Levy

The concept of a public figure features prominently in modern FIRST AMENDMENT law involving libel suits. NEW YORK TIMES V. SULLIVAN (1964) prevented public officials (officeholders and candidates for office) from recovering damages for defamation without proof of actual malice, that is, proof that the statement was made with the knowledge that it was false or with reckless disregard whether it was or not. In *Curtis Publishing Company v. Butts* (1967) the Supreme Court extended the actual malice rule to public figures, described by the Court as private persons in positions of considerable influence or able to attract attention because they had thrust themselves into public controversies. A public figure commands public interest and therefore has sufficient access to the mass media to be able, like an officeholder, to publicize his response to falsehoods about him. He invites comment and his remarks make news. The Justices unanimously agreed that for the sake of a robust FREEDOM OF THE PRESS, the actual malice rule applies to public figures, but they disagreed in specific cases on the question whether a particular person, such as the former wife of the scion of a famous family is a public figure, the question before the court in *Time Incorporated v. Firestone* (1976). The Court has tended to deny the press's claim that the party suing for damages is a public figure.

GERTZ v. ROBERT WELCH, INC.

418 U.S. 323 (1974)

Leonard W. Levy

In this major case on LIBEL AND THE FIRST AMENDMENT, the Supreme Court in an opinion by Justice LEWIS F. POWELL held, 5–4, that the rule of NEW YORK TIMES v. SULLIVAN (1964) did not apply when the party seeking damages for libel is not a public official or a public figure. *New York Times* had applied the rule of "actual malice": the First Amendment bars a public official from recovering damages for a defamatory falsehood relating to his conduct in office unless he proves that the publisher or broadcaster made the statement knowing it to be false or "with reckless disregard of whether it was false or not." The Court had extended that rule in 1967 to PUBLIC FIGURES. In *Rosenbloom v. Metromedia, Inc.* (1971) a plurality ruled that if the defamation concerned a public issue the actual malice rule extended also to private individuals, who were not public figures. In *Gertz* the Court, abandoning that rule, held that a private plantiff had to prove actual malice only if seeking punitive damages; the FIRST AMENDMENT did not require him to produce such proof merely to recover actual damages for injury to reputation.

Powell reasoned that public officers and public figures had a far greater opportunity to counteract false statements than private persons. Moreover, an official or a candidate for public office knowingly exposes himself to close public scrutiny and criticism, just as public figures knowingly invite attention and comment. The communications media cannot, however, assume that private persons similarly expose themselves to defamation. Powell declared that they "are not only more vulnerable to injury than public officials and public figures; they are also more deserving of recovery." Their only effective redress is resort to a state's libel laws. So long as a state does not permit the press or a broadcaster to be held liable without fault and applies the actual malice rule to requests for punitive damages, the Court held that the First Amendment requires a "less demanding showing than that required by *New York Times*" and that the states may decide for themselves the appropriate standard of liability for media defendants who defame private persons.

Each of the dissenting Justices wrote a separate opinion. The dissents covered a wide spectrum from greater concern for the defamed party to alarm about the majority's supposedly constrictive interpretation of the First Amendment. Chief Justice WARREN E. BURGER worried that the party libeled in this case was a lawyer who ought not to be invidiously identified with his client. Justice WILLIAM O. DOUGLAS thought all libel laws to be unconstitutional. Justice WILLIAM J. BRENNAN preferred the actual malice test to be applied to private individuals in matters of public concern. Justice BYRON R. WHITE, opposing the Court's restriction of the COMMON LAW of libels, condemned the nationalization of so large a part of libel law.

DUN & BRADSTREET, INC. v. GREENMOSS BUILDERS, INC.

472 U.S.   (1985)

Kenneth L. Karst

The PLURALITY OPINION in this case may portend significant changes in the constitutional DOCTRINE governing LIBEL AND THE FIRST AMENDMENT. Dun & Bradstreet, a credit reporting business, falsely and negligently reported to five subscribers that Greenmoss had filed a petition in bankruptcy, and also negligently misrepresented Greenmoss's assets and liabilities. In an action for defamation, Greenmoss recovered substantial compensatory and punitive damages. Vermont's highest court held that the principle of GERTZ v. ROBERT WELCH, INC. (1974) did not apply in actions against defendants who were not part of the press or broadcast media. A fragmented Supreme Court avoided this question but affirmed, 5–4.

Justice LEWIS F. POWELL, for a three-Justice plurality, concluded that *Gertz* —which had held, among other things, that punitive damages could not be awarded against a magazine without proof of knowing or reckless disregard of the falsity of the statement—was applicable only to "expression on a matter of public concern." Justice Powell spoke only generally about the content of the "matter of public concern" standard, but hinted that "media" speech might qualify automatically for protection under *Gertz*. Dun & Bradstreet's report, however, involved "matters of purely private concern." Although such speech is "not wholly unprotected" by the FIRST AMENDMENT, he concluded, it can be the basis of a punitive damages award even absent a showing of reckless disregard of the truth. Chief Justice WARREN E. BURGER and Justice BYRON R. WHITE, in separate CONCURRING OPINIONS, expressed willingness to abandon *Gertz* altogether, but meanwhile agreed with this radical surgery on *Gertz*.

In a footnote pregnant with meaning, Justice Powell remarked that some kinds of constitutionally protected speech are entitled only to "reduced protection"—COMMERCIAL SPEECH, for example. But he did not place Dun & Bradstreet's report in the latter category, and thus raised speculation that the majority may be prepared to adopt a "sliding scale" for the FREEDOM OF SPEECH, with varying (and, as yet, unspecified) degrees of constitutional protection for each kind of speech, depending on the Justices' determinations about the value of the speech and the context in which it is uttered.

Justice WILLIAM J. BRENNAN, for the four dissenters, agreed that credit reports were not central to First Amendment values, but argued nonetheless that the *Gertz* requirements should apply to this case: credit and bankruptcy information was "of public concern." Justice Brennan noted with satisfaction that six Justices (the dissenters and authors of the concurring opinions) had rejected a distinction between the First Amendment rights of "media defendants" and of others sued for defamation.

PRIVACY AND THE FIRST AMENDMENT

Melville B. Nimmer

William L. Prosser has listed four categories of invasion of privacy: intrusion upon the plaintiff's seclusion or solitude, or into his private affairs; public disclosure of embarrassing private facts about the plaintiff; publicity which places the plaintiff in a false light in the public eye; and appropriation, for the defendant's advantage, of the plaintiff's name or likeness. Absent the communication of information disclosed by the intrusion, the first category of invasion raises no FIRST AMENDMENT issue.

The second category, the public disclosure of embarrassing private facts, clearly does raise a First Amendment issue. When does the FREEDOM OF THE PRESS to report "news" outbalance the individual's RIGHT TO PRIVACY, even if the disclosure is of embarrassing private facts? Thus far, the Supreme Court has only partially answered that question. In Cox BROADCASTING CORPORATION v. COHN (1975) the Court held that the state could not impose liability for invasion of privacy by reason of the defendant's television news disclosure of the name of a rape victim. The Court held that the First Amendment immunized the press from such liability where the information disclosed was truthful and had already been publicly disclosed in court records. Subsequent decisions have indicated that such a First Amendment privilege applies as well to the publication of material in at least some official records designated confidential—for example, information about a criminal proceeding involving a juvenile, even though it was obtained from sources other than the public record. But what of intimate private fact disclosures that do not involve criminal proceedings, or other official action? Or suppose the disclosure of private facts is embarrassing to the subject, but does not injure reputation. Which prevails, the plaintiff's right of privacy or the defendant's FREEDOM OF SPEECH? The Supreme Court thus far has been silent on these issues, and the lower courts have offe.ed no satisfactory answers.

The third category, known as "false light" privacy, was the subject of the Supreme Court's decision in *Time, Inc. v. Hill* (1967). Defendant's report in *Life* magazine of plaintiffs' encounter with gangsters was in part false, though not reputation injuring. The Supreme Court held that the defendant was entitled to a First Amendment defense in a false-light privacy action unless the defendant knew the matter reported was false or published with reckless disregard of the truth. The Court acknowledged that this standard was borrowed from the First Amendment defense to DEFAMATION which it had fashioned in NEW YORK TIMES v. SULLIVAN (1964). Where *Sullivan* had involved statements about a public official, *Hill* seemingly extended the First Amendment privilege to statements about "a matter of public interest." The First Amendment defamation defense was later expanded in GERTZ v. ROBERT WELCH, INC. (1974) to apply to reports involving "public figures" as well as "public officials," and to require at least a negligence standard of liability as regards defamation of nonpublic figures. The Supreme Court has not had occasion to reconsider the impact of the First Amendment upon "false light" privacy cases since its decision in *Gertz*.

The fourth category is more generally referred to as the "right of publicity." It differs fundamentally from the other categories in that the injury does not consist of embarrassment and humiliation. It is based rather upon the wrongful appropriation of a person's (usually a celebrity's) name or likeness for commercial purposes. The measure of recovery is based upon the value of the use, not the injury suffered from mental distress. The only Supreme Court decision to consider the impact of the First Amendment upon the right of publicity has been *Zacchini v. Scripps-Howard Broadcasting Co.* (1977). The plaintiff performed a "human cannonball" act at a county fair. The defendant photographed his entire act and broadcast it in a local television news program. Plaintiff sued for infringement of his right of publicity. The Supreme Court held that the defendant was not entitled to a First Amendment defense. The Court regarded this as "the strongest case" for the right of publicity because it involved "the appropriation of the very activity by which the entertainer acquired his reputation in the first place." Even in the usual case, where a celebrity's name or likeness is used in order to sell a product, the lower courts have not found the First Amendment to constitute a defense, and it seems unlikely that the Supreme Court would take a contrary view. On the other hand, where the name or likeness is used as a part of an informational work, such as a biography or a biographical motion picture, in most cases the First Amendment would appear to constitute a valid defense.

Bibliography

NIMMER, MELVILLE B.   1968   The Right to Speak from *Times* to *Time:* First Amendment Theory Applied to Libel and Misapplied to Privacy. *California Law Review* 56:935–967.

PROSSER, WILLIAM L.   1971   *Torts,* 4th ed. St. Paul, Minn.: West Publishing Co.

COX BROADCASTING CORP. v. COHN

420 U.S. 469 (1975)

Steven Shiffrin

In *Cox Broadcasting Corp. v. Cohn* the Supreme Court held that broadcasting the name of a rape victim, derived from public court documents open to public inspection, could not constitutionally be made the basis for civil liability. The Court left open the questions whether liability could be imposed for a similar broadcast if the name had been obtained in an improper fashion, or if the name had not been directly derived from the public record, or if the name had not appeared in a public record open to public inspection, or if the public record were inaccurate.

OBSCENITY

Steven Shiffrin

Obscenity laws embarrass ALEXIS DE TOCQUEVILLE's claim that there is "hardly a political question in the United States which does not sooner or later turn into a judicial one." It is not merely that the obscenity question became a serious judicial issue rather much later than sooner. It is that the richness of the questions involved have been lost in their translation to the judicial forum.

Obscenity laws implicate great questions of political theory including the characteristics of human nature, the relationship between law and morals, and the appropriate role of the state in a democratic society. But these questions were barely addressed when the Court first seriously considered a constitutional challenge to obscenity laws in the 1957 cases of ROTH V. UNITED STATES and *Alberts v. California.*

The briefs presented the Court with profoundly different visions of FIRST AMENDMENT law. Roth argued that no speech including obscenity could be prohibited without meeting the CLEAR AND PRESENT DANGER test, that a danger of lustful thoughts was not the type of evil with which a legislature could be legitimately concerned, and that no danger of antisocial conduct had been shown. On the other hand, the government urged the Court to adopt a balancing test that prominently featured a consideration of the value of the speech involved. The government tendered an illustrative hierarchy of nineteen speech categories with political, religious, economic, and scientific speech at the top; entertainment, music, and humor in the middle; and libel, obscenity, profanity, and commercial PORNOGRAPHY at the bottom. The government's position was that the strength of public interest needed to justify speech regulation diminished as one moved down the hierarchy and increased as one moved up.

In response to these opposing contentions, the Court took a middle course. Relying on cases like BEAUHARNAIS V. ILLINOIS (1952), the Court seemed to embrace what HARRY KALVEN, JR., later called the TWO-LEVEL THEORY of the First Amendment. Under this theory, some speech is beneath the protection of the First Amendment; only that speech within the amendment's protection is measured by the clear and present danger test. Thus some speech is at the bottom of a two-level hierarchy, and the *Roth* Court sought to explain why obscenity deserved basement-level nonprotection.

History, tradition, and consensus were the staple of the Court's argument. Justice WILLIAM J. BRENNAN explained that all "ideas having even the slightest redeeming social importance" deserve full First Amendment protection. But, he said, "implicit in the history of the First Amendment is the rejection of obscenity as utterly without redeeming social importance." Then he pointed to the consensus of fifty nations, forty-eight states, and twenty obscenity laws passed by the Congress from 1842 to 1956. Finally, relying on an OBITER DICTUM from CHAPLINSKY v. NEW HAMPSHIRE (1942), the Court explained that obscene utterances "are of such slight social value as a step to truth that any benefit that may be derived from them is clearly outweighed by the social interest in order and morality."

From the perspective of liberal, conservative, or feminist values, the Court's reliance on the *Chaplinsky* quotation amounts to a cryptic resolution of fundamental political questions. Liberals would advance several objections. Some would suggest that the Court underestimates the contribution to truth made by sexually oriented material. David Richards, for example, has suggested that

pornography can be seen as the unique medium of a vision of sexuality . . . a view of sensual delight in the erotic celebration of the body, a concept of easy freedom without consequences, a fantasy of timelessly repetitive indulgence. In opposition to the Victorian view that narrowly defines proper sexual function in a rigid way that is analogous to ideas of excremental regularity and moderation, pornography builds a model of plastic variety and joyful excess in sexuality. In opposition to the sorrowing Catholic dismissal of sexuality as an unfortunate and spiritually superficial concomitant of propagation, pornography affords the alternative idea of the independent status of sexuality as a profound and shattering ecstasy [1974, p. 81].

Even some liberals might find these characterizations overwrought as applied to Samuel Roth's publications, such as *Wild Passion* and *Wanton by Night*. Nonetheless, many of them would argue that even if such publications have no merit in the MARKETPLACE OF IDEAS, individuals should be able to decide for themselves what they want to read. Many would argue along with John Stuart Mill that "[T]he only purpose for which power can be rightfully exercised over any member of a civilized community, against his will, is to prevent harm to others." Such a principle is thought to advance the moral nature of humanity, for what distinguishes human beings from animals is the capacity to make autonomous moral judgments. From this perspective, the *Roth* opinion misunderstands the necessity for individual moral judgments and diminishes liberty in the name of order without a proper showing of harm.

Conservatives typically agree that humans are distinguished from animals by their capacity to make rational moral judgments. They believe, however, that liberals overestimate human rational capacity and underestimate the importance of the state in promoting a virtuous citizenry. Moreover, they insist that liberals do not sufficiently appreciate the morally corrosive effects of obscenity. From their perspective, obscenity emphasizes the base animality of our nature, reduces the spirituality of humanity to mere bodily functions, and debases civilization by transforming the private into the public. As Irving Kristol put it, "When sex is a public spectacle, a human relationship has been debased into a mere animal connection."

Feminists typically make no objection to erotic material and make no sharp separation between reason and passion. Their principal objection is to the kind of sexually oriented material that encourages male sexual excitement in the domination of women. From their perspective, a multibillion dollar industry promotes antifemale propaganda encouraging males to get, as Susan Brownmiller put it, a "sense of power from viewing females as anonymous, panting playthings, adult toys, dehumanized objects to be used, abused, broken and discarded." From the feminist perspective, the *Roth* opinion's reference to the interests in order and morality obscures the interest in equality for women. From the conservative perspective, the opinion is underdeveloped. From the liberal perspective, it is wrong-headed.

Liberals gained some post-*Roth* hope from the Court's treatment of the obscenity question in STANLEY v. GEORGIA (1969). In *Stanley* the Court held that the possession of obscenity in the home could not be made a criminal offense without violating the First Amendment. More interesting than the holding, which has since been confined to its facts, was the Court's rationale. The Court insisted that "our whole constitutional heritage rebels at the thought of giving government the power to control men's minds." It denied the state any power "to control the moral content of a person's thoughts." It suggested that the only interests justifying obscenity laws were that obscene material might fall into the hands of children or that it might "intrude upon the sensibilities or privacy of the general public."

Many commentators thought that *Stanley* would be extended to protect obscene material where precautions had been taken to avoid exposure to children or nonconsenting adults. Indeed such precautions were taken by many theaters, but the Supreme Court (the composition of which had changed significantly since *Stanley*) reaffirmed *Roth* and expanded on its rationale in *Paris Adult Theatre I v. Slaton* (1973).

The Court professed to "hold that there are legislative interests at stake in stemming the tide of commercialized obscenity, even assuming it is feasible to enforce effective safeguards against exposure to the juvenile and the passerby. These include the interest of the public in the quality of life and the total community environment, the tone of commerce in the great city centers, and, possibly, the public safety itself."

The Court did not suggest that the link between obscenity and sex crimes was anything other than arguable. It did insist that the "States have the power to make a morally neutral judgment that public exhibition of obscene material, or commerce in such material, has a tendency to injure the community as a whole . . . or to jeopardize, in Chief Justice Earl Warren's words, the State's 'right . . . to maintain a decent society.' "

Several puzzles remain after the Court's explanation is dissected. First, "arguable" connections to crime do not ordinarily suffice to justify restrictions of First Amendment liberties. A merely arguable connection to crime supports restriction only if the speech involved is for some other reason outside First Amendment protection. Second, as the Court was later to recognize in YOUNG V. AMERICAN MINI THEATRES, INC. (1976), the reference to quality of life, the tone of commerce in the central cities, and the environment have force with respect to all sexually oriented bookstores and theaters whether or not they display obscene films or sell obscene books. The Court in MILLER V. CALIFORNIA (1973) limited the definition of obscenity to that material which the "average person, applying contemporary community standards" would find that "taken as a whole appeals to the prurient interest" and "depicts and describes, in a patently offensive way, sexual conduct specifically defined by the applicable state law"; and which, "taken as a whole, lacks serious literary, artistic, political, or scientific value." No one has suggested that these restrictions on the definition bear any relationship to the tone of commerce in the cities.

Moreover, if the intrusive character of public display were the issue, mail order sales of obscene material should pass muster under the First Amendment; yet there is no indication that the Court is prepared to protect such traffic. As interpreted in the *Paris Adult Theatre* opinion, *Stanley v. Georgia* appears to protect only those obscene books and films created and enjoyed in the home; the right to use in the home amounts to no more than that. There is no right to receive obscene material—even in plain brown wrappers.

Perhaps least convincing is the Court's attempt to harmonize its *Paris Adult Theatre* holding with liberal thought. It claims to have no quarrel with the court's insistence in *Stanley* that the state is without power "to control the moral content of a person's thoughts." Because obscene material by the Court's definition lacks any serious literary, artistic, political, or scientific value, control of it is said to be "distinct from a control of reason and the intellect." But this is doubletalk. The power to decide what has serious artistic value is the power to make moral decisions. To decide that material addressing "reason" or the "intellect" is all that is important to human beings is ultimately to make a moral decision about human beings. Implicit in the latter idea, of course, is the belief that the enjoyment of erotic material for its own sake is unworthy of protection. But the view is much more general. The Court supposes that human beings have a rational side and an emotional side, that the emotional side needs to be subordinated and controlled, and that such suppression or control is vital to the moral life. That is why the Court believes that the contribution of obscenity to truth is outweighed by the state's interest in morality. The Court's insistence on the right to maintain a decent society is in fact an insistence on the state's interest in the control of the "moral content of a person's thoughts."

Finally, it is simply dazzling for the Court to suggest that the states are engaged in a "morally neutral" judgment when they decide that obscene material jeopardizes the right to maintain a decent society. When states decide that "a sensitive key relationship of human existence, central to family life, community welfare, and the development of human personality can be debased and distorted by commercial exploitation of sex," they operate as moral guardians, not as moral neutrals. Nonetheless, the Courts' bows to liberal theory in *Paris Adult Theatre* are revealing, and so are the guarded compromises of the obscenity test adopted in *Miller v. California*. The bows and compromises reflect, as do the opinions of the four dissenting Justices in *Paris Adult Theatre,* that America is profoundly divided on the relationship of law to morality and on the meaning of free speech. Since *Paris Adult Theatre* and *Miller,* and despite those decisions, the quantity of erotic material has continued to grow. At the same time, feminist opposition to pornography has ripened into a powerful political movement. The Supreme Court's decisions have neither stemmed the tide of commercial pornography nor resolved the divisions of American society on the issue. These political questions will continue to be judicial questions.

Bibliography

CLOR, HARRY M.   1969   *Obscenity and Public Morality.* Chicago: University of Chicago Press.

KALVEN, HARRY, JR.   1960   The Metaphysics of the Law of Obscenity. *Supreme Court Review* 1960:1–45.

LEDERER, LAURA, ed.   1980   *Take Back the Night: Women on Pornography.* New York: Bantam Books.

RICHARDS, DAVID A. J.   1974   Free Speech and Obscenity Law: Toward a Moral Theory of the First Amendment. *University of Pennsylvania Law Review* 123:45–99.

ULYSSES, A BOOK NAMED, UNITED STATES v.

5F. Supp. 182 (1933); 72 F.2d 705 (1934)

Samuel Krislov

Although it was not a decision of the Supreme Court, *Ulysses* was not merely a case involving a famous book and prominent judges but also a harbinger of modern decisions on OBSCENITY. Its standards for construing the COMMON LAW terms embodied in federal customs regulations were transmuted in UNITED STATES v. ROTH (1957) into constitutional principles for testing both federal and state legislation on the subject.

The handful of early obscenity cases that reached the Supreme Court mainly presented claims of technical error in the trials below. *Ulysses* presented clear questions of substantive standards for adjudging obscenity and lewdness. The established reputation of the book insured careful attention; Judge John M. Woolsey's lower court opinion was unmistakably written for the anthologies it ultimately graced. Judge AUGUSTUS N. HAND's appellate majority opinion was straightforward, but Judge Martin T. Manton's dissent was somewhat verbose.

Woolsey declared that the book successfully showed "how the screen [sic] of consciousness with its ever-shifting kaleidoscopic impression carries, as it were on a plastic palimpsest, . . . a penumbral zone residual of past impressions . . . not unlike the result of a double or, if that is possible, a multiple exposure on a cinema film. . . ."

The relevant statute on importation of books prohibited not pandering but obscenity. Woolsey announced without discussion that the test for obscenity required examination of the whole work. The standard was the effect on "what the French would call *l'homme moyen sensuel* — who plays, in this branch of legal inquiry . . . the same role . . . as does the "reasonable man in the law of torts. . . ." With this standard he found the book "somewhat emetic, nowhere . . . an aphrodisiac." He also found Joyce to have been sincere and lacking pornographic intent or the "leer of the sensualist."

At the appellate level Augustus Hand for himself and LEARNED HAND managed to come to grips with the central legal issue—whether isolated passages could render a work of art obscene. This was the test derived from *Regina v. Hicklin* (1868), the classic British case, and, they conceded, followed in *United States v. Bennett* (1879), a CIRCUIT COURT decision by Justice SAMUEL BLATCHFORD. They discounted other alleged precedents and argued that the isolated passages concept was not followed for works of science or medicine and should not be followed for literature either. They cited state decisions embracing the "dominant effect" notion, and read that test (together with their definition of the relevant audience) into the statute, concluding that other readings would be impractical and overrestrictive.

Manton, dissenting, insisted that federal decisions in the past had accepted the "isolated passages" test. As literature was for amusement only, the community could reasonably demand that it meet moral standards—those of average, not exceptional, individuals.

Bibliography

LOCKHART, WILLIAM B. and McCLURE, ROBERT C.   1954 Literature, the Law of Obscenity, and the Constitution. *Minnesota Law Review* 38:295–395.

ROTH v. UNITED STATES

354 U.S. 476 (1957)
ALBERTS v. CALIFORNIA
354 U.S. 476 (1957)

Kim McLane Wardlaw

Until *Roth* and *Alberts,* argued and decided on the same days, the Supreme Court had assumed that the FIRST AMENDMENT did not protect OBSCENITY. Squarely confronted with the issue by appeals from convictions under the federal obscenity statute (in *Roth*) and a California law outlawing the sale and advertising of obscene books (in *Alberts*), the Court held that obscenity was not constitutionally protected speech.

Justice WILLIAM J. BRENNAN, for the majority, relied on historical evidence that the Framers of the First Amendment had not intended to protect all speech, but only speech with some redeeming social value. Thus, the First Amendment protected even hateful ideas that contributed toward the unfettered exchange of information that might result in desired political and social change. Obscenity, however, was utterly without redeeming social importance, and was not constitutionally protected.

Neither statute before the Court defined obscenity; nor did the Court examine the materials to determine whether they were obscene. The Court nevertheless rejected the appellants' due process objections on the grounds that the statutes had given sufficient warning as to the proscribed conduct and the trial courts had applied the proper standard for judging obscenity.

The Court rejected the widely used test based on *Queen v. Hicklin* (1868) which judged a work's obscenity by the effect of an isolated excerpt upon particularly susceptible persons. The proper standard was "whether to the average person, applying contemporary community standards, the dominant theme taken as a whole appeals to prurient interest," that is, has a tendency to excite lustful thoughts. Because the obscenity of the materials involved in *Roth* was not at issue, the Court escaped the task of applying its definition. Ironically, the definition of obscenity was to preoccupy the Court for the next sixteen years. The Court, having designated a category of speech that could be criminally proscribed, now confronted the critical task of delineating that category.

Chief Justice EARL WARREN and Justice JOHN MARSHALL HARLAN, separately concurring, sought to limit the scope of the majority opinion.

Warren, concurring in the result, agreed that the defendants' conduct in commercially exploiting material for its appeal to prurient interest was constitutionally punishable. Harlan, concurring in *Alberts* and dissenting in *Roth,* believed the Court was required to examine each work individually to determine its obscene character, and argued that the Constitution restricted the federal government in this field more severely than it restricted the states. Justices WILLIAM O. DOUGLAS and HUGO L. BLACK, dissenting in both cases, enunciated the positions they were to take in the wave of obscenity cases soon to overwhelm the Court: obscenity, like every other form of speech, is absolutely protected by the First Amendment.

KINGSLEY INTERNATIONAL PICTURES CORP. v. REGENTS

360 U.S. 684 (1959)

Steven Shiffrin

In *Kingsley International Pictures Corp. v. Regents* the state of New York had refused to issue a license for the motion picture *Lady Chatterley's Lover* because it "alluringly portrays adultery as proper behavior." There was no claim that the film constituted an INCITEMENT TO UNLAWFUL CONDUCT. Without deciding whether all licensing schemes for motion pictures were unconstitutional the Supreme Court held that the refusal to grant this license violated the FIRST AMENDMENT. The Court reaffirmed that motion pictures were within the scope of the First Amendment and proclaimed that the amendment's "basic guarantee" is "the freedom to advocate ideas," including the idea that adultery may in some cases be justified.

JACOBELLIS v. OHIO

378 U.S. 184 (1964)

Kim McLane Wardlaw

The Supreme Court reversed Jacobellis's conviction for possessing and exhibiting an obscene motion picture, finding the movie not obscene under ROTH v. UNITED STATES (1957). Justice WILLIAM J. BRENNAN's plurality opinion announced two significant constitutional developments and presaged a third. First, in any case raising the issue whether a work was obscene, the Court would determine independently whether the material was constitutionally protected. Second, in judging the material's appeal to prurient interests against "contemporary community standards," courts were to apply a national standard, not the standards of the particular local community from which the case arose. Finally, purporting to apply standards based on *Roth* and foreshadowing his opinion in MEMOIRS v. MASSACHUSETTS (1965), Brennan noted that a work could not be proscribed unless it was " 'utterly' without social importance."

Jacobellis is best known, however, for Justice POTTER J. STEWART's concurring opinion. Contending that only hard-core pornography constitutionally could be proscribed, Stewart declined to define the material that term included, stating only, "I know it when I see it."

MEMOIRS v. MASSACHUSETTS

383 U.S. 413 (1966)

Kim McLane Wardlaw

Nine years after ROTH v. UNITED STATES, still unable to agree upon a constitutional definition of OBSCENITY, the Supreme Court reversed a state court determination that John Cleland's *Memoirs of a Woman of Pleasure*, commonly known as *Fanny Hill*, was obscene. The three-Justice PLURALITY OPINION, written by Justice WILLIAM J. BRENNAN, held that the constitutional test for obscenity was: "(a) the dominant theme of the material taken as a whole appeals to a prurient interest in sex; (b) the material is patently offensive because it affronts contemporary community standards relating to the description or representation of sexual matters; and (c) the material is utterly without redeeming social value."

Despite an OBITER DICTUM in JACOBELLIS v. OHIO (1964), it was believed—and the Massachusetts courts had held—that *Roth* did not require unqualified worthlessness before a book might be deemed obscene. Justice Brennan twisted the *Roth* reasoning (that obscenity was unprotected because it was utterly worthless) into a constitutional test that was virtually impossible to meet under criminal standards of proof. Thus a finding of obscenity would become rare, even where the requisite prurient interest appeal and offensiveness could be demonstrated.

The Massachusetts courts had tried the book in the abstract; a host of literary experts testified to its social value. The circumstances of the book's production, sale, and publicity were not admitted. Justice Brennan noted that evidence that distributors commercially exploited *Fanny Hill* solely for its prurient appeal could have justified a finding, based on the purveyor's own evaluation, that *Fanny Hill* was utterly without redeeming social importance.

Justices HUGO L. BLACK, WILLIAM O. DOUGLAS, and POTTER J. STEWART concurred in the result, Black and Douglas adhering to their view that obscenity is protected expression. Stewart reiterated his view that the First Amendment protected all but "hard-core pornography."

Justice TOM C. CLARK, dissenting, rejected the importation of the "utterly without redeeming social value" standard into the obscenity test, which he believed would give the "smut artist free rein." Reacting against the continuous flow of pornographic materials to the Supreme

Court, he reasserted that the Court should apply a "sufficient evidence" standard of review of lower courts' obscenity decisions.

Justice JOHN MARSHALL HARLAN, dissenting, argued that although the federal government could constitutionally proscribe only hard-core pornography, the states could prohibit material under any criteria rationally related to accepted notions of obscenity.

Justice BYRON R. WHITE, also dissenting, argued that *Roth* counseled examination of the predominant theme of the material, not resort to minor themes of passages of literary worth to redeem obscene works from condemnation.

STANLEY v. GEORGIA

394 U.S. 557 (1969)

Kim McLane Wardlaw

Authorized by a SEARCH WARRANT, federal and state agents entered and searched Stanley's home for evidence of bookmaking activities. Instead they found film, which was used to convict him for possession of obscene material. The Supreme Court reversed, holding that mere possession of obscenity in one's home cannot constitutionally be made a crime.

Prior OBSCENITY decisions had recognized a legitimate state interest in regulating public dissemination of obscene materials. In *Stanley,* however, the Court recognized two fundamental constitutional rights that outweighed the state interest in regulating obscenity in a citizen's home: the FIRST AMENDMENT right to receive information and ideas, regardless of their social worth, and the constitutional right to be free from unwanted government intrusion into one's privacy.

As justification for interfering with these important individual rights, the state asserted the right to protect individuals from obscenity's effects. The Court rejected that argument, viewing such "protection" as an attempt to "control . . . a person's thoughts," a goal "wholly inconsistent with the philosophy of the First Amendment."

Justices POTTER J. STEWART, WILLIAM J. BRENNAN, and BYRON R. WHITE concurred in the result, on the ground that the SEARCH AND SEIZURE were outside the lawful scope of the officers' warrant, and thus violated Stanley's FOURTH AMENDMENT rights.

MILLER v. CALIFORNIA

413 U.S. 15 (1973)

PARIS ADULT THEATRE I v. SLATON

413 U.S. 49 (1973)

Kim McLane Wardlaw

For the first time since ROTH v. UNITED STATES (1957), a Supreme Court majority agreed on a definition of OBSCENITY. The Court had adopted the practice of summarily reversing obscenity convictions when at least five Justices, even if not agreeing on the appropriate test, found the material protected. The states were without real guidelines; and the requirements of JACOBELLIS v. OHIO (1964) that each Justice review the material at issue had transformed the Court into an ultimate board of censorship review.

To escape from this "intractable" problem, the *Miller Court* reexamined obscenity standards. Chief Justice WARREN E. BURGER's majority opinion, reaffirming *Roth,* articulated specific safeguards to ensure that state obscenity regulations did not encroach upon protected speech. The Court announced that a work could constitutionally be held to be obscene when an affirmative answer was appropriate for each of three questions:

(a) whether "the average person applying contemporary community standards" would find that the work, taken as a whole, appeals to the prurient interest . . .;
(b) whether the work depicts or describes, in a patently offensive way, sexual conduct specifically defined by the applicable state law; and
(c) whether the work, taken as a whole, lacks serious literary, artistic, political or scientific value.

Three aspects of the *Miller* formula are noteworthy. First, the work need not be measured against a single national standard, but may be judged by state community standards. Second, state obscenity regulations must be confined to works that depict or describe sexual conduct. Moreover, the states must specifically define the nature of that sexual conduct to provide due NOTICE to potential offenders. Third, the Court rejected the "utterly without redeeming social value" standard of MEMOIRS v. MASSACHUSETTS (1966). To merit FIRST AMENDMENT protection, the work, viewed as a whole, must have serious social value. A token political or social comment will not redeem an otherwise obscene work; nor will a brief erotic passage condemn a serious work.

In a COMPANION CASE, *Paris Adult Theater I*, the Court held that regulations concerning the public exhibition of obscenity, even in "adult" theaters excluding minors, were permissible if the *Miller* standards were met. The prohibition on privacy grounds against prosecuting possession of obscene material in one's home, recognized in STANLEY v. GEORGIA (1969), does not limit the state's power to regulate commerce in obscenity, even among consenting adults.

Justice WILLIAM J. BRENNAN, joined by Justices POTTER J. STEWART and THURGOOD MARSHALL, dissented in both cases. Abandoning the views he expressed in *Roth* and *Memoirs*, Brennan concluded that the impossibility of definition rendered the outright suppression of obscenity irreconcilable with the First Amendment and the FOURTEENTH AMENDMENT. The Court's inability to distinguish protected speech from unprotected speech created intolerable fair notice problems and chilled protected speech. Furthermore, "institutional stress" had resulted from the necessary case-by-case Supreme Court review. Instead of attempting to define obscenity, Brennan would balance the state regulatory interest against the law's potential danger to free expression. He recognized the protection of juveniles or unconsenting adults as a state interest justifying the suppression of obscenity. Justice WILLIAM O. DOUGLAS, separately dissenting, also denounced the vague guidelines that sent persons to jail for violating standards they could not understand, construe, or apply.

The Court's attempt to articulate specific obscenity standards was successful to the extent it reduced the number of cases on the Supreme Court docket. Nevertheless, as Justice Brennan noted, and the history of obscenity decisions confirms, any obscenity definition is inherently vague. The Court thus remains the ultimate board of censorship review.

Bibliography

LOCKHARD, WILLIAM B.   1975   Escape from the Chill of Uncertainty: Explicit Sex and the First Amendment. *Georgia Law Review* 9:533–587.

BROCKETT v. SPOKANE ARCADES, INC.
472 U.S.   (1985)

Kenneth L. Karst

The *Brockett* opinion refined the DOCTRINE of OVERBREADTH in FIRST AMENDMENT cases. A Washington statute provided both civil and criminal sanctions against "moral nuisances"—businesses purveying "lewd" matter. Various purveyors of sexually oriented books and films sued in federal district court for a DECLARATORY JUDGMENT that the law was unconstitutional and an INJUNCTION against its enforcement. That court denied relief, but the court of appeals held the law INVALID ON ITS FACE. The defect, the court said, was the law's definition of "lewd" matter, which followed the Supreme Court's formula defining OBSCENITY, but defined the term "prurient" to include material that "incites lasciviousness or lust." That definition was substantially overbroad, the court said, because it included material that aroused only a normal, healthy interest in sex.

A 6–2 Supreme Court reversed, in an opinion by Justice BYRON R. WHITE. The Court agreed that, under MILLER v. CALIFORNIA (1973), a work could not be held obscene if its only appeal were to "normal sexual reactions" and accepted the lower court's interpretation that "lust" would embrace such a work. However, Justice White said, these plaintiffs were not entitled to a facial invalidation of the law. They had alleged that their own films and books were not obscene, but were constitutionally protected. In such a case, there is "no want of a proper party to challenge the statute, no concern that an attack on the statute will be unduly delayed or protected speech discouraged." The proper course would be to declare the statute's partial invalidity—here, to declare that the law would be invalid in application to material appealing to "normal . . . sexual appetites." In contrast, when the state seeks to enforce such a partially invalid statute against a person whose own speech or conduct is constitutionally *unprotected*, the proper course, assuming the law's substantial overbreadth, is to invalidate the law entirely. The result is ironic, but explainable. In the latter case, if the court did not hold the law invalid on its face, there would be a serious risk of a CHILLING EFFECT on the potential protected speech of others who were not in court.

The propriety of partial invalidation depended on the SEVERABILITY of the Washington statute, but that issue was easily resolved: the law contained a severability clause, and surely the legislature would not have abandoned the statute just because it could not be applied to material appealing to normal sexual interests.

Justice SANDRA DAY O'CONNOR joined the OPINION OF THE COURT but argued separately, joined by Chief Justice WARREN E. BURGER and Justice WILLIAM H. REHNQUIST, that the case was appropriate for federal court ABSTENTION, awaiting guidance from the state courts on the statutory meaning of "lust." Justice WILLIAM J. BRENNAN, joined by Justice THURGOOD MARSHALL, dissented, agreeing with the court of appeals.

GINSBERG v. NEW YORK

390 U.S. 629 (1968)

Robert H. Mnookin

In *Ginsberg* the Supreme Court upheld the validity under the FIRST AMENDMENT and FOURTEENTH AMENDMENT of a New York criminal statute that prohibited the sale to persons under seventeen years of age of sexually explicit printed materials that would not be obscene for adults. Drawing upon the criteria suggested in ROTH v. UNITED STATES (1957) and MEMOIRS v. MASSACHUSETTS (1966), the New York statute broadly defined sexually explicit descriptions or representations as "harmful to minors" when the material: "(i) predominantly appeals to the prurient, shameful or morbid interest of minors, and (ii) is patently offensive to prevailing standards in the adult community as a whole with respect to what is suitable material for minors, and (iii) is utterly without redeeming social importance for minors." Convicted for selling two "girlie" magazines to a sixteen-year-old, Ginsberg claimed that the statute was unconstitutional because the state was without the power to deny persons younger than seventeen access to materials that were not obscene for adults. Justice WILLIAM J. BRENNAN, for the 6–3 majority, rejected this challenge by introducing the concept of "variable obscenity." According to the majority, the New York statute had "simply adjust[ed] the definition of OBSCENITY to social realities by permitting the appeal of this type of material to be assessed in terms of the sexual interests . . . of such minors."

Although the decision rests on the legitimacy of protecting children from harm, the Court found it unnecessary to decide whether persons under seventeen were caused harm by exposure to materials proscribed by the statute. After suggesting that scientific studies neither proved nor disproved a causal connection, the majority held that it was "not irrational" for the New York legislature to find that "exposure to material condemned by the statute is harmful to minors."

To what extent does a minor's own First Amendment rights constrain the state's power to limit a minor's access to written or pictorial materials? Because of the nature of Ginsberg's challenge to the statute, the Court did not concern itself with the question whether a minor might have the constitutional right to buy "girlie" magazines. In ERZNOZNIK v. JACKSONVILLE (1975) the Court later indicated that while the First Amendment rights of minors are not coextensive with those of adults, "minors are entitled to a significant measure of First Amendment protection" and that under the *Ginsberg* variable obscenity standard "all nudity" in films "cannot be deemed as obscene even as to minors."

NEW YORK v. FERBER

458 U.S. 747 (1982)

Kenneth L. Karst

This decision demonstrated the BURGER COURT's willingness to add to the list of categories of speech excluded from the FIRST AMENDMENT's protection. New York, like the federal government and most of the states, prohibits the distribution of material depicting sexual performances by children under age 16, whether or not the material constitutes OBSCENITY. After a New York City bookseller sold two such films to an undercover police officer, he was convicted under this law. The Supreme Court unanimously affirmed his conviction.

Justice BYRON R. WHITE, for the Court, denied that state power in this regulatory area was confined to the suppression of obscene material. The state's interest in protecting children against abuse was compelling; to prevent the production of such materials, it was necessary to forbid their distribution. Child PORNOGRAPHY—the visual depiction of sexual conduct by children below a specified age—was "a category of material outside the protection of the First Amendment."

The Court also rejected the argument that the law was overbroad, thus abandoning a distinction announced in BROADRICK v. OKLAHOMA (1973) to govern OVERBREADTH challenges. Henceforth the overbreadth doctrine would apply only in cases of "substantial overbreadth," whether or not the state sought to regulate the content of speech.

KINGSLEY BOOKS, INC. v. BROWN

354 U.S. 436 (1957)

Kim McLane Wardlaw

Kingsley authorized broad civil remedies to control the merchandising of OBSCENITY. The Supreme Court upheld a New York statute permitting state officials to obtain INJUNCTIONS against the sale of allegedly obscene materials before a judicial determination that the materials were obscene and, after trial, to seize and destroy any material found to be obscene. Rejecting assertions that the statutory scheme was an unconstitutional PRIOR RESTRAINT, the majority concluded that the scheme in actual application did not differ from the criminal remedies sanctioned in *Alberts v. California* (1957), decided the same day. (See ROTH V. UNITED STATES, 1957.)

The dissenters argued that numerous procedural defects rendered the statute unconstitutional. The seizure and destruction of the obscene books were tantamount to "book burning," according to Chief Justice EARL WARREN, for books were judged outside the context of their use. Justices WILLIAM O. DOUGLAS and HUGO L. BLACK, jointly dissenting, argued that an injunction before trial was censorship. They also would have required a finding of obscenity for each publication of the condemned work rather than regulating speech like "diseased cattle and impure butter." Justice WILLIAM J. BRENNAN contended that the statute was vastly defective for permitting a judge, rather than a jury, to determine a work's obscenity.

FREEDMAN v. MARYLAND

380 U.S. 51 (1965)

Kenneth L. Karst

Although the Supreme Court often remarks that the FIRST AMENDMENT imposes a heavy presumption against the validity of any system of PRIOR RESTRAINT on expression, the Court has tolerated state censorship of motion pictures through advance licensing. Typically, such a law authorizes a censorship board to deny a license to a film on the ground of OBSCENITY. Other substantive standards ("immoral," "tending to corrupt morals") have been held invalid for VAGUENESS. In addition, the Court insists that the licensing system's procedures follow strict guidelines designed to avoid the chief evils of censorship. *Freedman* is the leading decision establishing these guidelines.

In a test case, a Baltimore theater owner showed a concededly innocuous film without submitting it to the state censorship board, and he was convicted of a violation of state law. The Supreme Court unanimously reversed the conviction. The *Freedman* opinion, by Justice WILLIAM J. BRENNAN, set three procedural requirements for film censorship. First, the censor must have the burden of proving that the film is "unprotected expression" (for example, obscenity). Second, while the state may insist that all films be submitted for advance screening, the censor's determination cannot be given the effect of finality; a judicial determination is required. Thus the censor must, "within a specified brief period, either issue a license or go to court to restrain showing of the film." Advance restraint, before the issue gets to court, must be of the minimum duration consistent with orderly employment of the judicial machinery. Third, the court's decision itself must be prompt. Maryland's statute failed all three parts of this test and accordingly was an unconstitutional prior restraint. Justices WILLIAM O. DOUGLAS and HUGO L. BLACK, concurring, would have held any advance censorship impermissible.

PORNOGRAPHY

Catherine Hancock

The Supreme Court's OBSCENITY decisions define the forms of pornography that are protected from censorship by the FIRST AMENDMENT. As a practical matter, this protection is quite broad. Most pornography is also a unique kind of speech: about women, for men. In an era when sexual equality is a social ideal, the constitutional protection of pornography is a vexing political issue. Should pornographic imagery of male dominance and female subordination be repudiated through censorship, or will censorship inevitably destroy our commitment to free speech?

In ROTH v. UNITED STATES (1957) the Court found obscene speech to be unworthy of First Amendment protection because it forms "no essential part of any exposition of ideas." Yet precisely because of pornography's ideational content, some of it was deemed harmful and made criminal. The Court could avoid examining the specific nature of this harm, once it had located obscenity conveniently outside the constitutional pale. But it could not avoid defining obscenity, and thereby identifying the justification for its censorship.

The essential characteristic of "obscene" pornography is its appeal to one's "prurient interest," which is a genteel reference to its capacity to stimulate physical arousal and carnal desire. But such pornography must also be "offensive," and so, to be censored, sex-stimulant speech must be both arousing and disgusting. The meaning of offensiveness depends upon the subjective judgment of the observer, and is best captured by Justice POTTER STEWART's famous aphorism in JACOBELLIS v. OHIO (1964): "I know it when I see it."

Given the limitations of the criminal process, obscenity laws did not make offensive pornography unavailable in the marketplace. As HARRY KALVEN, JR. pointed out, few judges took the evils of obscenity very seriously, although constitutional rhetoric made the law appear to be "solemnly concerned with the sexual fantasies of the adult population." The Court's chief goal was the protection of admired works of art and literature, not the elimination of pornographic magazines at the corner drug store. Sporadic obscenity prosecutions may occur in jurisdictions where the "contemporary community standard" of offensiveness allows convictions under MILLER v. CALIFORNIA (1973). But the constitutional validity of a legal taboo on "hard-core" pornography became largely irrelevant to its suppliers and consumers, even as that material became sexually explicit and more violent in its imagery during the 1970s.

That same decade saw a legal revolution in equality between the sexes, embodied in judicial decisions based on the guarantees of EQUAL PROTECTION and DUE PROCESS. Women won legal rights to control and define their own sexuality, through litigation establishing rights to contraception and abortion, and through legislative reforms easing restrictions on prosecutions for sexual assault. Pornography also became a women's issue, as feminists such as Catharine MacKinnon attacked it as "a form of forced sex, a practice of sexual politics, an institution of gender inequality." Women marched and demonstrated against films and magazines portraying them as beaten, chained, or mutilated objects of sexual pleasure for men. In 1984, their protests took a legal form when MacKinnon and Andrea Dworkin drafted an ordinance adopted by the Indianapolis City Council, outlawing some types of pornography as acts of SEX DISCRIMINATION.

By using the concept of equal protection as a basis to attack pornographic speech, the council set up a dramatic assault upon First Amendment doctrine, making embarrassed enemies out of old constitutional friends. As a strategic matter, however, the council needed a COMPELLING STATE INTEREST to justify censorship of speech that did not fall into the obscenity category. The ordinance defined offensive pornography more broadly than *Miller'*s standards allow, because it went beyond a ban on displays of specific human body parts or sexual acts. Instead, it prohibited the "graphic sexually explicit subordination of women" through their portrayals as, for example, "sexual objects who enjoy pain or humiliation," or "sexual objects for domination, conquest, violation, exploitation, possession or use."

As a philosophical matter, sex discrimination is a good constitutional metaphor for the harms attributed to pornography, namely, the loss of equal CITIZENSHIP status for women through the "bigotry and contempt" promoted by the imagery of subordination. But as a matter of DOCTRINE, the causal link between the social presence of pornography and the harms of discrimination is fatally remote. Free speech gospel dictates that "offensive speech" may be censored only upon proof of imminent, tangible harm to individuals, such as violent insurrection (BRANDENBURG v. OHIO, 1969), a physical assault (COHEN v. CALIFORNIA, 1971), or reckless tortious injury to reputation (NEW YORK TIMES v. SULLIVAN, 1964). The closest historical analogue to the creation of a cause of action for classwide harm from speech is the criminal GROUP LIBEL statute upheld by a 5–4 Supreme Court in BEAUHARNAIS v. ILLINOIS (1952). But this remedy has been implicitly discredited by *New York Times* and *Brandenburg,* given its CHILLING EFFECT upon uninhibited criticism of political policies and officials.

It came as no surprise when early court decisions struck down Indianapolis-type ordinances as void for vagueness, as an unlawful PRIOR

RESTRAINT on speech, and as an unjustified restriction of protected speech as defined by the earlier obscenity decisions. The courts could accept neither the equal protection rationale nor the breadth of the ordinances' scope, as both would permit too great an encroachment upon the freedoms of expression and consumption of art, literature, and political messages. Ironically, it is the potentially endemic quality of the imagery of women's subordination that defeats any attempt to place a broad taboo upon it.

Eva Feder Kittay has posed the question, "How is it that within our society, men can derive a sexual charge out of seeing a woman brutalized?" Her answer to that loaded question is that our conceptions of sexuality are permeated with conceptions of domination, because we have eroticized the relations of power: men eroticize sexual conquering, and women eroticize being possessed. Pornography becomes more than a harmless outlet for erotic fantasies when it makes violence appear to be intrinsically erotic, rather than something that is eroticized. The social harm of such pornography is that it brutalizes our moral imagination, "the source of that imaginative possibility by which we can identify with others and hence form maxims having a universal validity."

The constitutional source for an analysis of brutalizing pornography lies in the richly generative symbols of First Amendment law itself. That law already contains the tolerance for insistence "on observance of the civic culture's norms of social equality," in the words of Kenneth L. Karst. Any acceptable future taboo would be likely to take the form of a ban on public display of a narrowly defined class of pictorial imagery, simply because that would be a traditional, readily enforceable compromise between free speech and equality. Any taboo would be mostly symbolic, but it would matter. Only by limiting the taboo can we avoid descending into the Orwellian hell where censorship is billed as freedom.

Bibliography

BRYDEN, DAVID   1985   Between Two Constitutions: Feminism and Pornography. *Constitutional Commentary* 2:147–189.

KALVEN, HARRY, JR.   1960   The Metaphysics of Obscenity. *Supreme Court Review* 1960:1–45.

KITTAY, EVA FEDER   1983   Pornography and the Erotics of Domination. Pages 145–174 in Carol C. Gould, ed., *Beyond Domination: New Perspectives on Women and Philosophy.* Totowa, N.J.: Rowman & Allanheld.

MACKINNON, CATHARINE A.   1984   Not a Moral Issue. *Yale Law & Policy Review* 2:321–345.

NOTE   1984   Anti-Pornography Laws and First Amendment Values. *Harvard Law Review* 98:460–481.

COHEN v. CALIFORNIA

403 U.S. (1971)

Martin Shapiro

Cohen was convicted of disturbing the peace. He wore a jacket bearing the words "Fuck the draft" while walking down a courthouse corridor. In overturning the conviction, a 5–4 Supreme Court held that the FIGHTING WORDS exception to FIRST AMENDMENT protection did not apply where "no individual . . . likely to be present could reasonably have regarded the words . . . as a direct personal insult," and there was no showing that anyone who saw Cohen was in fact violently aroused or that . . . [he] . . . intended such a result." Both majority and dissenters suggested that the failure to show that violence was imminent as the result of the words was fatal to the state's case. The Court thus made clear that words, in the abstract, cannot be read out of the First Amendment; the "fighting words" doctrine depends on the context in which words are uttered.

The state's assertion of other justifications for punishing Cohen were similarly rejected: the jacket's message was not OBSCENITY, because it was not erotic; the privacy interests of offended passers-by were insubstantial in this public place, and anyone offended might look away; there was no CAPTIVE AUDIENCE.

Cohen's chief doctrinal importance lies in its rejection of the notion that speech can constitutionally be prohibited by the state because it is offensive. Because offensiveness is an "inherently boundless" category, any such prohibition would suffer from the vice of VAGUENESS. And the First Amendment protects not only the cool expression of ideas but also "otherwise inexpressible emotions."

YOUNG v. AMERICAN MINI THEATRES, INC.

427 U.S. 50 (1976)

Steven Shiffrin

In *Young v. American Mini Theatres, Inc.* the Supreme Court upheld a Detroit ZONING ordinance requiring adult theaters to be located certain distances from residential areas and specified businesses. Four Justices led by Justice JOHN PAUL STEVENS argued that adult movies ranked low in the hierarchy of FIRST AMENDMENT values. Four dissenting Justices led by Justice POTTER STEWART argued that the First Amendment recognized no hierarchy for types of protected speech. Justice LEWIS F. POWELL agreed with the dissent, but voted to uphold the ordinance, arguing that the theater owners had asserted no First Amendment interest of their own and that the First Amendment interests of others, including moviemakers and potential audiences, were not endangered.

FEDERAL COMMUNICATIONS COMMISSION v. PACIFICA FOUNDATION

438 U.S. 726 (1978)

Steven Shiffrin

In *FCC v. Pacifica Foundation* the Court held that limited civil sanctions could constitutionally be invoked against a radio broadcast containing many vulgar words. The Court stressed that its holding was limited to the particular context, that is, to civil sanctions applied to indecent speech in an afternoon radio broadcast when, the Court assumed, children were in the audience. The opinion did not address criminal sanctions for televised or closed circuit broadcasts or late evening presentations, nor did it illuminate the concept of indecent speech except to suggest that occasional expletives and Elizabethan comedies may be decent enough even in the early afternoon.

COMMERCIAL SPEECH

Benno C. Schmidt, Jr.

Until 1976 "commercial speech"—a vague category encompassing advertisements, invitations to deal, credit or financial reports, prospectuses, and the like—was subject to broad regulatory authority, with little or no protection from the FIRST AMENDMENT. The early decisions, epitomized by *Valentine v. Chrestensen* (1942), followed the then characteristic judicial approach of defining certain subject-matter categories of expression as wholly outside the scope of First Amendment protection. Under this TWO-LEVEL THEORY, a "definitional" mode of First Amendment adjudication, commercial speech was considered to be, along with FIGHTING WORDS, OBSCENITY, and LIBEL, outside First Amendment protection.

When facing combinations of unprotected commercial speech and protected political speech in subsequent cases, the Court made First Amendment protection turn on the primary purpose of the advertisement. Thus, in MURDOCK V. PENNSYLVANIA (1943), the Court struck down an ordinance requiring solicitors of orders for goods to get a license and pay a fee as it applied to Jehovah's Witnesses who sold religious pamphlets while seeking religious converts. On the other hand, in *Bread v. Alexandria* (1951) the Court held that a door-to-door salesman of national magazine subscriptions was subject to a town ordinance barring such sales techniques, because his primary purpose was to sell magazines rather than to disseminate ideas.

The "primary purpose" test unraveled in NEW YORK TIMES V. SULLIVAN (1964), more prominently known for another rejection of the definitional approaches in its holding that defamation is not beyond First Amendment protection. In *Sullivan*, the *New York Times* had printed an allegedly defamatory advertisement soliciting funds for civil rights workers. Although the advertisement's primary purpose was, arguably, to raise money, the Court held that it was protected by the First Amendment because it "communicated information, expressed opinion, recited grievances, protested claimed abuses, and sought financial support on behalf of a movement whose existence and objectives are matters of the highest public interest and concern."

Recent decisions have gone well beyond *Sullivan* and moved advertising and other commercial speech—political or not—within the protection of the First Amendment. In the leading case, VIRGINIA PHARMACY BOARD V. VIRGINIA CITIZENS CONSUMER COUNCIL (1976), the Court struck down a state ban on prescription drug price advertising. The Court rejected the state's "highly paternalistic approach," preferring a system in which "people will perceive their own best interests if only they are well enough informed, and that the best means to that end is to open the channels of communication rather than to close them." The Court cautioned, however, that because untruthful speech has never been protected for its own sake government may take effective action against false and misleading advertisements. And it indicated a greater scope for regulating false or misleading commercial speech than is permitted in relation to false political statements, such as defamations of public officials, because advertising is more easily verifiable and is less likely to be "chilled" by regulation because it is a commercial necessity.

Virginia Pharmacy Board fixed the principle that advertising may be controlled when it is false, misleading, or takes undue advantage of its audience; but the case left open the issue whether whole categories of commercial speech deemed inherently misleading or difficult to police can be suppressed. This issue divided the Supreme Court with respect to lawyers' advertising, when a narrow majority extended First Amendment protection to price advertising of routine legal services, rejecting the dissenters' claim that the complex and variegated nature of legal services gave lawyers' advertising a high potential for deception and impeded effective regulation of particular deceptions. However, the Court held that "ambulance chasing"—in-person solicitation of accident victims for pecuniary gain—could be barred entirely because of its potential for deception and overbearing.

Where regulation of commercial expression is not directed at potential deception but intended to advance other interests such as aesthetics or conservation, the Supreme Court has followed a relatively permissive approach to state regulatory interests, while becoming hopelessly fragmented about the First Amendment principles that ought to govern. Thus, in METROMEDIA, INC. v. SAN DIEGO (1981) a shifting majority coalition of Justices made clear that commercial billboards could be entirely banned in a city for aesthetic or traffic safety reasons. Recent decisions, following CENTRAL HUDSON GAS & PUBLIC SERVICE COMMISSION (1980), have fashioned a four-part test to appraise the validity of restrictions on commercial speech. Protection will not be extended to commercial speech that is, on the whole, misleading or that encourages unlawful activity. Even protected commercial speech may be regulated if the state has a substantial interest, if the regulation directly advances that interest, and if the regulation is no broader than necessary to effectuate the state's interest. The elastic properties of this four-part test in actual application have generated considerable disarray within the Supreme Court.

The commercial speech decisions of the BURGER COURT have made clear that freedom of expression principles extend beyond political and religious expression, protecting not only the MARKETPLACE OF IDEAS but expression in the marketplace itself. Second, in affirming relatively broad regulatory power over commercial speech, even though it is deemed to be protected by the First Amendment, the Court has reinforced the notion that the First Amendment extends different levels of protection to different types of speech. The commercial speech decisions thus lend support to Justice ROBERT H. JACKSON's OBITER DICTUM in KOVACS v. COOPER (1949) that under the First Amendment each type and medium of expression "is a law unto itself."

Bibliography

JACKSON, THOMAS H. and JEFFRIES, J. C., JR.   1979 Commercial Speech: Economic Due Process and the First Amendment. *Virginia Law Review* 65:1–41.

WEINBERG, JONATHAN   1982   Constitutional Protection of Commercial Speech. *Columbia Law Review* 82:720–750.

VIRGINIA STATE BOARD OF PHARMACY v. VIRGINIA CITIZENS CONSUMERS COUNCIL

425 U.S. 748 (1976)

Martin Shapiro

Traditionally COMMERCIAL SPEECH was assumed to lie outside the FIRST AMENDMENT's protection. This decision made clear that this assumption was obsolete. Virginia's rules governing professional pharmacists forbade the advertising of prices of prescription drugs. The Supreme Court, 7–1, held this rule invalid at the behest of a consumers' group, thus promoting the notion of a "right to receive" in the FREEDOM OF SPEECH. (See LISTENERS' RIGHTS.) The Court's opinion indicated that false or misleading commercial advertising might be regulated—a rule the Court would never apply to political speech. For a few years, this decision stood as the Court's principal commercial speech precedent, only to be assimilated in the comprehensive opinion in CENTRAL HUDSON GAS v. PUBLIC SERVICE COMMISSION (1980).

Prior Restraint

PRIOR RESTRAINT AND CENSORSHIP

Benno C. Schmidt, Jr.

History has rooted in our constitutional tradition of freedom of expression the strongest aversion to official censorship. We have learned from the English rejection of press licensing and from our own experiences that the psychology of censors tends to drive them to excess, that censors have a stake in finding things to suppress, and that—in systems of wholesale review before publication—doubt tends to produce suppression. American law tolerated motion picture censorship for a time, but only because movies were not thought to be "the press" in FIRST AMENDMENT terms. Censorship of the movies is now virtually dead, smothered by stringent procedural requirements imposed by unsympathetic courts, by the voluntary rating system, and, most of all, by public distaste for the absurdities of censorship in operation.

American law has tolerated requirements of prior official approval of expression in several important areas, however. No one may broadcast without a license, and the government issues licenses without charge to those it believes will serve the "public interest." Licensing is also grudgingly tolerated—because of the desirability of giving notice and of avoiding conflicts or other disruptions of the normal functions of public places—in the regulation of parades, demonstrations, leafleting, and other expressive activities in public places. But the courts have taken pains to eliminate administrative discretion that would allow officials to censor PUBLIC FORUM expression because they do not approve its message.

Notwithstanding these areas where censorship has been permitted, the clearest principle of First Amendment law is that the least tolerable form of official regulation of expression is a requirement of prior official approval for publication. It is easy to see the suffocating tendency of prior restraints where all expression—whether or not ultimately deemed protected by the First Amendment for publication—must be submitted for clearance before it may be disseminated. The harder question of First Amendment theory has been whether advance prohibitions on expression in specific cases should be discredited by our historical aversion to censorship. The question has arisen most frequently in the context of judicial INJUNCTIONS against publication. Even though injunctions do not involve many of the worst vices of wholesale licensing and censorship, the Supreme court has tarred them with the brush of "prior restraint."

The seminal case was NEAR v. MINNESOTA (1931), handed down by a closely divided Court but never questioned since. A state statute provided for injunctions against any "malicious, scandalous, and defamatory newspaper," and a state judge had enjoined a scandal sheet from publishing anything scandalous in the future. The Minnesota scheme did not require advance approval of all publications, but came into play only after a publication had been found scandalous, and then only to prevent further similar publications. Nevertheless, the majority of the Justices concluded that to enjoin future editions under such vague standards in effect put the newspaper under judicial censorship. Chief Justice CHARLES EVANS HUGHES's historic opinion made clear, however, that the First Amendment's bar against prior restraint was not absolute. Various exceptional instances would justify prior restraints, including this pregnant one: "No one would question but that a government might prevent actual obstruction to its recruiting service or the publication of the sailing dates of transports or the number and location of troops."

It was forty years before the scope of the troop ship exception was tested. The *Pentagon Papers* decision of 1971, NEW YORK TIMES Co. v. UNITED STATES, reaffirmed that judicial injunctions are considered prior restraints and are tolerated only in the most compelling circumstances. This principle barred an injunction against publication of a classified history of the government's decisions in the Vietnam war, although—unlike *Near*—the government had sought to enjoin only readily identifiable material, not unidentified similar publications in the future. Ten different opinions discussed the problem of injunctions in national security cases, and the only proposition commanding a majority was the unexplained conclusion that the government had not justified injunctive relief.

The central theme sounded in the opinions of the six majority Justices was reluctance to act in such difficult circumstances without guidance from Congress. Accepting the premise that there was no statutory authority for an injunction, several considerations support the Court's refusal to forge new rules concerning the disclosure of national secrets. First, the Court's tools are inadequate for the task; ad hoc evaluations of executive claims of risk are not easily balanced against the First Amendment's language and judicial interpretation. Second, dissemination of secret information often arises in the context of heated disagreements about the proper direction of national policy. One's assessment of the disclosure's impact on security will depend on one's reaction to the policy. Third, it would be particularly unsatisfactory to build a judge-made system of rules in an area where much litigation must be done *in camera*.

Thus, general rules about specific categories of defense-related information cannot be fashioned by courts. The best hope in a nuclear age for accommodating the needs of secrecy and the public's RIGHT TO KNOW lies in the legislative process where, removed from pressures of adjudicating particular cases, general rules can be fashioned. The courts' proper role in this area is to review legislation, not try to devise rules of secrecy case by case.

Chilling this victory for freedom of the press were admonitions, loosely endorsed by four Justices, that the espionage statutes might support criminal sanctions against the *New York Times* and its reporters. No journalists were indicted, but the prosecutions of Daniel Ellsberg and Anthony Russo rested on a view of several statutes that would reach the press by punishing news-gathering activities necessarily incident to publication. Since the dismissal of these cases for reasons irrelevant to these issues, the extent of possible criminal liability for publishing national security secrets remains unclear.

The *Pentagon Papers* case underlines how little the United States has relied on law to control press coverage of national defense and foreign policy matters. For most of our history the press has rarely tested the limits of its rights to publish. Secrets were kept because people in and out of government with access to military and diplomatic secrets shared basic assumptions about national aims. The Vietnam war changed all that. The *Pentagon Papers* dispute marked the passing of an era in which journalists could be counted on to work within understood limits of discretion in handling secret information.

The third major decision striking down a judicial order not to publish involved neither national security nor scandal but the right of a criminal defendant to a fair trial. A state court enjoined publication of an accused's confession and some other incriminating material on the ground that if prospective jurors learned about it they might be incapable of impartiality. In NEBRASKA PRESS ASSOCIATION V. STUART (1976) the Supreme Court decided that the potential prejudice was speculative, and it rejected enjoining publication on speculation. The majority opinion examined the evidence to determine the nature and extent of pretrial publicity, the effectiveness of other measures in mitigating prejudice, and the effectiveness of a prior restraint in reducing the dangers. This opinion determined that the impact of pretrial publicity was necessarily speculative, that alternative measures short of prior restraint had not been considered by the lower courts, and that prior restraint would not significantly reduce the dangers presented.

On one issue of considerable importance, the Court seemed to be in full agreement. The opinions endorsed controls on parties, lawyers, witnesses, and law enforcement personnel as sources of information for journalists. These GAG ORDERS have been controversial among many journalists and publishers who think the First Amendment should guarantee the right to gather news. Although freeing the press from direct control by limiting prior restraint, the Court approved an indirect method of reaching the same result, guaranteeing that the press print no prejudicial publicity, by approving direct controls on sources of prejudicial information. The Court has subsequently held that pretrial motions may be closed to the public and the press with the consent of the prosecutor and the accused but over the objection of the press, in GANNETT CO. v. DePASQUALE (1979). This case involved access to judicial proceedings, not prior restraints on the press, and was decided largely on Sixth Amendment grounds. The Court reached the opposite result with respect to trials in RICHMOND NEWSPAPERS V. VIRGINIA (1980), but acknowledged that the right of access to trials is not absolute.

These decisions and others have firmly established that the First Amendment tolerates virtually no prior restraints. This DOCTRINE is one of the central principles of our law of FREEDOM OF THE PRESS. On the surface, the doctrine concerns only the form of controls on expression. It bars controls prior to publication, even if imposition of criminal or civil liability following publication would be constitutional. But, as with most limitations of form, the prior restraint doctrine has important substantive consequences. Perhaps the most important of these consequences is that the doctrine is presumably an absolute bar to any wholesale system of administrative licensing or censorship of the press, which is the most repellent form of government suppression of expression. Second, the prior restraint doctrine removes most of the opportunities for official control of those types of expression for which general rules of control are difficult to formulate. The message of the prior restraint doctrine is that if you cannot control expression pursuant to general legislative standards, you cannot control it at all—or nearly at all, as the *Pentagon Papers* decision suggests, by suggesting an exception allowing an injunction in a truly compelling case of national security. A third effect of the doctrine is that by transferring questions of control over expression from the judiciary to the legislatures, it provides an enormously beneficial protection for the politically powerful mass media, if not for other elements of society with strong First Amendment interests but weaker influence in the legislative process.

Although the Supreme Court has exceeded its historical warrant in subjecting judicial injunctions to the full burden of our law's traditional aversion to prior restraints, there are sound reasons for viewing all prior controls—not only wholesale licensing and censorship—as dangerous to free expression. Generally it is administratively easier to prevent expression in advance than to punish it after the fact. The inertia of public officials in responding to a *fait accompli*, the chance to look at whether expression has actually caused harm rather than speculate about the matter, public support for the speaker, and the interposition of juries and other procedural safeguards of the usual criminal or civil process all tend to reinforce tolerance when expression can only be dealt with by subsequent punishment. Moreover, all prior restraint systems, including injunctions, tend to divert attention from the central question of whether expression is protected to the subsidiary problem of promoting the effectiveness of the prior restraint system. Once a prior restraint is issued, the authority and prestige of the restraining agent are at stake. If it is disobeyed, the legality of the expression takes a back seat to the enforcement of obedience to the prior restraint process. Moreover, the time it takes a prior restraint process to decide produces a systematic delay of expression. On the other hand, where law must wait to move against expression after it has been published, time is on the side of freedom. All in all, even such prior restraints as judicial injunctions—which are more discriminating than wholesale censorship—tend toward irresponsible administration and an exaggerated assessment of the dangers of free expression.

Bibliography

BLASI, VINCENT   1981   Toward a Theory of Prior Restraint: The Central Linkage. *Minnesota Law Review* 66:11.
EMERSON, THOMAS   1955   The Doctrine of Prior Restraint *Law and Contemporary Problems* 20:648.
SCHMIDT, BENNO C., JR.   1977   Nebraska Press Association: An Expansion of Freedom and Contraction of Theory. *Stanford Law Review* 29:431.

NEAR v. MINNESOTA

283 U.S. 697 (1931)

Martin Shapiro

Although GITLOW V. NEW YORK (1925) had accepted for the sake of argument that the FIRST AMENDMENT'S FREEDOM OF SPEECH guarantees were applicable to the states through the DUE PROCESS clause of the FOURTEENTH AMENDMENT, *Near* was the first decision firmly adopting the INCORPORATION DOCTRINE and striking down a state law in its totality on free speech grounds. Together with STROMBERG V. CALIFORNIA (1931), decided in the same year and also with a 5–4 majority opinion by Chief Justice CHARLES EVANS HUGHES, *Near* announced a new level of Supreme Court concern for freedom of speech.

A Minnesota statute authorizing injunctions against a "malicious, scandalous and defamatory newspaper, magazine or other periodical" had been applied against a paper that had accused public officials of neglect of duty, illicit relations with gangsters, and graft. Arguing that hostility to PRIOR RESTRAINT AND CENSORSHIP are the very core of the First Amendment, the Court struck down the statute. Yet *Near,* the classic precedent against prior restraints, is also the doctrinal starting point for most defenses of prior restraint. The Court commented in OBITER DICTUM that "the protection even as to previous restraint is not absolutely unlimited," and listed as exceptions wartime obstruction of recruitment and publication of military secrets, OBSCENITY, INCITEMENTS to riot or forcible overthrow of the government, and words that "may have all the effect of force."

In emphasizing the special First Amendment solicitude for criticisms of public officials, whether true or false, *Near* was an important way station between *Gitlow*'s implicit acceptance of the constitutional survival in the United States of the English COMMON LAW concept of SEDITIOUS LIBEL and the rejection of that concept in NEW YORK TIMES V. SULLIVAN (1964).

NEW YORK TIMES CO. v.
UNITED STATES

403 U.S. 713 (1971)

Frederick F. Schauer

New York Times Co. v. United States, more commonly known as the Pentagon Papers case, is one of the landmarks of contemporary prior restraint
doctrine. Only NEAR v. MINNESOTA (1931) rivals it as a case of central
importance in establishing the FIRST AMENDMENT's particular and extreme aversion to any form of official restriction applied prior to the
act of speaking or the act of publication.

The dramatic facts of the case served to keep it before the public
eye even as it was being litigated and decided. On June 12, 1971, the
New York Times commenced publication of selected portions of a 1968
forty-seven-volume classified Defense Department study entitled "History of United States Decision Making Process on Vietnam Policy" and
a 1965 classified Defense Department study entitled "The Command
and Control Study of the Tonkin Gulf Incident Done by the Defense
Department's Weapons Systems Evaluation Group in 1965." Collectively
these documents came to be known as the Pentagon Papers. Within a
few days other major newspapers, including the *Washington Post,* the
Los Angeles Times, the *Detroit Free Press,* the *Philadelphia Inquirer,* and
the *Miami Herald* also commenced publication of the Pentagon Papers.
The papers had been provided to the *New York Times* by Daniel Ellsberg,
a former Defense Department official and former government consultant. Ellsberg had no official authority to take the Pentagon Papers;
his turning over the papers to the *New York Times* was similarly unautho-
rized.

When the newspapers commenced publication, the United States
was still engaged in fighting the VIETNAM WAR. Claiming that the publication of the Pentagon Papers jeopardized national security, the government sought an INJUNCTION against any further publication of the papers,
including publication of scheduled installments yet to appear. In the
United States District Court for the Southern District of New York,
Judge Murray Gurfein issued a temporary restraining order against
the *New York Times,* but then denied the government's request for a
preliminary injunction against publication, finding that, in light of the
extremely high hurdle necessary to justify a prior restraint against a

newspaper, "the publication of these historical documents would [not] seriously breach the national security." (See PRIOR RESTRAINT AND CENSORSHIP.) The United States immediately appealed, and the Court of Appeals for the Second Circuit, on June 23, 1971, remanded the case for further consideration in light of documents filed by the United States indicating that publication might pose "grave and immediate danger to the security of the United States." The Second Circuit continued to enforce the stay it had previously issued, in effect keeping the *Times* under the restraint of the temporary restraining order. On the same day, however, the United States Court of Appeals for the District of Columbia Circuit, in a case involving the *Washington Post's* publication of the Pentagon Papers, affirmed a decision of the district court refusing to enjoin further publication. On June 24, the *New York Times* filed a petition for a WRIT OF CERTIORARI and motion for expedited consideration in the Supreme Court, and on the same day the United States asked that Court for a stay of the District of Columbia circuit's ruling in the *Washington Post* case. The two cases were consolidated and accelerated, with briefs filed on June 26, oral argument the same day, and a decision of the Supreme Court on June 30, only seventeen days after the first publication of the papers in the *New York Times*.

In a brief PER CURIAM opinion, the Supreme Court affirmed the District of Columbia Circuit, reversed the Second Circuit, and vacated the restraints. Noting the "heavy presumption" against prior restraints, and the consequent "heavy burden of . . . justification" necessary to support a prior restraint, the Court found that the United States had not met that especially heavy burden.

The Court's per curiam opinion was accompanied by a number of important separate opinions by individual Justices. Justices HUGO L. BLACK and WILLIAM O. DOUGLAS made it clear that in their view prior restraints were never permissible. Justice WILLIAM J. BRENNAN would not go this far, but found it noteworthy that "never before has the United States sought to enjoin a newspaper from publishing information in its possession." For him "only governmental allegation and proof that publication must inevitably, directly, and immediately cause the occurrence of an evil kindred to imperiling the safety of a transport already at sea [citing *Near v. Minnesota*] can support even the issuance of an interim restraining order." In agreeing that the restraint was improper, Justice THURGOOD MARSHALL emphasized the absence of statutory authorization for governmental action to enjoin a newspaper. And Justice JOHN MARSHALL HARLAN, joined by Chief Justice WARREN E. BURGER and Justice HARRY A. BLACKMUN, dissented. The dissenters were disturbed by the alacrity of the proceedings, and in addition thought that the executive's "constitutional primacy in the field of FOREIGN AFFAIRS" justified a restraint at least long enough to allow the executive to present its complete case for the necessity of restriction. The most doctrinally illuminating opinions, however, were those of Justices POTTER J. STEWART and BYRON R. WHITE. For them only the specific nature of the restriction rendered it constitutionally impermissible. Had the case involved criminal or civil sanctions imposed after publication—subsequent punishment rather than prior restraint—they indicated that the First Amendment would not have stood in the way.

As highlighted by the opinions of Justices Stewart and White, therefore, the *Pentagon Papers* case presents the problem of prior restraint in purest form. The judges had the disputed materials in front of them, and thus there was no question of a restraint on materials not before a court, or not yet published. And the evaluation of the likely effect of the materials was made by the judiciary, rather than by a censorship board, other administrative agency, or police officer. Under these circumstances, why might a prior restraint be unconstitutional when a subsequent punishment for publishing the same materials would be upheld? What justifies a constitutional standard higher for injunctions than for criminal sanctions? It cannot be that prior restraints in fact "prevent" more things from being published, for the deterrent effect of a criminal sanction is likely to inhibit publication at least as much as an injunction. Someone who is willing knowingly to violate the criminal law, in order to publish out of conscience, may also be willing to violate an injunction. Is the special aversion against prior restraint, visible in the Pentagon Papers case, based on principle, or is it little more than an anachronism inherited from John Milton and WILLIAM BLACKSTONE, and transferred from a milieu in which prior restraint was synonymous with unreviewable determinations of an administrative censorship board?

The result in the Pentagon Papers case was not inconsistent with prior cases. The case did, however, present more clearly the puzzling nature of the virtually absolute prohibition against prior restraints under circumstances in which subsequent punishment of the very same material would have been permissible. Yet the case is also significant for reasons that transcend the doctrine of prior restraint. When confronted with a constitutional objection to a governmental policy, a court typically must evaluate the justification for the policy, and assess the likelihood of some consequences that the policy is designed to prevent. When that consequence and the governmental attempt to forestall it relates to war, national security, or national defense, judicial deference to governmental assertions of likely consequences has traditionally been greatest, even if the putative restriction implicates activities otherwise protected by the Constitution. When national security has been invoked, constitutional protection has often been more illusory than real. At every level in the Pentagon Papers case the courts conducted their own independent assessments of the likely dangers to national security and to troops overseas.

The Supreme Court's decision was at least partly a function of the Justices' unwillingness to accept governmental incantation of the phrase "national security" as dispositive. Certainly executive determinations concerning the effect of publications on national security still receive greater deference than do other executive predictions about the effect of publications. But the Pentagon Papers case stands for the proposition that even when national security is claimed the courts will scrutinize for themselves the necessity of restriction. The decision, therefore, speaks not only to prior restraint but also, and more pervasively, to the courts' willingness to protect constitutional rights even against wartime governmental restrictions imposed in the name of national security.

Bibliography

HENKIN, LOUIS   1971   The Right to Know and the Duty to Withhold: The Case of the Pentagon Papers. *University of Pennsylvania Law Review* 120:271–280.

JUNGER, PETER   1971   Down Memory Lane: The Case of the Pentagon Papers. *Case Western Reserve Law Review* 23:3–75.

KALVEN, HARRY, JR.   1971   Foreword: Even When a Nation Is at War. *Harvard Law Review* 85:3–36.

NEBRASKA PRESS ASSOCIATION v. STUART

427 U.S. 539 (1976)

Kim McLane Wardlaw

In *Nebraska Press Association v. Stuart* the Court addressed for the first time the constitutionality of a prior restraint on pretrial publicity about a criminal case. Noting the historic conflict between the FIRST and Sixth AMENDMENTS, the Court refused to give either priority, recognizing that the accused's right to an unbiased jury must be balanced with the interests in a free press. At issue was a narrowly tailored GAG ORDER in a sensational murder case restraining the press from publishing or broadcasting accounts of the accused's confessions or admissions or "strongly implicative" facts until the jury was impaneled.

Applying the standard of DENNIS v. UNITED STATES (1951) and inquiring whether "the gravity of the 'evil,' discounted by its improbability justified such invasion of free speech as is necessary to avoid the danger," the Court struck down the gag order. To determine whether the record supported the extraordinary measure of a prior restraint on publication, the Court considered the nature and extent of pretrial news coverage, the likelihood that other measures would mitigate the effects of unrestrained pretrial publicity, and the effectiveness of a restraining order to prevent the threatened danger, and, further, analyzed the order's terms and the problems of managing and enforcing it. The gag order was critically flawed because it prohibited publication of information gained from other clearly protected sources.

Justice WILLIAM J. BRENNAN, joined by Justices POTTER J. STEWART and THURGOOD MARSHALL, concurring, argued that a prior restraint on the press is an unconstitutionally impermissible method for enforcing the Sixth Amendment. Refusing to view the First and Sixth Amendments as in irreconcilable conflict, he noted that there were numerous less restrictive means by which a fair trial could be ensured. Justice BYRON R. WHITE doubted whether prior restraints were ever justifiable, but did not believe it wise so to announce in the first case raising that question. Justice LEWIS F. POWELL emphasized the heavy burden resting on a party seeking to justify a prior restraint.

LOVELL v. CITY OF GRIFFIN

303 U.S. 444 (1938)

Richard E. Morgan

A municipal ordinance prohibited the distribution of circulars or any other literature within Griffin without a permit from the city manager. Chief Justice CHARLES EVANS HUGHES, for a unanimous Court, held the Griffin ordinance unconstitutional. The ordinance provided no standards to guide the city manager's decision. To vest an official with absolute discretion to issue or deny a permit was an unconstitutional prior restraint that violated the FIRST AMENDMENT. Because the ordinance was INVALID ON ITS FACE, Lovell was entitled to distribute her literature without seeking a permit, and to challenge the ordinance's validity when she was charged with its violation.

COX v. NEW HAMPSHIRE

312 U.S. 569 (1941)

Martin Shapiro

In this seminal decision, Chief Justice CHARLES EVANS HUGHES, writing for a unanimous Supreme Court, synthesized a series of cases involving speeches, parades, and meetings in parks and on streets. He held that there was a "right of assembly . . . and . . . discussion of public questions immemorially associated with resort to public places," but that such a right was limited by the authority of local government to make reasonable regulations governing "the time, place and manner" of such speech, if the regulations did not involve "unfair discrimination" among speakers. The Court upheld a state law requiring parade licenses issued by local governments on the grounds that, as construed by the state supreme court, it authorized only such reasonable and nondiscriminatory regulations. *Cox* is one of the building blocks in the creation of the doctrine of the PUBLIC FORUM.

This case took on renewed importance in the context of the CIVIL RIGHTS demonstrations of the 1960s. The crucial problem under the *Cox* test is often whether a law purporting to be a neutral regulation of traffic and noise control is actually a façade behind which local authorities seek to deny a public forum to speakers whose speech they dislike.

WALKER v. BIRMINGHAM
388 U.S. 307 (1967)

Kenneth L. Karst

The Supreme Court, 5–4, upheld criminal contempt convictions of eight black ministers, including MARTIN LUTHER KING, JR., for holding a CIVIL RIGHTS protest parade in violation of an INJUNCTION issued by an Alabama state court. The injunction, which forbade them from engaging in street parades without a permit, was issued EX PARTE, two days before the intended march. The order was based on a city ordinance that the Court later held unconstitutional for VAGUENESS in *Shuttlesworth v. Birmingham* (1969), a case arising out of the same events.

For the majority, Justice POTTER STEWART concluded that the ministers, once enjoined by a court order, were not entitled to disregard the injunction even if it had been granted unconstitutionally. Rather, they were obliged to ask the court to modify the order, or to seek relief from the injunction in another court.

Justice WILLIAM J. BRENNAN, for the four dissenters, pointed out that, in the absence of a court order, the FIRST AMENDMENT would have entitled the marchers to disregard the ordinance, which was INVALID ON ITS FACE. It was incongruous, he argued, to let the state alter this result simply by obtaining "the ex parte stamp of a judicial officer on a copy of the invalid ordinance." These views were echoed in separate dissents by Chief Justice EARL WARREN and Justice WILLIAM O. DOUGLAS. The *Walker* principle, though much criticized, remains the DOCTRINE of the Court.

Symbolic
Expression

SYMBOLIC SPEECH

Melville B. Nimmer

Does communication by conduct rather than by words constitute "speech" within the FIRST AMENDMENT's guarantee of FREEDOM OF SPEECH? The status of communicative conduct, as with most free speech questions, is usually presented in an emotion-laden context: does the burning of a flag, or of a draft card, constitute a First-Amendment-protected activity? Is the act of marching in a public DEMONSTRATION (as distinguished from the placards which the marchers carry) a form of protected "speech?" Are school or other governmental regulations of hair styles an abridgment of freedom of speech? Does nude dancing constitute a form of First Amendment "speech?" Although the lower federal and state courts frequently have wrestled with all of these questions, the United States Supreme Court has yet to articulate a theoretical base that explains the status of symbolic speech under the First Amendment.

At least since STROMBERG V. CALIFORNIA (1931), the Supreme Court has assumed that "speech" within the meaning of the First Amendment's guarantee of "freedom of speech" includes more than merely verbal communications. In *Stromberg* the Court declared invalid a California statute that prohibited the public display of "any flag, badge, banner or device . . . as a sign, symbol or emblem of opposition to organized government." Among other decisions applying the First Amendment to nonverbal conduct, perhaps the most striking was TINKER V. DES MOINES INDEPENDENT COMMUNITY SCHOOL DISTRICT (1969). The Court there upheld the right of high school students to wear black armbands as a protest against American participation in the VIETNAM WAR, calling their conduct "the type of symbolic act that is within the Free Speech Clause of the First Amendment."

But if conduct sometimes constitutes protected "speech," sometimes it does not. UNITED STATES V. O'BRIEN (1968) affirmed a conviction for draft card burning. Chief Justice EARL WARREN, speaking for the Court, answered the defendant's symbolic speech defense by opining, "We cannot accept the view that an apparently limitless variety of conduct can be labeled 'speech' whenever the person engaging in the conduct intends thereby to express an idea."

Any attempt to disentangle "speech" from conduct that is itself communicative will not withstand analysis. The speech element in symbolic speech is entitled to no lesser (and also no greater) degree of protection than that accorded to so-called pure speech. Indeed, in one sense all speech is symbolic. At this moment the reader is observing black markings on paper which curl and point in various directions. We call such markings letters, and in groups they are referred to as words. What is being said in this sentence is meaningful only because the reader recognizes these markings as symbols for particular ideas. The same is true of oral speech which is simply the use of symbolic sounds. Outside the science fiction realm of mind-to-mind telepathic communication, all communications necessarily involve the use of symbols.

But because all expression necessarily requires the use of symbols, it does not necessarily follow as a matter of logic that First Amendment protection is or should be available for all symbolic expressions. The "speech" protected by the First Amendment might be limited to expressions in which the symbols employed consist of conventional words. The Supreme Court has found so restrictive a reading of the First Amendment to be unacceptable. Significantly, in First Amendment cases, the Court often refers to "freedom of expression" as the equivalent of freedom of speech. Justice OLIVER WENDELL HOLMES's "free trade in ideas" may not be reduced to mere trade in words. It is the freedom to express ideas and feelings, not merely the freedom to engage in verbal locutions, that must be protected if the First Amendment's central values are to be realized.

In COHEN v. CALIFORNIA (1971) the Supreme Court held that the emotive form of speech is as entitled to First Amendment protection as is its cognitive content. Emotive expression can be fully as important as intellectual, or cognitive, content in the competition of ideas for acceptance in the marketplace. Of course, most communications encompass both cognitive and emotive content. But even if a communication is substantially devoid of all cognitive content, its emotive content surely lies within the First Amendment scope. Symphonic compositions or nonrepresentational art are protected against governmental censorship, notwithstanding their lack of verbal or cognitive content.

Of course, not all conduct should be regarded as "speech" within the meaning of the First Amendment. Not even the most ardent free speech advocate would contend that all legislation regulating human conduct is subject to First Amendment restrictions. If, as the Court stated in the O'Brien opinion, the First Amendment is not to apply to a "limitless variety of conduct," what standards should be applied in determining whether given restrictions on conduct constitute First Amendment abridgment of symbolic speech?

If government's purpose in restricting is to suppress the message conveyed by the conduct, then the state should not be heard to deny the actor's claim that the conduct in question was intended to communicate a message. Such a message-restricting motivation by the state should also establish that the conduct in question constitutes symbolic speech. But such a conclusion does not necessarily imply that the speech is entitled to First Amendment protection. Even speech in words may in some circumstances be subordinated to a counter-speech interest. Likewise, no First Amendment ABSOLUTISM will protect communicative conduct. In some contexts symbolic speech may be overbalanced by counter-speech interests. If, however, the asserted or actual counter-speech interest is simply commitment to a particular view of the world—political, ethical, aesthetic, or otherwise—this interest will not justify abridgment of the right to express a contrary view, either by words or by conduct.

Just as First Amendment principles apply equally to expression in the symbols of the English or French languages, for example, the same principles govern when the symbols are of neither of these languages, nor of any conventional language. The crucial question under the First Amendment is whether meaningful symbols are being employed by one who wishes to communicate to others.

The courts have resisted equating symbolic speech with verbal speech because of a fear of immunizing all manner of conduct from the controls of the law. This fear is unjustifiable; it stems from a false premise as to the First Amendment protection accorded to verbal speech. In fact, speech in words is not immune from regulation. For example, an interest in excluding trespassers will justify abridging the verbal speech of those who wish to speak on property from which they may properly be excluded. Similarly, words that presage an imminent and likely BREACH OF THE PEACE will justify regulation just as much as if the idea be conveyed by nonverbal symbols. These are but two of many instances when verbal speech is subordinated to counter-speech interests.

According full and equal status to symbolic speech under the First Amendment will not open the floodgates to abuses, immunizing O'Brien's "apparently limitless variety of conduct" from legal regulation. Recognition of such equality of forms of expression would mean that no one will be penalized because he chooses to communicate—or is able to communicate—only in a language other than conventional words. We shall all be the richer for such recognition.

Bibliography

NIMMER, MELVILLE B.   1973   The Meaning of Symbolic Speech to the First Amendment. *UCLA Law Review* 21:29–62.

DRAFT CARD BURNING

Norman Dorsen

The burning of Selective Service registration certificates—or "draft cards"—was a brief and dramatic episode that punctuated the early opposition to the VIETNAM WAR. Many draft registrants, often before television cameras, publicly burned their cards to demonstrate their refusal to participate in the draft. These events attracted wide attention and often served as a rallying point for war protesters.

Congress responded in 1965 by amending the Universal Military Training and Service Act to make it a FELONY when any person "knowingly destroys [or] knowingly mutilates" his registration certificate. This law was challenged by David O'Brien with the aid of the AMERICAN CIVIL LIBERTIES UNION. O'Brien had burned his registration certificate before a sizable Boston crowd, including several FBI agents. He was indicted, tried, convicted, and sentenced to prison in the Massachusetts District Court, but the United States Court of Appeals held that the 1965 law unconstitutionally abridged FREEDOM OF SPEECH because it interfered with O'Brien's "symbolic" protest against the war.

In *United States v. O'Brien* (1968), the Supreme Court in an opinion by Chief Justice EARL WARREN reversed the Court of Appeals and upheld the challenged law and O'Brien's conviction. The Court first ruled that the Government has a "substantial interest in assuring the continued availability" of draft cards—for example, so that the individual can prove he has registered and so communication between registrants and local boards can be facilitated, particularly in an emergency. Second, in a more far-reaching holding, the Court rejected O'Brien's claim that the 1965 amendment was unconstitutional because Congress sought to suppress freedom of speech. The Court did not determine whether that in fact was Congress's purpose. Instead it ruled that such a purpose would not invalidate the law in light of the principle that courts may not "restrain the exercise of lawful [congressional] power on the assumption that a wrongful purpose or motive has caused the power to be exercised." (See McCRAY v. UNITED STATES, 1903.)

Only Justice WILLIAM O. DOUGLAS dissented from the Court's decision, in an opinion that dwelt less on draft card burning than on the power of Congress to initiate a peacetime draft. The *O'Brien* case led to a sharp curtailment of draft card burning and opponents of the Vietnam War turned to other forms of protest.

Bibliography

ALFANGE, DEAN, JR.   1968   Free Speech and Symbolic Conduct: The Draft Card Burning Case. *Supreme Court Review* 1968:1–52.

O'BRIEN, UNITED STATES v.

391 U.S. 367 (1968)

Kenneth L. Karst

The *O'Brien* opinion is today widely cited in briefs and judicial opinions defending governmental action against claims of violation of the FREEDOM OF SPEECH. In 1965 Congress amended the SELECTIVE SERVICE ACT to make it a crime to destroy or mutilate a draft registration card. The amendment's legislative history made clear that it was aimed at antiwar protest, but the Supreme Court nonetheless upheld, 8–1, the conviction of a protester for DRAFT CARD BURNING, rejecting his FIRST AMENDMENT claims.

Writing for the Court, Chief Justice EARL WARREN assumed that SYMBOLIC SPEECH of this kind was entitled to First Amendment protection. However, he announced a doctrinal formula now dear to the hearts of government attorneys, a formula that seemed to apply generally to all First Amendment cases: "[W]e think it clear that a government regulation is sufficiently justified if it is within the constitutional power of the Government; if it furthers an important or substantial governmental interest; if the governmental interest is unrelated to the suppression of free expression; and if the incidental restriction on alleged First Amendment freedoms is no greater than is essential to the furtherance of that interest."

This very case seemed appropriate for application of the formula to overturn the protesters' conviction, but it was not to be. Here, Warren said, the power of the federal government to "conscript manpower" was clear; further, he placed great importance on the government's interests in keeping draft cards intact. As for the purpose to suppress expression, the Chief Justice took away what he had just given to First Amendment challengers: the Court should not inquire, he said, into possible improper congressional motivations for an otherwise valid law. (See LEGISLATION.) Finally, he said, the government's interests could not be served by any less restrictive means.

It is hard to avoid the conclusion that the Justices, embattled on political fronts ranging from SEGREGATION to school prayers, thought it prudent not to add to the Court's difficulties a confrontation with Congress and the President over the VIETNAM WAR. Justice WILLIAM O. DOUGLAS, however, dissented alone on the ground that the Court should

264

consider the constitutionality of military CONSCRIPTION in the absence of a DECLARATION OF WAR by Congress.

Bibliography

ELY, JOHN HART   1975   Flag Desecration: A Case Study in the Roles of Categorization and Balancing in First Amendment Analysis. *Harvard Law Review* 88:1482–1508.

NIMMER, MELVILLE B.   1973   The Meaning of Symbolic Speech under the First Amendment. *UCLA Law Review* 21:29–62.

TINKER v. DES MOINES INDEPENDENT COMMUNITY SCHOOL DISTRICT

393 U.S. 503 (1969)

Kenneth L. Karst

Tinker is a leading modern decision on the subjects of SYMBOLIC SPEECH and CHILDREN'S RIGHTS. A group of adults and students in Des Moines planned to protest the VIETNAM WAR by wearing black armbands during the 1965 holiday season. On learning of this plan, the public school principals adopted a policy to forbid the wearing of armbands. Two high school students and one junior high school student wore armbands to school, refused to remove them, and were suspended until they might return without armbands. They sued in federal court to enjoin enforcement of the principals' policy and for nominal damages. The district court dismissed the complaint, and the court of appeals affirmed by an equally divided court. The Supreme Court reversed, 7–2, in an opinion by Justice ABE FORTAS.

The wearing of these armbands was "closely akin to 'pure speech' " and protected by the FIRST AMENDMENT. The school environment did imply limitations on the freedom of expression, but here the principals lacked justification for imposing any such limitations. The authorities' "undifferentiated fear" of disturbance was insufficient. While student expression could be forbidden when it materially disrupted school work or school discipline, these students had undertaken "a silent, passive expression of opinion, unaccompanied by any disorder or disturbance." Furthermore, only this "particular symbol . . . was singled out for prohibition"; political campaign buttons had been allowed, and even "the Iron Cross, traditionally a symbol of Nazism." (Justice Fortas may have been unaware of the vogue among surfers and their inland imitators.)

Justice HUGO L. BLACK dissented, accusing the majority of encouraging students to defy their teachers and arguing that the wearing of the armbands had, in fact, diverted other students' minds from their schoolwork. He did not ask how much the principals' reaction to the planned protest might have contributed to that diversion.

FLAG DESECRATION

Norman Dorsen

The American flag, as a unique symbol embodying national pride and patriotism, evidences the unity and diversity which the country represents, and the varying ideals and hopes of its people. By the same token, the flag has frequently been used by those who wish to communicate opposition to—or even ridicule of—government policies.

Congress has enacted statutes that prescribe how the flag may be displayed and disposed of, and how and for what purposes it may be used. Many state laws prohibit flag "desecration" (casting "contempt" on a flag by "mutilating, defacing, defiling, burning or trampling upon" it) and "improper use" of flags (placing on a flag "any word, figure, mark, picture, design, drawing or advertisement").

In *Halter v. Nebraska* (1907) the Supreme Court upheld a state statute prohibiting flag desecration and use of the flag for advertising purposes. But that decision was rendered twenty years before the Court applied the FIRST AMENDMENT to the States, and it was not dispositive when protesters later challenged the constitutionality of flag desecration statutes.

In *Smith v. Gorguen* (1973), the Court reversed a conviction for wearing an American flag on the seat of the pants, ruling that the Massachusetts flag desecration statute was void for VAGUENESS. In *Spence v. Washington* (1974) the Court invalidated a Washington statute prohibiting the affixing of a symbol to the flag, holding that the display of a flag with a peace symbol superimposed on it was protected free expression. The *Spence* decision was consistent with other cases in which the Supreme Court recognized SYMBOLIC SPEECH as a form of activity protected by the First Amendment. On the other hand, the Court has upheld statutes forbidding flag burning, concluding as in *Sutherland v. Illinois* (1976) that they rested on a "valid governmental interest unrelated to expression—that is, the prevention of breaches of the peace and the preservation of public order."

Public Order and the Public Forum

BREACH OF THE PEACE

John E. Nowak

Breach of the peace statutes are today popularly called disorderly conduct statutes. The wording of breach of the peace or disorderly conduct statutes varies significantly from one city or state to another. Generally, such statutes are violated if a person commits acts or makes statements likely to promote violence or disturb "good order" in a public place. Under modern statutes, as under the older COMMON LAW, it is possible to be guilty of committing a breach of the peace solely through the use of words likely to produce violence or disorder.

When a person is prosecuted for breach of the peace for his or her physical actions there is no significant FIRST AMENDMENT issue. Thus, if a person commits a breach of the peace by punching or shoving other persons in public no First Amendment issue arises. However, if a mixture of expression and physical activity forms the basis for the prosecution, the court must ask whether the person is being punished for the physical activity alone. Thus, a person might be convicted of a breach of the peace for using SOUNDTRUCKS OR AMPLIFIERS if the statute punished any use of a sound amplification device, regardless of the message communicated.

When a person is accused of committing a breach of the peace by speaking to others, a court must determine whether the guarantees of FREEDOM OF SPEECH and assembly have been violated. In addition, the court must determine whether the statute is tailored to avoid punishing constitutionally protected speech.

Although the Supreme Court has held that the First Amendment does not prohibit the punishment of FIGHTING WORDS, it has upheld few convictions for breach of the peace based solely upon verbal conduct. A considerable number of breach of the peace and disorderly conduct statutes have been held unconstitutional under the doctrine of VAGUENESS and OVERBREADTH.

A breach of the peace or disorderly conduct statute that can be constitutionally applied to persons who physically interfere with police officers engaged in police functions cannot constitutionally serve as the basis for punishing the use of insulting or annoying language to a police officer, short of actual interference with the officer's ability to perform police functions.

A person engaged in lawful speech in a public place may sometimes be confronted by a HOSTILE AUDIENCE. In such a situation the police must attempt to protect the individual speaker, or disperse the crowd, before ordering the speaker to cease his or her advocacy of the unpopular message. If it appears that the officers cannot otherwise prevent violence, they may order the speaker or speakers to cease their speech or assembly, and a refusal to comply can constitutionally be punished as disorderly conduct. Breach of the peace statutes may also be applied as consistent with the First Amendment to prohibit conduct that would interfere with the use of government property not traditionally open to speech. Thus, the state might prohibit activities near jails or school buildings if those activities interfere with the government's ability to operate the school or jail.

Bibliography

MONAGHAN, HENRY P.   1981   Overbreadth. *The Supreme Court Review* 1981:1–40.

NOWAK,   JOHN   E.;   ROTUNDA,   RONALD   D.;   and   YOUNG,   J. NELSON 1983 *Constitutional Law.* Pages 954–958, 973–987. St. Paul, Minn.: West Publishing Co.

CANTWELL v. CONNECTICUT

310 U.S. 296 (1940)

Richard E. Morgan

Newton Cantwell and his sons, Jesse and Russell, were arrested in New Haven, Connecticut. As Jehovah's Witnesses and, by definition, ordained ministers, they were engaged in street solicitation. They distributed pamphlets, made statements critical of the Roman Catholic Church, and offered to play for passers-by a phonograph record including an attack on the Roman Catholic religion. The Cantwells were convicted of violating a Connecticut statute that prohibited persons soliciting money for any cause without a certificate issued by the state secretary of the Public Welfare Council. Jesse Cantwell was also convicted of the COMMON LAW offense of inciting a BREACH OF THE PEACE.

Justice OWEN J. ROBERTS delivered the opinion of a unanimous Court: although Connecticut had a legitimate interest in regulating the use of its streets for solicitation, the means the state had chosen infringed upon the RELIGIOUS FREEDOM of solicitors. The secretary appeared to have unlimited discretion to determine the legitimacy of a religious applicant and either issue or withhold the certificate. If issuance had been a "matter of course," the requirement could have been maintained, but so wide an official discretion to restrict activity protected by the free exercise clause was unacceptable. (See PRIOR RESTRAINT.)

The conviction of Jesse Cantwell for inciting breach of the peace was also constitutionally defective. Justice Roberts noted that the open-endedness of the common law concept of breach of the peace offered wide discretion to law enforcement officials. When such a criminal provision was applied to persons engaging in FIRST AMENDMENT-protected speech or exercise of religion there must be a showing of a CLEAR AND PRESENT DANGER of violence or disorder. Although Cantwell's speech was offensive to his listeners, it had not created such a danger.

As a religious freedom precedent, *Cantwell* is important in two ways: first, it made clear that the free exercise clause of the First Amendment applied to the states through the DUE PROCESS clause of the FOURTEENTH AMENDMENT; second, it suggested (in contrast to previous case law, for example, REYNOLDS V. UNITED STATES, 1879) that the free exercise clause protected not only beliefs but also some actions. The protection of belief was absolute, Roberts wrote, but the protection of action was not; it must give way in appropriate cases to legitimate government regulation. The implication was that at least some government regulations of religion-based conduct would be impermissible.

FEINER v. NEW YORK

340 U.S. 315 (1951)

Martin Shapiro

Feiner was convicted of BREACH OF THE PEACE for derogatory remarks concerning President HARRY S. TRUMAN which provoked hostility and some threats from a "restless" crowd. Two police officers, fearing violence, ordered Feiner to stop. When he refused, they arrested him. Feiner marked the post-1920s Court's first use of the CLEAR AND PRESENT DANGER rule to uphold the conviction of a speaker. Chief Justice FRED M. VINSON spoke for the majority. JUSTICE FELIX FRANKFURTER's concurrence urged a balancing approach to replace the danger rule. This case, like TERMINIELLO v. CHICAGO (1949), raised the HOSTILE AUDIENCE problem.

HOSTILE AUDIENCE

Kenneth L. Karst

Nothing is more antagonistic to the FREEDOM OF SPEECH than a mob shouting a speaker into silence. For state officials to suppress speech merely because the audience is offended by the speaker's message is a violation of the FIRST AMENDMENT. Although some lower courts have experimented with the notion of a heckler's First Amendment right, there is no place in our constitutional order for what HARRY KALVEN called the "heckler veto." The duty of the police, when the audience is hostile, is to protect the speaker so long as that is reasonably possible. Similarly, the potential hostility of an audience—even its potential violence—will not justify denying a license to meet or parade in a PUBLIC FORUM.

When police protection is inadequate, however, and audience hostility poses an immediate threat of violence, the police may constitutionally order a speaker to stop, even though the speech does not amount to INCITEMENT TO UNLAWFUL CONDUCT, and is otherwise protected by the First Amendment. The Supreme Court so held in FEINER v. NEW YORK (1951), a case involving no more than "some pushing, shoving and milling around" in an audience hostile to a speaker in a park. The principle retains vitality, although *Feiner* itself, on its facts, seems an insecure precedent.

The constitutionality of police action requiring someone to stop addressing a hostile audience depends on one form of the CLEAR AND PRESENT DANGER test: the police may not stop the speaker unless the threat of violence is immediate and police resources are inadequate to contain the threatened harm. Thus, if the speaker refuses to stop and is charged with BREACH OF THE PEACE, the court must look beyond the arresting officers' good faith—a point emphasized by the Supreme Court in *Feiner* —to the objective likelihood of violence. Appellate courts, too, in reviewing convictions in such cases, must closely examine lower courts' findings of fact. An important difference between *Feiner* and *Edwards v. South Carolina* (1963), where the Court reversed breach of peace convictions of civil rights demonstrators facing a hostile audience, lay in the *Edwards* Court's willingness to scrutinize the record and reject the state courts' findings of danger.

Bibliography

KALVEN, HARRY, JR. 1965 *The Negro and the First Amendment*. Pages 139–145. Columbus: Ohio State University Press.

PUBLIC FORUM

Vincent Blasi

Laws that regulate the time, place, and manner of speech are not considered inherently problematic under the FIRST AMENDMENT, in contrast to laws that regulate the content of speech. As a general matter, would-be speakers can be denied the use of a particular public space for their expressive activities if other proper uses of that space would be unduly disturbed and if different speakers with different messages also would be denied use of the space.

The "public forum" DOCTRINE represents an important gloss on the general doctrine that accords government fairly wide authority to regulate speech in public places. For spaces that are designated public forums—streets, parks, and sidewalks, for example—the regulatory authority of government is subject to careful scrutiny under the First Amendment. Public forums, unlike other public spaces, cannot be devoted entirely to nonexpressive uses; some accommodation of the claims of would-be speakers must be made. In addition, when the content of the speech is taken into account in governing the use of a public forum, as when political criticism or commercial advertising but not expression of a labor grievance is disallowed on a public sidewalk, an especially strong presumption of invalidity stalks the regulation. Even content-neutral regulations regarding the time and manner of speech in a public forum pass muster under the First Amendment only if they are "narrowly tailored to serve a significant government interest, and leave open ample alternative channels of communication."

The historical derivation of the public forum doctrine can be traced to an oft-quoted OBITER DICTUM by Justice OWEN J. ROBERTS in HAGUE v. CIO (1939):

Wherever the title of streets and parks may rest, they have immemorially been held in trust for the use of the public and, time out of mind, have been used for purposes of assembly, communicating thoughts between citizens, and discussing public questions. The privilege of a citizen of the United States to use the streets and parks for communication of views on national questions may be regulated in the interest of all; it is not absolute, but relative, and must be exercised in subordination to the general comfort and convenience, and in consonance with peace and good order; but it must not, in the guise of regulation, be abridged or denied.

The dictum repudiated the doctrine, endorsed by the Supreme Court forty years earlier, that government's ownership of the land on which

277

streets and parks are situated gave officials the nearly plenary authority of a private landlord to regulate access to those spaces. The phrase "public forum" was first employed as a legal term of art by HARRY KALVEN, JR., in an influential article on the topic of speech in public places. The Supreme Court's most comprehensive discussion of the public forum doctrine is in PERRY EDUCATION ASSOCIATION v. PERRY LOCAL EDUCATORS' ASSOCIATION (1983).

Public streets, parks, state capitol grounds, and sidewalks have been held by the Court to be "quintessential" public forums. Public auditoriums and meeting rooms, state fair grounds, and public school classrooms have also been held to be public forums, although the tenor of judicial opinions suggests that officials may have somewhat more regulatory authority to preserve the special character of such places than may be exercised over open spaces such as streets and parks. The Court has denied public forum status to a jailyard, a military base portions of which were open to the public, residential mailboxes, and an internal communications system used for delivering messages and posting notices within a school district. The most important criterion for deciding whether a space constitutes a public forum is the traditional use of that type of space, not necessarily in the particular locale but rather as a general practice nationwide. Some Justices have contended that the dominant consideration should be whether the use of the space for expressive purposes is basically incompatible with other legitimate uses, but that position has not won acceptance by a majority of the Court.

The public forum doctrine has been criticized, primarily on two counts. First, it is claimed that the analytical device of categorizing public places on the basis of their general characteristics fails to give sufficient weight to considerations peculiar to each particular dispute over the use of public property for expressive purposes. Case-by-case variations in the degree to which expressive and regulatory values are implicated tend, so this criticism goes, to be overshadowed by the characterization of a place in gross as either a public forum or not. Particularly as applied to places that do not qualify as public forums, the categorization approach of the public forum doctrine permits government to regulate speech that may be highly appropriate in the particular circumstances and that may not impose serious burdens on other uses of the public space.

Second, and somewhat in tension with the first criticism, it is sometimes maintained that the public forum doctrine is misleading in that the designation of a place as a public forum or not has little resolving power in actual cases. Thus, the regulation of speech based on its content is highly disfavored, even as applied to places that are not public forums. It is not clear what the public forum doctrine adds to the presumption against regulation based on content. In addition, because a COMPELLING STATE INTEREST can justify the regulation of speech in a public forum and because places that are not public forums typically are devoted to activities that conflict somewhat with the use of such places for expressive purposes, it is not obvious that the public forum designation alters dramatically the balancing of conflicting uses that must take place in all disputes over access to public land.

Probably the most important aspect of the public forum doctrine is the principle that public forums cannot be closed off entirely to marches, DEMONSTRATIONS, rallies, and individual acts of expression. In contrast, uniformly enforced blanket prohibitions on expressive activities in places that are not public forums are permissible as a general matter under the First Amendment. Apart from this issue of blanket prohibitions, the significance of the public forum doctrine lies mainly in the tendency of courts to weigh competing particularistic considerations more favorably to speakers when the situs in dispute is a public forum.

Bibliography

KALVEN, HARRY, JR.   1965   The Concept of the Public Forum. *Supreme Court Review* 1965:1–32.

STONE, GEOFFREY   1974   Fora Americana: Speech in Public Places. *The Supreme Court Review* 1974:233–280.

COX v. LOUISIANA

379 U.S. 536 (1965)
379 U.S. 559 (1965)

Martin Shapiro

Some black students were jailed in a courthouse for PICKETING segregated lunch counters. About 2,000 other black students marched there and, in accordance with police instructions, lined a sidewalk 101 feet away. Whites gathered. Cox made a speech that elicited some grumbling from whites; the police ordered the demonstration broken up; the students were dispersed.

Justice ARTHUR GOLDBERG writing for the Supreme Court reversed Cox's BREACH OF THE PEACE conviction, finding that Cox's actions threatened no violence and that the police could have handled any threat from the whites. The Court also held the breach of peace statute unconstitutionally vague and overbroad as construed by the state supreme court to define breach as "to arouse from a state of repose . . . to disquiet."

In striking down Cox's conviction for obstruction of public passages because the statute's actual administration had vested discretion in city officials to forbid some parades and allow others, the Court emphasized that violation of nondiscriminatory traffic laws would not be protected by the FIRST AMENDMENT. The court reversed Cox's conviction for picketing near a courthouse because the police, by directing the demonstrators to a particular sidewalk, had led them to believe that it was not near the courthouse within the terms of the statute so that a subsequent conviction created a "sort of entrapment," in violation of DUE PROCESS. Nevertheless, in dictum it invoked the old doctrine that picketing was subject to reasonable regulation as "speech plus" and supported the authority of a state legislature to forbid picketing near a courthouse because of its danger to the administration of justice.

Although *Cox* is often cited as a case establishing the concept of a PUBLIC FORUM, the Court went out of its way to say "We have no occasion . . . to consider the constitutionality of the . . . non-discriminatory application of a statute forbidding all access to streets and other public facilities for parades and meetings."

DEMONSTRATIONS

Vincent Blasi

The FIRST AMENDMENT guarantees the right of persons to congregate peaceably in large numbers in appropriate public spaces in order to communicate ideas or grievances. In *Edwards v. South Carolina* (1963) the Court described an assemblage of 187 protesters on the grounds of a state capitol as "an exercise of . . . basic constitutional rights in their most pristine and classic form." Mass demonstrations cannot be prohibited simply on account of their size or their need to occupy public land.

Constitutional litigation over demonstrations tends to focus on three issues. First is the question of what public spaces must be made available to demonstrators. By virtue of the number of persons involved, mass demonstrations can be disruptive of other activities even when the demonstrators remain peaceable and orderly. When must those other activities give way to the First Amendment claims of persons who wish to engage in a mass demonstration?

The Supreme Court has never given a definitive and comprehensive answer to that question, and probably never could. The Court has indicated, however, that demonstrations in PUBLIC FORUMS such as streets, sidewalks, and parks cannot be subjected to a blanket prohibition. On the other hand, the Court has upheld regulations that entirely prohibited demonstrations in a jailyard and in areas of a military base otherwise open to the public.

Second, the issue has arisen whether a demonstration can be prohibited or postponed on the ground that audience hostility to the demonstrators threatens to produce a BREACH OF THE PEACE. The Court has inveighed against any such "heckler's veto" in OBITER DICTUM, and has reversed disorderly conduct convictions of speakers who continued their orderly protests in the face of potentially threatening crowds. In language quoted many times in the United States Reports, the Court stated in TERMINIELLO V. CHICAGO (1949):

[A] function of free speech under our system of government is to invite dispute. It may indeed best serve its high purpose when it induces a condition of unrest, creates dissatisfaction with conditions as they are, or even stirs people to anger. Speech is often provocative and challenging. It may strike at prejudices and preconceptions and have profound unsettling effects as it presses for acceptance of an idea. That is why freedom of speech . . . is . . . protected against censorship or punishment, unless shown likely to produce a clear and present danger of a serious substantive evil that rises far above public inconvenience, annoyance, or unrest.

Despite strong dicta and case outcomes favorable to speakers, it cannot be said with assurance that a hostile audience can in no circumstances provide a basis for disallowing a demonstration. The Court has yet to decide a case in which the regulatory authority was confined by a narrowly drawn statute and the police could not contain the HOSTILE AUDIENCE by the exercise of due diligence. There is also the unresolved question of whether demonstrators who wish to proceed in the face of a hostile audience have a First Amendment right to do so on repeated occasions, or whether at some point the mounting costs of police protection for the demonstrators might justify a prohibition on the continuation of their expressive activity.

A third set of issues that arise frequently in disputes over demonstrations concerns the doctrine of prior restraint. Demonstrators who wish to assemble in large numbers can be required to obtain permits in advance, despite the general presumption in First Amendment law against licensing. Officials who administer permit systems for marches and rallies are required to rule upon permit requests expeditiously, and to validate denials in court on a strict timetable. Thus, administrative delay is not permitted to serve as an indirect means of prohibiting mass demonstrations. If a permit request is under administrative or judicial consideration by the time a demonstration is scheduled to take place, the demonstrators may be permitted to proceed without a permit and defend against a prosecution on the ground that they exhausted all channels of prior approval and were entitled under the First Amendment to have their permit request granted. However, demonstrators who do not both apply for a permit and pursue all channels of appeal may be prosecuted for holding a march or rally without a permit, despite the fact that had they applied for a permit they would have been entitled under the Constitution to have it issued.

A fourth issue concerning demonstrations that has not generated a great deal of litigation to date but could do so in the future is whether persons who engage in mass demonstrations can be made to pay the costs of municipal services that attend the event. The Court has indicated in dictum that reasonable costs for such services as clean-up, police protection, and the provision of toilets can be assessed against the demonstrators. However, such assessments can be quite large for major events and can be used as a means of discouraging demonstrations. This issue of cost assessment was important in the litigations during the 1970s over the proposed march of American Nazis in the predominantly Jewish community of Skokie, Illinois, and could emerge as a focus of controversy in other cases.

Bibliography

BAKER, C. EDWIN   1983   Unreasoned Reasonableness: Mandatory Parade Permits and Time, Place, and Manner Regulations. *Northwestern University Law Review* 78:937–1024.

BOLLINGER, LEE C.   1982   The Skokie Legacy: Reflections on an "Easy Case" and Free Speech Theory. *Michigan Law Review* 80:617–633.

SOUNDTRUCKS AND AMPLIFIERS

Dennis J. Mahoney

When the Framers of the FIRST AMENDMENT wrote a ban on laws "abridging" FREEDOM OF SPEECH into the Constitution, the range of the human voice was relatively limited. The invention of electronic sound amplification equipment in the twentieth century potentially extended that range even into distant buildings and behind locked doors. Loudspeakers and bullhorns, whether stationary or mobile, present a particular problem of speech regulation: to what extent does the right to speak override the expectation of peace and privacy enjoyed by members of the public? Especially troubling are soundtrucks, amplifier-equipped motor vehicles that blare political slogans or advertising messages while roving the streets of residential neighborhoods.

The problem of soundtrucks and amplifiers was addressed by the Supreme Court in two famous cases. In *Saia v. New York* (1948) a 5–4 Court struck down a city ordinance requiring permission of the chief of police before a soundtruck could be used within the city limits. The ordinance provided no standard for the police chief to apply in granting or withholding permission. Eight months later, in KOVACS V. COOPER (1949), a five-Justice majority (including the *Saia* dissenters) upheld an ordinance prohibiting the operation within a city of soundtrucks that emitted "loud or raucous noises." The plurality thought the "loud and raucous" test an adequate standard of regulation, while two concurring Justices understood the ordinance as a ban on all soundtrucks.

The danger of public regulation of amplified speech is that restrictions ostensibly directed to the time, place, and manner of speaking will be used as a pretext for controlling the content of speech. But, as technology makes the outside world ever more intrusive into the realm of individual privacy, the right of the people to provide themselves freedom from loud and raucous utterance, whatever its content, can only become more valuable.

TRESPASS

John E. Nowak

A person commits trespass when he or she enters or remains on the property of another without the permission of the property owner. Violation of trespass laws may result in civil action by the property owner or criminal prosecution. Constitutional issues arise in civil or criminal trespass actions when a defendant claims that the basis for his or her exclusion from the property violates the Constitution. A defendant may assert that she was excluded from the property because she engaged in an activity protected by the Constitution (such as the FREEDOM OF SPEECH protected by the FIRST AMENDMENT) or because she is a member of a constitutionally protected class (such as a racial group) disfavored by the property owner.

If a property owner uses the property to perform a public function or if the property owner has become associated with the government in the operation of a business located on the property, the owner may not exclude persons on a basis that is incompatible with constitutional values. A public function is an activity that traditionally has been within the exclusive province of government, such as the operation of a municipality. When a state allowed a private company to own and operate a company town, which included residential and business districts, the First Amendment protection for freedom of speech prohibited exclusion of a woman who wished to distribute religious literature within the town. Operation of a store or SHOPPING CENTER on privately owned property is not held to be a public function. Thus, the First Amendment is not violated when a shopping center owner relies on trespass laws to exclude persons from the shopping mall who wish to engage in speech, PICKETING, or distribution of leaflets.

The Supreme Court will not allow trespass laws to be used to exclude persons from private property because of their race or political activity if the property owner has been directed or encouraged by the government to use the trespass laws in such a discriminatory manner. The Court has held that statutes requiring or specifically allowing a restaurant owner to provide separate areas for customers of different races encouraged racial segregation so that the owner could not use the trespass laws to exclude persons seeking service on a race neutral, integrated basis. Similarly, the owner of a restaurant operated in a government building could not exclude persons from the premises because of their race.

Federal statutes or state law may also limit the use of trespass laws. The National Labor Relations Board, for example, may order store or shopping center owners to allow labor picketers to walk on privately owned sidewalks or parking lots adjacent to businesses involved in a labor dispute. A state supreme court may interpret its state constitution to prohibit shopping center owners from excluding persons who wish to engage in political speech. These state and federal limitations on property owners' use of the trespass laws to exclude persons from their property do not violate any right guaranteed the property owners by the United States Constitution.

Bibliography

NOWAK, JOHN E.; ROTUNDA, RONALD D.; and YOUNG, J. NELSON 1983 *Constitutional Law.* Pages 497–525. St. Paul, Minn.: West Publishing Co.

VAN ALSTYNE, WILLIAM W. and KARST, KENNETH L. 1961 State Action. *Stanford Law Review* 14:3–58.

ADDERLEY v. FLORIDA
385 U.S. 39 (1966)
Martin Shapiro

A 5–4 Supreme Court, speaking through Justice Hugo L. Black, upheld
TRESPASS convictions of CIVIL RIGHTS advocates demonstrating in a jail
driveway, holding that where public property is devoted to a special
use, FREEDOM OF SPEECH constitutionally may be limited in order to "preserve the property . . . for the use to which it is lawfully dedicated."
This case signaled a new attention to the extent to which speakers have
a right to carry their expressive activity onto private property and non-
PUBLIC FORUM public property. It was also one of the first cases in which
Justice Black exhibited the increasingly critical attitude toward demonstrations and other nontraditional forms of speech that marked his last
years.

WIDMAR v. VINCENT

454 U.S. 263 (1981)

Kenneth L. Karst

In order to avoid activity that might constitute an ESTABLISHMENT OF RELIGION, the University of Missouri at Kansas City barred a student religious group from meeting on the campus for religious teaching or worship. The Supreme Court, 8–1, held that the University, having "created a forum generally open for use by student groups," was forbidden by the FIRST AMENDMENT's guarantee of the FREEDOM OF SPEECH to exclude the religious group. Because the exclusion was based on the content of the group's speech, it was unconstitutional unless necessary to serve a COMPELLING STATE INTEREST. The exclusion was not necessary to avoid establishment clause problems, for no state sponsorship of religion was implied when the university provided a forum generally open to all student groups.

Justice JOHN PAUL STEVENS, concurring, said that any university necessarily makes many distinctions based on speech content. Here, however, the university discriminated on the basis of the viewpoint of particular speakers, and that was forbidden by the First Amendment.

Justice BYRON R. WHITE dissented, arguing that the state could constitutionally "attempt to disentangle itself from religious worship."

PERRY EDUCATION ASSOCIATION v. PERRY LOCAL EDUCATORS' ASSOCIATION

460 U.S. 37 (1983)

Kenneth L. Karst

Perry provided the leading modern opinion setting guidelines governing FIRST AMENDMENT claims of access to the PUBLIC FORUM. A school district's collective bargaining agreement with a union (PEA) provided that PEA, but no other union, would have access to the interschool mails and to teacher mailboxes. A rival union (PLEA) sued in federal district court, challenging the constitutionality of its exclusion from the school mails. The district court denied relief, but the court of appeals held that the exclusion violated the EQUAL PROTECTION clause and the First Amendment. The Supreme Court reversed, 5–4, rejecting both claims.

Justice BYRON R. WHITE wrote for the Court, setting out a three-category analysis that set the pattern for later "public forum" cases such as CORNELIUS v. NAACP LEGAL DEFENSE AND EDUCATIONAL FUND, INC. (1985). First, the streets and parks are "traditional" public forums, in which government cannot constitutionally forbid all communicative activity. Any exclusion of a speaker from such a traditional public forum based on the content of the speaker's message must be necessary to serve a COMPELLING STATE INTEREST. Content-neutral regulations of the "time, place, and manner" of expression in such places may be enforced when they are narrowly tailored to serve significant state interests and they leave open "ample alternative channels" of communication.

Second, the state may open up other kinds of public property for use by the public for expressive activity. The state may close such a "designated" public forum, but so long as it remains open it must be made available to all speakers, under the same constitutional guidelines that govern traditional public forums.

Third, communicative uses of public property that is neither a traditional nor a designated public forum may be restricted to those forms of communication that serve the governmental operation to which the property is devoted. The only constitutional limits on such restrictions on speech are that they be reasonable, and that they not be imposed in order to suppress a particular point of view. The *Perry* case, said Justice White, fit this third category: the school mail system was neither a traditional public forum nor designated for public communicative use; rather it could be limited to school-related communications, including those from PEA, the teachers' elected bargaining agent. Such a limitation did not exclude PLEA because of its point of view.

Justice WILLIAM J. BRENNAN, for the four dissenters, argued that the exclusion of PLEA was "viewpoint discrimination," and thus that the case did not turn on the characterization of the school mails as a public forum.

The *Perry* formula capped a process of doctrinal development focused on what HARRY KALVEN, JR., named "the concept of the public forum." In its origin, the concept expanded the First Amendment's protections of speech. *Perry* marks the success of a campaign, highlighted by Justice WILLIAM H. REHNQUIST's opinion in *United States Postal Service v. Greenburgh Civic Association* (1981), to convert the public forum concept into a preliminary hurdle for would-be speakers to clear before they can establish their claims to the FREEDOM OF SPEECH on government property or in government-managed systems of communication.

CORNELIUS v. NAACP LEGAL DEFENSE AND EDUCATIONAL FUND, INC.

473 U.S.   (1985)

Kenneth L. Karst

This decision demonstrated how cumbersome the Supreme Court's analysis of PUBLIC FORUM issues has become since its decision in PERRY EDUCATION ASSOCIATION v. PERRY LOCAL EDUCATORS' ASSOCIATION (1983).

A 1983 EXECUTIVE ORDER limited the Combined Federal Campaign (CFC), a charity drive among federal employees, to charities that provide direct health and welfare services, and expressly excluded legal defense and advocacy groups. Seven such groups sued in federal district court, challenging their exclusion as a violation of the FIRST AMENDMENT. That court agreed, and issued an INJUNCTION forbidding exclusion of the groups from CFC. The court of appeals affirmed, but the Supreme Court reversed, 4–3, in an opinion by Justice SANDRA DAY O'CONNOR.

The Court held that the government had not designated either the federal workplace or CFC in particular as a public forum, in the sense of the *Perry* opinion. Rather, each of these was a "nonpublic forum"—a government operation in which communications could be limited to those promoting the operation's mission. CFC's purpose was to provide a means for government employees to lessen the government's burden in meeting human health and welfare needs, by making their own contributions to those ends. It was not necessary, in excluding the plaintiffs from CFC, to show that their solicitations would be incompatible with the goals of CFC; the relevant standard was the reasonableness of the exclusion. The President could reasonably conclude that money raised for direct provision of food or shelter was more beneficial than money raised for litigation or advocacy on behalf of the needy. Furthermore, the government could properly avoid the appearance of political favoritism by excluding all such groups. Those organizations had alternative means for raising funds from government employees, including direct mail advertising and in-person solicitation outside the workplace.

The Court, recognizing that other groups not in the business of direct provision of health and welfare services had been allowed to participate in CFC, remanded the case for determination whether the government had excluded the plaintiff groups for the purpose of suppressing their particular viewpoints.

Justice HARRY A. BLACKMUN, joined by Justice WILLIAM J. BRENNAN, dissented, arguing that any governmental exclusion of a class of speakers from any forum must be justified by a showing that the would-be speakers' intended use of the forum was incompatible with the relevant governmental operation. Here no such incompatibility had been shown, he said. Justice JOHN PAUL STEVENS, also dissenting, expressed skepticism about the value of a DOCTRINE founded on a series of categories of forum. In this case, he said, the government's own arguments supported "the inference of bias" against the excluded groups.

CITY COUNCIL OF LOS ANGELES *v.* TAXPAYERS FOR VINCENT

466 U.S. 789 (1984)

Kenneth L. Karst

A Los Angeles ordinance prohibited the posting of signs on public property. Supporters of a candidate for city council sued to enjoin city officials from continuing to remove their signs from utility poles; they were joined as plaintiffs by the company that made and posted the signs for them. Of the 1,207 signs removed during one week of the campaign, 48 supported the candidate; most were commercial signs. The Supreme Court, 6–3, rejected constitutional attacks on the ordinance on its face and as applied.

The case seemed to call for analysis according to the principles governing rights of access to the PUBLIC FORUM—rights particularly valuable to people of limited means. Instead, Justice JOHN PAUL STEVENS, for the Court, applied the set of rules announced in UNITED STATES v. O'BRIEN (1968), suggesting the possibility that those rules might in the future be applied routinely to FIRST AMENDMENT cases involving regulations that are not aimed at message content. Here the government interest in aesthetic values was substantial; the city had no purpose to suppress a particular message; and the law curtailed no more speech than was necessary to its purpose. In a bow to public forum reasoning, Stevens noted that other means of communication remained open to the plaintiffs.

The dissenters, led by Justice WILLIAM J. BRENNAN, argued that the assertion of aesthetic purposes deserved careful scrutiny to assure even-handed regulation, narrowly tailored to aesthetic objectives that were both comprehensively carried out and precisely defined. The City had made no such showing here, they contended.

Critics of the decision have suggested that it is part of a larger inegalitarian trend in BURGER COURT decisions concerning the FREEDOM OF SPEECH and FREEDOM OF THE PRESS, a trend exemplified by BUCKLEY v. VALEO (1976) and HUDGENS v. N.L.R.B. (1976).

MARSH v. ALABAMA

326 U.S. 501 (1946)

Martin Shapiro

When a person sought to distribute religious literature on the streets of a company town, the Supreme Court, 5–3, upheld her FIRST AMENDMENT claim against the owner's private property claims. Stressing the traditional role of free speech in town shopping districts open to the general public, Justice HUGO L. BLACK for the Court noted that, aside from private ownership, this town functioned exactly as did other towns which were constitutionally forbidden to ban leafleting. *Marsh* served as the basis for the later attempt, aborted in HUDGENS v. NLRB (1976), to extend First Amendment rights to users of privately owned SHOPPING CENTERS.

SHOPPING CENTERS

Kenneth L. Karst

By the 1960s, shopping centers accounted for more than one-third of the nation's retail sales. Crowds of shoppers made the centers attractive places for the exercise of FIRST AMENDMENT rights such as PICKETING, leafleting, and the circulation of petitions. Two decades earlier, in MARSH v. ALABAMA (1946), the Supreme Court had assimilated the "company town" to the First Amendment DOCTRINE governing the use of an ordinary city street as a PUBLIC FORUM. When shopping center owners sought to prevent the use of their property for communications they had not approved, the question arose whether the centers, too, would be assimilated to the public forum doctrine.

The problem first came to the Supreme Court near the zenith of WARREN COURT activism in the defense of CIVIL LIBERTIES. In *Amalgamated Food Employees Union v. Logan Valley Plaza, Inc.* (1968), a bare majority held that union picketing of a store in a shopping center was protected by the First Amendment. Justice THURGOOD MARSHALL, for the Court, described the shopping center as the functional equivalent of the business district of the company town in *Marsh.* The author of the *Marsh* opinion, Justice HUGO L. BLACK, led the four dissenters.

When the issue returned to the Court, President RICHARD M. NIXON's four appointees were sitting. A new 5–4 majority now held, in *Lloyd Corp v. Tanner* (1972), that the distribution of leaflets opposing the VIETNAM WAR could be forbidden by a shopping center's private owner. Justice LEWIS F. POWELL, for the majority, distinguished *Logan Valley:* the leafleting here had no relation to the center's activities, and here alternative means of communication were reasonably available on nearby streets. Justice Marshall led the dissenters.

The circle closed four years later, when a 7–2 majority, speaking through Justice POTTER STEWART (a *Lloyd Corp.* dissenter), said that *Lloyd Corp.* really had overruled *Logan Valley.* HUDGENS V. N.L.R.B. (1976), like *Logan Valley,* was a union picketing case. Justice Stewart pointed out that *Lloyd Corp.* had drawn an untenable distinction based on the content of messages being conveyed; because that distinction failed, it was necessary to make a yes-or-no decision on the assimilation of shopping centers to the doctrine governing company towns—and the majority's answer was "no."

Some passages in the *Lloyd Corp.* opinion had suggested that a shopping center owner had a constitutionally protected property right to exclude leafleters. That argument was flatly rejected by the Court in PRUNEYARD SHOPPING CENTER v. ROBBINS (1980). California's supreme court had ruled that the state constitution protected the right to collect signatures for a petition in a shopping center. The U.S. Supreme Court unanimously held that this principle of state constitutional law did not violate any federal constitutional rights.

Bibliography

TRIBE, LAURENCE H.   1978   *American Constitutional Law.* Pages 693–696, 1163–1167. Mineola, N.Y.: Foundation Press.

SIT-IN

Kenneth L. Karst

The CIVIL RIGHTS movement of the 1960s embraced more than lawsuits aimed at ending racial SEGREGATION in southern public institutions. It also included several forms of direct action, such as "freedom rides," in which blacks would ride on buses and trains, refusing to confine themselves to places set aside for black passengers. The quintessential form of direct action was the sit-in demonstration. The practice began in Greensboro, North Carolina, in 1960. Four black college freshmen went to a dime store lunch counter and ordered coffee. When they were told they would not be served, they sat at the counter, waiting, in silent protest against the indignity of RACIAL DISCRIMINATION. The next week they returned, joined by increasing numbers of students, white and black. Soon the sit-in technique spread to lunch counters throughout the South.

The impact of the sit-ins was enormous. Many stores and restaurants abandoned their discriminatory policies within a matter of weeks. Most, however, held out, and called the police. Sit-in demonstrators by the hundreds were arrested and charged with criminal TRESPASS. From 1960 to 1964, the problem of the sit-ins came to the Supreme Court over and over again.

When the segregating restaurant was a state operation (for example, a lunch counter in a courthouse), the Court could reverse the conviction by analogy to BROWN v. BOARD OF EDUCATION (1954). Even when the lunch counter was privately owned, the Court would reverse the conviction if it could find some public policy in the background, requiring or encouraging segregation. During the early 1960s the Court was pressed to abandon, or drastically alter, the STATE ACTION limitation, so as to create an equivalent FOURTEENTH AMENDMENT right to be free from racial discrimination in all privately owned PUBLIC ACCOMMODATIONS, irrespective of any state participation. The issue reached a climax—but not a resolution—in BELL v. MARYLAND (1964), when the Court again struck down a conviction on a narrow ground, without deciding the larger constitutional issue.

The Court was relieved of the need to face that issue when Congress adopted the CIVIL RIGHTS ACT OF 1964, which included a broad prohibition against racial discrimination in public accommodations. The Supreme Court quickly upheld the law's constitutionality in HEART OF

ATLANTA MOTEL V. UNITED STATES (1964). Further, the Court held that the 1964 act applied with retroactive force, invalidating trespass convictions for sit-ins at public accommodations before the law's effective date (*Hamm v. City of Rock Hill*, 1964).

Bibliography

LEWIS, THOMAS P.   1963   The Sit-In Cases: Great Expectations. *Supreme Court Review* 1963:101–151.

PAULSEN, MONRAD G.   1964   The Sit-In Cases of 1964: But Answer Came There None. *Supreme Court Review* 1964:137–170.

PICKETING

Theodore J. St. Antoine

Picketing typically consists of one or more persons patrolling or stationed at a particular site, carrying or wearing large signs with a clearly visible message addressed to individuals or groups approaching the site. Some form of confrontation between the pickets and their intended addressees appears an essential ingredient of picketing. Congress and the National Labor Relations Board have distinguished between picketing and handbilling, however, and merely passing out leaflets without carrying a placard does not usually constitute picketing. What stamps picketing as different from more conventional forms of communication, for constitutional and other legal purposes, ordinarily seems to be the combination of a sign big enough to be seen easily and a confrontation between picketer and viewer.

Constitutional determinations concerning picketing have usually involved LABOR unions that are advertising a dispute with employers and appealing to the public or fellow employees for support. The assistance sought might be a refusal by customers to patronize the picketed business or a refusal by workers to perform services or make deliveries there. In addition, picketing has often been a weapon of CIVIL RIGHTS demonstrators, political and religious activists, environmentalists, and other interest groups.

The leading Supreme Court decision upholding picketing as an exercise of FREEDOM OF SPEECH protected by the FIRST AMENDMENT is THORNHILL V. ALABAMA (1940). In striking down a state antipicketing statute, Justice FRANK MURPHY declared that an abridgment of the right to publicize through picketing or similar activity "can be justified only where the clear danger of substantive evils arises under circumstances affording no opportunity to test the merits of ideas by competition for acceptance in the market of public opinion." Despite this sweeping language, the actual holding in *Thornhill* was narrow. The Alabama courts were prepared to apply a criminal statute to prohibit a single individual from patrolling peacefully in front of an employer's establishment carrying a sign stating truthfully that the employer did not employ union labor.

Following *Thornhill* two principal themes have dominated the Supreme Court's analysis of the constitutional status of picketing. One is the "unlawful objectives" test and the other is the concept of picketing as "speech plus." Under the first approach, as illustrated by GIBONEY v. EMPIRE STORAGE & ICE CO. (1949), even peaceful picketing may be proscribed if its "sole, unlawful immediate objective" is the violation of a valid public policy or statutory mandate. Picketing is treated like any other type of communication, oral or written, which may also be forbidden if it produces a CLEAR AND PRESENT DANGER of, or a direct INCITEMENT to, substantive evils that government is entitled to prevent. A message delivered by pickets, however, might constitute a clearer and more present danger than the same message in a newspaper advertisement, for picketing physically confronts the addressee at the very moment of decision.

A conceptual weakness of the "unlawful objectives" test is that it can sustain almost any restriction on picketing by too loose a characterization of the pickets' purpose as illegal. In *Teamsters Local 695 v. Vogt, Inc.* (1957), a 5–3 Supreme Court upheld a state court INJUNCTION against peaceful organizational picketing on the ground that its purpose was to coerce the employer to force its employees to join the union. Even so, in *Amalgamated Food Employees Union v. Logan Valley Plaza* (1968) Justice THURGOOD MARSHALL could sum up the prior DOCTRINE by declaring that the cases in which picketing bans had been approved "involved picketing that was found either to have been directed at an illegal end . . . or to have been directed to coercing a decision by an employer which, although in itself legal, could validly be required by the State to be left to the employer's free choice."

Picketing as "speech plus" refers to two elements that arguably distinguish it from pure speech. First, it involves physical activity, usually the patrolling of a particular location. It is therefore subject to TRESPASS laws, and to other laws governing the time, place, and manner of expression, such as laws limiting sound levels, regulating parades, or forbidding the obstruction of public ways. Furthermore, picketing enmeshed with violence or threats of violence may be enjoined or prosecuted as assault and battery. Second, picketing may serve as a "signal" for action, especially by organized groups like labor unions, without regard to the ideas being disseminated. Some scholars have challenged the "pure speech/speech plus" dichotomy, contending that all speech, oral or written, has certain physical attributes, and can evoke stock responses from a preconditioned audience.

A further strand of Supreme Court free speech analysis is the notion that government may not engage in "content control." Thus, in POLICE DEPARTMENT OF CHICAGO v. MOSLEY (1972) the Court invalidated a city ordinance that forbade all picketing next to any school while it was in session, but exempted "peaceful picketing of any school involved in a labor dispute." That constituted "an impermissible distinction between labor and other peaceful picketing." The "no content control" doctrine obviously must be qualified by the "unlawful objectives" test.

In 1980 the Supreme Court extended the "unlawful objectives" test so far as to strip it of any practical limitations. A 6–3 majority held in *NLRB v. Retail Employees Local 1001* (*Safeco*) that picketing asking customers not to buy a nonunion product being distributed by a second party was an unlawful BOYCOTT of the distributor. Six Justices considered the prohibition justified constitutionally by Congress's purpose of blocking the "coercing" or "embroiling" of neutrals in another party's labor dispute. In *Safeco,* for the first time ever, the Supreme Court clearly sustained a ban on peaceful and orderly picketing addressed to, and calling for seemingly lawful responses by, individual consumers acting on their own.

Safeco might be explained on the basis that labor picketing is only "economic speech," like commercial advertising, and thus subject to lesser constitutional safeguards than political or ideological speech. Although such a distinction would contradict both established precedent and the traditional recognition of picketing as the working person's standard means of communication, at least it would preserve full-fledged free speech protections for picketing to promote political and ideological causes.

Bibliography

Cox, Archibald 1951 Strikes, Picketing and the Constitution. *Vanderbilt Law Review* 4:574–602.

Gregory, Charles O., and Katz, Harold A. (1946) 1979 *Labor and the Law.* New York: Norton.

Jones, Edgar A., Jr. 1956 Free Speech: Pickets on the Grass, Alas!—Amidst Confusion, a Consistent Principle. *Southern California Law Review* 29:137–181.

THORNHILL v. ALABAMA

310 U.S. 88 (1940)

Martin Shapiro

This case involved a FIRST AMENDMENT challenge to convictions under an Alabama antipicketing statute. Normally one has STANDING only to plead one's own constitutional rights. In *Thornhill,* however, the Supreme Court did not ask whether the particular activity in which the pickets had engaged was constitutionally protected. Instead it asked whether the statute itself, rather than its application to these particular persons, violated the First Amendment. Because the statute was INVALID ON ITS FACE, it could be challenged, even by a union that itself might have engaged in violent picketing not protected by the First Amendment. The theory was that the statute's general ban on all labor dispute picketing would threaten peaceful picketers as well, even though no peaceful picketers had even been prosecuted.

Justice FRANK MURPHY acknowledged that the state legislature legitimately might have written a narrowly drawn statute that condemned only violent or mass picketing. Instead it wrote a general ban on all picketing in labor–management disputes. "The existence of such a statute . . . which does not aim specifically at evils within the allowable area of state control but, on the contrary, sweeps within its ambit other activities that in ordinary circumstances constitute an exercise of freedom of speech . . . readily lends itself to . . . discriminatory enforcement by local prosecuting officials [and] results in a continuous and pervasive unconstitutional restraint on all freedom of discussion." Subsequently the Court was to speak of the unconstitutional CHILLING EFFECT of such "facially overbroad" statutes.

POLICE DEPARTMENT OF CHICAGO *v.* MOSLEY

408 U.S. 92 (1972)

Kenneth L. Karst

Mosley is the leading modern decision linking EQUAL PROTECTION doctrine with the FIRST AMENDMENT. Chicago adopted an ordinance prohibiting PICKETING within 150 feet of a school during school hours, but excepting peaceful labor picketing. Earl Mosley had been picketing on the public sidewalk adjoining a high school, carrying a sign protesting "black discrimination," and after the ordinance was adopted he sought declaratory and injunctive relief, arguing that the ordinance was unconstitutional. The Supreme Court unanimously agreed with him.

Justice THURGOOD MARSHALL, for the Court, concluded that the exemption of labor picketing violated the equal protection clause of the FOURTEENTH AMENDMENT. This conclusion followed the lead of Justice HUGO L. BLACK, concurring in COX v. LOUISIANA (1965). Yet Justice Marshall's opinion speaks chiefly to First Amendment values and primarily cites First Amendment decisions. "[A]bove all else, the First Amendment means that government has no power to restrict expression because of its message, its ideas, its subject matter, or its content." As Chief Justice WARREN E. BURGER noted in a brief concurrence, so broad a statement is not literally true; the Court has upheld regulations of speech content in areas ranging from DEFAMATION to OBSCENITY. Yet *Mosley* properly stakes out a presumption in favor of "equality of status in the field of ideas"—a phrase borrowed from ALEXANDER MEIKLEJOHN.

The *Mosley* opinion makes two main points. First, regulations of message content are presumptively unconstitutional, requiring justification by reference to state interests of compelling importance. Second, "time, place, and manner" regulations that selectively exclude speakers from a PUBLIC FORUM must survive careful judicial scrutiny to ensure that the exclusion is the minimum necessary to further a significant government interest. Together, these statements declare a principle of major importance: the principle of equal liberty of expression.

Bibliography

KARST, KENNETH L. 1976 Equality as a Central Principle of the First Amendment. *University of Chicago Law Review* 43:20–68.

BOYCOTT

Theodore J. St. Antoine

A boycott is a group refusal to deal. Such concerted action is an effective way for society's less powerful members, such as unorganized workers or racial minorities, to seek fair treatment in employment, public accommodations, and public services. But as the Supreme Court recognized in *Eastern States Retail Lumber Dealers' Association v. United States* (1914): "An act harmless when done by one may become a public wrong when done by many acting in concert, for it then takes on the form of a conspiracy."

Boycotts by private entrepreneurs were illegal at common law as unreasonable restraints on commercial competition. The Sherman Act of 1890 made it a federal offense to form a "combination . . . in restraint of trade." The Supreme Court has interpreted that prohibition as covering almost every type of concerted refusal by business people to trade with others. The constitutionality of outlawing commercial boycotts has never seriously been questioned.

Employee boycotts may be either "primary" or "secondary." A primary boycott involves direct action against a principal party to a dispute. A union seeking to organize a company's work force may call for a strike, a concerted refusal to work, by the company's employees. A secondary boycott involves action against a so-called neutral or secondary party that is doing business with the primary party. The union seeking to organize a manufacturing company might appeal to the employees of a retailer to strike the retailer in order to force the retailer to stop handling the manufacturer's products.

Although early American law regarded most strikes as criminal conspiracies, modern statutes like the WAGNER NATIONAL LABOR RELATIONS ACT (NLRA) treat primary strikes in the private sector as "protected" activity, immune from employer reprisals. Even so, the Supreme Court has never held there is a constitutional right to strike. Furthermore, the Court sustained the constitutionality of statutory bans on secondary boycott strikes or related picketing in *Electrical Workers Local 501 v. NLRB* (1951). The use of group pressure to enmesh neutrals in the disputes of others was sufficient to enable government to declare such activity illegal.

Consumer boycotts present the hardest constitutional questions. Here group pressure may not operate directly, as in the case of a strike.

Instead, the union or other protest group asks individual customers, typically acting on their own, not to patronize the subject firm. Yet if the appeal is to customers of a retailer not to shop there so long as the retailer stocks a certain manufacturer's goods, a neutral party is the target. The NLRA forbids union PICKETING to induce such a secondary consumer boycott. The Supreme Court held this limited prohibition constitutional in *NLRB v. Retail Clerks Local 1001* (1980), although there was no majority rationale. A plurality cited precedent concerning secondary employee boycotts, ignoring the differences between individual and group responses.

On the other hand, when a civil rights organization conducted a damaging boycott against white merchants to compel them to support demands upon elected officials for racial equality, the Supreme Court declared in *NAACP v. Claiborne Hardware Co.* (1982) that a state's right "to regulate economic activity could not justify a complete prohibition against a nonviolent, politically motivated boycott designed to force governmental and economic change and to effectuate rights guaranteed by the Constitution itself." The Court relied on the FIRST AMENDMENT rights of FREEDOM OF SPEECH, FREEDOM OF ASSEMBLY AND ASSOCIATION, and FREEDOM OF PETITION. The emphasis on the right to petition government raises the possibility of a different result if the merchants themselves, rather than the public officials, had been the primary target of the boycott. But that would appear incongruous. The Court needs to refine its constitutional analysis of consumer boycotts.

Bibliography

HARPER, MICHAEL C. 1984 The Consumer's Emerging Right to Boycott: *NAACP v. Claiborne Hardware* and Its Implications for American Labor Law. *Yale Law Journal* 93:409–454.

KENNEDY, RONALD E. 1982 Political Boycotts, the Sherman Act, and the First Amendment: An Accommodation of Competing Interests. *Southern California Law Review* 55:983–1030.

Special Problems of the Print and Broadcast Media

GROSJEAN v. AMERICAN PRESS CO., INC.

297 U.S. 233 (1936)

Leonard W. Levy

In this unique case the Court unanimously held unconstitutional, as abridgments of the FREEDOM OF THE PRESS, any "taxes on knowledge"—a phrase, from British history, used to designate any punitive or discriminatory tax imposed on publications for the purpose of limiting their circulation. Louisiana, under the influence of Governor Huey Long, exacted a license tax (two percent of gross receipts) on newspapers with a circulation exceeding 20,000 copies weekly. By no coincidence the tax fell on thirteen publications, twelve of which were critics of Long's regime, and missed the many smaller papers that supported him. The large publishers sued to enjoin enforcement of the license tax and won a permanent INJUNCTION.

Justice GEORGE SUTHERLAND, writing for the Court, reviewed the history of taxes on knowledge, concluding that mere exemption from PRIOR RESTRAINT was too narrow a view of the freedom of the press protected by the FIRST and FOURTEENTH AMENDMENTS. In addition to immunity from censorship, that freedom barred any government action that might prevent the discussion of public matters. Sutherland declared that publishers were subject to the ordinary forms of taxation, but the tax here was an extraordinary one with a long British history, known to the framers of the First Amendment, of trammeling the press as a vital source of public information. Similarly, Louisiana's use of the tax showed it to be a deliberate device to fetter a selected group of newspapers. To allow a free press to be fettered, Sutherland said, "is to fetter ourselves." Deciding that the tax abridged the freedom of the press made unnecessary a determination whether it also denied the EQUAL PROTECTION OF THE LAWS. In subsequent cases the Court sustained nondiscriminatory taxes on publishers but extended the principle of *Grosjean* to strike down taxes inhibiting RELIGIOUS LIBERTY.

REPORTER'S PRIVILEGE

Benno C. Schmidt, Jr.

The reporter's privilege issue posed in BRANZBURG v. HAYES (1972) is a microcosm of the difficulties of both journalism and law in accommodating traditional procedures and principles to the development of widespread disenchantment and disobedience in American society. For knowledge about dissident groups we must depend on the efforts of journalists, efforts that will be impeded if the subjects believe that reporters' information will become available to law enforcement agencies. Yet the legal system has important interests in prompt detection and prosecution of crimes. Anglo-American judges have long boasted that no person is too high to escape the obligation of testifying to a GRAND JURY. This obligation is an important guarantee of equality in the operation of criminal law. Thus, courts have historically been unsympathetic to claims that certain kinds of information should be privileged from disclosure before the grand jury. Only the RIGHT AGAINST SELF-INCRIMINATION and the attorney–client privilege have achieved general recognition from American courts.

In *Branzburg,* three cases joined for decision, three reporters had declined to provide requested information to a grand jury. The reporters argued for a special privilege, arguing that compulsory testimony would significantly diminish the flow of information from news sources.

The opinions of a closely divided Supreme Court spanned the spectrum of possible FIRST AMENDMENT responses. Justice BYRON R. WHITE's majority opinion rejected the notion of a journalist's claim of privilege, calling the journalists' fear speculative. Even assuming some constriction in the flow of news, White argued, the public interest in investigating and prosecuting crimes reported to the press outweighs that in the dissemination of news about those activities when the dissemination rests upon confidentiality.

After seemingly rejecting both the theoretical and the empirical arguments for a journalist's privilege, the majority opinion concluded with an enigmatic suggestion that the door to the privilege might not be completely closed. "Newsgathering," the majority noted obliquely, "is not without its First Amendment protection": "[G]rand jury investigations if instituted or conducted other than in good faith, would pose wholly different issues for resolution under the First Amendment. Official harassment of the press undertaken not for purposes of law enforcement

310

but to disrupt a reporter's relationship with his news sources would have no justification."

Moreover, the majority opinion made clear that the subject of reporter's privilege is an appropriate one for legislative or executive consideration. It noted that several states already had passed SHIELD LAWS embodying a journalist's privilege of the kind sought.

In a brief but important concurring opinion, Justice LEWIS F. POWELL emphasized that "we do not hold that . . . state and federal authorities are free to 'annex' the news media as an investigative arm of government." No "harassment" of newsmen will be tolerated, Powell continued, if a reporter can show that the grand jury investigation is "not being conducted in good faith" or if he is called upon for information "bearing only a remote and tenuous relationship to the subject of the investigation." Lower courts have generally followed the Powell approach to claims of reporter's privilege.

Four Justices dissented. For Justice WILLIAM O. DOUGLAS, the First Amendment offered immunity from appearing or testifying before a grand jury unless the reporter were implicated in a crime. Justice POTTER J. STEWART, for himself and Justices WILLIAM J. BRENNAN and THURGOOD MARSHALL, wrote a careful but impassioned dissent. From the right to publish Stewart deduced corollary right to gather news. This right, in turn, required protection of confidential sources. Stewart recognized that the interest of the government in investigating crime could properly outweigh the journalist's privilege if the government could show that the information sought were "clearly relevant to a precisely defined subject of governmental inquiry"; that the reporter probably had the relevant information; and that there were no other available source for the information.

Later decisions have uniformly rejected claims of special privilege for reporters in other factual settings. In ZURCHER V. STANFORD DAILY (1978) the Supreme Court denied that the First Amendment gave any special protection to newsrooms against police searches and seizures. And in HERBERT V. LANDO (1979) the Court rejected a claim that journalists should be privileged not to respond to questions about the editorial processes or their subjective state of mind concerning stories involved in libel actions. Thus the Court has left the question of reporter's privilege to legislative treatment through shield laws and to prosecutorial discretion.

Bibliography

BLASI, VINCENT   1971   The Newsman's Privilege: An Empirical Study. *Michigan Law Review* 70:229.

BRANZBURG v. HAYES

408 U.S. 665 (1972)

Steven Shiffrin

Branzburg v. Hayes combined several cases in which reporters claimed a FIRST AMENDMENT privilege either not to appear or not to testify before grand juries, although they had witnessed criminal activity or had information relevant to the commission of crimes. The reporters' chief contention was that they should not be required to testify unless a GRAND JURY showed that a reporter possessed information relevant to criminal activity, that similar information could not be obtained from sources outside the press, and that the need for the information was sufficiently compelling to override the First Amendment interest in preserving confidential news sources.

Justice BYRON R. WHITE's opinion for the Court not only rejected these showings but also denied the very existence of a First Amendment testimonial privilege. Despite the asserted lack of any First Amendment privilege, the White opinion allowed that "news gathering" was not "without its First Amendment protections" and suggested that such protections would bar a grand jury from issuing SUBPOENAS to reporters "other than in good faith" or "to disrupt a reporter's relationship with his news sources." White rejected any requirement for a stronger showing of relevance, of alternative sources, or of balancing the need for the information against the First Amendment interest.

Nevertheless, Justice LEWIS F. POWELL, who signed White's 5–4 OPINION OF THE COURT, attached an ambiguous CONCURRING OPINION stating that a claim to privilege "should be judged on its facts by the striking of a proper balance between FREEDOM OF THE PRESS" and the government interest. Most lower courts have read the majority opinion through the eyes of Justice Powell. An opinion that emphatically denied a First Amendment privilege at various points seems to have created one after all.

SHIELD LAWS

Benno C. Schmidt, Jr.

In BRANZBURG V. HAYES (1972) and later decisions relating to an asserted REPORTER'S PRIVILEGE, the Supreme Court rejected the claim that the FIRST AMENDMENT should privilege reporters from having to respond to proper inquiries incident to legal proceedings. However, before and after *Branzburg,* more than half the states have passed legislation, called shield laws, that give reporters such a privilege. These laws vary considerably, as has their reception in the state courts. Some laws privilege reporters as to all information gathered in the course of their journalistic activities. Others privilege reporters only as to information gathered from confidential informants. Some laws make an exception to the privilege if a reporter has witnessed the commission of a crime.

A number of state courts have found state constitutional grounds for cutting back on shield laws. Thus one California decision held that a shield law could not immunize a reporter from having to answer a judge's questions about who had violated a judicial GAG ORDER against informing the press about evidence in a notorious criminal trial. And New Jersey's supreme court held that the state's law could not shield a reporter from inquiries by a defendant in a criminal case concerning information relevant to his defense.

ZURCHER v. STANFORD DAILY

436 U.S. 547 (1978)

Steven Shiffrin

In *Zurcher v. Stanford Daily* the police chief of Palo Alto, California, appealed from a federal district court decision declaring that a search of a college newspaper's office conducted pursuant to a duly authorized search warrant had infringed upon FOURTH AMENDMENT and FIRST Amendment rights. There was no contention that the newspaper or any of its staff was reasonably suspected of the commission of a crime, nor was it contended that weapons, contraband, or fruits of a crime were likely to be found on the premises. Rather, the police secured a warrant on a showing of PROBABLE CAUSE for the conclusion that photographic evidence of a crime was to be found somewhere on the premises. The Supreme Court thus addressed the general question of the standards that should govern the issuance of warrants to search the premises of persons not themselves suspected of criminal activity and the specific question whether any different standards should apply to press searches.

The Court ruled that the innocence of the party to be searched was of no constitutional importance. So long as there was probable cause to believe that evidence of a crime was to be found on premises particularly described, no further showing was needed. Specifically, the Court declined to "reconstrue the Fourth Amendment" to require a showing that it would be impracticable to secure a subpoena *duces tecum* before a warrant could be issued.

That the party to be searched was a newspaper the Court regarded as of some moment but not enough to prefer subpoenas over warrants. Instead, the Court observed that warrant requirements should be applied with "particular exactitude when First Amendment interests would be endangered by the search."

The Court expressed confidence that magistrates would safeguard the interests of the press. Magistrates could guard against the type of intrusions that might interfere with the timely publication of a newspaper or otherwise deter normal editorial and publication decisions. Nor, said the Court, "will there be any occasion or opportunity for officers to rummage at large in newspaper files." The Court asserted that "the warrant in this case authorized nothing of this sort." Yet, as the *Zurcher* opinion discloses, the police searched "the Daily's photographic laboratories, filing cabinets, desks, and wastepaper baskets." The Court's application of the particular exactitude standard seems neither particular nor exact.

Zurcher is the first case squarely to authorize the search and seizure of mere evidence from an innocent party; it has raised difficult questions of Fourth Amendment reasonableness as applied to searches of other innocent third parties such as lawyers and judges. By suggesting that press values be considered in an assessment of reasonableness, it opens the door for further distinctions between searches of media and nonmedia persons. By suggesting that the reasonableness of a search is a requirement that may go beyond probable cause and specificity, it reopens discussion about the relationship between the two clauses of the Fourth Amendment.

RIGHT TO KNOW

Steven Shiffrin

The phrase "right to know" does not appear in the text of the FIRST AMENDMENT, nor has it been used as an organizing category in Supreme Court opinions. Nonetheless, the phrase captures several major themes in First Amendment law, and its frequent appearance in editorials concerning FREEDOM OF THE PRESS attests to its rhetorical appeal. The phrase conjures up the citizen critic responsible for democratic decision making and a vigilant press acting as public trustee in gathering and disseminating vital information. It recalls the companion ideas of LISTENERS' RIGHTS and the MARKETPLACE OF IDEAS.

The "right to know" is a slogan, but it is not empty and its content is not exhausted by conceptions of self-government, the marketplace of ideas, or listeners' rights. To be sure, such conceptions provide rationales for a right to know. Most court decisions preventing government from interfering with speakers' liberty have the effect of protecting the right to know. Some decisions are explicitly founded upon theories of listeners' rights, and, indeed, listeners have occasionally been the plaintiffs challenging the offending government action. Not every decision protecting a speaker's liberty, however, is appropriately characterized as protecting a right to know. For example, opinions in which the court has used the OVERBREADTH DOCTRINE to invalidate convictions for using fighting words find little support in any claim of a right to know. A police officer may learn something by being exposed to insulting language, but protection of speech in such decisions rests on a defense of speaker liberty for its own sake, wholly apart from anything the audience may learn.

If decisions protecting speaker's liberty are not always premised upon a right to know, neither are claims of the right to know limited to assertions of speaker's liberty. Indeed, the most intriguing question begged by the expression "right to know" is the scope of such a right. Does the public have a constitutional right to know anything that speakers themselves are unwilling to provide? To date, there is no judicial authority for the proposition that the public or the press has any First Amendment right to information voluntarily withheld by private actors. Indeed, even though the press is sometimes said to act as trustee for the public in getting information, the public has no constitutional right to compel the press to disclose any information it may choose to withhold.

The fighting issue is the extent to which the public or press has a constitutional right to know information that government officials wish to withhold. For a long time it appeared there was no such right. By 1978, no Supreme Court holding contradicted Chief Justice WARREN E. BURGER's contention in *Houchins v. KOED* that "neither the First not Fourteenth Amendment mandates a right of access to government information or sources of information within the government's control." Or, as Justice POTTER STEWART put it in an often-quoted statement, "[T]he First Amendment is neither a Freedom of Information Act nor an Official Secrets Act."

RICHMOND NEWSPAPERS, INC. v. VIRGINIA (1980) constituted the Court's first break with its past denials of constitutional rights of access to information within government control. The Court held that in the absence of some overriding consideration requiring closure, the public possessed a First Amendment right to be present at a criminal trial. Some of the Justices in *Richmond Newspapers* would have opted for a general right of access to governmental information subject to a degree of restraint dictated by the nature of the information and the strength of the government's interests in nondisclosure. Other Justices would have confined the right of access to places traditionally open to the public. What *Richmond Newspapers* makes clear, however, is that the First Amendment is a sword as well as a shield and that the right to know promises to be a developing area of First Amendment law.

Bibliography

BeVIER, LILLIAN   1980   An Informed Public, an Informing Press: The Search for a Constitutional Principle. *Stanford Law Review* 68:482–517.

EMERSON, THOMAS I.   1976   Legal Foundations of the Right to Know. *Washington University Law Quarterly* 1976:1–24.

FREE PRESS/FAIR TRIAL

Benno C. Schmidt, Jr.

Although press coverage has challenged the fairness and dignity of criminal proceedings throughout American history, intensive consideration of free press/fair trial issues by the Supreme Court has mainly been a product of recent decades. The first free press/fair trial issue to receive significant attention was the extent of press freedom from judges' attempts to hold editors and authors in contempt for criticizing or pressuring judicial conduct in criminal proceedings. The next category of decisions to receive attention, reversals of convictions to protect defendants from pretrial publicity, began rather gingerly in 1959, but in the years following the 1964 Warren Commission Report the Supreme Court reversed convictions more readily and dealt in considerable detail with the appropriate treatment of the interests of both the press and defendants when those interests were potentially in conflict. More recently, the Court has considered whether the press can be enjoined from publishing prejudicial material, and whether the press can be excluded from judicial proceedings.

In view of the large number of free press/fair trial decisions handed down over the years by the Supreme Court, this particular corner of the law of FREEDOM OF THE PRESS is probably the best developed of any, and offers a particularly instructive model of how the Supreme Court seeks to accommodate colliding interests of constitutional dimension. Overall, the Court has sought a balance that respects Justice HUGO L. BLACK'S OBITER DICTUM in the seminal case of BRIDGES v. CALIFORNIA (1941) that "free speech and fair trial are two of the most cherished policies of our civilization, and it would be a trying task to choose between them."

In one of our history's pivotal FIRST AMENDMENT cases, the Supreme Court in 1941 sharply restricted the power of state judges to hold persons in contempt for publishing material that attacked or attempted to influence judicial decisions. By a 5–4 vote in *Bridges* the Supreme Court struck down two contempt citations, one against a newspaper based on an editorial that stated that a judge would "make a serious mistake" if he granted probation to two labor "goons," the second against a union leader who had sent a public telegram to the secretary of labor criticizing a judge's decision against his union and threatening to strike if the decision was enforced. Black's majority opinion held that the First

Amendment protected these expressions unless they created a CLEAR AND PRESENT DANGER of interfering with judicial impartiality. From the start, this test as applied to contempt by publication has been virtually impossible to satisfy. Black insisted that "the substantive evil must be extremely serious and the degree of imminence extremely high before utterances can be punished," and, in order to remove predictions about the likelihood of interference from the ken of lower courts, the Court reinforced the strictness of this standard by using an apparently IRREBUTTABLE PRESUMPTION that judges would not be swayed by adverse commentary. "[T]he law of contempt," wrote Justice WILLIAM O. DOUGLAS in *Craig v. Harney* (1947), echoing a position taken in *Bridges,* "is not made for the protection of judges who may be sensitive to the winds of public opinion. Judges are supposed to be men of fortitude, able to thrive in a hardy climate." Under these decisions, it seems doubtful that anything short of a direct and credible physical threat against a judge would justify punishment for contempt.

For general First Amendment theory and more specifically for the rights of the press in free press/fair trial contexts, the chief significance of the contempt cases is the emergence of a positive conception of protected expression under the First Amendment. As Black put it in *Bridges,* "it is a prized American privilege to speak one's mind, although not always with perfect good taste, on all public questions." Drawing upon the decisions in NEAR v. MINNESOTA (1931) and DE JONGE v. OREGON (1937), which stressed the Madisonian conception of free expression as essential to political democracy, opinions in the contempt cases shifted the clear and present danger rule toward a promise of constitutional immunity for criticism of government. The contempt cases are thus the primary doctrinal bridge between the Court's unsympathetic approach to political dissent during and after World War I and the grand conception of NEW YORK TIMES CO. v. SULLIVAN (1964) that the central meaning of the First Amendment is "the right of free discussion of the stewardship of public officials." Beyond this, the contempt cases make it clear that protecting expressions about judges and courts is itself a core function of the First Amendment. Douglas put it this way in *Craig,* in words that have echoed in later free press/fair trial cases: "A trial is a public event. What transpires in the court room is public property. . . . There is no special perquisite of the judiciary which enables it, as distinguished from other institutions of democratic government, to suppress, edit, or censor events which transpire in proceedings before it."

Although the contempt cases focused on the rights of the press and others who sought to publicize information about trials, the next set of free press/fair trial cases, without dealing with the right to publish, looked with a sympathetic eye toward defendants who might have been convicted because of prejudice caused by such publications. Although individual Justices had objected bitterly to the prejudicial effects of media coverage on jurors, not until 1959 did the Supreme Court reverse a federal conviction because of prejudicial publicity. The first reversal of a state court conviction followed two years later in IRVIN V. DOWD (1961), where 268 of 430 prospective jurors said during their VOIR DIRE examination that they had a fixed belief in the defendant's guilt, and 370 entertained some opinion of guilt. News media had made the trial a "cause célèbre of this small community," the Court noted, as the press had reported the defendant's prior criminal record, offers to plead guilty, confessions, and a flood of other prejudicial items.

In 1963, the special problems of television were introduced into the pretrial publicity fray by *Rideau v. Louisiana,* producing another reversal by the Supreme Court of a state conviction. A jailed murder suspect was filmed in the act of answering various questions and of confessing to the local sheriff, and the film was televised repeatedly in the community that tried and convicted him. The Supreme Court held that "[a]ny subsequent court proceedings in a community so pervasively exposed to such a spectacle could be but a hollow formality." Two years later, in ESTES V. TEXAS (1965), a narrowly divided Court held that, at least in a notorious case, the presence of television in the courtroom could generate pressures that added up to a denial of due process.

In the mid-1960s the Court took a more categorical and more aggressive stance against prejudicial publicity. The shift was consistent with the WARREN COURT's growing impatience toward ad hoc evaluations of fairness in its review of state criminal cases. This period of heightened concern for the defendant was triggered by the disgraceful media circus that surrounded the murder trial of Dr. Sam Sheppard. Before Sheppard's trial, most of the print and broadcast media in the Cleveland area joined in an intense publicity barrage proclaiming Sheppard's guilt. During the trial, journalists swarmed over the courtroom in a manner that impressed upon everyone the spectacular notoriety of the case. "The fact is," wrote Justice TOM C. CLARK in his most memorable opinion for the Court, "that bedlam reigned at the courthouse during the trial and newsmen took over practically the entire courtroom, hounding most of the participants in the trial, especially Sheppard." The deluge of publicity outside the courtroom, and the disruptive behavior of journalists inside, combined to make the trial a " 'Roman holiday' for the news media" that "inflamed and prejudiced the public."

In *Sheppard v. Maxwell* (1966) Clark adumbrated the techniques by which trial judges may control prejudicial publicity and disruptions of the judicial process by the press. The opinion is a virtual manual for trial judges, suggesting proper procedures initially by listing the particular errors in the case: that Sheppard was not granted a continuance or a change of VENUE, that the jury was not sequestered, that the judge merely requested jurors not to follow media commentary on the case rather than directing them not to, that the judge failed "to insulate" the jurors from reporters and photographers, and that reporters invaded the space within the bar of the courtroom reserved for counsel, created distractions and commotion, and hounded people throughout the courthouse.

But the *Sheppard* opinion went beyond these essentially traditional judicial methods for coping with publicity and the press. The Court identified the trial judge's "fundamental error" as his view that he "lacked power to control the publicity about the trial" and insisted that "the cure lies in those remedial measures that will prevent the prejudice at its inception." Specifically, Clark admonished trial judges to insulate witnesses from press interviews, to "impos[e] control over the statements made to the news media by counsel, witnesses, and especially the Coroner and police officers," and to "proscrib[e] extrajudicial statements by any lawyer, party, witness, or court official which divulged prejudicial matters. . . ."

Sheppard left open the central question whether the courts could impose direct restrictions on the press by INJUNCTIONS that would bar publications that might prejudice an accused. In NEBRASKA PRESS ASSOCI-ATION v. STUART (1976) the Supreme Court, unanimous as to result though divided in rationale, answered this question with a seemingly definitive No. The Nebraska state courts had ordered the press and broadcasters not to publish confessions or other information prejudicial to an accused in a pending murder prosecution. Some of the information covered by the injunction had been revealed in an open, public preliminary hearing, and the Supreme Court made clear that a state could in no event bar the publication of matters disclosed in open judicial proceedings. As to other information barred from publication by the state courts, Chief Justice WARREN E. BURGER's majority opinion went by a curious and circuitous route to the conclusion that the impact of prejudicial publicity on prospective jurors was "of necessity speculative, dealing . . . with factors unknown and unknowable." Thus, the adverse effect on the fairness of the subsequent criminal proceeding "was not demonstrated with the degree of certainty our cases on PRIOR RESTRAINT require." Burger's opinion made much of the fact that the state court had not determined explicitly that the protections against prejudicial publicity set out in *Sheppard* would not suffice to guarantee fairness, as if trial court findings to this effect might make a difference in judging the validity of a prior restraint against publication. And Burger said again and again that he was dealing with a particular case and not laying down a general rule. But because Burger termed the evils of prejudicial publicity "of necessity speculative," and viewed the prior restraint precedents as requiring a degree of certainty about the evils of expression before a prior restraint should be tolerated, his opinion for the Court seems to be, in the guise of a narrow and particularistic holding, a categorical rejection of prior restraints on pretrial publicity. Lower courts have read the decision as an absolute bar to judicial injunctions against the press forbidding the publication of possibly prejudicial matters about pending criminal proceedings.

Beyond its rejection of prior restraints against the press to control pretrial publicity, the *Nebraska Press Association* decision emphatically affirmed all the methods of control set out in *Sheppard,* including the validity of judicial orders of silence directed to parties, lawyers, witnesses, court officers, and the like not to reveal information about pending cases to the press. Such orders, indeed, have flourished in the lower courts since the *Nebraska Press Association* decision.

The free press/fair trial conundrum has also presented the Supreme Court with the only occasion it has accepted to shed light on the very murky question whether the First Amendment protects the right to gather information, as against the right to publish or refuse to publish. No doubt in response to the Supreme Court's rejection of direct controls on press publication, either by injunctions or by the CONTEMPT POWER, several lower courts excluded news reporters and the public from preliminary hearings and even from trials themselves to prevent the press from gathering information whose publication might be prejudicial to current or later judicial proceedings. Initially, in GANNETT CO. V. DE PASQUALE (1979), reviewing a closing of a preliminary hearing dealing with the suppression of EVIDENCE, the Supreme Court found no guarantee in the Sixth Amendment of public and press presence. The decision produced an outcry against secret judicial proceedings, and only a year later, in one of the most precipitous and awkward reversals in its history, the Court held in RICHMOND NEWSPAPERS v. VIRGINIA (1980) that the First Amendment barred excluding the public and the press from criminal trials except where special considerations calling for secrecy, such as privacy or national security, obtained. The decision marks the first and only occasion to date in which the Court has recognized a First Amendment right of access for purposes of news gathering, and the Court was careful to limit its holding by resting on the long tradition of open judicial proceedings in English and American law. One year later, in *Chandler v. Florida* (1981), the Court held that televising a criminal trial was not invariably a denial of due process, thus removing *Estes* as an absolute bar to television in the courtroom.

The pattern of constitutional law formed by the free press/fair trial decisions has several striking aspects. While direct judicial controls on the right of publication have been firmly rejected, the courts have proclaimed extensive power to gag sources of information. (See GAG ORDERS.)

Participants in the process can be restrained from talking, but the press cannot be restrained from publishing. However, the broad power to impose secrecy on sources does not go so far as to justify closing judicial proceedings, absent unusual circumstances. The interests of freedom of expression and control over information to enhance the fairness of criminal trials are accommodated not by creating balanced principles of general application but rather by letting each interest reign supreme in competing aspects of the problem. Moreover, the principles fashioned in the cases tend to be sweeping, as if the Supreme Court were acting with special confidence in fashioning First Amendment standards to govern the familiar ground of the judicial process. And in dealing with its own bailiwick, the judicial process, the Supreme Court has acted not defensively but with a powerful commitment to freedom of expression.

Bibliography

FRIENDLY, ALFRED and GOLDFARB, RONALD   1967 *Crime and Publicity.* New York: Twentieth Century Fund.

JAFFE, LOUIS   1965   Trial by Newspaper. *New York University Law Review* 40:504–524.

LEWIS, ANTHONY   1980   A Public Right to Know about Public Institutions: The First Amendment as Sword. *Supreme Court Law Review* 1980:1–25.

SCHMIDT, BENNO C., JR.   1977   Nebraska Press Association: An Expansion of Freedom and Contraction of Theory. *Stanford Law Review* 29:431–476.

TAYLOR, TELFORD   1969   *Two Studies in Constitutional Interpretation.* Evanston, Ill.: Northwestern University Press.

RICHMOND NEWSPAPERS, INC. v. VIRGINIA

448 U.S. 555 (1980)

Aviam Soifer

Richmond Newspapers recognized a constitutional right of access to criminal trials. It marked the first time a majority embraced any such FIRST AMENDMENT claim. Yet division and bitterness obviously remained from the splintered decision a year earlier in GANNETT V. DEPASQUALE, which had held that the Sixth Amendment did not preclude closing a pretrial suppression hearing to the press and public.

In *Richmond Newspapers,* a 7–1 majority distinguished *Gannett* and held that the press and public share a right of access to actual criminal trials, though the press may enjoy some preference. In the PLURALITY OPINION, Chief Justice WARREN E. BURGER found a right to attend criminal trials within "unarticulated rights" implicit in the First Amendment rights of speech, press, and assembly, as well as within other constitutional language and the uninterrupted Anglo-American tradition of open trials. This right to an open trial prevailed over efforts by Virginia courts to close a murder trial, premised on the defendant's request to do so. The trial judge had made no particularized finding that a FAIR TRIAL could not be guaranteed by means less drastic than total closure.

Justice WILLIAM H. REHNQUIST was alone in dissent, but only Justices BYRON R. WHITE and JOHN PAUL STEVENS concurred in Burger's opinion. Justice LEWIS F. POWELL took no part in the decision. Four Justices concurred separately in the JUDGMENT. They differed about whether *Gannett* actually was distinguishable, what weight to give history, and what particular constitutional basis mandated the result.

Richmond Newspapers decided only the UNCONSTITUTIONALITY of a total ban on public access to actual criminal trials when there is no demonstration that alternative means could not guarantee a fair trial. Yet the decision is significant for its recognition of a First Amendment right to gather newsworthy information; moreover, some Justices identified a broad right to receive information about government, including the activities of the judicial branch.

BROADCASTING

Monroe E. Price

Broadcasting is the electronic transmission of sounds or images from a single transmitter to all those who have the appropriate receiving equipment. It is thus a powerful medium for communicating ideas, information, opinions, and entertainment. In many countries broadcasting has become an arm of government. In the United States, however, Congress established the Federal Radio Commission in 1927 and then the Federal Communications Commission (FCC) in 1934 to award broadcasting licenses to private parties. Although a number of licenses were also designated for "public broadcasting," most were allocated to qualified applicants who promised to serve the public interest by acting as public trustees of the airwaves.

The asserted basis for government intervention in the United States was, initially, to eliminate the interference created when many different parties broadcast over the same frequency in the same area. Yet this chaos could have been eliminated with a mere registration requirement and the application of property rights concepts, allocating broadcast licenses by deed, as land is allocated. Instead, the potential interference was used to justify a complex and comprehensive regulatory scheme, embodied in the COMMUNICATIONS ACT of 1934.

In 1952, the FCC established a pattern of allocating television licenses to ensure that the maximum number of local communities would be served by their own local broadcast stations, a departure from the more centralized broadcasting systems of most other countries. Although this decision has added additional voices of local news in many communities, most local television stations affiliated with national networks to share the cost of producing programs of higher technical quality. Thus, while broadcast regulation always has been premised on the primacy of these local outlets, much of it has focused on the relationship between local stations and the powerful national broadcasting networks.

Government regulation of broadcasting obviously presents dangers to the FREEDOM OF SPEECH. Notwithstanding a statutory prohibition on censorship in the Communications Act, the existence of the licensing scheme has significantly influenced the content of programs. Holders of valuable licenses are careful not to offend the FCC, lest they jeopardize their chances of a license renewal. Raised eyebrows and stated concerns about aspects of content prevent station management from acting as freely as newspapers or magazines do. (See FAIRNESS DOCTRINE.) Indeed, only in the last quarter-century have broadcasters come to understand the dominant role that they can play in the distribution of news and information in the United States.

Until recently, the distinct constitutional status of broadcast regulation was premised on the assumption that only a limited number of broadcasting frequencies existed and on the right of the federal government to insure that this scarce commodity was used in the public interest. But recent technological developments have belied this basis for special intervention. Clearly, policy and not physics created the scarcity of frequencies, and now that economic conditions have made alternative media practical, the FCC has begun to open the broadcasting spectrum to new entrants, such as direct broadcast satellites, low-power television, and microwave frequencies.

Nevertheless, in FCC v. PACIFICA FOUNDATION (1978) the Supreme Court suggested that the extraordinary impact of broadcasting on society is itself a possible basis for special rules, at least during hours when children are likely to be listening and watching. This rationale appears to be the only remaining basis for giving broadcasting special constitutional treatment. Technology is rendering obsolete all other distinctions between broadcasting and printed material. For the receiver of ideas at a home console, all manner of data—words and hard copy and soft images—will come through the atmosphere, or over cables, or both. Distinctions based on the mode of delivery of information will have less and less validity. FCC efforts to repeal broadcast regulations, however, have often met with congressional disapproval.

Bibliography

COASE, R. H.   1959   The Federal Communications Commission. *Journal of Law & Economics* 2:1–40.

COMMUNICATIONS ACT

48 Stat. 1064 (1934)

Dennis J. Mahoney

The Communications Act of 1934, enacted under Congress's COMMERCE POWER, provides the statutory basis for federal regulation of BROADCASTING and electronic communication. The act describes the electromagnetic spectrum as a national resource and permits private parties to use portions of it only as trustees in the public interest. To administer its provisions the act established the seven-member Federal Communications Commission (FCC), authorizing it to make regulations with the force of law and to issue licenses to broadcasters that may be granted, renewed, or revoked in accordance with "public interest, convenience, and necessity." Under the authority of the act the FCC has promulgated the FAIRNESS DOCTRINE, requiring broadcasters to provide equal time for replies to controversial messages, as well as regulations to prohibit the broadcasting of OBSCENITY.

The act was based on both technological and ideological considerations. The assumption that broadcasting channels are extremely limited has been disproved by improvements in technology; however, the ideological bias in favor of public ownership and regulation has not yet been overcome. Because of the Supreme Court's deference to Congress's findings of LEGISLATIVE FACT regarding the scarcity of broadcasting channels, as embodied in the Communications Act, in the face of the manifest reality that such channels are far more numerous than, for example, presses capable of producing a major metropolitan newspaper or an encyclopedia, the protection afforded broadcasters' FREEDOM OF SPEECH and FREEDOM OF THE PRESS is significantly reduced.

FAIRNESS DOCTRINE

Monroe E. Price

Born out of a progression of decisions by the Federal Communications Commission (FCC) and then codified by Congress in 1959, the fairness doctrine requires a BROADCASTING license holder "to operate in the public interest and to afford reasonable opportunity for the discussion of conflicting views on issues of public importance." Although the doctrine was upheld against a FIRST AMENDMENT challenge in RED LION BROADCASTING COMPANY v. FCC (1969), it has been perceived increasingly as an intrusive exception to the First Amendment, with diminishing justification.

The doctrine, applicable to radio and television licensees and to some cable operators, requires a licensee that presents a controversial issue to provide a reasonable amount of time for contrasting viewpoints. A less frequently litigated aspect of the doctrine requires affirmative coverage of issues important to the public. Finally, the doctrine assures persons who are disparaged on the airwaves a limited right to respond.

The doctrine reflects a distinction in the way Congress and the courts have conceived of newspapers, on the one hand, and broadcasters on the other. Thus, in MIAMI HERALD v. TORNILLO (1974) the Supreme Court held unconstitutional on First Amendment grounds a Florida statute that required a newspaper to grant a right of reply to persons attacked in its columns. The Court did not distinguish *Red Lion* but ignored it.

Recently a campaign to narrow, if not eliminate, the fairness doctrine has gained momentum. When the fairness doctrine was in full sway, its justification was a supposed scarcity of the channels available for transmission of broadcast signals. Those who wished to communicate by the printed word were not curtailed by government action or the rationing of resources. On the other hand, the number of channels for radio and television transmission was demonstrably limited. Cable television and other new technologies have undermined the "scarcity" justification for regulation by providing abundant new channels.

Some have argued that the spectrum of broadcasting channels is a public resource, and thus that the federal government can insist that a private user of that resource give voice to many speakers. In another perspective, emphasis on the right of the licensee to be an unencumbered editor is misplaced. Expressing this view, in *Red Lion*, the Court said that "it is the right of the viewers and listeners, not the right of broadcasters, which is paramount." (See LISTENERS' RIGHTS.)

Recent commentary has proposed quite a different solution to the "fairness" issue: setting aside segments of broadcast time, or even whole channels, for public access. Owners of broadcasting stations would have no editorial control over these "soapboxes of the air." Broadcasters generally consider the fairness doctrine a badge of second-class citizenship in the ranks of the press. The FCC, in the early 1980s, confined the fairness doctrine's scope and considered its repeal. As an interim measure the FCC announced that asserted violations would not be adjudicated individually, but would be considered when a broadcaster sought renewal of a license. Still, despite these limits, the doctrine continues to influence the culture of television. Producers of national and local television news programs take great care to present at least two sides of important controversial issues.

Bibliography

BOLLINGER, LEE 1976 Freedom of the Press and Public Access: Toward a Theory of Partial Regulation of the Mass Media. *University of Michigan Law Review* 75:1–42.

COLUMBIA BROADCASTING SYSTEM v. DEMOCRATIC NATIONAL COMMITTEE

412 U.S. 94 (1973)

Steven Shiffrin

The Supreme Court here considered a FIRST AMENDMENT challenge to a broadcaster's refusal to accept editorial advertisements except during political campaigns. Some Justices maintained that the broadcaster's action did not amount to governmental action, but the Court did not reach the question. Even assuming STATE ACTION, it held that the First Amendment permitted broadcasters to discriminate between commercial and political advertisements. Broadcasters, the Court observed, were obligated by the FAIRNESS DOCTRINE to cover political issues, and their choice to cover such issues outside of commercials protected CAPTIVE AUDIENCES and avoided a threat that the wealthy would dominate broadcast decisions about political issues.

MIAMI HERALD PUBLISHING COMPANY v. TORNILLO

418 U.S. 241 (1974)

Martin Shapiro

It may be argued that FREEDOM OF SPEECH is meaningless unless it includes access to the mass media so that the speech will be heard. Here the Supreme Court unanimously struck down a Florida statute requiring a newspaper to provide a political candidate free space to reply to its attacks on his personal character. Noting that the statute infringed upon "editorial control and judgment," the Court held that "any [governmental] compulsion to publish that which 'reason' tells . . . [the editors] . . . should not be published is unconstitutional."

Tornillo was a major blow to proponents of a right of access. When compared to RED LION BROADCASTING COMPANY v. FEDERAL COMMUNICATIONS COMMISSION (1969), it raises the question whether the FIRST AMENDMENT provides greater protection for the press than for the electronic media. In light of the large number of one-newspaper towns, the scarcity rationale for allowing government to compel access to broadcast channels would seem to apply even more strongly to the print media. Ultimately the distinction may be between the public ownership of the channels and the private ownership of the print media. If so, the Court has not explained or defended this linking of speech rights to property rights.

Freedom of Association; Rights of Government Employees

NAACP v. ALABAMA
357 U.S. 449 (1958)

Kenneth L. Karst

In this decision the Supreme Court first recognized a FREEDOM OF ASSOCIATION guaranteed by the FIRST AMENDMENT. Alabama, charging that the NAACP had failed to qualify as an out-of-state CORPORATION, had sought an INJUNCTION preventing the association from doing business in the state. In that proceeding, the state obtained an order that the NAACP produce a large number of its records. The association substantially complied, but refused to produce its membership lists. The trial court ruled the NAACP in contempt and fined it $100,000. The state supreme court denied review, and the U.S. Supreme Court unanimously reversed.

Justice JOHN MARSHALL HARLAN wrote for the Court. First, the NAACP had STANDING to assert its members' claims; to rule otherwise would be to require an individual member to forfeit his or her political privacy in the act of claiming it. On the constitutional merits, Harlan wrote: "Effective advocacy . . . is undeniably enhanced by group association"; thus "state action which may have the effect of curtailing the freedom to associate is subject to the closest scrutiny." The privacy of association may be a necessary protection for the freedom to associate "where a group espouses dissident beliefs." Here, disclosure of NAACP membership in Alabama during a time of vigorous civil rights activity had been shown to result in members' being fired from their jobs, physically threatened, and otherwise harassed. Only a COMPELLING STATE INTEREST could justify this invasion of political privacy. That compelling interest was not shown here. The names of the NAACP's rank-and-file members had no substantial bearing on the state's interest in assuring compliance with its corporation law.

This same technique—solemnly accepting the state's account of its purposes, ignoring possible improper motives, and concluding that those state interests were not "compelling"—was employed in other cases involving efforts by southern states to force disclosures of NAACP membership such as *Bates v. Little Rock* (1960) and *Shelton v. Tucker* (1960).

PUBLIC EMPLOYEES

Johnathan D. Varat

The government may regulate public employees more extensively than citizens at large because legitimate employer interests in controlling job-related behavior supplement the government's general constitutional power to control the behavior of private citizens. Government employers constitutionally are less free than private employers to control their employees, however, for the simple reason that the Constitution primarily limits government, not private, power. Eligibility criteria, work rules, and myriad personnel decisions take on constitutional dimensions in public sector employment that are absent from the private sector.

The competing analogies of government as citizen-regulator and government as private employer raise related questions. How much more power may the government exercise over its employees than over citizens at large? What constitutional limits bind public employers that do not bind private employers? The two questions tend to converge because, inevitably, the government affects its employees as regulator and employer simultaneously.

The constitutional issues comprise both substance and process. What substantive freedoms may the government require its employees to forgo as a condition of employment and what are the permissible and impermissible bases for disadvantaging public employees? Procedurally, when, how, and with what opportunity to respond, must government employers inform their employees of the reasons for adverse personnel actions?

The constitutional values at stake clash and mesh in complex ways. Government workers have individual rights to exercise substantive freedoms without improper penalty and to be treated fairly by the government. These often vie with government interests in effective, honest, efficient, and democratic management of the public's business. The government also has interests in employee loyalty and in the confidential execution of public policy. These may war with the value of freedom for dissident employees to bring important information to public attention and to check abuse of government power by other officials. Inevitably, public employees have greater opportunities than ordinary citizens both to impede legitimate government action and to prevent government abuse.

Public employees' own rights and the implication of their activities for public governance make the constitutional balance important and intricate, especially given this century's extensive increase in public employment. The existence of 3 million federal employees and 13 million more state and local government workers makes sacrifices of their constitutional freedoms of considerable consequence, both personal and societal. Yet their numbers create a potent political force able to secure statutory job protection and to fend off arbitrary treatment as a group, diminishing the need for constitutional protection. In addition, the size of the public work force increases legitimate government claims to constitutional flexibility in employee management.

Speaking in broad historical terms, Supreme Court decisions on the constitutional status of public employees reflect varying sensitivity to one or a combination of these competing considerations at different periods. Three major themes are discernible, however. The earliest, simplest, and perhaps most powerful is broad deference to government employment prerogatives. This deference rests on the common understanding that the Constitution creates no constitutional right to government employment. The frequently invoked corollary is that those who want the privilege of government work may be compelled to forgo exercising constitutional rights that the government cannot deny private citizens. Justice OLIVER WENDELL HOLMES, then still a state court judge, succinctly expressed this RIGHT–PRIVILEGE DISTINCTION theme in *McAuliffe v. Mayor of New Bedford* (1892). Holmes rejected a policeman's claim that his discharge for political activity violated his right of free expression, commenting that the officer "may have a constitutional right to talk politics, but he has no constitutional right to be a policeman."

The Supreme Court invoked this theme before and after *McAuliffe*. At very different stages of constitutional development over the past century, the Court has consistently upheld government power to foster a nonpartisan civil service by requiring vast numbers of public employees to refrain from active participation in politics, a cherished right of the citizenry at large. The Court has also upheld government requirements that public employees vow to uphold and defend the federal and state constitutions and not attempt their unlawful overthrow, that they live in the employing JURISDICTION, and that national security employees not publish writings about their work until the intended publication is screened to cull out classified information. In the early 1950s, moreover, the Court tolerated government efforts to disqualify from public jobs people who had advocated the forceful overthrow of the government, or who belonged to groups that did, or who refused to reveal their association with such groups, even in circumstances in which private citizens could not be punished for saying or doing the same things.

The right–privilege distinction remains a powerful influence, but Cold War hysteria and McCarthy-era purges of government employees suspected of subversive beliefs provoked the realization that adverse

personnel decisions may involve more than legitimate government interests in employee relations, worker loyalty, bureaucratic neutrality, and
government efficiency. The Court began to impose constitutional limits
narrowly designed to protect public employees from invidiously selective
maltreatment. This second theme protects against improper government
motivation, but not against broad impact. Restrictions on the political
freedom of numerous public employees are tolerated for the legitimate
advantages of having a nonpartisan bureaucracy, but government may
not penalize even a few for constitutionally unacceptable reasons, such
as dislike of their beliefs. In UNITED STATES V. LOVETT (1946), for example, the Court struck down as a BILL OF ATTAINDER a provision of an
appropriations law prohibiting payment of the salaries of three named
government employees declared guilty of SUBVERSIVE ACTIVITY not by
a court but by a House of Representatives subcommittee. Similarly, WIE-
MANN V. UPDEGRAFF (1952) took a stand against GUILT BY ASSOCIATION
and held that government employment could not be denied for membership in a group advocating unlawful overthrow of the government if
the member lacked knowledge of the group's unlawful aim.

With the advent of the WARREN COURT, constitutional protection
for public employees expanded with the gradual adoption of a third,
more complex approach that perceived several values at risk in government treatment of public employees. Increased solicitude for the employees' personal freedom, heightened awareness that jobs often carry some
sense of entitlement, and growing appreciation of the part that government workers play in citizen self-government, intensified objections to
blatant instances of ideologically discriminatory treatment. Reports of
the death of the right–privilege distinction may have been exaggerated,
but its hold weakened considerably. Various methods used to weed out
allegedly subversive public employees, especially LOYALTY OATHS and
compelled disclosure of an individual's associations, were invalidated
on VAGUENESS and OVERBREADTH grounds, because the Court thought
those methods of employment disqualification would excessively inhibit
freedom of expression and association. Those developments paralleled
the Warren Court's general expansion of citizen immunity from regulation affecting individual liberty and culminated in a series of decisions
between 1966 and 1968, including ELFBRANDT V. RUSSELL (1966) and
KEYISHIAN V. BOARD OF REGENTS (1967), that forbade public employers
from requiring their employees as a condition of employment to relin-
quish the expanded constitutional freedoms they enjoyed as citizens.
Pickering v. Board of Education (1968) appeared to complete the rejection
of Holmes's view in *McAuliffe* by holding that a teacher could not be
dismissed for speaking on issues of public concern involving her employer.

After the Warren Court era ended, the broadest implications of the demise of the right–privilege distinction were curtailed when the Court reaffirmed the constitutionality of government efforts to keep the civil service broadly—and neutrally—apolitical. The opposition to narrower but selective disadvantaging based on ideological viewpoint remained, however. The Court has disallowed the firing of public employees for belonging to the wrong political party, except where party affiliation is a legitimate qualification for the particular job. The political patronage practice may distort the political beliefs of public employees, but because it represents discrimination against ideologically disfavored viewpoints, it also elicits the narrower concern for preventing selective arbitrariness. In 1983 the Court drew an uncertain line between a worker grievance and a citizen complaint, allowing dismissal of public employees without constitutional restraint for employee speech on matters of personal interest, but retaining *Pickering*'s FIRST AMENDMENT protection against dismissal for speech as a citizen on matters of public concern. It endorsed neither government's right to impose any conditions on public employment it chooses, nor the employees' personal rights of self-expression. Rather, the Court stressed the government's need for flexibility in employee discipline and the public, not personal, value of employee freedoms.

Protection against employment sanctions imposed for constitutionally unacceptable reasons also underlies the Court's public employees PROCEDURAL DUE PROCESS decisions. Significantly, these protections developed after, not before, the Court established substantive limits on the reasons the government legitimately could invoke to disadvantage its employees. The possibility of intentional government arbitrariness, rather than government indifference to valuable employment opportunities, seems to have prompted the development of procedural protections surrounding the loss of government employment benefits.

The development was part of the procedural due process revolution of the Warren Court. Government benefits that did not have to be granted at all, including employment, could not be taken away once awarded without providing certain constitutionally imposed minimum procedures. Rejecting both extremes, the Court never recognized a right to government work but also denied the government the unrestricted freedom to withhold it. Nor has the Court required that reasons and a fair process always be provided before an individual loses an employment opportunity. Instead, the Court has let the government decide whether to hold out a job as offering some job protection or security of employment. If the government bestows no entitlement by statute or practice, several rules apply. No reason is needed to discharge or refuse to hire. If defamatory reasons nonetheless are given for an adverse personnel action, the employee must have an opportunity to defend against the charge. In any event, constitutionally illegitimate reasons may not form the public basis of the adverse action. If the government does hold out a job as offering employment security of any sort, moreover, the Court disallows deprivation of the secured position until constitutionally adequate notice, reasons, and other procedures are followed. The government worker may not be deprived of employment prospects either for illegitimate reasons or for legitimate reasons that do not apply to his circumstances.

The constitutional law of public employee regulation inevitably affects the efficiency of government operations, the personal freedoms of the workers, and the public interest in checking government abuse and being apprised of how public policy is being enforced. Accommodating these interests is, and will remain, an important and complex constitutional problem.

Bibliography

NOTE   1984   Developments in the Law—Public Employment. *Harvard Law Review* 97:1611, 1738–1800.

VAN ALSTYNE, WILLIAM W.   1969   The Constitutional Rights of Public Employees. *UCLA Law Review* 16:751–772.

HATCH ACT

53 Stat. 1147 (1939)
54 Stat. 767 (1940)

Daniel H. Lowenstein

The Hatch Act prohibits most federal employees from engaging in any of a broad range of partisan political activities. It was adopted in 1939, but its antecedents go back well into the nineteenth century. The act has twice been challenged on FIRST AMENDMENT, VAGUENESS, and OVERBREADTH grounds, and has twice been upheld: CIVIL SERVICE COMMISSION V. NATIONAL ASSOCIATION OF LETTER CARRIERS (1973) and UNITED PUBLIC WORKERS V. MITCHELL (1947). Similar state legislation was upheld in BROADRICK V. OKLAHOMA (1973).

Although public employee organizations are among the most formidable lobbies in Congress and state legislatures, laws like the Hatch Act severely restrict the individual employee's political activities. These restrictions have been justified as assuring impartiality in public service, preventing the incumbent party from constructing a political machine, and preventing coercion of public employees.

The Hatch Act cases contrast sharply with later BURGER COURT decisions such as BUCKLEY V. VALEO (1976), protecting unlimited campaign spending, and FIRST NATIONAL BANK OF BOSTON V. BELLOTTI (1978), protecting corporate spending in ballot measure campaigns.

These decisions, in combination with the Hatch Act cases, suggest that, in the Burger Court's view, no liberty may be sacrificed to prevent unfair grasping of power by the use of concentrated wealth, but a great deal of liberty may be sacrificed to prevent unfair grasping of power by a mass-based device such as political patronage.

Bibliography

COMMISSION ON POLITICAL ACTIVITY OF GOVERNMENT PERSONNEL 1968 *A Commission Report.*

ROSE, HENRY 1962 A Critical Look at the Hatch Act. *Harvard Law Review* 75:510–526.

BROADRICK *v.* OKLAHOMA
413 U.S. 601 (1973)

Kenneth L. Karst

The FIRST AMENDMENT doctrine of OVERBREADTH, developed by the WAR-REN COURT in the 1960s, came under increasing criticism from within the Supreme Court. In *Broadrick,* that criticism culminated in the invention of a "substantial overbreadth" DOCTRINE.

Oklahoma law restricted the political activities of state civil servants; such employees were forbidden to "take part in the management or affairs of any political party or in any political campaign," except to vote or express opinions privately. Three civil servants sued in a federal district court for a declaration that the law was unconstitutional for VAGUENESS and overbreadth. The district court upheld the law, and on direct review the Supreme Court affirmed, 5–4.

Justice BYRON R. WHITE, for the majority, concluded that the overbreadth doctrine should not be used to invalidate a statute regulating conduct (as opposed to the expression of particular messages or viewpoints) unless the law's overbreadth is "substantial, . . . judged in relation to the statute's plainly legitimate sweep." Although Oklahoma's law was theoretically capable of constitutionally impermissible application to some activities (the use of political buttons or bumper stickers were arguable examples), it was not substantially overbroad—not likely to be applied to a substantial number of cases of constitutionally protected expression. Thus the law's overbreadth did not threaten a significant CHILLING EFFECT on protected speech, and could be cured through "case-by-case analysis" rather than invalidation on its face. Appellants had conceded that their own conduct (campaigning for a superior state official) could be prohibited under a narrowly drawn statute.

Justice William J. Brennan, for three dissenters, called the decision "a wholly unjustified retreat" from established principles requiring facial invalidation of laws capable of applications to prohibit constitutionally protected speech. Justice WILLIAM O. DOUGLAS, dissenting, generally attacked the validity of laws restricting public employees' political activity.

On the same day the Court reaffirmed, 6–3, the validity of the HATCH ACT, which similarly restricts federal civil servants, in *Civil Service Commission v. National Association of Letter Carriers* (1973).

PARKER v. LEVY

417 U.S. 733 (1974)

Michael E. Parrish

In a celebrated trial of the VIETNAM WAR era, Captain Howard Levy, an Army physician, was convicted by COURT MARTIAL for violating provisions of the UNIFORM CODE OF MILITARY JUSTICE that penalized willful disobedience of the lawful command of a superior officer, "conduct unbecoming an officer and a gentleman," and conduct "to the prejudice of good order and discipline in the armed forces." The Third Circuit Court of Appeals had held that these provisions were unconstitutionally vague in violation of the DUE PROCESS clause of the Fifth Amendment and overbroad in violation of the FIRST AMENDMENT.

Justice WILLIAM H. REHNQUIST, for the Supreme Court, reversed and upheld Levy's conviction. Rehnquist's opinion rejected the contention that the provisions of the Uniform Code of Military Justice were too vague and overbroad. "The fundamental necessity for obedience, and the consequent necessity for imposition of discipline, may render permissible within the military that which would be constitutionally impermissible outside it," he wrote. Justices WILLIAM O. DOUGLAS, WILLIAM J. BRENNAN, THURGOOD MARSHALL, and POTTER STEWART dissented. The last wrote, "I cannot believe that such meaningless statutes as these can be used to send men to prison under a Constitution that guarantees due process of law."

HAIG v. AGEE

453 U.S. 280 (1981)

Leonard W. Levy

Philip Agee, a former employee of the Central Intelligence Agency (CIA) who was familiar with its covert intelligence gathering, revealed the identities of its agents and sources, disrupting the intelligence operations of the United States, and exposing CIA operatives to assassination. The secretary of state revoked Agee's passport because his activities abroad damaged national security. Agee objected that revocation of his passport violated his constitutional RIGHT TO TRAVEL, FREEDOM OF SPEECH, and PROCEDURAL DUE PROCESS. An 8–2 SUPREME COURT found his claims meritless, because his freedom to travel abroad was subordinate to national security considerations, his disclosures obstructed intelligence operations and therefore were unprotected by the FIRST AMENDMENT, and his right to due process was satisfied by the opportunity for a prompt hearing after revocation. The dissenters did not rely on constitutional grounds.

SNEPP *v.* UNITED STATES

444 U.S. 507 (1980)

Kim McLane Wardlaw

A former Central Intelligence Agency (CIA) employee, Frank W. Snepp III, published a book containing unclassified information about CIA activities in South Vietnam. Snepp did not submit the book to the CIA for prepublication review, in breach of his express employment agreement not to publish any information without the agency's prior approval or to disclose any *classified* information. In a decision remarkable for its procedural setting and for its failure to meet head-on the FIRST AMENDMENT issues implicated by the prior restraint, the Supreme Court, PER CURIAM, sanctioned the imposition of a constructive trust on all proceeds from the book's sales.

The Court recognized, as the government conceded, that Snepp had a First Amendment right to publish unclassified information. The Court found, however, that by virtue of his employment as a CIA agent, Snepp had entered a fiduciary relationship with the agency. Snepp breached the special trust reposed in him by failing to submit *all* material, whether classified or not, for prepublication review. That breach posed irreparable harm to the CIA's relationships with foreign governments and its ability to perform its statutory duties. The constructive trust remedy was thereby warranted.

Justice JOHN PAUL STEVENS, joined by Justices WILLIAM J. BRENNAN and THURGOOD MARSHALL, dissented, arguing that the remedy was unsupported by statute, the contract, or case law. He urged that the contract be treated as an ordinary employment covenant. On this theory, its enforcement would be governed by a rule of reason that would require a balancing of interests, including Snepp's First Amendment rights, and might justify an equity court's refusal to enforce the prepublication review covenant. Further, the alleged harm suffered by the government did not warrant the Court's "draconian" remedy, especially because the government had never shown that other remedies were inadequate. Stevens noted that the Court seemed unaware that it had fashioned a drastic new remedy to enforce a species of prior restraint on a citizen's right to criticize the government.

Political Parties and Elections

POLITICAL PARTIES IN CONSTITUTIONAL LAW

David W. Adamany

"No America without democracy, no democracy without politics, no politics without parties. . . ." So begins Clinton Rossiter's commentary on American political parties. Nonetheless, the Supreme Court has said in *Elrod v. Burns* (1976) that "partisan politics bears the imprimatur only of tradition, not the Constitution." Despite the absence of constitutional reference to political parties, the Constitution has had substantial influence in shaping the two-party system and in defining the contested boundary between governmental authority and political party autonomy.

Frank Sorauf has observed that "[t]he major American political parties are in truth three-headed political giants, tripartite systems of interactions. . . . As a political structure they include a party organization, a party in office, and a party in the electorate. . . ." All three branches of political parties are defined, limited, and authorized, at least in part, by constitutional DOCTRINE. All three are shaped in part by specific constitutional arrangements.

Two-party politics, which has persisted throughout the nation's history, began in the struggle between Federalists and Anti-Federalists over the RATIFICATION OF THE CONSTITUTION. Provisions of the Constitution have reinforced the two-party system, especially Article II, section 1, empowering each state to select presidential electors, and the TWELFTH AMENDMENT, requiring an absolute majority of the ELECTORAL COLLEGE or, failing that, of state delegations in the House of Representatives for election of the President. The majority rule tends to compel the coalition of disparate factions into two parties, because only the establishment of broad coalitions offers any prospect of securing the majority necessary for election of the President.

Although no constitutional rule requires that members of the House of Representatives be elected by plurality vote or from single-member districts, these understandings soon took root after ratification of the Constitution. The popular election of the United States senators mandated by the SEVENTEENTH AMENDMENT has the effect of creating single-member districts for the selection of members of that house. These constitutional practices strengthen the two-party system, requiring broad coalitions to secure a majority, the only guarantee of electoral victory under these rules.

The Constitution's provision for a federal structure of government also shapes the party system. Unlike the majority rule's incentive for factions to consolidate into two parties, the federal structure encourages wide dispersion of influence within the party ranks. Because offices and powers at the state and local levels are more accessible and often more important than those in the national government, party organizations in each state and locale grow independent of one another and are largely free from sanctions imposed by any national party organization. This dispersion of party organization is heightened by the mandate of Article I, section 1, and the Twelfth Amendment for state-by-state selection of the electors who choose the President.

States began to regulate political parties in the late eighteenth century, and these regulations became commonplace during the Progressive era. The STATE POLICE POWER was regarded as a sufficient basis for the imposition of governmental authority upon the parties. The state-prescribed Australian ballot, antifusion legislation, and state-operated primaries were introduced at the same time as laws regulating the structure and activities of political parties. All of these were intended to curb political "bosses" and "machines."

By the beginning of World War II, the constitutions of seventeen states and the statutes in virtually all states referred to political parties—conferring rights on them, regulating their activities, or both. State regulatory schemes went beyond prescribing the methods by which parties would select nominees for office and the qualifications of parties for places on the ballot. Many states also regulated the selection and composition of district, county, and state political party committees, the authority and duties of those committees, and the rules for their operation.

Whether the national government has similar authority to regulate political parties has seldom been tested, for Congress has not chosen to enact legislation recognizing party associations or regulating their structure and activities. Any such federal power could, however, be thought to derive from several constitutional sources.

Article IV, section 1, of the Constitution grants Congress a broad power to regulate the time, place, and manner of electing senators and representatives. In UNITED STATES v. CLASSIC (1941) the Supreme Court construed this provision to allow Congress to regulate individual conduct and also to modify those state regulations of federal elections that the Constitution authorizes. The Court has also cited the NECESSARY AND PROPER CLAUSE as an additional source of congressional authority over federal elections, and in EX PARTE YARBROUGH (1884) it declared that Congress has the power, as an attribute of republican government, to pass laws governing federal elections, especially to protect them against fraud, violence, and other practices that undermine their integrity. And, although no constitutional provision explicitly extends the authority of Congress to regulate presidential elections, the Court affirmed this power in *Burroughs v. United States* (1934), OREGON V. MITCHELL (1970), and BUCKLEY V. VALEO (1976).

Congressional power to regulate elections does not necessarily imply power to regulate political parties. But the Supreme Court has taken a major step in that direction by bringing federal PRIMARY ELECTIONS, which are principally a party process for selecting candidates, within the ambit of Article I. In *United States v. Classic* the Justices held that: "Where state law has made the primary an integral part of the procedure of choice, or where in fact the primary effectively controls the choice, the right of the elector to have his ballot counted at the primary is . . . included in the right [to vote in congressional elections] protected by Article I, sec. 2." This right to vote in congressional elections may be protected by Congress under Article I, section 4. Subsequently, the Court has treated *Classic* as recognizing a general congressional power to regulate primary elections for federal offices.

A wholly distinct doctrinal technique for imposing judicial limits upon party affairs, which may extend congressional legislative authority to party activities, grew out of the White Primary Cases. In NIXON V. HERNDON (1927) the Supreme Court held that because the sponsorship of a primary election by a state was STATE ACTION subject to the FOURTEENTH AMENDMENT, the exclusion of black voters from such a primary was unconstitutional. Even when the state authorized the party executive committee to determine party membership, NIXON V. CONDON (1932) held the ensuing primary to constitute state action. State authorization of a ballot position for candidates selected in party-sponsored primaries, without any state-prescribed primary rules or state operation of the primary, was held in SMITH V. ALLWRIGHT (1944) to be state action in violation of the FIFTEENTH AMENDMENT.

Many commentators and judges regard TERRY V. ADAMS (1953)— the last of the White Primary Cases—as extending constitutional limitation to party activities beyond primary elections. In *Terry* the Supreme Court held that the Fifteenth Amendment prohibited a local group, the Jaybird Democratic Association, from excluding blacks from a preprimary straw vote, paid for and operated exclusively by the association, to endorse candidates to run in the statutorily recognized Democratic party primary. The four-member plurality of the *Terry* Court concluded that the Jaybirds were part of the Democratic party. Only three Justices said that the Jaybird straw vote was limited by the Fifteenth Amendment because it was "an integral part, indeed the only effective part, of the electoral process."

Nonetheless, most judicial decisions now treat party organizations as state-affiliated agencies. State laws often closely prescribe the structure, organization, and duties of local, district, and state party units. Hence, the lower federal court cases have held that the EQUAL PROTECTION CLAUSE governs the selection and apportionment of members of local, district, and state party committees and conventions. Several decisions of the Court of Appeals for the District of Columbia have also applied the Fourteenth Amendment to national party conventions, because those conventions are integral parts of the process of selecting the President. But in at least one case that court suggested that the developing law of "state action," as defined by the Supreme Court, had excluded party conventions from the scope of the Fourteenth Amendment.

In defining the scope of the Fourteenth and Fifteenth Amendments, and thus the scope of congressional power to enforce those amendments, several appellate courts have distinguished between parties' candidate selection activities and their management of "internal affairs." Ronald Rotunda has suggested "a functional standard" in which "all integral steps in an election for public office are public functions and therefore state action subject to some judicial scrutiny." The functional distinction, though plausible and attractive, is difficult to apply in practice. Party activists often seek to influence the selection of party candidates, presumably to assure that party nominees reflect the policies of the party organization. Working through party organizations, they endorse candidates in the primary, expend money on their behalf, and mobilize primary voters for them. These activities could easily be construed as part of the selection of candidates; yet it seems unlikely that they fall within the reach of the prohibitions of the Fourteenth and Fifteenth Amendments—and thus the reach of Congress's power to enforce those amendments.

One further source of governmental authority to regulate political parties is the power to attach restrictions to special statuses or benefits accorded to candidates and parties under federal and state laws. Generally, the Supreme Court has rejected legislation that requires the surrender of constitutional rights as a condition for attaining a governmental benefit. (See UNCONSTITUTIONAL CONDITIONS.) Although it recognized in *Buckley v. Valeo* (1976) that political expenditures constitute protected speech under the FIRST AMENDMENT, the Supreme Court nonetheless upheld the PRESIDENTIAL ELECTION CAMPAIGN FUND ACT's limits on political party expenditures for nomination conventions and on candidate spending in presidential nomination and general election campaigns subsidized by federal money. This decision has broad implications for state regulatory authority in the thirteen states that provide public grants to candidates and political parties.

In virtually all states political parties receive automatic access to the ballot if they obtain a certain percentage of votes cast in a prior election. And in every state the ballot carries the party label to identify the candidates nominated by qualified political parties. These state benefits to political parties may justify state regulation of the structure, organization, and operation of political parties. Moreover, these benefits may strengthen claims that party activities constitute state action, thus bringing them within the ambit of both judicial and congressional authority under the Civil War amendments.

Although the Constitution has been interpreted to allow government to extend special recognition to political parties, especially major parties, governmental assistance to parties is circumscribed by constitutional limits. In *Buckley v. Valeo* the Supreme Court not only held that financial subventions were within congressional authority under the GENERAL WELFARE CLAUSE; it also sustained definitions of eligibility that tended to reinforce the position of the major parties. Full public financing is available only to a party whose presidential candidate in the previous election received at least 25 percent of the popular vote. Some minor parties and candidates are eligible for lesser funding; others are not.

The party, seen as part of the electorate, is recognized by state eligibility requirements for voter participation in primary elections. Connecticut's closed party primary survived the challenge that it abridged independent voters' right to vote and freedom of association. A lower federal court held that the state law validly served "to protect party members from 'intrusion by those with adverse political principles,' and to preserve the integrity of the electoral process," and the Supreme Court affirmed in *Nader v. Schaffer* (1976). The courts have not decided whether political parties' freedom of association protects them from intrusion into the nominating process by persons who are not party members.

State authority to protect the integrity of party membership rolls is limited by the Fourteenth Amendment. A voter's freedom to associate with a party is apparently abridged if state-mandated enrollment rules unduly delay participation in a party primary. In *Kusper v. Pontikes* (1973) the Supreme Court invalidated a law requiring party enrollment twenty-three months in advance of a primary in which the voter wished to participate.

States also have power to protect the integrity of party nominating procedures by limiting independent or third-party candidacies by those who have been affiliated with another party. Hence, in *Storer v. Brown* (1974) the Supreme Court sustained a state law requiring an independent or new-party candidate to disaffiliate from his prior party at least a year in advance of his new party's primary. And in *American Party of Texas v. White* (1974) the Justices upheld a state law prohibiting persons who had voted in a party's most recent primary from signing petitions to qualify another party's candidate or an independent candidate for the ballot. The Court has also intimated that it would sustain "sore loser" statutes which prohibit a candidate who has participated in a party's nominating contest from subsequently qualifying as an independent candidate or opposition party aspirant in the same election. But in the same case, *Anderson v. Celebrezze* (1983), the Court held that states may not protect established parties by setting early filing deadlines that bar independent candidates arising from opposition to the platforms or candidates of major parties, when those become known.

The Constitution has been interpreted to allow preferred ballot access to established parties. Hence, in *Jennes v. Fortson* (1971) the Court sustained a statute giving automatic ballot access to parties that had obtained twenty percent or more of the vote in the prior election, while requiring others to gain ballot placement by obtaining petition signatures equivalent to five percent of those eligible to vote in the prior election. Nonetheless, in *Williams v. Rhodes* (1968) the Court rejected statutory schemes so complex or burdensome as to make it virtually impossible for any but the Democratic and Republican parties to obtain ballot access.

Promotion of political parties through minimal restrictions on the First Amendment right to associate and on the right to vote are justified by a wide array of governmental interests. The Supreme Court has said that states may protect political parties in order to assure "stability of the political system," to avoid confusion or deception, to "avoid frivolous or fraudulent candidacies prompted by short-range political goals, pique, or personal quarrel." Congress, in providing public financing of parties and candidates, can seek to avoid funding hopeless candidacies with large sums of public money or fostering proliferation of splinter parties. In the aggregate these justifications represent a constitutional hospitality toward political parties, at least when legislators grant them special statuses.

Several developments in constitutional doctrine suggest that long-established governmental regulation of political parties may now stand on treacherous ground. The 1950s saw the emergence of an independent First Amendment freedom of association, principally in cases involving dissident or oppressed groups, especially the Communist party. As early as 1952, in *Ray v. Blair*, the Supreme Court sustained a Democratic party requirement that candidates for presidential elector swear to vote for the presidential and vice-presidential candidates selected by the national Democratic party. Such an oath "protects a party from intrusion by those with adverse political principles." But until the 1970s there was little other judicial recognition that the freedom of association might secure rights of major political parties against governmental regulation.

In *Cousins v. Wigoda* (1975) and *Democratic Party v. LaFollette* (1981) the Supreme Court specifically announced that the First Amendment protected national party conventions in their establishment of rules for the selection of delegates, even in the face of contrary state laws or local party practices. In both cases, the Supreme Court announced that "the National Democratic party and its adherents enjoy a constitutionally protected right of political association." Both cases also applied the traditional standard in First Amendment cases; only a COMPELLING STATE INTEREST warranted abridgment of the "rights of association" of the national Democratic party.

In *LaFollette* the Court concluded that Article II, section 1, of the Constitution, which empowers each state to "appoint" presidential electors in the manner directed by the legislature, bears such a "remote and tenuous" connection to "the means by which political party members in a State associate to elect delegates to party nominating conventions . . . as to be wholly without constitutional significance." This conclusion sets aside one possible constitutional basis for state power to regulate party activities in selecting presidential nominees. Together, *Cousins* and *LaFollette* signal judicial reluctance to sweep every stage in the candidate selection process, especially those conducted by the parties themselves, within the scope of governmental regulation.

Indeed, in *Cousins* the Supreme Court specifically declined to "decide" or to "intimate" decisions on several critical issues of governmental authority to regulate parties, thus suggesting that large areas of the law remain open despite the assumption of past practices and of lower court decisions that party affairs are subject to extensive regulation. First, the Court did not decide "whether the decisions of a National Political Party in the area of selection constitute state or governmental action" limited by the Fourteenth and Fifteenth Amendments, and thus subject to congressional regulation. Second, the Justices left open the question "whether national political parties are subject to the principles of the REAPPORTIONMENT decisions, or other constitutional restraints, in their methods of delegate selection or allocation." Third, the Court did not decide "whether or to what extent national political parties and their nominating conventions are regulable by, or only by, Congress."

Although the sweeping associational rights of political parties recognized in *Cousins* and *LaFollette* have sometimes been regarded as limited by the Supreme Court's reference to the special "national interest" in presidential nominating conventions, the Court has relied on those decisions to protect party autonomy below the national level. In *Rivera-Rodriguez v. Popular Democratic Party* (1982) the Court cited *Cousins* and *LaFollette* in holding that a territorial political party, empowered by law to select a replacement for a deceased territorial legislator originally elected on the party ticket, was "entitled to adopt its own procedures to select . . . [a] replacement" and "was not required to include nonmembers in what can be analogized to a party primary election."

These developments suggest that the emerging First Amendment rights of parties may give them broad autonomy to order their affairs. At a minimum, party organizations can make a strong claim to order the selection, structure, and operation of party committees and conventions free from state regulation, even if those committees and conventions participate actively in candidate selection primaries. The federal courts have held that a state law prohibiting party committees from endorsing candidates in primaries violated First Amendment speech and associational rights; they avoided deciding, however, whether party campaign activities such as contributing money were similarly protected in those primary contests. If party assemblies actually select candidates, they may claim autonomy under *Cousins* and *LaFollette,* which held that party rules overrode contrary state laws in prescribing the selection of delegates to national party nominating conventions.

At the farthest reaches, the First Amendment might be construed to allow parties a substantial role in prescribing party membership and qualifying candidates for participation in party primaries established by the states. A state has a legitimate interest in an orderly election process that encourages qualified persons to participate in elections free of fraud, intimidation, and corruption; but its interests do not warrant limitations on the First Amendment associational rights of political parties. Parties may therefore establish voter enrollment and candidate eligibility rules to prevent the intrusion into party primaries of candidates and voters who do not share the party's goals. These party rules would, of course, be subject to the limits that the Supreme Court has already imposed to protect the constitutional rights to vote and associate. Such a theory of party autonomy is consistent with the modern understanding of the First Amendment and with contemporary Supreme Court declarations of party associational rights. It is a theory awaiting full explication and recognition.

Bibliography

GEYH, CHARLES   1983   "It's My Party and I'll Cry If I Want To": State Intrusions upon the Associational Freedoms of Political Parties. *Wisconsin Law Review* 1983:211–240.

GOTTLIEB, STEPHEN E.   1982   Rebuilding the Right of Association: The Right to Hold a Convention as a Test Case. *Hofstra Law Review* 11:191–247.

KESTER, JOHN G.   1974   Constitutional Restrictions on Political Parties. *Virginia Law Review* 60:735–784.

NOTE   1978   Equal Representation of Party Members on Political Party Central Committees. *Yale Law Journal* 88:167–185.

ROSSITER, CLINTON L.   1960   *Parties and Politics in America.* Ithaca, N.Y.: Cornell University Press.

ROTUNDA, RONALD D.   1975   Constitutional and Statutory Restrictions on Political Parties in the Wake of *Cousins v. Wigoda. Texas Law Review* 53:935–963.

SORAUF, FRANK J.   1980   *Party Politics in America.* Boston: Little, Brown.

CAMPAIGN FINANCE

David W. Adamany

Enlargement of the electorate and development of modern communications have heightened the importance of campaign funds for communicating with voters, a purpose less patently wicked or easily regulated than vote-buying and bribery, which have long been illegal.

Modern attempts to regulate campaign financing, which raise sweeping constitutional issues, have been largely centered on the FEDERAL ELECTION CAMPAIGN ACT of 1971 and its various amendments. Federal law has developed along six identifiable lines: prohibitions of bribery and corrupt practices; disclosures of campaign contributions and expenditures; limits on the amount of contributions from individuals and groups; prohibitions against contributions from certain sources, such as corporate or union treasuries; limits on total expenditures; and public financing.

Although the regulation of bribery and corrupt practices does not generally raise significant constitutional issues, all of the other elements of the Federal Election Campaign Act and of comparable state laws do. In BUCKLEY v. VALEO (1976), the landmark case on the constitutionality of political finance regulations, the Supreme Court held that expenditures to advocate the election or defeat of candidates are constitutionally protected speech and may not be limited. Subsequent decisions have held that no limit may be imposed on expenditures in REFERENDUM or INITIATIVE campaigns. And in *Common Cause v. Schmitt* (1982) an evenly divided Court sustained a lower court ruling that limits on expenditures by groups or individuals, acting independently, were impermissible, even when the candidate has agreed to limits as a condition for obtaining campaign public subsidies.

Campaign contributions embody a lesser element of constitutionally protected speech, but they are also an exercise of FREEDOM OF ASSEMBLY AND ASSOCIATION guaranteed in the FIRST AMENDMENT. Contributions may be limited to achieve COMPELLING STATE INTERESTS, such as avoidance of "the actuality and appearance of corruption." The Supreme Court has not yet identified any other compelling interest that justifies limits on campaign contributions. Hence, in *Buckley* the Court voided limits on a candidate's contributions to his own campaign and, in *Citizens Against Rent Control v. Berkeley* (1981), invalidated limits on contributions in referendum campaigns, because in neither case did the contributions pose a danger of corrupting candidates.

The rule against expenditures by and contributions from CORPORA-TIONS, labor unions, and other specified sources has not yet been tested in court, but its justification is largely undermined by FIRST NATIONAL BANK OF BOSTON V. BELLOTTI (1978), which struck down limits on referendum expenditures by corporations because First Amendment speech rights extend to corporations. Presumably the speech and association rights inherent in making contributions attach to corporations, unions, and other associations, and only limits necessary to avoid the actuality or appearance of corruption could be applied.

Public subsidies of campaigns and parties have been adopted by Congress and several states. In *Buckley* the Court held that such expenditures are within the ambit of the spending power of the general welfare clause. The Court also sustained a limit on expenditures for candidates who voluntarily accept public subsidies. No unconstitutional discrimination was found in limiting eligibility for subsidies to parties that had received a specified percentage of the vote in a prior election.

The Court has acknowledged that some persons may be deterred from making contributions and others may be subject to harassment if they exercise their constitutional right to make contributions, but substantial governmental interests warrant disclosure because it assists voters to evaluate candidates, deters corruption, and facilitates enforcement of contribution limits. Minor parties and independent candidates, however, because they have only a modest likelihood of coming to power and because they are often unpopular, need show only "a reasonable probability that compelled disclosure . . . of contributors will subject them to threats, harassment, or reprisals" in order to obtain relief from the disclosure requirements. Minor-party expenditures were also held exempt from disclosure, in BROWN V. SOCIALIST WORKERS '74 CAMPAIGN COMMITTEE (1982), to protect First Amendment political activity.

Equality and liberty, both values rooted in the Constitution, come into conflict in regulation of political finance. Limitations on contributions and expenditures have been justified as efforts to equalize the influence of citizens and groups in the political process. Money and the control of technology, especially communications media, pose special problems of scale; the magnitude of potential inequality between citizens far exceeds that which occurs in traditional or conventional political participation.

In balancing First Amendment liberties and the concern for political equality, the Supreme Court has, in the area of campaign finance, consistently given preference to speech and association rights, with little reference to the inequality this may produce between citizens. The Court has sustained limits on contributions only to avoid corruption, not to achieve equality. Similarly, the Court has permitted public subsidies, which equalize funds available to candidates, and expenditure limits attached to such subsidies, which create an equal ceiling on spending. But equality is not the controlling principle; the Court has made clear that candidate participation in public subsidy-and limitation schemes must be voluntary and that such schemes do not impose ceilings on expenditures by persons acting independently of candidates.

Although equality in the political process has constitutional imprimatur in voting, contemporary constitutional doctrines relating to campaign finance neither acknowledge the validity of equality interests nor provide means for effecting them.

Bibliography

NICHOLSON, MARLENE   1977   Buckley v. Valeo: The Constitutionality of the Federal Election Campaign Act Amendments of 1974. *Wisconsin Law Review* 1977:323–374.

FEDERAL ELECTION CAMPAIGN ACTS

Presidential Election Campaign Fund Act
85 Stat. 497 (1971)

Federal Election Campaign Act
86 Stat. 3 (1971)

Federal Election Campaign Act
88 Stat. 1263 (1974)

Dennis J. Mahoney

The success of constitutional democracy depends upon the integrity and autonomy of the electoral process. But whether that integrity is threatened more seriously by wealthy individuals and organizations than by regulations that prevent individuals and organizations from using their resources to promote candidates and policies is a matter for debate. During the 1970s several attempts at campaign finance "reform" were enacted, resulting in an almost complete switch from private to public financing at least of the presidential general election campaigns.

Two reform statutes were enacted in 1971: the Federal Election Campaign Act (FECA) and the Presidential Election Campaign Fund Act. The former required any committee receiving or spending more than $1,000 in a campaign for federal office to register with the federal government and publish reports of contributions and expenditures. It also prohibited contributions under names other than that of the actual donor and limited total expenditures on campaign advertising. The second statute created a fund of public money to replace private contributions in financing presidential election campaigns. By means of a "check-off" device, taxpayers would nominally designate one dollar of their annual federal income tax payment for the election campaign fund. Acceptance of these public funds precluded a party or campaign committee from accepting any private contributions.

The FECA of 1974 was an extremely comprehensive effort to regulate the "time, place, and manner" of electing federal officials. Among the provisions of the 1974 act were: maximum spending limits for presidential nominating and general election campaigns; federal matching funds for qualifying candidates in major party nominating campaigns; complete federal funding of major party candidates in the general election campaign; limits on contributions of individuals, organizations, and political action committees to campaigns for Congress and for the presidential nominations; limits on campaign spending per state in presidential nomination campaigns; and rigorous accounting and reporting requirements for campaign finance committees. In addition, the 1974 act created a six-member Federal Elections Commission to enforce the other provisions of the act; the commission was to comprise members appointed by the President, the speaker of the House of Representatives, and the president pro tempore of the Senate.

The Supreme Court heard major constitutional challenges to the 1974 act even as the first campaign was being conducted under it. In BUCKLEY v. VALEO (1976) the Court held unconstitutional the method of appointment of the commission (because the Constitution grants to the President alone the power to appoint federal officers) and all the spending limitations imposed other than as a condition for receiving federal matching funds. The rationale for the latter holding was that the commitment of funds in support of a candidate or cause was a form of expression protected under the FIRST AMENDMENT.

The tendency toward public financing of electoral campaigns, with accompanying regulation, works to the advantage of incumbents and to the disadvantage of challengers, who usually need to spend more than their opponents to overcome the advantages of incumbency. The scheme for financing and regulating the presidential election campaigns serves to insulate the two major parties from challenges by third parties or independent candidates. While claiming to protect the people from the "fat cats," federal politicians have taken steps to protect themselves from the people.

Bibliography

ALEXANDER, HERBERT E.   1980   *Financing Politics: Money, Elections and Political Reform.* Washington, D.C.: Congressional Quarterly.

BUCKLEY v. VALEO

424 U.S. 1 (1976)

Martin Shapiro

In *Buckley* the Supreme Court dealt with a number of constitutional challenges to the complex provisions of the FEDERAL ELECTIONS CAMPAIGN ACT. The act provided for a Federal Elections Commission, members of which were to be appointed variously by the President and certain congressional leaders. The Court held the congressional appointment unconstitutional; Article 2, section 2, prescribes a process for appointing all officers who carry out executive and quasi-judicial duties: appointment by the President, with confirmation by the Senate. Congress subsequently amended the statute to meet the Court's objections.

Rejecting both FIRST AMENDMENT and EQUAL PROTECTION challenges, the Court upheld, 7–2, the provision of public funds for presidential campaigns in amounts that favored major parties over minor parties.

The Court used a BALANCING TEST in considering First Amendment challenges to the provisions limiting expenditures by candidates and contributions to candidates in congressional elections. For both expenditures and contributions the Court defined the government's interest as preventing corruption and appearance of corruption.

The Court placed the interest of the candidate in FREEDOM OF SPEECH on the other side of the balance in striking down the expenditure provisions. Limiting expenditure limited the amount of speech a candidate might make. The Court rejected the argument that another legitimate purpose of the statute was to equalize the campaign opportunities of rich and poor candidates. The PER CURIAM opinion said that the government might not seek to equalize speech by leveling down the rights of rich speakers. High expenditures by rich candidates created no risk of corruption. Indeed, the opinion demonstrated that such a candidate was not dependent on others' money.

In upholding the contribution limits, the Court characterized the First Amendment interest of contributors not as freedom of speech but freedom of association. It reasoned that the initial contribution of $1,000 allowed by the statute completed the act of association and that further contributions did not significantly enhance the association. Further contributions did, however, increase the risk of corruption.

The statute's requirement that all contributions over $100 be a matter of public record were challenged as violating the right to anonymous political association previously recognized in NAACP v. ALABAMA (1958). The Court upheld the reporting provisions but said that individual applications to contributors to small unpopular parties might be unconstitutional.

Bibliography

POLSBY, DANIEL D.   1976   Buckley v. Valeo: The Special Nature of Political Speech. *Supreme Court Review* 1976:1–44.

FIRST NATIONAL BANK OF BOSTON v. BELLOTTI

435 U.S. 765 (1978)

Martin Shapiro

Although the Supreme Court had extended FIRST AMENDMENT protections to newspapers that were organized as CORPORATIONS, this was the first case to hold explicitly that the FREEDOM OF SPEECH was not a "purely personal" right such as the RIGHT AGAINST SELF-INCRIMINATION and so might be claimed by corporations. In this case and in VIRGINIA STATE BOARD OF PHARMACY v. VIRGINIA CITY CONSUMER COUNCIL (1976), the Justices adopted the position that where there is a willing speaker, he may be protected by the First Amendment not so much because of his own speech interest but because of the societal interest in maximizing the stock of information upon which the public may draw. Thus a banking corporation was held to have speech rights because limiting its speech would limit the electorate's access to vital information.

After defeat of a REFERENDUM authorizing a personal income tax, which was attributed by some to corporation-funded advertising, Massachusetts adopted a statute forbidding a corporation to spend money for the purpose of influencing the vote on referenda not directly affecting the corporation, including referenda on individual income taxation. In the face of this obvious attempt of protax legislators to muzzle their opponents, Justice LEWIS F. POWELL for the Court had little trouble concluding under a BALANCING TEST that the asserted state interests in preserving the integrity of the electoral process were not compelling and that the statute was not narrowly drawn to protect the interests of stockholders.

The dissent by Justices BYRON R. WHITE, WILLIAM J. BRENNAN, and THURGOOD MARSHALL sounds the theme of a legitimate state interest in limiting the influence of money on elections raised in BUCKLEY v. VALEO (1976). Justice WILLIAM H. REHNQUIST dissented alone on STATES' RIGHTS grounds.

With the recognition of corporate speech rights and the recognition of some First Amendment protection for COMMERCIAL SPEECH, the Court set the stage for a whole new area of freedom-of-speech jurisprudence, particularly in the light of the high levels of corporate institutional and issue advertising engendered by environmental, energy, and deregulation policies. Among the difficult problems are the rights of stockholders who oppose advertised corporate stances and the extent to which laws against false and misleading advertising constitutionally can be applied to advertisements that do more than offer a product for sale.

Religion: The Establishment Clause

ESTABLISHMENT OF RELIGION

Leonard W. Levy

The FIRST AMENDMENT begins with the clause, "Congress shall make no law respecting an establishment of religion. . . ." There are two basic interpretations of what the framers meant by this clause. In EVERSON v. BOARD OF EDUCATION (1947), the first decision on the clause, the Supreme Court unanimously adopted the broad interpretation, although the Justices then and thereafter disagreed on its application. (See SEPARATION OF CHURCH AND STATE.) Justice HUGO L. BLACK declared that the clause means not only that government cannot set up a church but also that government cannot aid all religions impartially or levy a tax for the support of any religious activities, institutions, or practices. "In the words of [THOMAS] JEFFERSON," Black said, "the clause against establishment of religion by laws was intended to erect 'a wall of separation between Church and State.' "

EDWARD S. CORWIN, a distinguished constitutional scholar who espoused the narrow view of the clause, asserted that the Court's interpretation was "untrue historically." What the clause does, he wrote, "and all that it does, is to forbid Congress to give any religious faith, sect, or denomination preferred status. . . . The historical record shows beyond peradventure that the core idea of 'an establishment of religion' comprises the idea of preference; and that any act of public authority favorable to religion in general cannot, without manifest falsification of history, be brought under the ban of that phase" (Corwin, "Supreme Court as National School Board," pp. 10, 20). Justice POTTER STEWART, dissenting in ENGEL v. VITALE (1962), endorsed the narrow view when he noted that a nondenominational school prayer did not confront the Court with "the establishment of a state church" or an "official religion."

The debate in the First Congress, which proposed the First Amendment, provides support for neither the broad nor the narrow interpretation. The history of the drafting of the clause, however, is revealing. Congress carefully considered and rejected various phrasings that embraced the narrow interpretation. At bottom the amendment was an expression of the intention of the Framers of the Constitution to prevent Congress from acting in the field of religion. The "great object" of the BILL OF RIGHTS, JAMES MADISON had said, when introducing his draft of amendments to the House, was to "limit and qualify the powers of Government" for the purpose of making certain that none of the powers granted could be exercised in forbidden fields, including religion. The history of the drafting of the establishment clause does not provide a clear understanding of what was meant by the phrase "an establishment of religion." But the narrow interpretation, which permits government aid to religion in general or on a nonpreferential basis, leads to the impossible conclusion that the First Amendment *added* to Congress's powers. The amendment meant to restrict Congress to the powers that it possessed, and since it had no power to legislate on matters concerning religion, and therefore could not support religion on any basis, Congress would have had no such power even in the absence of the First Amendment. To suppose that an express prohibition on power vests or creates power is capriciously unreasonable. The Bill of Rights, as Madison said, was not framed "to imply powers not meant to be included in the enumeration."

Congress did not define "an establishment of religion" because its members knew from common experience what they meant. At the time of the framing of the amendment, six states maintained or authorized establishments of religion. That amendment denied to Congress the power to do what those states were doing, and since *Everson* the states come under the same ban. An establishment meant to the framers of the amendment what it meant in those states. Thus, reference to the American experience with establishments at the time of the framing of the Bill of Rights is essential to any understanding of what the clause in question meant.

The narrow interpretation is based on European precedents but the European form of an establishment was not the American form, except in the Southern colonies before the American Revolution, and the European meaning of establishment was not the American meaning. The revolution triggered a pent-up movement for separation of church and state in the nine states that had establishments. Of these nine, North Carolina (1776), New York (1777), and Virginia (1786) separated church and state. Each of the remaining six states made concessions to anti-establishment sentiment by broadening their old establishments. After the Revolution, none maintained a single or exclusive establishment. In all six an establishment of religion was not restricted to a state church or a system of public support of one denomination; in all an establishment meant public support of all denominations and sects on a nonpreferential basis.

Three of these six states were in New England. The MASSACHUSETTS CONSTITUTION (1780) authorized its towns and parishes to levy taxes for the support of Protestant churches, provided that each taxpayer's money go to the support "of his own religious sect or denomination" and added that "no subordination of any one sect or denomination to the other shall ever be established by law." An establishment in Massachusetts meant government support of religion. Congregationalists, for a few decades, benefited the most, because they were the most numerous and resorted to various tricks to fleece non-Congregationalists out of their share of religious taxes. But the fact remains that Massachusetts had a multiple, not a single, establishment under which Baptist, Episcopalian, Methodist, and Unitarian churches were publicly supported until the establishment ended in 1833. In 1784 Connecticut and New Hampshire modeled their multiple establishments after that of Massachusetts, ending them in 1818 and 1819, respectively.

In the South, where the Episcopal Church was the sole established church before the revolution, three states either maintained or permitted establishments of religion, and in each the multiple form was the only legal one. Maryland (1776) permitted its legislature to tax for the support of "the Christian religion," with the proviso that every person had the right to designate the church of his choice, making every Christian church an established church on a nonpreferential basis. The legislature sought to pass an enabling act in 1785, but the nonpreferential system was denounced as an establishment and defeated. The situation in Georgia was the same as in Maryland, and a revised constitution (1789), which was in effect when the First Amendment was adopted, continued the multiple establishment system, allowing each person to support only his own church. South Carolina restricted its multiple nonpreferential establishment to Protestant churches. The last Southern establishment died in 1810. Virginia sought to emulate the Maryland system, but a general assessment bill benefiting all Christian churches failed, thanks to the opposition of most non-Episcopal denominations and to MADISON'S MEMORIAL AND REMONSTRANCE; the VIRGINIA STATUTE OF RELIGIOUS FREEDOM (1786) then separated church and state.

In none of the six states maintaining or allowing establishments at the time of the framing of the First Amendment was any church but a Christian one established. The multiple establishments of that time comprehended the churches of every denomination and sect with a sufficient number of adherents to form a church. Where Protestantism was established it was synonymous with religion; there were either no Jews or no Roman Catholics or too few of them to make a difference. Where Christianity was established, as in Maryland, which had a significant Roman Catholic minority, Jews were scarcely known. To contend that exclusive establishments of one religion existed in each of the six states ignores the novel American experiment with multiple establishments on an impartial basis. Europe knew only single-church establishments. An establishment of religion in the United States at the time of the First Amendment included nonpreferential government recognition, aid, or sponsorship of religion. The framers of the amendment looked to their own experience, not Europe's.

Bibliography

ANTIEAU, CHESTER JAMES, ET AL.   1964   *Freedom from Federal Establishment: Formation and Early History of the First Amendment Religion Clauses.* Milwaukee, Wisc.: Bruce Publishing Co.

COBB, SANFORD H.   1902   *The Rise of Religious Liberty in America.* New York: Macmillan.

CORWIN, EDWARD S.   1949   The Supreme Court as National School Board. *Law and Contemporary Problems* 14:3–22.

LEVY, LEONARD W.   1986   *The Establishment Clause: Religion and the First Amendment.* New York: Macmillan.

SEPARATION OF CHURCH AND STATE

Jesse Choper

The first provision of the BILL OF RIGHTS—known as the establishment clause—states that "Congress shall make no law respecting an ESTABLISHMENT OF RELIGION. . . ." This constitutional mandate seeks to assure the separation of church and state in a nation characterized by religious pluralism.

Justice WILEY B. RUTLEDGE observed in EVERSON V. BOARD OF EDUCATION (1947) that "no provision of the Constitution is more closely tied to or given content by its generating history than the religious clause of the FIRST AMENDMENT." Justice HUGO L. BLACK recounted in *Everson* that in the old world, "with the power of government supporting them, at various times and places, Catholics had persecuted Protestants, Protestants had persecuted Baptists, Protestant sects had persecuted other Protestant sects, Catholics of one shade of belief had persecuted Catholics of another shade of belief, and all of these had from time to time persecuted Jews." And, he added, "these practices of the old world were transplanted to and began to thrive in the soil of the new America." For example, in Massachusetts, Quakers, Baptists, and other religious minorities suffered harshly and were taxed for the established Congregational Church. In 1776, the Maryland "Declaration of Rights" stated that "only persons professing the Christian religion" were entitled to religious freedom, and not until 1826 were Jews permitted to hold public office. The South Carolina Constitution of 1778 stated that "the Christian Protestant religion shall be deemed . . . the established religion of this state."

The specific historical record, rather than disclosing a coherent "intent of the Framers," suggests that those who influenced the framing of the First Amendment were animated by several distinct and sometimes conflicting goals. Thus, THOMAS JEFFERSON believed that the integrity of government could be preserved only by erecting "a wall of separation" between church and state. A sharp division of authority was essential, in his view, to insulate the democratic process from ecclesiastical depradations and excursions. JAMES MADISON shared this view, but also perceived church–state separation as benefiting religious institutions. Even more strongly, ROGER WILLIAMS, one of the earliest colonial proponents of religious freedom, posited an evangelical theory of separation, believing it vital to protect the sanctity of the church's "garden" from the "wilderness" of the state. Finally, there is evidence that one purpose of the establishment clause was to protect the existing state-established churches from the newly ordained national government. (Indeed, although disestablishment was then well under way, the epoch of state-sponsored churches did not close until 1833 when Massachusetts separated church and state.)

Even if the Framers' intent were unanimous and unambiguous, it still could not provide ready answers for many contemporary problems. First, a number of present-day church–state issues were not foreseen by the founders. For example, public education was virtually unknown in the eighteenth century; the Framers could have no position on the matter of RELIGION IN PUBLIC SCHOOLS—one of the most frequently adjudicated modern establishment clause questions. Second, implementing the Framers' precise thinking, even if discernible, might jeopardize values now considered secured by the establishment clause. As Justice WILLIAM J. BRENNAN speculated in ABINGTON TOWNSHIP SCHOOL DISTRICT V. SCHEMPP (1963), perhaps because the nation has become more religiously heterogeneous, "practices which may have been objectionable to no one in the time of Jefferson and Madison may today be highly offensive to . . . the deeply devout and the non-believers alike."

The varied ideologies that prompted the founders do, however, disclose a dominant theme: according constitutional status to RELIGIOUS LIBERTY and the integrity of individual conscience. Moreover, one of the main practices seen by many Framers as anathema to religious freedom was forcing the people to support religion through compulsory taxation. Jefferson viewed this as "sinful and tyrannical," and Madison found it abhorrent to compel "a citizen to contribute three pence only of his property" to a religious cause. The founders recognized that although government subsidy of religion may not directly influence people's beliefs, it coerces citizens either to contribute to their own religions or, worse, to support sectarian doctrines antithetical to their convictions.

By its terms, the establishment clause applies only to the federal government ("*Congress* shall make no law . . ."), but in *Everson* (1947) the Court ruled that the FOURTEENTH AMENDMENT made the clause applicable to the states. Before then, only two Supreme Court decisions had produced any significant consideration of the establishment clause. *Bradfield v. Roberts* (1899) had upheld federal appropriations to a Roman Catholic hospital for care of indigent patients. *Quick Bear v. Leupp* (1908) had sustained federal disbursement of funds, held in trust for the Sioux Indians, to Roman Catholic schools designated by the Sioux for payment of tuition. Neither opinion, however, attempted any comprehensive definition of the nonestablishment precept, an effort first undertaken in *Everson* where the Court stated:

The "establishment of religion" clause of the First Amendment means at least this: Neither a state nor the Federal government can set up a church. Neither can pass laws which aid one religion, aid all religions, or prefer one religion over another. Neither can force nor influence a person to go to or to remain away from church against his will or force him to profess a belief or disbelief in any religion. No person can be punished for entertaining or professing religious beliefs or disbeliefs, for church attendance or nonattendance. No tax in any amount, large or small, can be levied to support any religious activities or institutions, whatever they may be called, or whatever form they may adopt to teach or practice religion. Neither a state nor the Federal Government can, openly or secretly, participate in the affairs of any religious organization or groups and *vice versa*. In the words of Jefferson, the clause against establishment of religion by law was intended to erect "a wall of separation between church and state."

Since then, there has been little agreement among the Justices, lower courts, and scholars as to what constitutes impermissible "aid" to, or "support" of, religion.

Beginning in the early 1960s and culminating in LEMON V. KURTZMAN (1971), the Court developed a three-part test for reviewing establishment clause challenges: "First, the statute must have a secular legislative purpose; second, its principal or primary effect must be one that neither advances nor inhibits religion . . . ; finally, the statute must not foster 'an excessive government entanglement with religion.'" The *Lemon* test, despite its consistent invocation by the Court, has not been a model of coherence. Indeed, in an unusually candid OBITER DICTUM in COMMITTEE FOR PUBLIC EDUCATION V. REGAN (1980) the Court conceded that its approach "sacrifices clarity and predictability for flexibility," a state of affairs that "promises to be the case until the continuing interaction between the courts and the states . . . produces a single, more encompassing construction of the Establishment Clause." A better approach would read the establishment clause to forbid government action when its purpose is religious *and* it is likely to impair religious freedom by coercing, compromising, or influencing religious beliefs.

One of the nation's most politically divisive issues has been the proper place of religion in public schools. Decisions in the early 1960s, holding that prayer and Bible reading violate the establishment clause, precipitated serious efforts to reverse the Court by constitutional amendment. Later legislative proposals have sought to strip the federal courts of JURISDICTION over cases challenging voluntary school prayer.

The first cases concerning religion in public schools involved RELEASED TIME. In McCOLLUM V. BOARD OF EDUCATION (1948) the Court invalidated an Illinois program of voluntary religious instruction in public school classrooms during school hours by privately employed teachers. Students whose parents signed "request cards" attended weekly classes in religion; others pursued secular studies elsewhere in the school during this period. The Court's opinion emphasized use of "the state's tax-supported public school buildings" and "the state's compulsory public school machinery." Four years later, in ZORACH v. CLAUSEN (1952), the Court upheld a New York City "off-premises" released time program. Released students attended classes at their respective religious centers; neither public funds nor public classrooms directly supported religion. In a much quoted and controversial passage, the Court observed: "We are a religious people whose institutions presuppose a Supreme Being. We guarantee the freedom to worship as one chooses. We make room for as wide a variety of beliefs and creeds as the spiritual needs of man deem necessary. . . . When the state encourages religious instruction or cooperates with religious authorities by adjusting the schedule of public events to sectarian needs, it follows the best of our traditions."

Neither *McCollum* nor *Zorach* propounded any specific STANDARD OF REVIEW. A decade later, in ENGEL v. VITALE (1962), the Court invalidated a New York law providing for recitation of a state-composed prayer at the beginning of each public school day. Although the prayer was denominationally "neutral," and students could remain silent or leave the room, the Court declared that this "breaches the constitutional wall of separation between Church and State," because "it is no part of the business of government to compose official prayers."

The Court's approach soon underwent a dramatic revision. In *Abington Township v. Schempp* the Court held it unconstitutional for public schools to conduct daily exercises of reading student-selected passages from either the Old or New Testaments (without teacher comment) and recitation of the Lord's Prayer. Drawing on its rationale in the SUNDAY CLOSING CASES (1961), the Court articulated a "test" for government action challenged under the establishment clause: "[W]hat are the purpose and the primary effect of the enactment? If either is the advancement or inhibition of religion then the enactment exceeds the scope of legislative power as circumscribed by the Constitution. That is to say that to withstand the strictures of the Establishment Clause there must be a secular legislative purpose and a primary effect that neither advances nor inhibits religion." The Court ruled that the "opening exercise is a religious ceremony," emphasizing, however, that "objective" study of the Bible (presumably for its literary and historical value) was constitutionally permissible.

There are two difficulties with the Court's declared willingness—reaffirmed regularly since *Schempp*—to invalidate government action solely on the basis of a nonsecular "purpose." First, although *Schempp* emphasized the establishment clause's requirement of a "wholesome neutrality" by the state toward religion, the Court has also made clear that the Constitution does not mandate an "untutored devotion" to this precept. Indeed, it has sometimes held that the free exercise clause *obliges* government to act with a nonsecular purpose—actually, to give a preference to religion—when the action is necessary to permit the unburdened exercise of religion.

Second, despite the *Schempp* test's condemnation of laws whose purpose is to "advance religion," the Court in *Zorach* had previously conceded that the released time program upheld had a nonsecular purpose: facilitation of religious instruction. *Zorach* has been specifically reaffirmed since *Schempp* was decided. Thus, the Court itself is not fully committed to its articulated doctrine that a religious purpose alone is sufficient to invalidate government action.

Although both *Engel* and *Schempp* declared that religious coercion was irrelevant under the establishment clause, the Court has nevertheless often carefully analyzed the elements of coercion and influence in programs it has considered. For example, in *Engel* the Court remarked on "the indirect coercive pressure upon religious minorities to conform to the prevailing officially approved religion." In *Zorach,* the Court emphasized its questionable conclusion that there was no "coercion to get public school students into religious classrooms." And in WIDMAR v. VINCENT (1981), in requiring a state university to provide student religious groups equal access to its facilities, the Court noted: "University students are . . . less impressionable than younger students and should be able to appreciate that the university's policy is one of neutrality towards religion."

The Court's sensitivity to religious coercion and influence in establishment clause challenges, its doctrinal pronouncements to the contrary notwithstanding, comports with an approach that recognizes that in accommodating the values underlying both the establishment and free exercise clauses, a nonsecular purpose cannot always be avoided, and that the primary offense to the establishment clause is some meaningful intrusion upon religious liberty.

Nearly two decades elapsed between *Schempp* and the BURGER COURT's first major decision on religion in public schools. In *Stone v. Graham* (1980) a Kentucky statute required posting a copy of the Ten Commandments (purchased with private funds) in all public school classrooms, with the notation: "The secular application of the Ten Commandments is clearly seen in its adoption as the fundamental legal code of Western Civilization and the COMMON LAW of the United States." Although the state court found that the legislature's purpose was not religious and sustained the law, the Supreme Court reversed.

The *Stone* opinion is significant for several reasons. First, it sheds further light on how the Court decides whether a legislative purpose is secular or religious. In *Schempp,* when the school board contended that the Bible reading program was not instituted for religious reasons (but rather to promote moral values, teach literature, and inspire student discipline), the Court brusquely replied that "surely, the place of the Bible as an instrument of religion cannot be gainsaid." In *Stone,* the Court stated that the Ten Commandments were not confined to "arguably secular matters" such as prohibition of murder and adultery but also prescribed religious duties such as observing the Sabbath and avoiding idolatry—adding that the law did not integrate the Bible or the commandments into an ethics, history, or comparative religion course. It quite peremptorily concluded that the program "serves no . . . educational function" and that "the Ten Commandments is undeniably a sacred text in the Jewish and Christian faiths, and no legislative recitation of a supposed secular purpose can blind us to that fact." *Stone* also reaffirms that a nonsecular purpose is itself enough to condemn a law under the establishment clause. Although the Court briefly considered the state program's potential for coercing or influencing children—observing that "if the posted copies of the Ten Commandments are to have any effect at all, it will be to induce the school children to read, meditate upon, perhaps to venerate and obey, the Commandments"—it nevertheless held that the law lacked a secular purpose and was invalid on that basis alone. This doctrine was vigorously reinforced in WALLACE V. JAFFREE (1985), which invalidated an Alabama statute authorizing a period of silence in public schools "for meditation or voluntary prayer," because the law was "entirely motivated by a purpose to advance religion." (The Justices plainly indicated that only a slightly different statutory formulation "protecting every student's right to engage in voluntary prayer during an appropriate moment of silence during the school day" would pass constitutional muster.)

Although regulatory laws allegedly enacted to aid religion have generated only a few Supreme Court decisions, they have significantly affected establishment clause jurisprudence. In McGowan v. Maryland (1961) the Court upheld prohibition of the sale of most merchandise on Sundays. The Court conceded that the original purpose of Sunday closing laws was to encourage observance of the Christian Sabbath. But it found that, as presently written and administered, most such laws "are of a secular rather than of a religious character," seeking "to set one day apart from all others as a day of rest, repose, recreation and tranquility." The choice of Sunday, "a day of particular significance for the dominant Christian sects," did not "bar the state from achieving its secular goals."

McGowan emphasized that a Sunday closing law might violate the establishment clause if its purpose were "to use the State's coercive power to aid religion." This warning was fulfilled in EPPERSON V. ARKANSAS

(1968), when the Court invalidated a law that excised the theory of human biological evolution from public school curricula. Reviewing the circumstances of its adoption in 1928, the Court found that "fundamentalist sectarian conviction was and still is the law's reason for existence."

Although Arkansas probably exceeded what the free exercise clause required for "accommodation" of fundamentalist religious doctrine, there was no indication that its anti-evolution statute coerced, compromised, or influenced school children to embrace fundamentalist doctrine. The Arkansas statute thus satisfied religious needs with no meaningful threat to religious liberty—the chief danger the establishment clause was intended to avoid. Yet, as in the Ten Commandments and moment-of-silence cases, a religious purpose alone proved fatal.

The Court first gave plenary consideration to the problem of public aid to church-related schools in *Everson v. Board of Education* (1947). A New Jersey township reimbursed parents for the cost of sending their children on public buses to and from schools, including Roman Catholic parochial schools. Although the Court asserted that "no tax . . . can be levied to support any religious activity or institution," it upheld the New Jersey program by a 5–4 vote. The majority conceded that without the program's subsidy some children might not be sent to church schools. But it reasoned that funding bus transportation for all pupils in both public and sectarian schools accomplished the "public purpose" of aiding parents in getting their children "safely and expeditiously to and from accredited schools." In this respect, New Jersey's aid program was similar to providing all schools with basic municipal services, such as fire and police protection. Furthermore, the state could not constitutionally exclude persons from its aid "because of their faith, or lack of it." (The *Everson* majority indicated that bus transportation might be the limit of permissible assistance.) The dissenters protested that the program aided children "in a substantial way to get the very thing which they are sent to [parochial schools] to secure, namely, religious training and teaching."

The Court did not again confront the issue of aid to church-related schools until BOARD OF EDUCATION V. ALLEN (1968). During the intervening two decades, the Court had developed the "secular purpose-secular effect" standard. *Allen* held that New York's lending secular textbooks, approved by local school boards, to all secondary school students, including those in church-related schools, had the secular purpose of furthering education and a primary effect that benefited students and parents, not religious schools.

The "excessive entanglement" prong of the Court's establishment clause test emerged two years later. WALZ V. TAX COMMISSION (1970) rejected the claim that New York's tax exemption for "real or personal property used exclusively for religious, educational or charitable purposes" supported religion in violation of the establishment clause. After finding that the exemption had the nonreligious purpose of avoiding inhibition on the activities of charities and other community institutions, the Court continued: "We must also be sure that the end result—the effect—is not an excessive government entanglement with religion. The test is inescapably one of degree. Either course, taxation of churches or exemptions, occasions some degree of involvement with religion. . . . [The question is] whether it is a continuing one calling for official and continuing surveillance leading to an impermissible degree of entanglement." The Court conceded that tax exemption accorded an indirect economic benefit to religion, but concluded that it gave rise to less government involvement than nonexemption. Taxing the churches would occasion "tax valuation of church property, tax liens, tax foreclosures, and the direct confrontations and conflicts that follow in the train of those legal processes."

In LEMON v. KURTZMAN (1971) the Court returned to the problem of church-related schools. Rhode Island subsidized public and private school teachers of secular subjects (not to exceed fifteen percent of their salaries); parochial school teachers agreed not to teach religion during the subsidy. The legislature had found that "the quality of education available in nonpublic elementary schools has been jeopardized [by] rapidly rising salaries." Pennsylvania reimbursed nonpublic schools for the salaries of teachers of "secular" subjects such as mathematics, physical science, physical education, and foreign languages. Church-related schools maintained accounts, subject to state audit, that segregated the costs of "secular educational service." Reimbursement for religiously oriented courses was prohibited.

The Court held that both programs violated the establishment clause. It acknowledged a secular purpose, but reasoned that the states' efforts to avoid a primary effect that advanced religion produced "excessive entanglement between government and religion." In the Court's view, church-related elementary and secondary schools had as their mission the inculcation of religious doctrine, especially among "impressionable" primary school pupils. Continuing state evaluation of school records "to establish the cost of secular as distinguished from religious instruction," and the state "surveillance necessary to ensure that teachers play a strictly nonideological role" were "pregnant with dangers of excessive government direction of Church schools and hence of Churches." Although this "administrative" entanglement was fatal, both laws risked another sort of entanglement: their "divisive political potential" along religious lines, given the likely demand for continuing and ever increasing annual appropriations.

The excessive entanglement criterion has been prominent in establishment clause adjudication since 1970; but it does not represent a value that either can or should be judicially secured by the establishment clause. The major fear of administrative entanglement between government and religion is that state regulation impairs the ability of religious groups to pursue their mission. This concern, however, is unfounded both doctrinally and empirically. At least since PIERCE v. SOCIETY OF SISTERS (1925) it has been understood that the Constitution permits the state to regulate church-related institutions whether or not it provides them financial assistance. Parochial school curricula, for example, have long been regulated without significant evidence of infringement of religious values. And if there were, the regulation would be invalid whether or not tied to monetary aid.

Another form of administrative entanglement regularly occurs when the state seeks to distinguish religion from nonreligion in order to grant an exemption from civil regulations. Although government scrutiny of religious beliefs is a sensitive task, the need for that scrutiny springs from the Constitution's explicit definition of religion as a subject for special treatment.

Similar objections can be raised to using "avoidance of political strife along religious lines" as a criterion for establishment clause adjudication. Indeed, if government were to ban religious conflict in the legislative process, serious questions of First Amendment political liberty would arise. But practical considerations, more than doctrinal ones, demonstrate the futility of making "political divisiveness" a constitutional determinant. Legislation does not violate the establishment clause simply because religious organizations support or oppose it. Religious groups have frequently differed on secular political issues—gambling, OBSCENITY, drug and gun control, CONSCRIPTION, PROHIBITION, abolition of slavery, racial integration, prostitution, sterilization, abortion, BIRTH CONTROL, divorce, the VIETNAM WAR, the EQUAL RIGHTS AMENDMENT, and CAPITAL PUNISHMENT, to name but a few. Churches and other religious groups have markedly influenced resolution of some of these matters. In the early 1980s, they actively debated the question of the nation's nuclear arms policy. Although a law may in fact promote a religious purpose, if the law serves genuinely secular ends—and impairs no one's religious liberty by coercing, compromising, or influencing religious beliefs—it should not be unconstitutional simply because its proponents and antagonists were divided along religious lines.

Moreover, even if government could or should eliminate religious fragmentation in the political arena, the establishment clause is an ineffective tool for the task. For example, forbidding aid to parochial schools does not effect a truce, but only moves the battleground; if children in parochial schools are excluded from school aid, their parents will tend to oppose increased funding of public schools.

The Court has viewed aid to church-related higher education more favorably than it has viewed aid to elementary and secondary schools. *Tilton v. Richardson* (1971), a companion case to *Lemon,* upheld federal construction grants to colleges for buildings and facilities that applicants agreed not to use for religious instruction. The government enforced this promise by on-site inspections. The Court easily found a secular purpose in the expansion of higher education opportunities. In reasoning that the subsidy's primary effect did not advance religion, it stated that, unlike elementary and secondary schools, church-related colleges were not "permeated" by religion. Their dominant motive is secular education; they normally afford a high degree of ACADEMIC FREEDOM for faculty and students; and their students are less susceptible to religious indoctrination than are school children. In sharp contrast to its generalized appraisal of parochial schools, the Court rejected a "composite profile" of a "typical sectarian" college. Instead, the Court found, on the record before it, that courses at the four recipient Roman Catholic institutions were taught according to professional academic standards. Moreover, the aid took the form of a one-time, single-purpose construction grant. Thus no appreciable governmental surveillance was required. Finally, the Court found the potential for "religious fragmentation in the political arena" lessened by the religious colleges' geographically diverse student bodies and the absence of religious affiliation of a majority of recipient colleges.

Decisions since *Tilton* have continued to sustain aid to religiously affiliated colleges. In *Hunt v. McNair* (1973) the Court upheld the use of South Carolina tax-exempt bonds to finance facilities for all colleges, so long as the facilities were limited to nonsectarian purposes. The Court placed the burden on those challenging the aid to establish that recipient colleges are "permeated" with religion. And in *Roemer v. Board of Public Works* (1976) the Court upheld Maryland grants of fifteen percent of the student cost in the state college system to all private colleges, if they certified that they used the funds for nonreligious purposes.

Subsequent decisions on aid to elementary and secondary schools have generally, but not unexceptionally, followed the path of *Lemon. Meek v. Pittenger* (1975) involved a program under which Pennsylvania lent instructional materials (such as maps, films, projectors, and laboratory equipment) to private schools, seventy-five percent of which were church-related. The Court agreed that the aid was ideologically neutral, but held that "when it flows to an institution in which religion is so pervasive that a substantial portion of its functions are subsumed in the religious mission," it has the primary effect of advancing religion. The Court also invalidated "auxiliary services" (such as standardized testing, speech therapy, and psychological counseling) by public employees for private school children on their schools' premises: "To be certain that auxiliary teachers remain religiously neutral . . . the State would have to impose limitations . . . and then engage in some form of continuing surveillance to ensure that those restrictions were being followed." In addition to this "administrative entanglement," the Court observed that the program promised to generate "political entanglement" in the form of "continuing political strife." (The Court reaffirmed this holding as to auxiliary services in 1985 in the COMPANION CASES of *Grand Rapids School District v. Ball* and AGUILAR v. FELTON.)

Two years after *Meek, Wolman v. Walter* (1977) illustrated how constitutionality may turn on slight changes in form. The Court upheld Ohio's provision of (1) speech, hearing, and psychological diagnostic services by public employees on private school premises; (2) therapeutic and remedial services by public employees at a "neutral site off the premises" of the private school (even if in an adjacent mobile unit); and (3) payment for standardized tests used in private schools (the dispositive factor being that the tests were drafted and scored by public employees). The Court distinguished *Meek* on paperthin grounds relating to the closeness of the connection between the services provided and the religious school's educational mission and to the likelihood that public employees would "transmit ideological views" to children.

Wolman invalidated state payment for field trips of private school pupils, distinguishing *Everson* on the basis of the school's control over the expenditure of the funds and the close relation of the expenditure to the school's curriculum. The Court also invalidated a program for lending instructional materials to students, but, as in *Meek,* reaffirmed *Allen* and upheld lending students secular textbooks.

COMMITTEE FOR PUBLIC EDUCATION v. REGAN (1980) upheld New York's reimbursing private schools for performing testing and reporting services mandated by state law. The tests were prepared by the state, but, unlike those in *Wolman,* some were administered and scored by private school personnel. Nevertheless, because the tests were mostly objective, the Court concluded that there was little risk of their religious use. The Court distinguished *Levitt v. Committee for Public Education* (1973), which had invalidated a similar New York statute because it did not provide for state audits to ensure that the public funds did not exceed the nonpublic school's actual cost. In *Regan,* the occasional audits were found adequate to prevent a religious effect but not so intrusive as to produce excessive entanglement.

As of the mid-1980s, the most effective way for government to assist elementary and secondary parochial schools is through the tax system. In COMMITTEE FOR PUBLIC EDUCATION v. NYQUIST (1973) the Court invalidated a New York program, which the Court agreed had a "secular purpose," that gave tuition grants to low-income parents and tax relief to middle-income parents of children in private schools. The Court held that this had the effect of aiding the religious functions of sectarian schools. The Court distinguished *Walz* on several grounds. First, unlike the *Nyquist* programs, tax exemptions for church property had ample historical precedent, being "widespread during colonial days" and currently "in force in all 50 states." Second, although property tax exemption tended to lessen involvement between church and state, the programs in *Nyquist* tended to increase it. Finally, the tax exemption in *Walz* went to a broad class of charitable, religious, and educational institutions, but the record in *Nyquist* showed that eighty-five percent of the children benefited attended sectarian schools, practically all run by the Roman Catholic Church.

A decade later, in MUELLER v. ALLEN (1983), the Court upheld a Minnesota program granting a state income tax deduction for parents with children in *any* nonprofit school, public or private. This deduction could be used for expenditures for tuition and transportation, as well as for textbooks and instructional materials and equipment (so long as they were not used to teach religion). The Court conceded that the "economic consequences" of the Minnesota program were "difficult to distinguish" from the New York program in *Nyquist*. But that it was difficult did not make it impossible. One difference the Court found was that *Mueller* involved "a genuine tax deduction," whereas the *Nyquist* tax credit was more like a direct grant than a tax benefit. The Court found most significant that the *Mueller* plan was available to all parents, not just those with children in private schools. Thus, the plan was "facially neutral" and its "primary effect" did not advance religion. The Court reached this conclusion even though ninety-six percent of the Minnesota deductions were taken by parents who sent their children to parochial schools—mainly Roman Catholic and Lutheran. As for the other four percent, there were only seventy-nine public school students who deducted tuition, which they paid because they attended public schools outside their districts for special reasons. Of course, children who attended public schools in their districts did get some deductions—for the cost of pencils, notebooks, and other incidentals not customarily provided.

The lesson to be drawn from all the elementary and secondary school decisions is that states wishing to provide significant financial assistance may do so simply by adopting the proper form. For example, New York could successfully revive its program invalidated in *Nyquist* by providing a tax benefit to all parents, including those whose children attend public schools, knowing that this would not appreciably increase the cost of the plan. But New York might be required to use the form of a tax deduction (rather than a tax credit or direct grant as in *Nyquist*), a difference of vital importance to parents with low incomes, who would obtain little benefit from a tax deduction.

Application of the Court's three-part test to the problem of GOVERN-

MENT AID TO RELIGIOUS INSTITUTIONS has generated ad hoc judgments incapable of being reconciled on a principled basis. The Court has assumed that the entire program of parochial schools is "permeated" with religion. But there is much dispute as to the facts. Some "secular" subjects in some parochial schools are unquestionably courses of religious indoctrination; other courses are truly secular; many probably fall between these polar characterizations. Thus, public aid incidentally benefits religion. But virtually all government services to church-related facilities—whether bus transportation, police and fire protection, sewage connections, sidewalks, tuition grants, or textbooks—incidentally benefit their sectarian functions by releasing church funds for religious purposes.

The critical inquiry should be whether direct or indirect government assistance to parochial schools exceeds the value of the secular educational service the schools render. If it does not, there is no use of tax-raised funds to aid religion, and thus no danger to religious liberty. This inquiry differs from the Court's approach, which has often invalidated laws with secular purposes because of their effects in advancing religion. A state program with both a secular purpose and a secular effect does not threaten values underlying the establishment clause. Furthermore, when the Court invalidates such a law simply because it incidentally furthers religious interests, the Justices assert the power to assess the multiple impacts of legislation, to separate religious from secular effects, and then to determine which are paramount. Ultimately the Justices must then rely on their own subjective notions of predominance.

In the mid-1980s, the Court was twice confronted with the problem of government practices that specifically acknowledge religion. MARSH v. CHAMBERS (1983) upheld Nebraska's paying a chaplain to open each legislative session with a prayer. Proceeding unusually, the Court did not apply its three-part test. Rather, it relied first on history and tradition—pointing out that paid legislative chaplains and opening prayers existed in the Continental Congress, the First Congress, and every Congress thereafter, as well as in most states today and in colonies such as Virginia and Rhode Island, both of which were bastions of religious liberty. Second, the Court rested on the intent of the Framers, noting that just three days after the First Congress had authorized paid chaplains it approved the Bill of Rights; this made it difficult to believe that the Framers could conceive of the establishment clause as prohibiting legislative chaplains. Thus, the practice survived challenge even though Nebraska's purpose was unquestionably religious and the Court's doctrine is that such purpose alone produces an establishment clause violation.

A year later, in LYNCH v. DONNELLY (1984), the Court sustained Pawtucket, Rhode Island's inclusion of a nativity scene in the city's annual Christmas season display. The cost was nominal, unlike the $320 expended monthly for Nebraska's chaplain in *Marsh*. The Court reasoned that the purpose and effect were not exclusively religious but, rather, that "the creche in the display depicts the historical origins of this traditional event long recognized as a National Holiday." The opinion also emphasized that our history was replete with government recognition of religion's role in American life and with government expressions of religious belief. As examples, it pointed to presidential proclamations of national days of prayer and of Thanksgiving and Christmas as national holidays, public funding of a chapel in the Capitol and of chaplains in the legislature and in the military, "In God We Trust" as our statutorily prescribed national motto, the language "One Nation under God" as part of the Pledge of Allegiance, and the plethora of religious paintings in publicly supported galleries and in public buildings. Stating that "this history may help explain why the Court consistently has declined to take a rigid, absolutist view of the Establishment Clause," the Court strongly suggested that all these deeply ingrained practices were constitutional.

The final important church–state separation issue concerns the tension between the First Amendment's two religion clauses, one forbidding government to promote or "establish" religion, the other forbidding government to abridge the "free exercise" of religion. As observed in *Walz,* both "are cast in absolute terms, and either . . . if expanded to a logical extreme, would tend to clash with the other." Charting a course that offends neither provision presents a continual challenge for the Court; yet its few direct confrontations with the problem have been unsatisfying.

The two most celebrated free exercise clause decisions illustrate the inherent conflict. In SHERBERT V. VERNER (1962) a Seventh-Day Adventist was discharged by her employer because she would not work on Saturday, her Sabbath. South Carolina denied her unemployment compensation for refusing "suitable work," that is, a job requiring Saturday labor. The Court held that this denial violated the free exercise clause by conditioning benefits on a violation of her religious faith. Although the Court's decision implements the free exercise clause, the purpose of its ruling—like the purpose of the released time program in *McCollum* —is clearly to facilitate religious practice. Thus, the exemption required by the Court in the name of the free exercise clause appears to violate the Court's establishment clause doctrine, which renders invalid any government action with a nonsecular purpose. The Court's conclusory response was that "plainly we are not fostering the 'establishment' of the Seventh-day Adventist religion" but rather governmental "neutrality in the face of religious differences."

In WISCONSIN V. YODER (1971) the Court held that application of school attendance requirements to the Old Order Amish violated the free exercise clause. In characterizing this as an "accommodation" for the Amish, the Court rejected the contention that this religious exemption violated the establishment clause: "The purpose and effect of such an exemption are not to support, favor, advance or assist the Amish, but to allow their centuries-old religious society . . . to survive free from the heavy impediment compliance with the Wisconsin compulsory-education law would impose."

In THORNTON V. CALDOR, INC. (1985), however, the Court ruled that a state had gone too far in "accommodating" religion. It held that a Connecticut law that required employers to give a day off to employees on their Sabbath, "no matter what burden or inconvenience this imposes on the employer or fellow workers," had the "primary effect" of advancing "a particular religious practice" and thus violated the establishment clause. The Court emphasized the "absolute and unqualified right not to work" afforded the employees, although this appeared to be little different from the exemption that the Court itself had ordered in *Sherbert*.

Although there is considerable overlap in the purposes of the establishment and free exercise clauses—their central function being to secure religious liberty—the decisions disclose that each has an identifiable emphasis. In the main, the free exercise clause protects adherents of religious faiths from secularly motivated laws whose effect burdens them because of their particular beliefs. When the Court finds a violation of the free exercise clause, the law is normally held invalid as applied; all that is required is an exemption for the claimant from the law's otherwise proper operation. In contrast, the principal thrust of the establishment clause concerns religiously motivated laws that pose the danger to believers and nonbelievers of being required to support their own religious observance or that of others. When the Court finds a violation of the establishment clause, ordinarily the offensive provision is entirely invalid and may not be enforced at all.

A better approach would reconcile the conflict between the clauses by interpreting the establishment clause to forbid only those laws whose purpose is to favor religion, and then only if such laws tend to coerce, compromise, or influence religious beliefs. Under this standard, the religious exemption that the Court required in *Sherbert* would itself be unconstitutional because it impairs religious liberty by supporting religion with funds raised by taxation. Although the core value of religious liberty may forbid government to interfere with Sherbert's practice of Seventh-Day Adventism, it similarly forbids forcing other citizens to subsidize a religious practice. On the other hand, the proposed alternative approach probably would not change the result in *Yoder;* it is doubtful that exempting the Amish from the compulsory education law (or giving employees a day off on their Sabbath, as in *Thornton*) would tend to coerce, compromise, or influence religious choice. Finally, the alternative approach would distinguish *Yoder* from those decisions—such as *McCol-*

lum, Engel, and *Schempp*—that have invalidated religious practices in public schools. Neither these programs nor the exemption in *Yoder* had a "secular" purpose. But, unlike *Yoder* and *Thornton,* the public school programs threatened religious liberty and were thus properly held to abridge the constitutional separation of church and state.

Bibliography

ANTIEAU, CHESTER J.; DOWNEY, ARTHUR T.; and ROBERTS, EDWARD C. 1964 *Freedom from Federal Establishment.* Milwaukee, Wisc.: Bruce Publishing Co.

CHOPER, JESSE H. 1963 Religion in the Public Schools: A Proposed Constitutional Standard. *University of Minnesota Law Review* 47:329–416.

———— 1968 The Establishment Clause and Aid to Parochial Schools. *California Law Review* 56:260–341.

———— 1980 The Religion Clauses of the First Amendment: Reconciling the Conflict. *University of Pittsburgh Law Review* 41:673–701.

CURRY, THOMAS 1986 *The First Freedoms.* New York: Oxford University Press.

HOWE, MARK D. 1965 *The Garden and the Wilderness.* Chicago: University of Chicago Press.

KURLAND, PHILIP B. 1962 *Religion and the Law.* Chicago: Aldine Publishing Co.

LEVY, LEONARD W. 1986 *An Establishment of Religion.* New York: Macmillan.

MURRAY, JOHN C. 1960 *We Hold These Truths.* Chap. 2. New York: Sheed & Ward.

NOWAK, JOHN E.; ROTUNDA, RONALD D.; and YOUNG, J. NELSON 1983 *Handbook on Constitutional Law,* 2nd ed. Pages 1229–1281. St. Paul, Minn.: West Publishing Co.

PFEFFER, LEO 1984 *Religion, State, and the Burger Court.* Buffalo, N.Y.: Prometheus Books.

SCHWARTZ, ALAN 1968 No Imposition of Religion: The Establishment Clause Value. *Yale Law Journal* 77:692–737.

STOKES, ANSON PHELPS 1950 *Church & State in the United States.* 3 Vols. New York: Harper.

TRIBE, LAURENCE H. 1978 *American Constitutional Law.* Chap. 14. Mineola, N.Y.: Foundation Press.

BLASPHEMY

Leonard W. Levy

Defaming religion by any words expressing scorn, ridicule, or vilification of God, Jesus Christ, the Holy Ghost, the doctrine of the Trinity, the Old or New Testament, or Christianity, constitutes the offense of blasphemy. In the leading American case, *Commonwealth v. Kneeland* (1838), Chief Justice LEMUEL SHAW of Massachusetts repelled arguments based on FREEDOM OF THE PRESS and on RELIGIOUS LIBERTY when he sustained a state law against blasphemy and upheld the conviction of a pantheist who simply denied belief in God, Christ, and miracles. In all the American decisions, the courts maintained the fiction that the criminality of the words consisted of maliciousness or the intent to insult rather than mere difference of opinion.

The Supreme Court has never decided a blasphemy case. In BURSTYN, INC. v. WILSON (1951) the Court relied on FREEDOM OF SPEECH to void a New York statute authorizing the censorship of "sacrilegious" films. Justice FELIX FRANKFURTER, concurring, observed that blasphemy was a far vaguer term than sacrilege because it meant "criticism of whatever the ruling authority of the moment established as the orthodox religious doctrine." In 1968, when the last prosecution of blasphemy occurred in the United States, an appellate court of Maryland held that the prosecution violated the First Amendment's ban on ESTABLISHMENT OF RELIGION and its protection of freedom of religion. Should a blasphemy case ever reach the Supreme Court, that Court would surely reach a similar result.

Bibliography

LEVY, LEONARD W. 1981 *Treason Against God: A History of the Offense of Blasphemy.* New York: Schocken Books.

MADISON'S "MEMORIAL AND REMONSTRANCE"

(1785)

Leonard W. Levy

This remonstrance is the best evidence of what JAMES MADISON, the framer of the FIRST AMENDMENT, meant by an ESTABLISHMENT OF RELIGION. In 1784 the Virginia legislature had proposed a bill that benefited "Teachers of the Christian Religion" by assessing a small tax on property owners. Each taxpayer could designate the Christian church of his choice as the recipient of his tax money; the bill allowed non-church members to earmark their taxes for the support of local schools, and it upheld the "liberal principle" that all Christian sects and denominations were equal under the law, none preferred over others. The bill did not speak of the "established religion" of the state as had an aborted bill of 1779, and it purported to be based on only secular considerations, the promotion of the public peace and morality rather than Christ's kingdom on earth. Madison denounced the bill as an establishment of religion, no less dangerous to RELIGIOUS LIBERTY than the proposal of 1779 and differing "only in degree" from the Inquisition.

In an elaborate argument of fifteen parts, Madison advocated a complete SEPARATION OF CHURCH AND STATE as the only guarantee of the equal right of every citizen to the free exercise of religion, including the freedom of those "whose minds have not yet yielded to the evidence which has convinced us." He regarded the right to support religion as an "unalienable" individual right to be exercised only on a voluntary basis. Religion, he contended, must be exempt from the power of society, the legislature, and the magistrate. In his trenchant assault on establishments including the one proposed by this mild bill—"it is proper to take alarm at the first experiment on our liberties"—and in his eloquent defense of separation, Madison stressed the point that separation benefited not only personal freedom but also the free state and even religion itself. His remonstrance, which circulated throughout Virginia in the summer of 1785, actually redirected public opinion, resulting in the election of legislators who opposed the bill, which had previously passed a second reading. Madison then introduced THOMAS JEFFERSON's proposal which was enacted into law as the VIRGINIA STATUTE OF RELIGIOUS FREEDOM.

Bibliography

BRANT, IRVING 1948 *James Madison, Nationalist 1780–1787*. Pages 343–355. Indianapolis: Bobbs-Merrill.

RELIGION IN PUBLIC SCHOOLS

Leo Pfeffer

For centuries in the Western world, organized education was church education; colonial schools established on the American shores therefore naturally reflected a religious orientation. Prior to the early nineteenth-century migration of Irish to this country, the orientation of these schools was Protestant—a fact that contributed to the establishment and growth of the Roman Catholic parochial school system. Nevertheless, when the RELEASED TIME plan for religious instruction was initiated in 1914, the majority of Roman Catholic children still attended public schools. The plan thus provided for separate religious instruction classes for Protestants, Roman Catholics, and Jews. Roman Catholic Church spokesmen condemned the Supreme Court's decision in McCOLLUM v. BOARD OF EDUCATION (1948) invalidating the program. Previously, however, Roman Catholics had protested against public school religious instruction with a Protestant orientation, and had instituted lawsuits challenging such programs' constitutionality. Public school authorities in New York chose to formulate their own "non-sectarian" prayer, which was submitted to and received the approval of prominent religious spokesmen of the three major faiths. The twenty-two-word prayer read: "Almighty God, we acknowledge our dependence upon Thee, and beg Thy blessings upon us, our parents, our teachers and our country."

The denominational neutrality of the prayer, the Supreme Court held in ENGEL v. VITALE (1962), was immaterial. Nor was it relevant that observance on the part of students was voluntary (nonparticipating students were not even required to be in the classroom or assembly hall while the prayer was recited). Under the establishment clause, the Court said, aid to all religions was as impermissible as aid to one religion, even if the aid was noncoercive. The constitutional prohibition against laws respecting an ESTABLISHMENT OF RELIGION means at least that it is "no part of the business of government to compose official prayers for any group of the American people to recite as part of a religious program carried on by government."

One year after *Engel,* the Court, in ABINGTON SCHOOL DISTRICT v. SCHEMPP, was called upon to rule on the constitutionality of two practices in the public schools common throughout the nation, prayer recitation and devotional Bible reading. In respect to the former it ruled immaterial the fact that, unlike *Engel,* the recited prayer had not been formulated by public school authorities, but was the Lord's Prayer taken from the Bible. The fatal flaw in the *Engel* regulation lay not in the authorship of the prayer but in the fact that its purpose and primary effect were the advancement of religion. This fact mandated invalidation of both Lord's Prayer recitation and devotional Bible reading. The Court rejected the claim that the purposes of the challenged program were the secular ones of promoting moral values, contradicting the materialistic trends of our time, perpetuating our institutions, and teaching literature. None of these factors, the Court said, justified use of the Bible as an instrument of religion or resort to a ceremony of pervasive religious character. Nothing in its decision, it concluded, was intended to cast doubt on the study of comparative religion or the study of the Bible for its literary and historic qualities, so long as these were presented as part of a secular program of education.

   McCollum, Engel, and *Schempp* involved efforts to introduce religious teachings or practices into the public schools. EPPERSON V. ARKANSAS (1968) presented the converse, that is, religiously motivated exclusion of secular instruction from the public school curriculum. A statute forbade teaching "the theory or doctrine that mankind ascended or descended from a lower order of animals." The Court held that the statute violated the establishment clause, because its purpose was to protect religious orthodoxy from inconsistent secular teaching of evolution.

   In *Stone v. Graham* (1980) the Court struck down a Kentucky statute requiring the posting of copies of the Ten Commandments (purchased with private contributions) on the walls of all the public school classrooms in the state. The statute, it held, had no secular purpose; unlike the second part of the Commandments, the first (worshiping God, avoiding idolatry, not taking the Lord's name in vain, and observing the Sabbath) concerned religious rather than secular duties.

   WIDMAR V. VINCENT (1981) manifests a more tolerant approach in respect to colleges than to elementary and secondary schools. With but one dissent, the Court held that where state university facilities were open to groups and speakers of all kinds, they must also be open for use by an organization of evangelical Christian students for prayer, hymns, Bible commentary, and discussion of religious views and experience. As construed by the Court, the establishment clause did not mandate such exclusion; on the contrary, the state's interest in enforcing its own constitution's church–state separation clause was not sufficiently "compelling" to justify content-barred discrimination forbidden by the FREEDOM OF SPEECH clause.

   However, in *Jaffree v. Board of School Commissioners* (1984) the Court affirmed without opinion a Court of Appeals decision ruling unconstitutional an Alabama law authorizing voluntary participation in a prayer formulated by the legislators; and a year later, in WALLACE v. JAFFREE (1985) it invalidated another section of the statute that required a one-minute period of silence for "meditation or voluntary prayer." The provision, the Court said, did not have a valid secular purpose, but rather one that sought to return prayer to the public schools.

Bibliography

PFEFFER, LEO   (1953)1967   Church, State and Freedom. Boston: Beacon Press.
STOKES, A. P. and PFEFFER, LEO   1964   Church and State in the United States. New York: Harper & Row.
TRIBE, LAURENCE H.   1984   American Constitutional Law. Chap. 14. Mineola, N.Y.: Foundation Press.

STATE OF TENNESSEE v. SCOPES

289 SW 363 (1925)

Michael E. Parrish

In 1925 Dayton, Tennessee, authorities arrested a local high school teacher, John T. Scopes, for violating the state's Butler Act, which prohibited public school instructors from teaching "any theory that denies the story of the Divine Creation of man as taught in the Bible, and to teach instead that man has descended from a lower order of animals." Scopes admitted to teaching about evolution from George Hunter's *Civic Biology*, a book approved by Tennessee's textbook commission. The Scopes trial, soon known throughout the nation as "the monkey trial," came in the middle of a decade punctuated by the Red Scare, increased urban–rural tensions, and the resurgence of the Ku Klux Klan. The Dayton courtroom soon became an arena of cultural and political conflict between fundamentalist Christians and civil libertarians.

The former, led by William Jennings Bryan, a three-time presidential candidate and ardent prohibitionist who joined the prosecution staff, argued that the Butler Act was a traditional exercise of STATE POLICE POWER with respect to public education, little different from mandating other curricula and fixing the qualifications of teachers. They also saw the statute as a defense of traditional folk values against the moral relativism of modern science and other contemporary religious beliefs. Scopes's defenders, including the AMERICAN CIVIL LIBERTIES UNION (ACLU) and the celebrated criminal lawyer Clarence Darrow, saw in the Butler Act a palpable threat to several constitutional guarantees, including SEPARATION OF CHURCH AND STATE and FREEDOM OF SPEECH.

The trial judge, John T. Raulston, rejected all constitutional attacks against the statute; he also declined to permit testimony by scientific and religious experts, many of whom hoped to argue the compatibility between evolution and traditional religious values, including the belief in a supreme being. The only issue for the jury, Raulston noted, was the narrow one of whether or not John Scopes had taught his class that man had descended from a lower form of animals. Because Scopes has already admitted doing so, the jury's verdict was never in doubt. Darrow and the defense gained a public relations triumph by putting Bryan on the stand to testify as an expert about the Bible. The Great

Commoner, who collapsed and died several days after the trial ended, affirmed his faith in biblical literalism, including the story of Jonah and the whale. The jury, however, found Scopes guilty and Raulston fined him the statutory minimum of $100.

Darrow and the ACLU encountered only frustration when they attempted to APPEAL the conviction. The state supreme court, with one judge dissenting, upheld the constitutionality of the Butler Act. However, they reversed Scopes's conviction on a technicality, holding that the Tennessee constitution prohibited trial judges from imposing fines in excess of $50 without a jury recommendation. The state supreme court also urged Tennessee officials to cease further prosecution of John Scopes—advice which the attorney general followed. The Butler Act remained on the Tennessee statute books but was not enforced against other educational heretics.

Bibliography

GINGER, RAY   1958   *Six Days or Forever? Tennessee v. John Thomas Scopes.* New York: Oxford University Press.

MCCOLLUM v. BOARD OF EDUCATION

333 U.S. 203 (1948)

Richard E. Morgan

During the late 1940s and 1950s "RELEASED TIME programs" were popular around the country. Public school boards and administrators cooperated with churches and synagogues to provide religious education for students according to their parents' choices. Under the arrangement in Champaign-Urbana, Illinois, students whose parents had so requested were excused from their classes to attend classes given by religious educators in the school buildings. Nonparticipating pupils were not excused from their regular classes.

McCollum, whose child Terry attended the public schools, challenged the Illinois practice on the grounds that it violated the establishment clause of the FIRST AMENDMENT. The case was the first church–state controversy to reach the Court since EVERSON v. BOARD OF EDUCATION the year before, and Justice HUGO L. BLACK again delivered the opinion of the Court.

Referring to the theory of strict separation announced as OBITER DICTUM in his *Everson* opinion, Black held that the Illinois arrangement fell squarely within the First Amendment's ban. He stressed particularly the utilization of tax-supported facilities to aid religious teaching.

Justice FELIX FRANKFURTER concurred in an opinion in which Justices ROBERT JACKSON, WILEY B. RUTLEDGE, and HAROLD H. BURTON joined. These four had dissented from *Everson*'s approval of state aid to the transportation of children to religious schools.

Justice Jackson also concurred separately, rejecting the sweeping separationism of the Black opinion. Pointing out that there was little real cost to the taxpayers in the Illinois program, he agreed that the Court should end "formal and explicit instruction" such as that in the Champaign schools, but cautioned against inviting ceaseless petitions to the Court to purge school curricula of materials that any group might regard as religious.

Justice STANLEY F. REED, the lone dissenter, had concurred in the result in *Everson*. Here he argued that the majority was giving "establishment" too broad a meaning; unconstitutional "aid" to religion embraced only purposeful assistance directly to a church, not cooperative relation-ships between government and religious institutions.

　　McCollum seemed to represent a deepening Supreme Court commit-ment to the theory of strict SEPARATION OF CHURCH AND STATE, but it was significantly limited by another released-time case, ZORACH v. CLAU-SEN (1952).

RELEASED TIME

Leo Pfeffer

Twice, in McCollum v. Board of Education (1948) and again in Zorach v. Clausen (1952), the Supreme Court considered First Amendment challenges to the practice of releasing public school pupils from their regular studies so that they might participate in programs for religious instruction.

The first such program, in Gary, Indiana, in 1914, provided that, with parental consent and cooperation of church authorities, children could be released for one or more periods each week to go to churches of their own faith and there participate in religious instruction, returning to the public school at the end of the period, or if the period was the last of the day, going home.

The idea spread to other communities, but, for a variety of reasons, quite slowly. In rural and small urban communities, such as Champaign, Illinois, it was found more effective to have the religious instruction take place within the public schools rather than in the church schools.

In Champaign in 1940, an interfaith council with Protestant, Roman Catholic, and Jewish representatives was formed to offer religious instruction within the public schools during regular school hours. Instructors of religion were to be hired and paid by or through the interfaith council, subject to the approval and supervision of the public school superintendent. Each term the public school teachers distributed to the children cards on which parents could indicate their consent to the enrollment of their children in the religion classes. Children who obtained such consent were released by the school authorities from the secular work for a period of thirty minutes weekly in the elementary schools and forty-five minutes in the junior high school. Only Protestant instruction was conducted within the regular classroom; children released for Roman Catholic or Jewish instruction left their classroom for other parts of the building. Nonparticipants were also relocated, sometimes accompanied by their regular teachers and sometimes not. At the end of each session, children who had participated in any religious instruction returned to the regular classroom, and regular class work was resumed.

McCollum v. Board of Education (1948) was a suit, brought in a state court by the mother of a fifth grader, challenging the constitutionality of Champaign's program. In the Supreme Court, counsel for the school authorities argued that the establishment clause did not apply to the states, and that the contrary HOLDING in EVERSON V. BOARD OF EDUCATION (1947) should be overruled. This the Court refused to do, reasserting *Everson*'s conclusion about the scope of the establishment clause.

No more successful was the argument that historically the establishment clause had been intended to forbid only preferential treatment of one faith over others, whereas the Champaign program was open equally to Protestants, Roman Catholics, and Jews. Here, too, the Court found no reason to reconsider its statement in *Everson* that the clause barred aid not only to one religion but equally to all religions.

Where, the Court said, pupils compelled by law to go to school for secular education are released in part from their legal duty if they attend religious classes, the tax-supported public school system's use to aid religious groups to spread their faiths falls squarely under the ban of the First Amendment. Not only are the public school buildings used for the dissemination of religious doctrines, but the state also affords sectarian groups an invaluable aid, helping to provide pupils for their religious classes through the use of the state's compulsory public school machinery. This, the Court concluded, was not SEPARATION OF CHURCH AND STATE.

Although the Court's language appeared to encompass in its determination of unconstitutionality released time plans providing for off-school religious instruction (and Justice HUGO L. BLACK who wrote the opinion so interpreted it), the majority reached a contrary conclusion in *Zorach v. Clausen* (1952).

Zorach involved New York City's program, which restricted public school participation to releasing children whose parents had signed consent cards and specifically forbade comment by any principal or teacher on the attendance or nonattendance of any pupil upon religious instruction. This situation, said the Court speaking through Justice WILLIAM O. DOUGLAS, differed from that presented in the *McCollum* case. There, the classrooms had been used for religious instruction and the influence of the public school used to promote that instruction. Here, the public schools did no more than accommodate their schedules to allow children, who so wished, to go elsewhere for religious instruction completely independent of public school operations. The situation, Douglas said, was not different from that presented when a Roman Catholic student asks his teacher to be excused to attend a mass on a Holy Day of Obligation or a Jewish student to attend synagogue on Yom Kippur.

Government, Justice Douglas said further, may not finance religious groups nor undertake religious instruction nor blend secular and sectarian education nor use secular institutions to force one or some religion on any person. Government, however, must be neutral in respect to religion, not hostile. "We are," he said, "a religious people whose institutions presuppose a Supreme Being. When the state encourages religious instruction or cooperates with religious authorities, it follows the best of our traditions. For it then respects the religious nature of our people and accommodates the public service to their spiritual needs."

On the basis of *McCollum* and *Zorach*, the present law is that released time programs are constitutional so long as the religious instruction is given off the public school premises and the public school teachers and authorities are involved in it only by releasing uncoerced children who choose to participate in it.

Bibliography

PFEFFER, LEO (1953)1967   *Church, State and Freedom.* Boston: Beacon Press.
Released Time for Religious Education in New York City Schools.   1949   Public Education Association.
STOKES, A. P. and PFEFFER, LEO 1964   *Church and State in the United States.* New York: Harper & Row.

ZORACH v. CLAUSEN

343 U.S. 306 (1952)

Richard E. Morgan

This was the Supreme Court's second encounter with a RELEASED TIME program. In McCOLLUM v. BOARD OF EDUCATION (1948), the Court had invalidated an arrangement by which teachers entered public schools to provide religious instruction. *Zorach* involved New York City's released time program in which instruction was offered off school premises. According to the requests of their parents, public school children were allowed to leave school for specific periods of time to go to church facilities. Nonparticipating students remained in their regular classrooms.

Justice WILLIAM O. DOUGLAS delivered the OPINION OF THE COURT sustaining the constitutionality of New York's program. Douglas emphasized that, as opposed to *McCollum,* no public facilities were used. The schools, Douglas said, were merely rearranging their schedules to accommodate the needs of religious people.

Justices HUGO L. BLACK, ROBERT H. JACKSON, and FELIX FRANKFURTER dissented. Black and Jackson argued that children were compelled by law to attend public schools and that to release them for religious instruction used governmental compulsion to promote religion. In a slap at Douglas's presumed presidential ambitions, Jackson said, "Today's judgment will be more interesting to students of psychology and of the judicial process than to students of constitutional law."

ENGEL v. VITALE

370 U.S. 421 (1962)

Richard E. Morgan

The Board of Regents of the State of New York authorized a short prayer for recitation in schools. The Regents were seeking to defuse the emotional issue of religious exercises in the classroom. The matter was taken out of the hands of school boards and teachers, and the blandest sort of invocation of the Deity was provided: "Almighty God, we acknowledge our dependence upon Thee, and beg Thy blessings upon us, our teachers, and our country." School districts in New York did not have to use the prayer, and if they did, no child was required to repeat it. But if there were any prayer in a New York classroom it would have to be this one. The Board of Education of New Hyde Park, New York, chose to use the Regents' Prayer and directed its principals to cause it to be said aloud at the beginning of each school day in every classroom.

Use of the prayer was challenged as an ESTABLISHMENT OF RELIGION. Justice HUGO L. BLACK, writing for the Court, concluded that neither the nondenominational nature of the prayer nor the fact that it was voluntary could save it from unconstitutionality under the establishment clause. By providing the prayer, New York officially approved theistic religion. With his usual generous quotations from JAMES MADISON and THOMAS JEFFERSON, Black found such state support impermissible.

Justice WILLIAM O. DOUGLAS concurred separately. He had more trouble than Black concluding that the prayer established religion "in the strictly historic meaning of these words." What Douglas feared was the divisiveness engendered in a community when government sponsored a religious exercise.

Only Justice POTTER STEWART dissented, concluding that "the Court has misapplied a great constitutional principle." Stewart could not see how a purely voluntary prayer could be held to constitute state adoption of an official religion. For Stewart, an official religion was the only meaning of "establishment of religion." He noted that invocations of the Deity in public ceremonies of all sorts had been a feature of our national life from its outset. Without quite saying so, Stewart asked his brethren how the Regents' Prayer could be anathematized on establishment clause grounds without scraping "In God We Trust" off the pennies.

Engel v. Vitale was the first of a series of cases in which the Court used the establishment clause to extirpate from the public schools the least-commondenominator religious invocations which had been a traditional part of public ceremonies—especially school ceremonies—in America.

The decision proved extremely controversial. It has been widely circumvented and there have been repeated attempts to amend the Constitution to undo the effect of *Engel*.

Bibliography

BERNS, WALTER   1976   *The First Amendment and the Future of American Democracy*. Pages 33–76. New York: Basic Books.

MUIR, WILLIAM K., JR.   1967   *Prayer in the Public Schools*. Chicago: University of Chicago Press.

ABINGTON TOWNSHIP SCHOOL DISTRICT v. SCHEMPP

374 U.S. 203 (1963)

Richard E. Morgan

A Pennsylvania statute required that at least ten verses from the Holy Bible be read, without comment, at the opening of each public school day. A child might be excused from this exercise upon the written request of his parents or guardian.

In ENGEL v. VITALE (1962) the school prayer held unconstitutional had been written by state officials. The question in *Schempp* was whether this made a difference—there being no claim that Pennsylvania was implicated in the authorship of the holy scripture.

Justice TOM C. CLARK concluded that the Pennsylvania exercise suffered from an establishment-clause infirmity every bit as grave as that afflicting New York's prayer. Clark's opinion in *Schempp* was the first strict separationist opinion of the Court not written by Justice HUGO L. BLACK, and Clark formulated a test for establishment clause validity with a precision that had eluded Black. A state program touching upon religion or religious institutions must have a valid secular purpose and must not have the primary effect of advancing or inhibiting religion. The Pennsylvania Bible reading program failed the test on both counts.

Justices WILLIAM O. DOUGLAS and WILLIAM J. BRENNAN concurred separately in opinions reflecting an even stricter separationism than Clark's. Justice ARTHUR J. GOLDBERG also filed a brief concurring opinion.

Justice POTTER STEWART dissented, as he had in *Engel,* arguing that religious exercises as part of public ceremonies were permissible so long as children were not coerced to participate.

Schempp, along with *Murray v. Curlett* (decided the same day), settled whatever lingering question there may have been about the constitutionality of RELIGION IN PUBLIC SCHOOLS.

EPPERSON *v.* ARKANSAS

393 U.S. 97 (1968)

Richard E. Morgan

Arkansas prohibited the teaching in its public schools "that mankind ascended or descended from a lower order of animals." In dealing with a challenge to the law based on establishment clause and FREEDOM OF SPEECH grounds, Justice ABE FORTAS, speaking for the Supreme Court, concluded that the Arkansas law violated the establishment clause. "There can be no doubt," he said, "that Arkansas sought to prevent its teachers from discussing the theory of evolution because it is contrary to the beliefs of some that the book of Genesis must be the exclusive source of the doctrine of the origin of man."

Justice HUGO L. BLACK and Justice POTTER STEWART concurred in brief opinions resting on VAGUENESS grounds. The Black opinion raised important GOVERNMENT SPEECH issues that are still unresolved.

WALLACE v. JAFFREE
472 U.S.   (1985)

Leonard W. Levy

A 6–3 Supreme Court, in an opinion by Justice JOHN PAUL STEVENS, held unconstitutional an Alabama statute that required public school children to observe a period of silence "for meditation or voluntary prayer." No member of the Court contested the constitutionality of the period of silence for meditation. As Justice SANDRA DAY O'CONNOR said in her CONCURRING OPINION, no threat to RELIGIOUS LIBERTY could be discerned from a room of "silent, thoughtful school children." Chief Justice WARREN E. BURGER added that there was no threat "even if they chose to pray." Burger willfully misunderstood or missed the point. Any student in any public school may pray voluntarily and silently at almost any time of the school day, if so moved. The state, in this case, sought to orchestrate group prayer by capitalizing on the impressionability of youngsters. Compulsory attendance laws and the coercive setting of the school provided a CAPTIVE AUDIENCE for the state to promote religion. Justice JOHN PAUL STEVENS emphasized the fact that the state act was "entirely motivated by a purpose to advance religion" and had "*no* secular purpose." The evidence irrefutably showed that. Accordingly, the Alabama act failed to pass the test of LEMON v. KURTZMAN (1971) used by the Court to determine whether a state violated the FIRST AMENDMENT's prohibition against an ESTABLISHMENT OF RELIGION.

Justice O'Connor, observing that Alabama already had a moment of silence law on its books, noted that during the silence, no one need be religious, no one's religious beliefs could be compromised, and no state encouragement of religion existed. "The crucial question," she wrote, "is whether the State has conveyed or attempted to convey the message that children should use the moment of silence for prayer." The only possible answer was that the state, by endorsing the decision to pray during the moment of silence, sponsored a religious exercise, thereby breaching the First Amendment's principle of SEPARATION OF CHURCH AND STATE.

GOVERNMENT AID TO RELIGIOUS INSTITUTIONS

Leo Pfeffer

Constitutionality of governmental aid to religious institutions, generally, though not exclusively, in the form of financial subsidies, is most often challenged under the FIRST AMENDMENT's ban on laws respecting an ESTABLISHMENT OF RELIGION. When the purpose of the subsidy is to finance obviously religious activities, such as the erection or repairing of a church building, UNCONSTITUTIONALITY is generally recognized. In large measure the purpose of the establishment clause was to forbid such grants, as is indicated by the Court's opinion and Justice WILEY RUTLEDGE's dissenting opinion in EVERSON v. BOARD OF EDUCATION (1947). On the other hand, where the funds are used for what would generally be considered secular activities, such as maintaining hospitals or providing meals for pupils in church-related (often called parochial) schools, constitutional validity is fairly unanimously assumed.

Constitutional controversy revolves largely around governmental financing of church-related schools that combine the inculcation of religious doctrines and beliefs with what is generally considered the teaching of secular subjects, substantially, though not necessarily entirely, as they are taught in public schools.

In *Everson,* the Court upheld as a valid exercise of the POLICE POWER a state statute financing bus transportation to parochial schools, on the ground that the legislative purpose was not to aid religion by financing the operations of the schools but to help insure the safety of children going to or returning from them. A law having the former purpose would violate the establishment clause, which forbids government to set up a church, aid one or more religions, or prefer one religion over others. "No tax in any amount, large or small," the Court said, "can be levied to support any religious activities or institutions, whatever they may be called, or whatever form they may adopt to teach or practice religion."

The *Everson,* or "no-aid," interpretation of the establishment clause as applied to governmental financing of religious schools next reached the Supreme Court in the case of BOARD OF EDUCATION v. ALLEN (1968).

There the Court upheld a New York statute providing for the loan to pupils attending nonpublic schools of secular textbooks authorized for use in public schools. The Court concluded that the statute did not impermissibly aid religious schools within the meaning of *Everson,* nor did it violate the establishment clause ban on laws lacking a secular legislative purpose or having a primary effect that either advances or inhibits religion, as that clause had been interpreted in ABINGTON SCHOOL DISTRICT V. SCHEMPP (1963). In upholding the New York law, the Court recognized that the police power rationale of *Everson* was not readily applicable to textbook laws, but it adjudged that the processes of secular and religious training are not so intertwined that secular textbooks furnished to students by the public are in fact instrumental in the teaching of religion.

It is fairly obvious that the *Allen* rationale could be used to justify state aid to religious schools considerably more extensive than mere financing of transportation or provision of secular textbooks. It could, for example, justify state financing of supplies other than textbooks, costs of maintenance and repair of parochial school premises, and, most important, salaries of instructors who teach the nonreligious subjects, which constitute the major part of the parochial school curriculum.

That this extension was intended by Justice BYRON R. WHITE, the author of the *Allen* opinion, is indicated by the fact that he thereafter dissented in all the decisions barring aid to church-related schools. The first of these decisions came in the companion cases of LEMON V. KURTZMAN and *Earley v. DiCenso* (1973). In *Lemon,* Pennsylvania purchased the services of religious schools in providing secular education to their pupils. In *DiCenso,* Rhode Island paid fifteen percent of the salaries of religious school teachers who taught only secular subjects.

A year earlier, in WALZ V. TAX COMMISSION (1970), the Court had expanded the purpose–effect test by adding a third dimension: a statute violated the establishment clause if it fostered excessive governmental entanglement with religion. The statutes involved in *Lemon* and *DiCenso* violated the clause, the Court held, because in order to insure that the teachers did not inject religion into their secular classes or allow religious values to affect the content of secular instruction, it was necessary to subject the teachers to comprehensive, discriminating, and continuing state surveillance, which would constitute forbidden entanglement of church and state.

In other cases the Court held unconstitutional laws enacted to reimburse religious schools for the cost of preparing, conducting, and grading teacher-prepared tests, of maintaining and repairing school buildings, of transporting students on field trips to museums and concerts as part of secular courses, and of purchasing instructional materials and equipment susceptible of diversion to religious use. The Court also held unconstitutional state tuition assistance to the parents of parochial school pupils, whether by direct grant or through state income tax benefits.

On the other hand, the Court has upheld the constitutionality of reimbursement for noninstructional health and welfare services supplied to parochial school pupils, such as meals, medical and dental care, and diagnostic services relating to speech, hearing, and psychological problems. In COMMITTEE FOR PUBLIC EDUCATION AND RELIGIOUS LIBERTY v. REGAN (1980) the Court allowed reimbursement for the expense of administering state-prepared and mandated objective examinations.

The Court has manifested a considerably more tolerant approach in cases challenging governmental aid to church-related institutions of higher education. While the purpose–effect–entanglement test is in principle equally applicable, the Court held that where a grant is used to finance facilities in colleges and universities used only for secular instruction, the primary effect of the law is not to advance religion. As for entanglement, religion does not necessarily so permeate the secular education provided by church-related colleges nor so seep into the use of their facilities as to require a ruling that in all cases excessive surveillance would be necessary to assure that the facilities were not used for religious purposes. The Court also gave consideration to the skepticism of college students, the nature of college and postgraduate courses, the high degree of academic freedom characterizing many church-related colleges, and their nonlocal constituencies. For all these reasons, in TILTON v. RICHARD-SON (1973) the Court sanctioned substantial governmental financing of church-related institutions of higher education.

In *Walz v. Tax Commission* the Court upheld the constitutionality of tax exemption accorded to property used exclusively for worship or other religious purposes. Exemption, it held, does not entail sponsorship of religion and involves even less entanglement than nonexemption, since it does not require the government to examine the affairs of the church and audit its books or records. The longevity of exemption, dating as it does from the time the Republic was founded, constitutes strong evidence of its constitutionality.

The Court, in *Walz,* did not hold that the free exercise clause would be violated if exemption were disallowed (although it was urged to do so in the AMICUS CURIAE brief submitted by the National Council of Churches). Nor, on the other hand, did it decide to the contrary. As of the present, therefore, it seems that governments, federal or state, have the constitutional option of granting or denying exemption.

Bibliography

MORGAN, RICHARD E.   1972   *The Supreme Court and Religion.* New York: Free Press.

PFEFFER, LEO   1967   *Church, State and Freedom.* Rev. ed. Boston: Beacon Press.
_____   1975   *God, Caesar and the Constitution.* Boston: Beacon Press.
TRIBE, LAURENCE   1978   *American Constitutional Law.* Chap. 14. Mineola, N.Y.:
    Foundation Press.

RELIGIOUS USE OF STATE PROPERTY

Leo Pfeffer

In WIDMAR V. VINCENT (1981) the Supreme Court ruled that a state university's exclusionary policy in respect to students' use for prayer or religious instruction of premises generally available to students for nonreligious use violated the FIRST AMENDMENT's guarantee of FREEDOM OF SPEECH.

Earlier, relevant decisions, mostly involving Jehovah's Witnesses, were handed down before the Court ruled in CANTWELL V. CONNECTICUT (1940) that the free exercise of religion clause, like the free speech clause, was applicable to the states no less than to the federal government. Quite naturally, therefore, it applied to religious meetings and conversionary efforts the CLEAR AND PRESENT DANGER (later COMPELLING STATE INTEREST) test formulated in SCHENCK V. UNITED STATES (1919) in respect to political speech and meetings and continued to do so after *Cantwell*.

In *Jamison v. Texas* (1943) the Court rejected a contention that a city's power over streets and parks is not limited to making reasonable regulations for the control of traffic and maintenance of order, but encompasses power absolutely to prohibit use for communication of ideas, including religious ones. No doubt, it ruled in NIEMOTKO V. MARYLAND (1951), a municipality may require a permit to hold religious meetings or, as in *Cox v. New Hampshire* (1941), public parades or processions, in streets and parks, but only to regulate time and place, and it may not refuse a permit by reason of the meeting's content, even if it includes verbal attacks upon some religions. This is so, the Court ruled in KUNZ V. NEW YORK (1941), even where prior missionary meetings had resulted in disorder because of the minister's scurrilous attacks on Roman Catholicism and Judaism, because the added cost of providing police to prevent possible violence does not justify infringement upon First Amendment rights.

Nor, as the Court held in *Schneider v. Irvington* (1939), may a municipality prohibit distribution of leaflets, including religious ones, on public streets and parks in order to prevent littering; the constitutional way to avoid littering is by arresting litterers, rather than restricting rights secured by the amendment. For the same reason, it reversed the conviction of a Jehovah's Witness who rang door bells to distribute religious handbills, in violation of an ordinance (enacted in part to prevent criminal entry) prohibiting ringing of doorbells or knocking on doors to distribute handbills.

The Court, in *Widmar,* did not hold that a state university must provide premises for student prayer and religious instruction, but only that it may not exclude such use if premises are provided for other noncurricular purposes. It is hardly likely that it intended thereby to overrule McCollum v. Board of Education (1948), wherein it outlawed religious instruction in public schools even where limited to pupils whose parents consent thereto. The distinction between the two situations lies in the fact that *McCollum* involved students of elementary and secondary school ages, whereas *Widmar* concerned students of college age who are generally less likely to be unduly influenced by on-premises prayer meetings.

In Lynch v. Donnelly (1984) the Court upheld the use of municipal funds to finance the cost of erecting and illuminating a life-size nativity scene in Pawtucket, Rhode Island, as part of an annual Christmas display. (Although the display was on private property, the Court made it clear that the result would have been the same had it been on town-owned property.) The Court based its decision on the recognition that Christmas had become a national secular holiday in American culture.

Bibliography

Pfeffer, Leo   1985   *Religion, State and the Burger Court.* Buffalo, N.Y.: Prometheus.

EVERSON v. BOARD OF EDUCATION

330 U.S. 1 (1947)

Richard E. Morgan

A New Jersey statute authorized local school boards to reimburse parents for the cost of public transportation of students to both public and private schools. Such reimbursement for the cost of transportation to church-related schools was challenged as an unconstitutional ESTABLISH-MENT OF RELIGION.

Justice HUGO L. BLACK delivered the opinion of a 5–4 Supreme Court. He began with a consideration of the background of the establishment clause, which relied heavily on the writings of JAMES MADISON and THOMAS JEFFERSON, but he had little to say about the actual legislative history of the FIRST AMENDMENT's language in the First Congress. Black concluded that the establishment clause "means at least this":

Neither a state nor the federal government can set up a church. Neither can pass laws which aid one religion, aid all religions or prefer one religion over another. . . . No tax in any amount, large or small, can be levied to support any religious activities or institutions, whatever they may be called, or whatever form they may adopt to teach and practice religion. . . . In the words of Jefferson, the clause against the establishment of religion by law was intended to erect "a wall of separation between church and State."

But after this sweeping separationist pronouncement, Justice Black pirouetted neatly and upheld the New Jersey program on the grounds that the state aid in that case was a public safety measure designed to protect students and could in no way be construed as aid to church-related schools.

Four dissenters were convinced that Justice Black had missed the point. Justice ROBERT H. JACKSON likened Black's MAJORITY OPINION to Byron's Julia who, "whispering I will ne'er consent, consented." What could be more helpful to a school, Jackson asked, than depositing the students at its door? Justice WILEY B. RUTLEDGE, with whom Justices Jackson, FELIX FRANKFURTER, and HAROLD BURTON joined, also filed a lengthy dissent. Justice Rutledge also made lavish use of the writings of Madison and Jefferson, and argued that the New Jersey program could not be justified as a public safety expenditure.

Everson stands at the entrance to the maze of law and litigation concerning participation by church-related schools in public programs. It was the first major utterance by the Supreme Court on the meaning of the establishment clause. Those favoring strict separation between religious institutions and government were pleased by Black's rhetoric and dismayed by his conclusion; those favoring a policy of flexibility or accommodation in church–state relations reacted the opposite way. That *Everson* satisfied no one and enraged many was portentous.

Bibliography

JOHNSON, RICHARD M.   1967   *The Dynamics of Compliance.* Evanston, Ill.: Northwestern University Press.
MORGAN, RICHARD E.   1972   *The Supreme Court and Religion.* Pages 76–122. New York: Free Press.

CHILD BENEFIT THEORY

Leo Pfeffer

Protagonists of aid to religious schools have sought to justify the practice constitutionally through what has become known as the child benefit theory. The establishment clause, they urge, forbids aid to the schools but not to the children who attend them. Recognizing that the schools themselves benefit from the action, they argue that the benefit is secondary to that received by the pupils, and note that the courts have long upheld governmental assistance to children as an aspect of the POLICE POWER.

The recognition is at least implicit in Supreme Court decisions through BOARD OF EDUCATION v. ALLEN (1968). Thus, in *Bradfield v. Roberts* (1899), the Court upheld the validity under the establishment clause of a grant of federal funds to finance the erection of a hospital in the DISTRICT OF COLUMBIA, to be maintained and operated by an order of nuns. The Court reasoned that the hospital corporation was a legal entity separate from its incorporators, and concluded that the aid was for a secular purpose. Later court decisions ignored this fiction, consistently upholding grants to religious organizations, corporate or noncorporate, to finance hospitals that, though owned and operated by churches, nevertheless were nonsectarian in their admission policies, and generally benefited the patients.

In EVERSON v. BOARD OF EDUCATION (1947) the Court upheld use of tax-raised funds to finance transportation to religious schools, in part because the program had the secular purpose to enable children to avoid the risks of traffic or hitchhiking in going to school. In COCHRAN v. LOUISIANA STATE BOARD OF EDUCATION (1930) and *Board of Education v. Allen* (1968) the Court similarly sustained laws financing the purchase of secular textbooks for use in parochial schools. The beneficiaries of the laws, the Court asserted, were not the schools but the children who attended them.

More recent decisions, however, manifest a weakening of the theory. In *Board of Education v. Nyquist* (1973) the Court refused to uphold a law to finance costs of maintenance and repair in religious schools, notwithstanding a provision that the program's purpose was to insure the health, welfare, and safety of the school children.

Two years later, in *Meek v. Pittenger,* the Court refused to extend *Allen* to encompass the loan of instructional materials to church-related schools, even though the materials benefited nonpublic school children and were provided for public school children. Finally, in WOLMAN v. WALTER (1977) the Court, unwilling to overrule either *Everson* or *Allen,* nevertheless refused to extend them to encompass educational field trip transportation to governmental, industrial, cultural, and scientific centers.

In these later cases, the Court has rejected the argument that if public funds were not used for these support services, many parents economically unable to pay for them would have to transfer their children to the public schools in violation of their own and of their children's religious conscience.

(SEE ALSO: Establishment of Religion; Separation of Church and State.)

Bibliography

DRINAN, ROBERT F., S.J.   1963   *Religion, the Courts, and Public Policy.* Chap. 5. New York: McGraw-Hill.

PFEFFER, LEO   1967   *Church, State and Freedom,* rev. ed. Chap. 14. Boston: Beacon Press.

WALZ v. TAX COMMISSION
397 U.S. 664 (1970)

David Gordon

In this 8–1 decision, the Supreme Court added a new element to the test for the constitutionality of financial aid to religious institutions. Chief Justice WARREN E. BURGER rejected Walz's claim that a state's grant of tax exemption to property used only for religious purposes violated the ESTABLISHMENT OF RELIGION clause of the FIRST AMENDMENT. Adding to tests already elaborated in ABINGTON SCHOOL DISTRICT V. SCHEMPP (1963), Burger required assurance that "the end result—the effect—[of a grant of tax exemption] is not an excessive government entanglement with religion. The test is inescapably one of degree." Commenting that "the course of constitutional neutrality in this area cannot be an absolutely straight line," he said that taxing a church would have involved even more "entanglement" than exempting them. Justice WILLIAM O. DOUGLAS, dissenting, believed that TORCASO V. WATKINS (1961) governed. He concluded that "a tax exemption is a subsidy."

LEMON v. KURTZMAN

403 U.S. 602 (1971) (I)
411 U.S. 192 (1973) (II)

Richard E. Morgan

This case involved one of the school aid statutes produced by state legislatures in the wake of BOARD OF EDUCATION v. ALLEN (1968). *Lemon* I stands for three cases joined for decision by the Court. Lemon challenged the constitutionality of a Pennsylvania statute that authorized the Superintendent of Public Instruction to reimburse nonpublic schools for teachers' salaries, textbooks, and instructional materials in secular subjects. *Erley v. DiCenso* and *Robinson v. DiCenso* (1971) challenged a Rhode Island statute that made available direct payments to teachers in nonpublic schools in amounts of up to fifteen percent of their regular salaries.

Both statutes were unconstitutional, Chief Justice WARREN BURGER concluded, and he set forth a threefold test which continues to be invoked in ESTABLISHMENT OF RELIGION cases: any program aiding a church-related institution must have an adequate secular purpose; it must have a primary effect that neither advances nor inhibits religion; and government must not be excessively entangled with religious institutions in the administration of the program. The Pennsylvania and Rhode Island schemes provided GOVERNMENT AID TO RELIGIOUS INSTITUTIONS. Burger argued that in order to see that these dollars were not used for religious instruction, the states would have to monitor compliance in ways involving excessive entanglement.

Lemon v. Kurtzman returned to the Court (*Lemon* II) two years later on the question of whether the Pennsylvania schools could retain the monies that had been paid out in the period between the implementation of law and the decision of the Supreme Court invalidating it in *Lemon* I. In a PLURALITY OPINION for himself and Justices HARRY BLACKMUN, LEWIS F. POWELL, and WILLIAM H. REHNQUIST, Chief Justice Burger held that they could. An unconstitutional statute, he suggested, is not absolutely void but is a practical reality upon which people are entitled to rely until authoritatively informed otherwise. Justice BYRON R. WHITE concurred. Justice WILLIAM O. DOUGLAS, joined by Justices WILLIAM J. BRENNAN and POTTER STEWART, dissented. Douglas argued that there was "clear warning to those who proposed such subsidies" that they were treading on unconstitutional ground. "No consideration of EQUITY," Douglas suggested, should allow them "to profit from their unconstitutional venture."

TUITION GRANTS

Kenneth L. Karst

While parents have a constitutional right to send their children to private rather than public schools (see PIERCE V. SOCIETY OF SISTERS, 1925), the exercise of that right costs money. Such parents not only bear their share of the taxes that support public schools but also pay tuition to their children's schools. Not surprisingly, a regular item of business in Congress and the state legislatures is a proposal to relieve this "double burden" through some form of governmental relief. Two types of constitutional problems beset such proposals. Governmental aid to private schools may be attacked as STATE ACTION that promotes racial SEGREGATION or as an unconstitutional ESTABLISHMENT OF RELIGION.

Soon after the decision in BROWN V. BOARD OF EDUCATION (1954–1955), a number of southern states adopted a series of devices aimed at evading DESEGREGATION. One such device was the payment of state grants to private schools or to parents of private school children. The assumption was that when public schools were ordered to desegregate, white children would be withdrawn and placed in private schools. Some states went so far as to give local school boards the option of closing public schools and even selling those schools' physical plants to the operators of private schools which would be supported by tuition subsidized by the state. These private schools, it was expected, would be limited to white students. (More recently, federal CIVIL RIGHTS legislation has been applied to forbid that type of "segregation academy" to refuse black applicants. See RUNYON V. MCCRARY, (1976.) The Supreme Court held these tuition grant programs unconstitutional as evasions of *Brown* in cases such as GRIFFIN V. COUNTY SCHOOL BOARD (1964) and *Poindexter v. Louisiana Financial Assistance Commission* (PER CURIAM, 1968).

More recently, private schools in the North and West have acquired new white students following orders desegregating urban school systems. "White flight" means not only the departure of white families for the suburbs but also the transfer of white students from public to private schools. Estimates in the late 1970s suggested that as many as one-fifth of all enrollments in the nation's private schools were the result of "white flight." Proposals for governmental aid to private school children and their parents must therefore face a challenge based on the likely racially discriminatory impacts of various proposed forms of aid. Such impacts would not, of themselves, establish a constitutional violation; they would, however, be some evidence of an improper governmental purpose. (See LEGISLATION.)

Tuition grants limited to low-income parents of children enrolled in religious schools were held to violate the establishment clause in COMMITTEE FOR PUBLIC EDUCATION v. NYQUIST (1973). That decision did not settle the question of the constitutionality of a hypothetical program in which the state gave *all* parents education vouchers, to be used to support schools of their choosing, public or private, religious or secular. (See GOVERNMENT AID TO RELIGIOUS INSTITUTIONS; MUELLER v. ALLEN, 1983.)

Proponents of voucher plans designed to aid private schools and their clienteles have gone to some lengths in an effort to tailor their proposals to meet these two types of constitutional objection. One proposal provides elaborate incentives for racial integration, such as bonuses for integrated schools. In the absence of strong incentives of some kind, it seems obvious that significant aid to private elementary and secondary education will have the effect of increasing racial segregation by increasing the educational mobility of middle class whites.

Bibliography

SUGARMAN, STEPHEN D.   1974   Family Choice: The Next Step in the Quest for Equal Educational Opportunity? *Law and Contemporary Problems* 38:513–565.

COMMITTEE FOR PUBLIC EDUCATION AND RELIGIOUS LIBERTY v. NYQUIST

413 U.S. 752 (1973)
SLOAN v. LEMON
413 U.S. 825 (1973)

Leonard W. Levy

These cases, said Justice Lewis F. Powell in his opinion for a 6–3 Supreme Court, "involve an intertwining of societal and constitutional issues of the greatest importance." After Lemon v. Kurtzman (1971), New York State sought to aid private sectarian schools and the parents of children in them by various financial plans purporting to maintain the separation of church and state. Avowing concern for the health and safety of the children, the state provided direct financial grants to "qualifying" schools for maintenance costs. But as Justice Powell observed, "virtually all" were Roman Catholic schools, and the grants had the inevitable effect of subsidizing religious education, thus abridging the First Amendment's prohibition against an establishment of religion. New York, as well as Pennsylvania, also provided for the reimbursement of tuition paid by parents who sent their children to nonpublic sectarian schools; New York also had an optional tax relief plan. The Court found that the reimbursement plans constituted grants whose effect was the same as grants made directly to the institutions, thereby advancing religion. The tax benefit plan had the same unconstitutional result, because the deduction, like the grant, involved an expense to the state for the purpose of religious education. The Court distinguished outright tax exemptions of church property for reasons given in Walz v. Tax Commission (1970). By distinguishing *Nyquist* in Mueller v. Allen (1983), the Court sustained the constitutionality of a tax benefit plan that aided the parents of children in nonpublic sectarian schools.

WOLMAN v. WALTER

433 U.S. 229 (1977)

Richard E. Morgan

Ohio's aid plan for independent schools had six components: (1) the loan of textbooks; (2) the supply of standardized testing and scoring material; (3) the provision of diagnostic services aimed at identifying speech, hearing, and psychological problems; (4) the provision, off non-public school premises, of therapeutic, guidance, and remedial services; (5) the loan to pupils of instructional materials such as slide projectors, tape recorders, maps, and scientific gear; and (6) the provision of transportation for field trips similar to the transportation provided public school students.

Justice HARRY BLACKMUN delivered what was in part an opinion of the Supreme Court and in part a PLURALITY OPINION in which only Chief Justice WARREN E. BURGER, Justice POTTER STEWART, and Justice LEWIS F. POWELL joined.

The Court upheld the loan of textbooks, the supply of testing materials, the therapeutic services, and the provision of diagnostic services on non-public school premises. The Court found unconstitutional the provisions for lending secular instructional materials and for field trip transportation.

This case indicated the extent to which the "wall between church and state" was in fact a blurred, indistinct, and variable barrier.

COMMITTEE FOR PUBLIC EDUCATION AND RELIGIOUS LIBERTY v. REGAN

444 U.S. 646 (1980)

Richard E. Morgan

A New York statute directed the reimbursement to nonpublic schools of costs incurred by them in complying with certain state-mandated requirements, including the administration of standardized tests. The participation of church-related schools in this program was challenged as an unconstitutional ESTABLISHMENT OF RELIGION, but the Supreme Court rejected the challenge.

Justice BYRON R. WHITE, writing for a narrowly divided Court, noted that a previous New York law authorizing reimbursement for test services performed by nonpublic schools had been found unconstitutional in *Levitt v. Committee* (1973). However, the new statute, unlike its predecessor, provided for state audit of school financial records to insure that public monies were used only for secular purposes.

Justice HARRY BLACKMUN, with whom Justices WILLIAM J. BRENNAN and THURGOOD MARSHALL joined, dissented. Blackmun stressed that New York's program involved direct payments by the state to a school engaged in a religious enterprise. Justice JOHN PAUL STEVENS also filed a brief dissent.

Committee v. Regan is another illustration of the blurred nature of the line the Court has attempted to draw between permissible and impermissible state support to church-related schools.

MUELLER v. ALLEN

463 U.S. 388 (1983)

Leonard W. Levy

In this major case on the SEPARATION OF CHURCH AND STATE, the Supreme Court altered constitutional law on the issue of state aid to parents of parochial school children. The precedents had established that a state may not aid parochial schools by direct grants or indirectly by financial aids to the parents of the children; whether those aids took the form of tax credits or reimbursements of tuition expenses did not matter. In this case the state act allowed taxpayers to deduct expenses for tuition, books, and transportation of their children to school, no matter what school, public or private, secular or sectarian.

Justice WILLIAM H. REHNQUIST for a 5–4 Court ruled that the plan satisfied all three parts of the purpose, effect, and no-entanglement test of LEMON V. KURTZMAN (1971). That all taxpaying parents benefited from the act made the difference between this case and the precedents, even though parents of public school children could not take advantage of the major tax deduction. Rehnquist declared that the state had not aided religion generally or any particular denomination and had not excessively entangled the state with religion even though government officials had to disallow tax deductions for instructional materials and books that were used to teach religion. According to the dissenters, however, the statute had not restricted the parochial schools to books approved for public school use, with the result that the state necessarily became enmeshed in religious matters when administering the tax deductions. The dissenters also rejected the majority point that the availability of the tax deduction to all parents distinguished this case from the precedents. The parents of public school children simply were unable to claim the large deduction for tuition. Consequently the program had the effect of advancing the religious mission of the private sectarian schools.

VALLEY FORGE CHRISTIAN COLLEGE v. AMERICANS UNITED FOR SEPARATION OF CHURCH AND STATE

454 U.S. 464 (1982)

Kenneth L. Karst

Severely limiting the precedent of FLAST v. COHEN (1968), the Supreme Court here tightened the requirements for STANDING in a TAXPAYER'S SUIT against the federal government.

Under a general power from Congress to dispose of surplus federal property, the Department of Health, Education and Welfare (HEW) transferred land and buildings worth over $500,000 to a religious college that trained students for the ministry. Because HEW calculated that the government benefited from the transfer at a rate of 100 percent, the college paid nothing.

Federal taxpayers sued to set aside the transfer, contending that it amounted to an ESTABLISHMENT OF RELIGION. The Supreme Court held, 5–4, that the taxpayers lacked standing. The majority distinguished *Flast,* which had upheld taxpayer standing to challenge federal subsidies to church schools: *Flast* challenged an act of Congress; here plaintiffs challenged a decision by HEW. Furthermore, *Flast* involved injury to the plaintiffs as taxpayers: tax money was to be spent unconstitutionally. Here the Court dealt not with Congress's spending power but with the power to dispose of property.

The dissenters emphasized what everyone knew: absent taxpayer standing, no one has standing to challenge government donations of property to churches. In such cases the establishment clause is enforceable in the consciences of government officials, but not in court.

RELIGIOUS TEST FOR PUBLIC OFFICE

Leo Pfeffer

As early as the seventeenth century ROGER WILLIAMS expressed his dissent from the common practice, inherited from England, of imposing a religious test for public office. However, by the beginning of the eighteenth century even Rhode Island had adopted the pattern prevailing among the other colonies and had enacted a law that limited CITIZENSHIP and eligibility for public office to Protestants.

Most liberal of these was Pennsylvania's law, which required a belief that God was "the rewarder of the good and punisher of the wicked." At the other extreme was that of North Carolina, which disqualified from office any one who denied "the being of God or the truth of the Protestant religion, or the divine authority of either the Old or New Testament."

After the Revolutionary War, however, the states began the process of disestablishment, including the elimination of religious tests. The 1786 VIRGINIA STATUTE OF RELIGIOUS LIBERTY, for example, asserted that "our CIVIL RIGHTS have no dependence on our religious opinions," and "the proscribing of any citizen as unworthy of being called to office of trust and emolument, unless he profess or renounce this or that religious opinion, is depriving him injuriously of those privileges and advantages to which in common with his fellow citizens he has a NATURAL RIGHT." The CONSTITUTIONAL CONVENTION OF 1787 unanimously adopted the clause of Article VI providing that "no religious Test shall ever be required as a qualification to any Office or public Trust under the United States."

The prohibition applies only to federal offices, and some states having religious tests in their constitutions or laws did not repeal them but contented themselves with limiting them to belief in the existence of God. One of these was Maryland, where an otherwise fully qualified appointee to the office of notary public was denied his commission for the office for refusing to sign the oath.

In TORCASO v. WATKINS (1961) the Supreme Court ruled the denial unconstitutional, relying upon both the no-establishment and the free exercise clauses of the FIRST AMENDMENT. As to the former, it asserted that the clause does not bar merely preferential treatment of one religion over others (although even such limited interpretation would require invalidation since the oath preferred theistic over nontheistic faiths such as "Buddhism, Taoism, Ethical Culture and Secular Humanism and others") but also preferential treatment of religion as against nonreligion. The opinion also invoked the free exercise clause in concluding that the provision invades "freedom of religion and belief."

The converse of religious tests for public office, reflecting a prevalent anticlericalism, was the disqualification of clergymen from serving in public office. A majority of the states had such provisions when the Constitution was written, but in *McDaniel v. Paty* (1978) the Supreme Court held such laws violative of the First Amendment's free exercise clause.

Bibliography

PFEFFER, LEO   (1953)1967   *Church, State and Freedom*. Boston: Beacon Press.
_____   1975   *God, Caesar and the Constitution*. Boston: Beacon Press.

LARKIN v. GRENDEL'S DEN, INCORPORATED

459 U.S. 116 (1982)

Leonard W. Levy

Dissenting alone, Justice WILLIAM H. REHNQUIST observed that "silly cases" like this one, as well as great or hard cases, make bad law. Chief Justice WARREN E. BURGER for the Court aimed its "heavy FIRST AMENDMENT artillery," in Rehnquist's phrase, at a statute that banned the sale of alcoholic beverages within 500 feet of a school or church, should either object to the presence of a neighboring tavern. Originally, Massachusetts had absolutely banned such taverns but found that the objective of the STATE POLICE POWER, promoting neighborhood peace, could be fulfilled by the less drastic method of allowing schools and churches to take the initiative of registering objections. In this case a church objected to a tavern located ten feet away. Burger held that vesting the church with the state's veto power breached the prohibition against an ESTABLISHMENT OF RELIGION, on the grounds that the church's involvement vitiated the secular purposes of the statute, advanced the cause of religion, and excessively entangled state and church. Rehnquist argued that a sensible statute had not breached the wall of SEPARATION OF CHURCH AND STATE.

SUNDAY CLOSING LAWS

Leo Pfeffer

The first compulsory Sunday observance law in what is now the United States was promulgated in Virginia in 1610. It made absence from church services punishable by death for the third offense. Although there is no record of any person suffering the death penalty, lesser penalties, including whipping, were in effect in all the colonies and were continued after independence. Implicit constitutional recognition of Sunday observance is found in Article I, section 7, which excepts Sundays from the ten days wherein the President is required to exercise his veto of bills adopted by Congress.

Before the Supreme Court ruled that the FIRST AMENDMENT was applicable to the states, it held, in *Hennington v. Georgia* (1896), that Georgia had not unconstitutionally burdened INTERSTATE COMMERCE by regulating the movement of freight trains on Sundays. Four years later, it held, in *Petit v. Minnesota* (1900), that the state had not denied DUE PROCESS in refusing to classify barbering as an act of necessity or charity that could legally be performed on Sundays.

In 1961, after the Court had ruled the First Amendment applicable to the states, it considered the constitutionality of three state Sunday closing laws under that Amendment in four cases, known collectively as the Sunday Closing Law Cases. Two, *McGowan v. Maryland* and *Two Guys from Harrison-Allentown, Inc. v. McGinley,* concerned owners of highway discount stores that were open for business seven days a week. The other two, *Gallagher v. Crown Kosher Super Market* and *Braunfeld v. Brown,* involved stores owned by Orthodox Jews, who, by reason of religious convictions, abstained from all business activities on Saturdays.

In these cases the statutes were challenged on three principal grounds: that the laws violated the ban on the ESTABLISHMENT OF RELIGION; that the statutes' crazy-quilt pattern of exemptions was arbitrary, constituting a denial of due process and the EQUAL PROTECTION OF THE LAWS (for example, in one of the states it was legal to sell fish and food stuffs wholesale, but not at retail; in another, merchandise customarily sold at beaches and amusement parks might be sold there, but not elsewhere); that, at least in respect to Jews, Seventh-Day Adventists, and others whose religions required rest on Saturday, the laws violated the constitutional protection of RELIGIOUS LIBERTY by making it economically difficult if not impossible for them to observe their own Sabbath when their competitors operated six days each week.

In all four cases the Court upheld the constitutionality of the challenged laws, with all the prevailing opinions written by Chief Justice EARL WARREN. He recognized that the laws challenged in these cases had been enacted in colonial times with the purpose of ensuring observance of the majoritarian Christian Sabbath as a religious obligation. However, he said, the religious origin of these statutes did not require their invalidation if their present purpose was secular.

Warren said that the modern purpose of the challenged statutes was to set aside a day for "rest, repose, relaxation, tranquillity"; the purpose was therefore secular rather than religious. The Maryland statutes, for example, permitted such Sunday activities as the operation of bathing beaches, amusement parks, and even pinball and slot machines, as well as the sale of alcoholic beverages and the performance of professional sports. That such exemptions are directly contrary to the religiosity of the Sabbath indicated clearly that the Sunday laws' present purpose was not religious.

Viewed as welfare legislation, the Sunday laws presented little constitutional difficulty. The Chief Justice noted in *McGowan* that numerous federal and state laws affecting public health, safety, conditions of labor, week-end diversion at parks and beaches, and cultural activities of various kinds, had long been upheld. To forbid a state from prescribing Sunday as a day of rest solely because centuries ago such laws had their genesis in religion would be a CONSTITUTIONAL INTERPRETATION based on hostility to the public welfare rather than the SEPARATION OF CHURCH AND STATE.

The Court had more difficulty in sustaining laws applied against persons observing a day other than Sunday as their divinely ordained day of rest. Six Justices agreed that state legislatures, if they so elected, could constitutionally exempt Sabbatarians from complying with Sunday law restrictions, but the free exercise clause did not mandate that they do so. However, a majority of the Court could not agree upon one opinion to that effect. The Chief Justice, speaking for a plurality of four, noted that while the clause secured freedom to hold any belief, it did not forbid regulation of secular practices merely because some persons might suffer economically if they obeyed the dictates of their religion. Income tax laws, for example, did not violate the clause even though they limited the amount of deductions for religious contributions. If a state regulated conduct by a general law, the purpose and effect of which were to advance secular goals, its action was valid despite its indirect burden on the exercise of religion unless the purpose could practicably be otherwise accomplished. A sabbatarian exemption would be hard to enforce, and would interfere with the goal of providing a uniform day of rest that as far as possible eliminated the atmosphere of commercial activity. The laws thus did not violate the free exercise clause.

In THORNTON v. CALDOR, INC. (1985) the Court went even further. It ruled unconstitutional, under the effect aspect of the purpose-effect-entanglement test of constitutionality under the establishment clause, a Connecticut law that accorded employees an absolute right not to work on their chosen Sabbath.

Bibliography

PFEFFER, LEO   (1953)1967   *Church, State and Freedom.* Boston: Beacon Press.
_____   1975   *God, Caesar, and the Constitution.* Boston: Beacon Press.
STOKES, ANSON PHELPS   1950   *Church and State in the United States.* New York: Harper & Brothers.

MARSH v. CHAMBERS

463 U.S. 783 (1983)

Leonard W. Levy

A 6–3 Supreme Court sustained the constitutionality of legislative chaplaincies as not violating the SEPARATION OF CHURCH AND STATE mandated by the FIRST AMENDMENT. Chief Justice WARREN E. BURGER for the Court abandoned the three-part test of LEMON V. KURTZMAN (1971) previously used in cases involving the establishment clause and grounded his opinion wholly upon historical custom. Prayers by tax-supported legislative chaplains, traceable to the FIRST CONTINENTAL CONGRESS and the very Congress that framed the BILL OF RIGHTS, had become "part of the fabric of our society." Justice JOHN PAUL STEVENS, dissenting, asserted that Nebraska's practice of having the same Presbyterian minister as the official chaplain for sixteen years preferred one denomination over others. Justices WILLIAM J. BRENNAN and THURGOOD MARSHALL, dissenting, attacked legislative chaplains generally as a form of religious worship sponsored by government to promote and advance religion and entangling the government with religion, contrary to the values implicit in the establishment clause—privacy in religious matters, government neutrality, freedom of conscience, autonomy of religious life, and withdrawal of religion from the political arena.

LYNCH v. DONNELLY

465 U.S. 668 (1984)

Leonard W. Levy

The Supreme Court significantly lowered the wall of SEPARATION OF CHURCH AND STATE by sanctioning an official display of a sacred Christian symbol. Pawtucket, Rhode Island, included a crèche, or nativity scene, in its annual Christmas exhibit in the center of the city's shopping district. The case raised the question whether Pawtucket's crèche violated the Constitution's prohibition of ESTABLISHMENT OF RELIGION.

Chief Justice WARREN BURGER for a 5–4 Court ruled that despite the religious nature of the crèche, Pawtucket had a secular purpose in displaying it, as evinced by the fact that it was part of a Christmas exhibit that proclaimed "Season's Greetings" and included Santa Claus, his reindeer, a Christmas tree, and figures of carolers, a clown, an elephant, and a teddy bear. That the FIRST AMENDMENT, Burger argued, did not mandate complete separation is shown by our national motto, paid chaplains, presidential proclamations invoking God, the pledge of allegiance, and religious art in publicly supported museums.

Justice WILLIAM BRENNAN, dissenting, construed Burger's majority opinion narrowly, observing that the question was still open on the constitutionality of a public display on public property of a crèche alone or of the display of some other sacred symbol, such as a crucifixion scene. Brennan repudiated the supposed secular character of the crèche; he argued that "[f]or Christians the essential message of the nativity is that God became incarnate in the person of Christ." The majority's insensitivity toward the feelings of non-Christians disturbed Brennan.

A spokesman for the National Council of Churches complained that the Court had put Christ "on the same level as Santa Claus and Rudolph the Red-Nosed Reindeer." Clearly, the Court had a topsy-turvy understanding of what constitutes an establishment of religion, because in LARKIN V. GRENDEL'S DEN (1982) it saw a forbidden establishment in a STATE POLICE POWER measure aimed at keeping boisterous patrons of a tavern from disturbing a church, yet here saw no establishment in a state-sponsored crèche.

Religion: The Free Exercise Clause

RELIGIOUS LIBERTY

Leo Pfeffer

Although the FIRST AMENDMENT's mandate that "Congress shall make no law respecting an ESTABLISHMENT OF RELIGION, or prohibiting the free exercise thereof" is expressed in unconditional language, religious liberty, insofar as it extends beyond belief, is not an absolute right. The First Amendment, the Supreme Court said in CANTWELL v. CONNECT-ICUT (1940), "embraces two concepts—freedom to believe and freedom to act. The first is absolute but, in the nature of things, the second cannot be. Conduct remains subject to regulation of society."

Although the Court has repeated this dualism many times, it does not explain what the free exercise clause means. There is no need for a constitutional guarantee protecting freedom to believe, for, as the COMMON LAW had it, "the devil himself knows not the thoughts of man." Even if freedom to believe encompasses freedom to express what one believes, the clause adds nothing, since FREEDOM OF SPEECH and FREEDOM OF THE PRESS are specifically guaranteed in the amendment. Indeed, before *Cantwell* was decided, the Court applied the free speech rather than free exercise guarantee to challenges against state laws allegedly impinging upon religious liberty. Moreover, the word "exercise" connotes action or conduct, thus indicating that the framers had in mind something beyond the mere expression of a belief even if uttered in missionary activities.

In America the roots of religious liberty can be traced to ROGER WILLIAMS, whose pamphlet, "The Bloudy Tenent of Persecution for cause of Conscience, discussed in a Conference between Truth and Peace," asserted that it was God's command that "a permission of the most Paganish, Jewish, Turkish, or Antichristian consciences and worships, be granted to all men in all Nations and Countries." Another source was THOMAS JEFFERSON's VIRGINIA STATUTE OF RELIGIOUS LIBERTY, adopted in 1786, which declared that no person should be compelled to frequent or support any religious worship nor suffer on account of religious opinions and beliefs.

By the time the First Amendment became part of the Constitution in 1791, practically every state in the Union, to a greater or lesser degree, had enacted constitutional or statutory provisions securing the free exercise of religion. Indeed, it was the absence of a BILL OF RIGHTS whose proponents invariably called for a guarantee of religious freedom, that was the most frequently asserted objection to the Constitution presented to the states for approval. The necessary approval was obtained only because the Constitution's advocates promised that such a bill would be added by amendment after the Constitution was adopted.

Although the First Amendment was framed as a limitation of congressional powers, Supreme Court decisions have made it clear that executive and judicial action were likewise restricted by the amendment. Thus in *Anderson v. Laird* (1971) the Supreme Court refused to review a decision that the secretary of defense violated the First Amendment in requiring cadets in governmental military academies to attend chapel. As to the judiciary, unquestionably a federal court could not constitutionally disqualify a person from testifying as a witness because he was an atheist. (See TORCASO V. WATKINS, 1961.)

Since the Court's decision in *Cantwell* the states are subject to the restrictions of the free exercise clause no less than the federal government. Because our federal system leaves to the states what is generally called the POLICE POWER, there were few occasions, prior to *Cantwell*, when the Supreme Court was called upon to define the meaning of the clause. The few that did arise involved actions in the TERRITORIES, which were subject to federal laws and thus to the First Amendment. Most significant of these was REYNOLDS V. UNITED STATES (1879), wherein the Supreme Court upheld the constitutionality of an act of Congress criminalizing POLYGAMY in any American territory. In rejecting the defense that polygamy was mandated by doctrines of the Holy Church of Latter-Day Saints (Mormons) and thus was protected by the free exercise clause, the Court stated what was later echoed in *Cantwell*, that although laws "cannot interfere with mere religious belief, they may with practice." It could hardly be contended, the Court continued, that the free exercise clause barred prosecution of persons who engaged in human sacrifice as a necessary part of their religious worship.

Since Reynolds was charged with practicing polygamy, the Court's decision did not pass upon the question whether teaching it as a God-mandated duty was "mere religious belief" and therefore beyond governmental interference. In DAVIS V. BEASON (1890) the Court decided that such teaching was "practice," and therefore constitutionally subject to governmental restrictions.

Teaching or preaching, even if deemed action, is however not beyond all First Amendment protection, which encompasses freedom of speech as well as religion. In GITLOW V. NEW YORK (1925) the Supreme Court declared for the first time that the free speech guarantee of the First Amendment was incorporated into the FOURTEENTH AMENDMENT by virtue of the DUE PROCESS clause in the latter and thus was applicable to the states. Accordingly, the Jehovah's Witnesses cases that first came to the Court in the 1930s were initially decided under the speech rather than the religion clause (LOVELL V. GRIFFIN, 1938; *Schneider v. Irvington,* 1939). It was, therefore, natural for the Court to decide the cases under the CLEAR AND PRESENT DANGER test that had first been announced in SCHENCK V. UNITED STATES (1919), a case involving prosecution for speaking against United States involvement in World War I.

In another sense, this too was quite natural since, like Schenck, the Witnesses were pacifists, at least in respect to wars in this world. (In *Sicurella v. United States,* the Court in 1955 ruled that a member of the sect was not disqualified from conscientious objector exemption because the sect's doctrines encompassed participation by believers in serving as soldiers in the Army of Christ Jesus at Armageddon.) Nevertheless, unlike Schenck and other opponents to American entry in World War I, the Witnesses (like the Friends) did not vocally oppose American entry into the war but limited themselves to claiming CONSCIENTIOUS OBJECTION status.

The Court did not apply the clear and present danger test in a case involving a member of the Jehovah's Witnesses whose child was expelled from public school for refusing to participate in the patriotic program of flag salute. In that case, *Minersville School District v. Gobitis* (1940), the Court, in an opinion by Justice FELIX FRANKFURTER, rejected the assertion as a defense of religious freedom. (See FLAG SALUTE CASES.) The antipolygamy law, he stated, was upheld in *Reynolds* not because it concerned action rather than belief, but because it was a valid general law, regulating the secular practice of marriage.

The majority of the Court, however, soon concluded that *Gobitis* had been incorrectly decided, and three years later the Court overruled it in *West Virginia State Board of Education v. Barnette* (1943). There the Court treated the Witnesses' refusal to salute the flag as a form of speech and therefore subject to the clear and present danger test. In later decisions, the Court returned to *Cantwell* and treated religious freedom cases under the free exercise rather than free speech clause, although it continued to apply the clear and present danger test.

Unsatisfied with that test, Justice Frankfurter prevailed upon his colleagues to accept a differently worded rule, that of BALANCING competing interests, also taken from Court decisions relating to other freedoms secured in the Bill of Rights. When a person complains that his constitutional rights have been infringed by some law or action of the state, it is the responsibility of the courts to weigh the importance of the particular right in issue as against the state's interest upon which its law or action is based. For example, the right of an objector not to violate his religious conscience by engaging in war must be weighed against the nation's interest in defending itself against foreign enemies, and, in such weighing, the latter interest may be adjudged the weightier.

The majority of the Court accepted this rule, but in recent years it has added an element that has almost turned it around. Justice Frankfurter believed that a citizen who challenged the constitutionality of state action had the burden of convincing the court that his interest was more important than the state's and should therefore be adjudged paramount. Establishing an individual's right superior to the state's interest was a particularly heavy burden to carry, but it was made even heavier by Justice Frankfurter's insistence that any doubt as to relative weights must be resolved in favor of the state, which would prevail unless its action were patently unreasonable. Recently, however, the Court has taken a more libertarian approach, requiring the state to persuade the courts that the values it seeks to protect are weightier. In the language of the decisions, the state must establish that there is a COMPELLING STATE INTEREST that justifies infringement of the citizen's right to the free exercise of his religion. If it fails to do so, its law or action will be adjudged unconstitutional. (See THOMAS V. REVIEW BOARD OF INDIANA, 1981; UNITED STATES V. LEE, 1982.)

In accord with this rule, the Court, in the 1972 case of WISCONSIN V. YODER, expressly rejected the belief–action test, holding that Amish parents could not be prosecuted for refusing to send their children to school after they had reached the age of fourteen. "Only those interests of the highest order," the Court said, "and those not otherwise served can overbalance the legitimate claim to the free exercise of religion."

Religious liberty is protected not only by the free exercise clause but also by the clause against ESTABLISHMENTS OF RELIGION. In EVERSON V. BOARD OF EDUCATION (1947) and later cases, the Court has stated that under the establishment clause, government cannot force a person to go to church or profess a belief in any religion. In later decisions, the Court has applied a three-pronged purpose–effect–entanglement test as a standard of constitutionality under the establishment clause. The Court has held, in *Committee for Public Education and Religious Liberty v. Nyquist* (1973), for example, that a challenged statute must have a primary effect that neither advances nor inhibits religion, and must avoid government entanglement with religion. (See SEPARATION OF CHURCH AND STATE.)

The Supreme Court's decisions in the arena of conflict between governmental concerns and individuals' claims to religious liberty can be considered in relation to the four categories suggested by the PREAMBLE to the Constitution: national defense, domestic tranquillity, the establishment of justice, and GENERAL WELFARE. In resolving the issues before it in these decisions the Court has spoken in terms of clear and present danger, balancing of competing interests, or determination of compelling governmental interests, depending upon the date of the decision rendered.

Probably no interest of the government is deemed more important than defense against a foreign enemy. Individual liberties secured by the Constitution must yield when the nation's safety is in peril. As the Court ruled in the SELECTIVE DRAFT LAW CASES (1918), the prohibition by the THIRTEENTH AMENDMENT of involuntary servitude was not intended to override the nation's power to conscript an army of—if necessary—unwilling soldiers, without which even the most just and defensive war cannot be waged.

By the same token, exemption of Quakers and others whose religious conscience forbids them to engage in military service cannot be deemed a constitutional right but only a privilege accorded by Congress and thus subject to revocation at any time Congress deems that to be necessary for national defense. However, even in such a case, Congress must exercise its power within the limitations prescribed by the First Amendment's mandate of neutrality among religions and by the EQUAL PROTECTION component of the Fifth Amendment's due process clause. Hence, in exercising its discretion, Congress could not constitutionally prefer some long-standing pacifist religions over others more recently established.

Exemption of specific classes—the newly betrothed, the newly married, the fainthearted, and others—goes back as far as Mosaic times (Deuteronomy 20:1–8). Since all biblical wars were theocratic, there was no such thing as religious exemption. In England, Oliver Cromwell believed that those whose religious doctrine forbade participation in armed conflict should constitute an exempt class. So too did the legislatures in some of the American colonies, the Continental Congress, and a number of the members of the Congress established under the Constitution. Madison's original draft of what became the SECOND AMENDMENT included a provision exempting religious objectors from compulsory militia duty; but that provision was deleted before Congress proposed the amendment to the states. The first national measure exempting conscientious objectors was adopted by Congress during the Civil War; like its colonial and state precedents, it was limited to members of well-recognized religious denominations whose articles of faith forbade the bearing of arms.

The SELECTIVE SERVICE ACT of 1917 exempted members of recognized denominations or sects, such as the Friends, Mennonites, and Seventh-Day Adventists, whose doctrine and discipline declared military service sinful. The 1940 act liberalized the requirements for exemption to encompass anyone who by "reason of religious training and belief" possessed conscientious scruples against "participation in war in any form." In 1948, however, the 1940 act was further amended, first, to exclude those whose objection to war was based on "essentially political, sociological or philosophical views or a mere personal code," and second, to define religion as a belief in a "Supreme Being."

In view of the Court's holding in *Torcaso v. Watkins* (1961) that the Constitution did not sanction preferential treatment of theistic religions over other faiths, limitation of exemption to persons who believe in a "Supreme Being" raised establishment clause issues. In UNITED STATES V. SEEGER (1965) the Court avoided these issues by interpreting the statute to encompass a person who possessed a sincere belief occupying a place in the life of its possessor parallel to that filled by the orthodox belief in God of one who clearly qualified for the exemption. Applying this definition to the three cases before it, the Court held that Selective Service boards had erroneously denied exemption: to one who expressed a "belief in and devotion to goodness and virtues for their own sakes, and a religious faith in a purely ethical creed"; to another who rejected a relationship "vertically towards Godness directly," but was committed to relationship "horizontally towards Godness through Mankind and the World"; and to a third who defined religion as "the supreme expression of human nature," encompassing "man thinking his highest, feeling his deepest, and living his best."

Because exemption of conscientious exemption is of legislative rather than constitutional origin, Congress may condition exemption on possession of belief forbidding participation in all wars, excluding those whose objection is selective and forbids participation only in what they personally deem unjust wars, such as that in Vietnam. The Court sustained such an act of Congress in *Gillette v. United States* (1971). However, independent of any statutory exemption, the Court held in *Thomas* that, at least in peacetime, disqualification of a person from unemployment insurance benefits for conscientious refusal to accept an offered job in a plant that manufactured arms violated the free exercise clause.

Closely related to military service as an aspect of national defense is national unity, cultural as well as political. The relevant constitutional issues reached the Supreme Court in 1923 in three cases involving Lutheran and Reformed schools, and, two years later, in two cases involving a Roman Catholic parochial and a nonsectarian private school. The former cases, reflecting post-World War I hostility to German-speaking Americans, were decided by the Court in MEYER V. NEBRASKA (1923) and two companion cases. These involved the conviction of teachers of German who violated statutes forbidding the teaching of a foreign language to pupils before they had completed eight grades of elementary schooling. The Court, in reversing the convictions, relied not only on the constitutional right of German teachers to pursue a gainful occupation not inherently evil or dangerous to the welfare of the community, but also the right of parents to have their children taught "Martin Luther's language" so that they might better understand "Martin Luther's dogma." The cases were decided long before the Court held that the free exercise clause was incorporated in the Fourteenth Amendment's due process clause and therefore were technically based upon the teachers' due process right to earn a livelihood and the parents' due process right to govern the upbringing of their children.

In PIERCE V. SOCIETY OF SISTERS and its companion case, *Pierce v. Hill Military Academy* (1925), the Court invalidated a compulsory education act that required all children, with limited exceptions, to attend only public schools. A single opinion, governing both cases, relied upon *Meyer v. Nebraska* and based the decision invalidating the law on the due process clause as it related to the school owners' contractual rights and the parents' right to control their children's education, rather than to the free exercise rights of teachers, parents, or pupils. Nevertheless, since the Court's ruling in *Cantwell* that the free exercise clause was applicable to the states, *Pierce* has often been cited by lawyers, scholars, and courts as a free exercise case, and particularly one establishing the constitutional rights of churches to operate parochial schools. Had *Pierce* been decided after *Cantwell* it is probable that free exercise would have been invoked as an additional ground in respect to the Society of Sisters' claim; the opinion as written did note that the child was not the mere creature of the state and that those who nurtured him and directed his destiny had the right, coupled with the high duty, to recognize and prepare him for additional obligations.

Reference has already been made to the Supreme Court's decision in *West Virginia State Board of Education v. Barnette* upholding the First Amendment right of Jehovah's Witnesses public school pupils to refrain from participating in flag salute exercises, although there the Court predicated its decision on the free speech rather than the free exercise mandate of the Amendment.

Jehovah's Witnesses' creed and conduct affected not only national defense through pacifism and alleged failure to pay respect to the flag but also governmental concern with domestic tranquillity. What aggravated hostility to the sect beyond its supposed lack of patriotism were its militant proselytizing methods, encompassing verbal attacks on organized religion in general and Roman Catholicism in particular. In their 1931 convention the Witnesses declared their mission to be "to inform the rulers and the people of and concerning Satan's cruel and oppressive organization, and particularly with reference to Christiandom, which is the most visible part of that visible organization." God's purpose was to destroy Satan's organization and bring quickly "to the obedient peoples of the earth peace and prosperity, liberty and health, happiness and life."

This is hardly new or surprising. Practically every new religion, from Judaism through Christianity and Islam to the present, has been predicated upon attacks against existing faiths; indeed, this is implied in the very term "Protestant." Clearly, those who wrote the First Amendment intended it to encompass attacks upon existing religions. (In BURS-

TYN V. WILSON, 1952, the Court invalidated a statute banning "sacrilegious" films.) Attacks on existing religions are almost invariably met with counterattacks, physical as well as verbal, by defenders of the accepted faiths.

The assaults upon the Jehovah's Witnesses were particularly widespread and intense for a number of reasons. Their conduct enraged many who felt that their refusal to salute the flag was unpatriotic, if not treasonous. Their attacks upon the Christian religion infuriated many others. The evidence in *Taylor v. Mississippi* (1943), for example, included a pamphlet suggesting that the Roman Catholic Church was responsible for flag saluting. The book *Religion,* by the Witnesses' first leader, Charles T. Russell, described their operations: "God's faithful servants go from house to house to bring the message of the kingdom to those who reside there, omitting none, not even the houses of the Roman Catholic hierarchy, and there they give witness to the kingdom because they are commanded by the Most High to do so. . . . They do not loot nor break into the houses, but they set up their phonographs before the doors and windows and send the message of the kingdom right into the ears of those who might wish to hear; and while those desiring to hear are hearing, some of the 'sourpusses' are compelled to hear."

The predictably resulting resort to violence and to law for the suppression of the Witnesses' activities gave rise to a host of Supreme Court decisions defining for the first time both the breadth and the limitations of the free exercise clause (and also, to some extent, the free speech clause). Most of the Jehovah's Witnesses cases were argued before the Supreme Court by Hayden Covington; his perseverance, as well as that of his client, was manifested by the fact that before *Minersville School District v. Gobitis* was decided, the Court had rejected his appeals in flag salute cases four times. The Court had accepted JURISDICTION in *Gobitis,* as well as its successor, *Barnette,* because, notwithstanding these previous rejections, the lower courts had decided both cases in the Witnesses' favor.

The Witnesses were not the only persons whose aggressive missionary endeavors and verbal attacks upon other faiths led to governmental actions that were challenged as a violation of the free exercise clause and were defended as necessary to secure domestic tranquillity. In KUNZ V. NEW YORK (1951), the Court held that a Baptist preacher could not be denied renewal of a permit for evangelical street meetings because his preachings, scurrilously attacking Roman Catholicism and Judaism, had led to disorder in the streets. The Court said that appropriate public remedies existed to protect the peace and order of the communities if the sermons should result in violence, but it held that these remedies did not include prior restraint under an ordinance that provided no standards for the licensing official.

Jehovah's Witnesses were the major claimants to religious liberty in the two decades between 1935 and 1955. During that period they brought to the Supreme Court a large number of cases challenging the application to them of a variety of laws forbidding disturbing the peace, peddling, the use of SOUNDTRUCKS, as well as traffic regulations, child labor laws, and revenue laws.

In *Cantwell v. Connecticut* (1940) the Court held that the First Amendment guaranteed the right to teach and preach religion in the public streets and parks and to solicit contributions or purchases of religious materials. Although a prior municipal permit might be required, its grant or denial might not be based upon the substance of what is taught, preached, or distributed but only upon the need to regulate, in the interests of traffic control, the time, place, and manner of public meetings. In COX v. NEW HAMPSHIRE (1940) the Court ruled that religious liberty encompassed the right to engage in religious processions, although a fee might be imposed to cover the expenses of administration and maintenance of public order. The Constitution, however, does not immunize from prosecution persons who in their missionary efforts use expressions that are lewd, obscene, libelous, insulting, or that contain "fighting" words which by their very utterance, the Court declared in CHAPLINSKY v. NEW HAMPSHIRE (1942), inflict injury or tend to incite an immediate breach of the peace. The Constitution also secures the right to distribute religious handbills in streets and at publicly owned railroad or bus terminals, according to the decision in *Jamison v. Texas* (1943), and, according to *Martin v. City of Struthers* (1943), to ring doorbells in order to offer house occupants religious literature although, of course, not to force oneself into the house for that purpose.

Related to the domestic tranquillity aspects of Jehovah's Witnesses claims to use public streets and parks are the claims of other feared or unpopular minority religious groups (often referred to as "sects" or, more recently, "CULTS") to free exercise in publicly owned areas. In HEFFRON v. INTERNATIONAL SOCIETY FOR KRISHNA CONSCIOUSNESS (ISKCON) (1981) the Court held that a state rule limiting to specific booths the sale or distribution of merchandise, including printed material, on public fair grounds did not violate the free exercise clause when applied to members of ISKCON whose ritual required its members to go into all public places to distribute or sell its religious literature and to solicit donations.

Discriminatory treatment, however, is not constitutionally permissible. Thus, in *Cruz v. Beto* (1972) the Supreme Court upheld the claim of a Buddhist prisoner in Texas that his constitutional rights were violated by denying him use of the prison chapel, punishing him for sharing his Buddhist religious materials with other prisoners, and denying him other privileges, such as receiving points for attendance at religious services, which enhanced a prisoner's eligibility for early parole consideration. While a prisoner obviously cannot enjoy the free exercise of religion to the same extent as nonprisoners, the Court said, he is protected by the free exercise clause subject only to the necessities of prison security and discipline, and he may not be discriminated against simply because his religious belief is unorthodox. This does not mean that every sect within a prison, no matter how few in number, must have identical facilities or personnel; but reasonable opportunities must be afforded to all persons to exercise their religion without penalty.

One of the most difficult problems facing a court arises when it is called upon to decide between free exercise and the state's interest in preventing fraud. The leading case on the subject is *United States v. Ballard* (1944), which involved a prosecution for mail fraud. The INDICT-MENT charged that the defendants, organizers of the "I Am" cult, had mulcted money from elderly and ill people by falsely representing that they had supernatural powers to heal and that they themselves had communicated personally with Heaven and with Jesus Christ.

The Court held that the free exercise clause would be violated if the state were allowed to seek to prove to a jury that the defendants' representations were false. Neither a jury nor any other organ of government had power to decide whether asserted religious experiences actually occurred. Courts, however, could constitutionally determine whether the defendant himself believed that what he recounted was true, and if a jury determined that he did not, they could convict him of obtaining money under false pretenses. The difficulty with this test, as Justice ROBERT H. JACKSON noted in his dissenting opinion, is that prosecutions in cases such as *Ballard* could easily degenerate into religious persecution; juries would find it difficult to accept as believed that which, by reason of their own religious upbringing, they deemed unbelievable.

In providing for "affirmation" as an alternative to "oath" in Article II, section 1, and Article VI, section 3, the framers of the Constitution, recognizing that religious convictions might forbid some persons (specifically Quakers) to take oaths, manifested their intention that no person in the judicial system—judge, lawyer, court official, or juryman—should be disqualified from governmental service on the ground of religion. In *Torcaso v. Watkins* (1961) the Court reached the same conclusion under the First Amendment as to state officials (for example, notaries public), and in *In re Jenison* (1963), the Court refused to uphold a conviction for contempt of court of a woman who would not serve on a jury because of the biblical command "Judge not that ye not be judged."

Resort to secular courts for resolution of intrachurch disputes (generally involving ownership and control of church assets) raises free exercise as well as establishment problems. As early as 1872 the Court held in *Watson v. Jones* that judicial intervention in such controversies was narrowly limited: a court could do no more than determine and enforce the decision of that body within the church that was the highest judicatory body according to appropriate church law. If a religious group (such as Baptist and Jewish) were congregational in structure, that body would be the majority of the congregation; if it were hierarchical (such as Roman Catholic or Russian Orthodox), the authority would generally be the diocesan bishop.

That principle was applied by the Supreme Court consistently until *Jones v. Wolf* (1979). There the court held that "neutral principles of law developed for use in all property disputes" could constitutionally be applied in church schism litigation. This means that unless the corporate charter or deeds of title provide that the faction loyal to the hierarchical church will retain ownership of the property, such a controversy must be adjudicated in accordance with the laws applicable to corporations generally, so that if recorded title is in the name of the local church, the majority of that body is entitled to control its use and disposition. The Court rejected the assertion in the dissenting opinion that a rule of compulsory deference to the highest ecclesiastical tribunal is necessary in order to protect the free exercise of those who formed the association and submitted themselves to its authority.

Where a conflict exists between the health of the community and the religious conscience of an individual or group, there is little doubt that the free exercise clause does not mandate risk to the community. Thus, as the Court held in JACOBSON v. MASSACHUSETTS (1905), compulsory VACCINATION against communicable diseases is enforceable notwithstanding religious objections to the procedure. So, too, fluoridation of municipal water supplies to prevent tooth cavities cannot be enjoined because of objection by some that drinking fluoridated water is sinful.

Where the life, health, or safety of individuals, rather than communities at large, is involved the constitutional principles are also fairly clear. When the individuals are children, a court may authorize blood transfusions to save their lives notwithstanding objection by parents (such as Jehovah's Witnesses) who believe that the procedure violates the biblical command against the drinking of blood. The underlying principle was stated by the Court in PRINCE v. MASSACHUSETTS (1944) upholding the conviction of a Jehovah's Witness for violating the state's child labor law in allowing her nine-year-old niece to accompany and help her while she sold the sect's religious literature on the city's streets. "Parents," the Court said, "may be free to become martyrs themselves. But it does not follow that they are free, in identical circumstances, to make martyrs of their children before they have reached the age of full and legal discretion when they can make that choice for themselves." It follows from this that unless mental incompetence is proved, a court may not authorize a blood transfusion upon an unconsenting adult.

The Court also balances competing interests in determining the constitutionality of enforcing compulsory Sunday laws against those whom religious conscience forbids labor or trade on the seventh rather than the first day of the week. In McGOWAN v. MARYLAND and *Two Guys from Harrison-Allentown v. McGinley* (1961) the Court upheld the general validity of such laws against an establishment clause attack. Although their origin may have been religious, the Court said, the laws' present purpose was secular: to assure a weekly day for rest, relaxation, and family companionship.

Two other cases, *Gallagher v. Crown Kosher Super Market* (1961) and *Braunfeld v. Brown* (1961), decided at the same time, involved Orthodox Jews who observed Saturday as their day of rest and refrained from business on that day. In these cases the Court rejected the argument that requiring a Sabbatarian either to abstain from engaging in his trade or business two days weekly or to sacrifice his religious conscience, while requiring his Sunday-observing competitors to abstain only one day, imposed upon the Sabbatarian a competitive disadvantage, thereby penalizing him for his religious beliefs in violation of the free exercise clause. Exempting Sabbatarians, the Court held, might be administratively difficult, might benefit non-Sabbatarians motivated only by a desire for a competitive advantage over merchants closing on Sundays, and might frustrate the legitimate legislative goal of assuring a uniform day of rest. Although state legislatures could constitutionally elect to grant an exemption to Sabbatarians, the free exercise clause does not require them to do so.

In SHERBERT v. VERNER (1963), however, the Court reached a conclusion difficult to reconcile with that in *Gallagher* and *Braunfeld.* Denial of unemployment insurance benefits to a Seventh-Day Adventist who refused to accept tendered employment that required working on Saturday, the Court held, imposed an impermissible burden on the free exercise of religion. The First Amendment, it said, forbids forcing an applicant to choose between following religious precepts and forfeiting government benefits on the one hand, or, on the other, abandoning the precepts by accepting Sabbath work. Governmental imposition of such a choice, the Court said, puts the same kind of burden upon the free exercise of religion as would a fine imposed for Saturday worship.

The Court upheld statutory tax exemptions for church-owned real estate used exclusively for religious purposes in WALZ v. TAX COMMISSION (1970), rejecting an establishment clause attack. In *Murdock v. Pennsylvania* (1943) and *Follett v. Town of McCormack* (1944), however, the Court ruled that under the free exercise clause a revenue-raising tax on the privilege of canvassing or soliciting orders for articles could not be applied to Jehovah's Witnesses who sold their religious literature from door to door; in the same cases, the Court stated that an income tax statute could constitutionally be applied to clergymen's salaries for performing their clerical duties.

In *United States v. Lee* (1982) the Court upheld the exaction of social security and unemployment insurance contributions from Amish employers. The employers argued that their free exercise rights had been violated, citing 1 Timothy 5:8: "But if any provide not . . . for those of his own house, he hath denied the faith, and is worse than an infidel." Compulsory contribution, the Court said, was nonetheless justified; it was essential to accomplish the overriding governmental interest in the effective operation of the social security system.

To sum up, the Supreme Court's decisions in the arena of religious liberty manifest a number of approaches toward defining its meaning, specifically clear and present danger, the balancing of competing interests, and the establishment of a compelling state interest justifying intrusion on free exercise. On the whole, the Court has been loyal to the original intent of the generation that wrote the First Amendment to accord the greatest degree of liberty feasible in our society.

Bibliography

GIANELLA, DONALD   1968   Religious Liberty: Non-Establishment and Doctrinal Development: Part I, The Religious Liberty Guarantee. *Harvard Law Review* 80:1381–1431.

HOWE, MARK DEWOLFE   1965   *The Garden and the Wilderness: Religion and Government in American Constitutional History.* Chicago: University of Chicago Press.

KAUPER, PAUL G.   1964   *Religion and the Constitution.* Baton Rouge: Louisiana State University Press.

MANWARING, DAVID R.   1962   *Render unto Caesar: The Flag Salute Controversy.* Chicago: University of Chicago Press.

PFEFFER, LEO   (1953) 1967   *Church, State and Freedom.* Boston: Beacon Press.

STOKES, ANSON P.   1950   *Church and State in the United States.* New York: Harper & Brothers.

———— and PFEFFER, LEO   1965   *Church and State in the United States.* New York: Harper & Row.

TRIBE, LAWRENCE H.   1978   *American Constitutional Law.* Mineola, N.Y.: Foundation Press.

MARYLAND
TOLERATION ACT
(April 2, 1649)

Leonard W. Levy

This landmark in the protection of liberty of conscience was the most liberal in colonial America at the time of its passage by the Maryland Assembly under the title, "An Act Concerning Religion," and it was far more liberal than Parliament's TOLERATION ACT of forty years later. Until 1776 only the Rhode Island Charter of 1663 and Pennsylvania's "Great Law" of 1682 guaranteed fuller RELIGIOUS LIBERTY.

Maryland's statute, framed by its Roman Catholic proprietor, Lord Baltimore (Cecil Calvert), was the first public act to use the phrase "the free exercise" of religion, later embodied in the FIRST AMENDMENT. More noteworthy still, the act symbolized the extraordinary fact that for most of the seventeenth century in Maryland, Roman Catholics and various Protestant sects openly worshiped as they chose and lived in peace, though not in amity. The act applied to all those who professed belief in Jesus Christ, except antitrinitarians, and guaranteed them immunity from being troubled in any way because of their religion and "the free exercise thereof." In other provisions more characteristic of the time, the act fixed the death penalty for blasphemers against God, Christ, or the Trinity, and it imposed lesser penalties for profaning the sabbath or for reproaching the Virgin Mary or the apostles. Another clause anticipated GROUP LIBEL laws by penalizing the reproachful use of any name or term such as heretic, puritan, popish priest, anabaptist, separatist, or antinomian.

At a time when intolerance was the law in Europe and most of America, Maryland established no church and tolerated all Trinitarian Christians, until Protestants, who had managed to suspend the toleration act between 1654 and 1658, gained political control of the colony in 1689.

Bibliography

HANLEY, THOMAS O'BRIEN 1959 *Their Rights and Liberties: The Beginnings of Religious and Political Freedom in Maryland.* Westminister, Md.: Newman Press.

TOLERATION ACT

1 William & Mary ch. 18 (1689)

Leonard W. Levy

The principle of RELIGIOUS LIBERTY denies that the state has any legitimate authority over the individual's religion or irreligion; the principle of toleration insists that a state which maintains an ESTABLISHMENT OF RELIGION indulge the existence of nonconformist religious groups. Toleration is a step between persecution and liberty. The Toleration Act, which accompanied the Glorious Revolution of 1688–1689, was a political necessity that restored peace to a religiously pluralistic England and ended a period of persecution during which thousands of nonconformist Protestant ministers had died in jail.

The act, entitled "A Bill of Indulgence," exempted most nonconformists from the penalties of the persecutory laws of the Restoration, leaving those laws in force but inapplicable to persons qualifying for indulgence. Subjects who took the requisite oaths to support the new king and reject the authority of the pope might have the privilege of worshipping as they pleased, because they were exempted from the penalties that had suppressed them. Baptists and Quakers received special indulgences. Thus the act had the effect of permitting the existence of lawful nonconformity, though nonconformists still had to pay tithes to the established church and endure many civil disabilities. One section of the act excluded from its benefits Roman Catholic recusants and Protestant antitrinitarians. England still regarded the former as political subversives, the latter as virtual atheists. For all its faults the statute of 1689 ushered in an era of toleration under the established church and ultimately benefited dissenters in those American colonies that maintained establishments of religion.

Bibliography

SEATON, A. (1911)1972 *The Theory of Toleration under the Later Stuarts.* Pages 92–236. New York: Octagon Books.

VIRGINIA STATUTE OF RELIGIOUS FREEDOM

(1786)

Leonard W. Levy

This historic statute, one of the preeminent documents in the history of RELIGIOUS LIBERTY, climaxed a ten-year struggle for the SEPARATION OF CHURCH AND STATE in Virginia. On the eve of the Revolution Baptists were jailed for unlicensed preaching, and JAMES MADISON exclaimed that the "diabolical Hell conceived principle of persecution rages." The Church of England (Episcopal) was the established church of Virginia, supported by public taxes imposed on all. The state CONSTITUTION of 1776 guaranteed that everyone was "equally entitled to the free exercise of religion," but the convention defeated a proposal by Madison that would have ended any form of an ESTABLISHMENT OF RELIGION. By the close of 1776 the legislature, responding to dissenter petitions, repealed all laws punishing any religious opinions or modes of worship, exempted dissenters from compulsory support of the established church, and suspended state taxation on its behalf. But the legislature reserved for future decision the question whether religion ought to be supported by voluntary contributions or by a new establishment of all Christian churches.

In 1779 an indecisive legislature confronted two diametrically opposed bills. One was a general assessment bill, providing that the Christian religion should be "the established religion" supported by public taxation and allowing every taxpayer to designate the church that would receive his money. The other was THOMAS JEFFERSON's Bill for Religious Freedom, which later provided the philosophical basis for the religion clauses of the FIRST AMENDMENT. The preamble, a classic expression of the American creed on intellectual as well as religious liberty, stressed that everyone had a "natural right" to his opinions and that religion was a private, voluntary matter of individual conscience beyond the scope of the civil power to support or restrain. Jefferson rejected the BAD TENDENCY TEST for suppressing opinions and proposed "that it is time enough for the rightful purposes of the civil government for its officers to interfere when principles break out into overt acts against peace and good order. . . ." The bill, which protected even freedom of irreligion, provided that no one should be compelled to frequent or support any worship. Neither Jefferson's bill nor the other could muster a majority, and for several years the legislature deadlocked.

Each year, however, support for an establishment grew. When a liberalized general assessment bill was introduced in 1784, omitting subscription to articles of faith and giving secular reasons for the support of religion, the Presbyterian clergy backed it. Madison angrily declared that they were "as ready to set up an establishment which is to take them in as they were to pull down that which shut them out." Only Madison's shrewd politicking delayed passage of the general assessment bill until the legislature had time to evaluate the state of public opinion. MADISON'S MEMORIAL AND REMONSTRANCE turned public opinion against the assessment; even the Presbyterian clergy now endorsed Jefferson's bill. Madison reintroduced it in late 1785, and it became law in early 1786, completing the separation of church and state in Virginia and providing a model for a nation.

Bibliography

STOKES, ANSON PHELPS   1950   *Church and State in the United States.* Vol. 1:366–394. New York: Harper & Row.

POLYGAMY

Kenneth L. Karst

Because polygamy was one of the early tenets of the Mormon Church, the movement to eradicate plural marriage became bound up with religious persecution. The Supreme Court has consistently held that the FIRST AMENDMENT's protections of RELIGIOUS LIBERTY do not protect the practice of plural marriage. Thus REYNOLDS V. UNITED STATES (1879) upheld a criminal conviction for polygamy in the Territory of Utah, and DAVIS V. BEASON (1880) upheld a conviction for voting in the Territory of Idaho in violation of an oath required of all registrants forswearing belief in polygamy. The corporate charter of the Mormon Church in the Territory of Utah was revoked, and its property forfeited to the government, in CHURCH OF JESUS CHRIST OF LATTER-DAY SAINTS V. UNITED STATES (1890). The church's First Amendment claim was waved away with the statement that belief in polygamy was not a religious tenet but a "pretense" that was "contrary to the spirit of Christianity."

It would be comforting if this judicial record were confined to the nineteenth century, but it was not. In *Cleveland v. United States* (1946), the Court upheld a conviction of Mormons under the MANN ACT for transporting women across state lines for the purpose of "debauchery" that took the form of living with them in polygamous marriage. The Court's opinion, citing the nineteenth-century cases and even quoting the "spirit of Christianity" language with approval, was written by none other than Justice WILLIAM O. DOUGLAS.

More recently, the Court has recognized a constitutional right to marry, and in a number of contexts has afforded protection for a FREEDOM OF INTIMATE ASSOCIATION. (See MARRIAGE AND THE CONSTITUTION.) With or without the ingredient of religious freedom, SUBSTANTIVE DUE PROCESS doctrine seems amply to justify an extension of these rights to plural marriage among competent consenting adults. Yet the force of conventional morality in constitutional adjudication should not be underestimated; the Supreme Court is not just the architect of principle but an institution of government. Polygamy is not on the verge of becoming a constitutional right.

Bibliography

LARSON, GUSTAVE O. 1971 *The "Americanization" of Utah for Statehood.* San Marino, Calif.: Huntington Library.

REYNOLDS v. UNITED STATES

98 U.S. 145 (1879)

Leonard W. Levy

This case established the principle that under the guarantee of RELIGIOUS LIBERTY, government may not punish religious beliefs but may punish religiously motivated practices that injure the public interest. Reynolds violated a congressional prohibition on bigamy in the territories and appealed his conviction in Utah on FIRST AMENDMENT grounds, alleging that as a Mormon he had a religious duty to practice POLYGAMY. Chief Justice MORRISON R. WAITE for a unanimous Supreme Court ruled that although government might not reach opinions, it could constitutionally punish criminal activity. The question, Waite declared, was whether religious belief could be accepted as justification of an overt act made criminal by the law of the land. Every government, he answered, had the power to decide whether polygamy or monogamy should be the basis of social life. Those who made polygamy part of their religion could no more be exempt from the law than those who believe that human sacrifice was a necessary part of religious worship. Unless the law were superior to religious belief, Waite reasoned, every citizen might become a law unto himself and government would exist in name only. He did not explain why polygamy and human sacrifice were analogous, nor did he, in his simplified exposition, confront the problem whether an uncontrollable freedom of belief had much substance if the state could punish the dictates of conscience: belief without practice is an empty right. Moreover, Waite did not consider whether belief should be as absolutely free as he suggested; if polygamy was a crime, its advocacy had limits.

DAVIS v. BEASON

130 U.S. 333 (1890)

Richard E. Morgan

Davis involved an Idaho territorial statute directed at POLYGAMY. The law required voters to foreswear membership in any organization that "teaches, advocates, counsels or encourages" its members to undertake polygamous relationships. Davis was convicted of swearing falsely.

Justice STEPHEN J. FIELD, speaking for the Supreme Court, saw the case as identical to REYNOLDS v. UNITED STATES (1879). The free exercise clause of the FIRST AMENDMENT protected religious beliefs not acts that prejudiced the health, safety, or good order of society as defined by the legislature operating under its POLICE POWER. Field concluded that if something is a crime, then to teach, advise, or counsel it cannot be protected by evoking religious tenets.

The decision became one of the principal underpinnings of what later came to be called the "secular regulation" approach to the free exercise clause whereby no religious exemptions are required from otherwise valid secular regulations.

CHURCH OF JESUS CHRIST OF LATTER DAY SAINTS v. UNITED STATES

136 U.S. 1 (1890)

Richard E. Morgan

The Mormon Church was granted a charter of incorporation in February 1851 by the so-called State of Deseret; later an act of the territorial legislature of Utah confirmed the charter. In 1887 Congress, having plenary power over the TERRITORIES, repealed the charter and directed the seizure and disposal of church property.

Justice JOSEPH P. BRADLEY wrote for the Court. He held that the power of Congress over the territories was sufficient to repeal an act of incorporation. He also held that once the Mormon Church became a defunct CORPORATION, Congress had power to reassign its property to legitimate religious and charitable uses, as near as practicable to those intended by the original donors. The claim of RELIGIOUS FREEDOM could not immunize the Mormon Church against the congressional conclusion that, because of its sponsorship of polygamy, it was an undesirable legal entity.

Chief Justice MELVILLE WESTON FULLER dissented, joined by Justice STEPHEN J. FIELD and Justice L. Q. C. LAMAR. Fuller objected to according Congress such sweeping power over property.

FLAG SALUTE CASES

MINERSVILLE SCHOOL DISTRICT v. GOBITIS
310 U.S. 586 (1940)
WEST VIRGINIA BOARD OF EDUCATION v. BARNETT
319 U.S. 624 (1943)

Richard E. Morgan

The Supreme Court's encounter in the early 1940s with the issue of compulsory flag salute exercises in the public schools was one of the turning points in American constitutional history. It presaged the civil libertarian activism that culminated in the WARREN COURT of the 1960s.

The flag salute ceremony developed in the latter half of the nineteenth century. In the original ceremony the participants faced the flag and pledged "allegiance to my flag and the republic for which it stands, one nation indivisible, with liberty and justice for all." While repeating the words "to my flag" the right hand was extended palm up toward the flag. Over the years the ceremony evolved slightly, with minor changes of wording and with the extended arm salute dropped in 1942 because of its similarity to the Nazi salute. At this point in its evolution, however, the salute had official standing; Congress had prescribed the form of words and substituted the right hand over the heart for the extended arm.

Beginning in 1898 with New York, some states began requiring the ceremony as part of the opening exercise of the school day. The early state flag salute laws did not make the ceremony compulsory for individual pupils, but many local school boards insisted on participation. Many patriotic and fraternal organizations backed the flag salute; opposition came from civil libertarians and some small religious groups. The principal opponents of the compulsory school flag salute were the Jehovah's Witnesses, a tightly knit evangelical sect whose religious beliefs commanded them not to salute the flag as a "graven image."

The Witnesses were blessed with legal talent. "Judge" Joseph Franklin Rutherford, who had become head of the sect, brought in Hayden Covington, who, as chief counsel for the Witnesses in the *Gobitis* litigation and in many other cases influenced the development of First Amendment doctrine.

460

The first flag salute case to reach the Supreme Court came out of Minersville, a small community in northwest Pennsylvania. Because of Rutherford's bitter opposition to required flag salute exercises, Lillian and William Gobitis stopped participating in the ceremony in their school and were expelled.

The argument for the Gobitis children was that requiring them to salute the flag, an act repugnant to them on religious grounds, denied that free exercise of religion protected against state action by the DUE PROCESS clause of the FOURTEENTH AMENDMENT. Arguments for the Minersville School Board relied on REYNOLDS V. UNITED STATES (1878), JACOBSON V. MASSACHUSETTS (1905), and the doctrine that a religious objection did not relieve an individual from the responsibility of complying with an otherwise valid secular regulation. The Gobitis children won in the lower federal courts, but the Supreme Court granted CERTIORARI.

The Court in the spring of 1940 had a very different cast from that which had survived FRANKLIN D. ROOSEVELT's effort to "pack" it three years before. Of the hard-core, pre-1937 conservatives only Justice JAMES C. MCREYNOLDS remained. Chief Justice CHARLES EVANS HUGHES and Justices HARLAN F. STONE and OWEN J. ROBERTS also remained. With them, however, were five Roosevelt appointees: FELIX FRANKFURTER, HUGO L. BLACK, WILLIAM O. DOUGLAS, STANLEY F. REED, and FRANK MURPHY. On three previous occasions the Court had sustained compulsory flag salutes against religious objection in PER CURIUM opinions. Whether because of the extraordinary persistence of the Jehovah's Witnesses or because of the nonconformance of the lower federal courts in this case, the Justices now gave the matter full dress consideration.

Speaking for the majority Justice Frankfurter concluded that "conscientious scruples have not, in the course of the long struggle for religious toleration, relieved the individual from obedience to a general law not aimed at the persecution or a restriction of religious beliefs."

To Justice Stone, dissenting, the crucial issue was that the Gobitis children were forced to bear false witness to their religion. The flag salute compelled the expression of a belief, and "where that expression violate[d] religious convictions," the free exercise clause provided protection.

The reaction to the decision in the law reviews was negative. In the popular press the reaction was mixed but criticism predominated. Most important, the decision seems to have produced a wave of persecution of Jehovah's Witnesses which swept through the country. *Gobitis* emboldened some school authorities. The State Board of Education of West Virginia in January 1942 made the salute to the flag mandatory in the classrooms of that state.

Meanwhile, new decisions of the Supreme Court, notably the 5–4 division of the Justices in *Jones v. Opelika,* raised the hopes of opponents of the mandatory flag salute. Hayden Covington sought an INJUNCTION barring enforcement of West Virginia's new rule against Walter Barnett and other Jehovah's Witness plaintiffs. After a three-judge District Court issued an injunction, the State Board of Education appealed to the Supreme Court.

The case was argued on March 11, 1943, and the decision came down on June 14. Justice ROBERT H. JACKSON, who had joined the Court after *Gobitis,* wrote for a 6–3 majority, overruling the prior decision. Chief Justice Stone was with Jackson, as were Justices Douglas, Black, and Murphy, who had changed their minds. Justice Frankfurter, the author of *Gobitis,* wrote a long and impassioned dissent.

For Justice Jackson and the majority the crucial point was that West Virginia's action, while not intended either to impose or to anathematize a particular religious belief, did involve a required affirmation of belief: "If there is any fixed star in our constitutional constellation, it is that no official, high or petty, can prescribe what shall be orthodox in politics, nationalism, religion, or other matters of opinion or force citizens to confess by word or act their faith therein." West Virginia was pursuing the legitimate end of enhancing patriotism, but had not borne the heavy burden of justifying its use of coercive power.

Justice Frankfurter began his dissent by noting that were the matter one of personal choice he would oppose compulsory flag salutes. But it was not for the Court to decide what was and was not an effective means of inculcating patriotism. West Virginia had neither prohibited nor imposed any religious belief. For Frankfurter this fact was controlling, and he reminded his brethren that a liberal spirit cannot be "enforced by judicial invalidation of illiberal legislation."

Barnett was a landmark decision in the strict sense of that overworked word. By 1943 the Roosevelt Court had largely completed its task of dismantling the edifice of SUBSTANTIVE DUE PROCESS erected by its predecessors to protect economic liberty. Now the Court set out on the path to a new form of JUDICIAL ACTIVISM in the service of individual rights. *Barnett* was the first long step on that path.

Barnett had doctrinal significance both for FREEDOM OF SPEECH and for RELIGIOUS LIBERTY. Jackson's opinion suggested that there were significant limitations on the kinds of patriotic affirmations that government might require, and the decision also moved away from the "secular regulation" rule that had dominated free exercise doctrine.

Barnett also had a significant effect on the Supreme Court. Justice Frankfurter was deeply offended by the majority's treatment of his *Gobitis* opinion and even more alarmed at what he regarded as a misuse of judicial power. The split between the activist disposition of Justices Black and Douglas and the judicial self-restraint championed by Frankfurter date from *Barnett.*

Bibliography

MANWARING, DAVID R.   1962   *Render unto Caesar: The Flag Salute Controversy.* Chicago: University of Chicago Press.

SHERBERT v. VERNER

374 U.S. 398 (1963)

Richard E. Morgan

Sherbert, a Seventh-Day Adventist, lost her job after the mill at which she had been working went on a six-day work week and she refused Saturday work. She filed for unemployment compensation, was referred to a job, but declined it because it would have required Saturday work. By declining proffered employment she was no longer "available for work" under South Carolina's rules and hence no longer eligible for unemployment benefits.

Justice WILLIAM J. BRENNAN, speaking for the Supreme Court, concluded that the disqualification imposed a burden on Mrs. Sherbert's free exercise of religion. The FIRST AMENDMENT, he declared, protected not only belief but observance. Even an incidental burdening of religion could be justified only if the state could show a COMPELLING STATE INTEREST in not granting an exemption.

This decision was a significant departure from the secular regulation approach to free exercise claims which had been affirmed by the Court as recently as *Braunfeld v. Brown* (1961). Brennan made little attempt to distinguish *Sherbert* from *Braunfeld*. Justice WILLIAM O. DOUGLAS, concurring, rejected the secular regulation approach.

Justice POTTER STEWART concurred in the result, disassociating himself from Brennan's reasoning. Stewart saw tension developing between the Court's interpretation of the free exercise and establishment clauses. To grant free exercise exemptions from otherwise valid secular regulations preferred religious over nonreligious people. In establishment clause cases, however, any governmental action that had the effect of advancing religion was forbidden. Stewart would have relieved the tension by relaxing the establishment clause rule.

Justice JOHN MARSHALL HARLAN, joined by Justice BYRON R. WHITE, dissented. For Harlan, the notion of a constitutional compulsion to "carve out an exception" based on religious conviction was a singularly dangerous one.

WISCONSIN v. YODER

406 U.S. 205 (1972)

Richard E. Morgan

Wisconsin's school-leaving age was sixteen. Members of the Old Order Amish religion declined, on religious grounds, to send their children to school beyond the eighth grade. Wisconsin chose to force the issue, and counsel for the Amish defendants replied that while the requirement might be valid as to others, the free exercise clause of the FIRST AMENDMENT required exemption in the case of the Amish.

Chief Justice WARREN E. BURGER, speaking for the Supreme Court, was much impressed by the Amish way of life. He rejected Wisconsin's argument that belief but not action was protected by the free exercise clause, and cited SHERBERT V. VERNER (1963). Nor was the Chief Justice convinced by the state's assertion of a COMPELLING STATE INTEREST. Nothing indicated that Amish children would suffer from the lack of high school education. Burger stressed that the Amish would have lost had they based their claim on "subjective evaluations and rejections of the contemporary social values accepted by the majority."

Justice BYRON R. WHITE filed a concurring opinion in which Justices WILLIAM J. BRENNAN and POTTER STEWART joined. White found the issue in *Yoder* much closer than Burger. White pointed out that many Amish children left the religious fold upon attaining their majority and had to make their way in the larger world like everyone else.

Justice WILLIAM O. DOUGLAS dissented in part. He saw the issue as one of CHILDREN'S RIGHTS in which Frieda Yoder's personal feelings and desires should be determinative. Justice Stewart, joined by Justice Brennan, filed a brief concurrence which took issue with Douglas on this point, and noted that there was nothing in the record which indicated that the religious beliefs of the children in the case differed in any way from those of the parents.

CONSCIENTIOUS OBJECTION

R. Kent Greenawalt

A conscientious objector is a person who is opposed in conscience to engaging in socially required behavior. Since the genuine objector will not be easily forced into acts he abhors and since compelling people to violate their own moral scruples is usually undesirable in a liberal society, those who formulate legal rules face the question whether conscientious objectors should be excused from legal requirements imposed on others. The issue is most striking in relation to compulsory military service: should those whose consciences forbid killing be conscripted for combat? Historically, conscientious objection has been considered mainly in that context, and the clash has been understood as between secular obligation and the sense of religious duty felt by members of pacifist sects. The Constitution says nothing directly about conscientious objection, and for most of the country's existence Congress was thought to have a free hand in deciding whether to afford any exemption and how to define the class of persons who would benefit. By now, it is evident that the religion clauses of the FIRST AMENDMENT impose significant constraints on how Congress may draw lines between those who receive an exemption from military service and those who do not. The Supreme Court has never accepted the argument that Congress is constitutionally required to establish an exemption from military service, but it has indicated that the Constitution does entitle some individuals to exemption from certain other sorts of compulsory laws.

The principle that society should excuse conscientious objectors from military service was widely recognized in the colonies and states prior to adoption of the Constitution. JAMES MADISON's original proposal for the BILL OF RIGHTS included a clause that "no person religiously scrupulous of bearing arms shall be compelled to render military service in person," but that clause was dropped, partly because conscription was considered a state function. The 1864 Draft Act and the SELECTIVE SERVICE ACT of 1917 both contained exemptions limited to members of religious denominations whose creeds forbade participation in war. The 1917 act excused objectors only from combatant service, but the War Department permitted some of those also opposed to noncombatant military service to be released for civilian service.

The 1940 Selective Service Act set the basic terms of exemption from the system of compulsory military service that operated during World War II, the KOREAN WAR, and the Vietnam War, and during the intervening periods of uneasy peace. A person was eligible "who, by reason of religious training and belief, [was] conscientiously opposed to participation in war in any form." Someone opposed even to noncombatant service could perform alternate civilian service. In response to a court of appeals decision interpreting "religious training and belief" very broadly, Congress in 1948 said that religious belief meant belief "in relation to a Supreme Being involving duties superior to those arising from any human relation. . . ." What Congress had attempted to do was relatively clear. It wanted to excuse only persons opposed to participation in all wars, not those opposed to particular wars, and it wanted to excuse only those whose opposition derived from religious belief in a rather traditional sense. The important Supreme Court cases have dealt with these lines of distinction.

By dint of strained interpretation of the statute, the Court has avoided a clear decision whether Congress could limit the exemption to traditional religious believers. First, in UNITED STATES v. SEEGER (1965), a large majority said that an applicant who spoke of a "religious faith in a purely ethical creed" was entitled to the exemption because his belief occupied a place in his life parallel to that of a belief in God for the more orthodox. Then, in *Welsh v. United States* (1970), four Justices held that someone who laid no claim to being religious at all qualified because his ethical beliefs occupied a place in his life parallel to that of religious beliefs for others. Four other Justices acknowledged that Congress had explicitly meant to exclude such applicants. Justice JOHN MAR-SHALL HARLAN urged that an attempt to distinguish religious objectors from equally sincere nonreligious ones constituted a forbidden ESTABLISH-MENT OF RELIGION; the three other Justices thought that Congress could favor religious objectors in order to promote the free exercise of religion. Because the plurality's view of the statute was so implausible, most observers have supposed that its members probably agreed with Justice Harlan about the ultimate constitutional issue, but this particular tension between "no establishment" and "free exercise" concepts has not yet been decisively resolved.

In *Gillette v. United States* (1971), a decision covering both religious and nonreligious objectors to the Vietnam War, the Court upheld Congress's determination not to exempt those opposed to participation in particular wars. Against the claim that the distinction between "general" and "selective" objectors was impermissible, the Court responded that the distinction was supported by the public interest in a fairly administered system, given the difficulty officials would have dealing consistently with the variety of objections to particular wars. The Court also rejected the claim that the selective objector's entitlement to free exercise of his religion created a constitutionally grounded right to avoid military service.

In other limited areas, the Court has taken the step of acknowledging a free exercise right to be exempt from a generally imposed obligation. Those religiously opposed to jury duty cannot be compelled to serve, and adherents of traditional religious groups that provide an alternative way of life for members cannot be required to send children to school beyond the eighth grade. (See WISCONSIN V. YODER, 1972.) Nor can a person be deprived of unemployment benefits when an unwillingness to work on Saturday is religiously based, though receptivity to jobs including Saturday work is a usual condition of eligibility. (See SHERBERT V. VERNER, 1963.) What these cases suggest is that if no powerful secular reason can be advanced for demanding uniform compliance, the Constitution may require that persons with substantial religious objections be excused. To this degree the Constitution itself requires special treatment for conscientious objectors. Beyond that, its recognition of religious liberty and of governmental impartiality toward religions provides a source of values for legislative choice and constrains the classifications legislatures may make.

Bibliography

FINN, JAMES, ED.   1968   *A Conflict of Loyalties.* New York: Pegasus.

GREENAWALT, KENT   1972   All or Nothing At All: The Defeat of Selective Conscientious Objection. *Supreme Court Review* 1971: 31–94.

SIBLEY, MULFORD QUICKERT and JACOB, PHILIP E.   1952   *Conscription of Conscience: The American State and the Conscientious Objector, 1940–1947.* Ithaca, N.Y.: Cornell University Press.

SEEGER, UNITED STATES v.

380 U.S. 163 (1965)

Richard E. Morgan

At issue in the *Seeger* case was Section 6(j) of the Universal Military Training and Service Act. Originally enacted in 1940, the act exempted those who, as a matter of "religious training and belief," were opposed to participation in a war. In 1948, Congress amended this provision and defined religious belief as "an individual's belief in a relation to a supreme being involving duties superior to those arising from any human relation, but [not including] essentially political, sociological, or philosophical views. . . ."

Despite the textual evidence of a congressional intent to condition exemption on the theistic belief, Justice TOM C. CLARK, for the Supreme Court, interpreted the provision as requiring only a sincere and meaningful belief occupying in the life of its possessor a place parallel to that filled by the belief in God of those admittedly qualified for the exemption. Seeger had argued that if section 6(j) granted exemptions only on the basis of conventional theistic belief, it amounted to an ESTABLISHMENT OF RELIGION. Facing the unattractive alternatives of finding section 6(j) unconstitutional or reading it in a sufficiently broad fashion so as to secularize the exemption, the majority chose the latter.

LEE, UNITED STATES v.

455 U.S. 252 (1982)

Kenneth L. Karst

Members of the Amish religion object, on religious grounds, to paying taxes or receiving benefits under the SOCIAL SECURITY ACT. An Amish employer of Amish workers claimed a constitutional right to refuse to pay Social Security taxes. The Supreme Court unanimously rejected that claim. Chief Justice WARREN E. BURGER, for the Court, accepted STRICT SCRUTINY as the appropriate STANDARD OF REVIEW in cases involving RELIGIOUS LIBERTY, but concluded that the government had established that mandatory participation was necessary to achieving the "overriding governmental interest" in maintaining the Social Security system. In a concurring opinion, Justice JOHN PAUL STEVENS argued against the strict scrutiny standard, saying that claimants of special religious exemptions from laws of general applicability must demonstrate "unique" reasons for being exempted—a standard that would be nearly impossible to meet.

RELIGION AND FRAUD

Leo Pfeffer

Few responsibilities are more sensitive and difficult to meet than drawing a line between punishable obtaining of property under false pretenses and constitutionally protected free exercise of religion. In the one major case to reach the Supreme Court, *United States v. Ballard* (1944), the Court split three ways in its decision.

Ballard involved the conviction of organizers of the "I Am" movement, indicted for using the mails to defraud because they falsely represented that they had supernatural powers to heal the incurably ill, and that as "Divine messengers" they had cured hundreds of afflicted persons through communication with Saint Germain, Jesus, and others. The trial court had instructed the jury that they should not decide whether these statements were literally true, but only whether the defendants honestly believed them to be true.

On appeal the majority of the Supreme Court agreed with the trial judge. Under the principles of SEPARATION OF CHURCH AND STATE and RELIGIOUS LIBERTY, it held, neither a jury nor any other organ of government had the competence to pass on whether certain religious experiences actually occurred. A jury could no more constitutionally decide that defendants had not shaken hands with Jesus, as they claimed, than they could determine that Jesus had not walked on the sea, as the Bible related. The limit of the jury's power was a determination whether defendants actually believed that what they recounted was true.

Chief Justice HARLAN FISKE STONE dissented on the ground that the prosecution should be allowed to prove that none of the alleged cures had been effected. On the other extreme Justice ROBERT H. JACKSON urged that the prosecution should not have been instituted in the first place, for few juries would find that the defendants honestly believed in something that was unbelievable. Nevertheless the majority decision remains the law, and is not likely to be OVERRULED after a half-century of acceptance.

Bibliography

PFEFFER, LEO (1953)1967 *Church, State and Freedom.* Boston: Beacon Press.

CULTS (RELIGIOUS) AND THE CONSTITUTION

Leo Pfeffer

The term "cult," currently used to designate a particular unpopular and feared new religious group often claiming a personal relationship between its leader and the Divinity, is not found explicitly in the original Constitution, the FIRST AMENDMENT's free exercise or establishment clause, or the FOURTEENTH AMENDMENT's EQUAL PROTECTION clause. Among the most prominent of these groups in recent times have been the Unification Church, the Worldwide Church of God, Inc., the Church of Scientology, and the International Society for Krishna Consciousness.

Cults, which have experienced varying degrees of discrimination and persecution by law enforcement officials, have consistently claimed that the Constitution does not sanction legal distinctions between them on the one hand and long-established and respected faiths on the other. They note, too, that historically most of the now well-established and fully respected faiths, including Baptists, Roman Catholics, Jews, Mormons, Christian Scientists, and Jehovah's Witnesses, have been subjected to governmental discrimination before achieving acceptability and equal treatment.

The claim to equal treatment was upheld in LARSON v. VALENTE (1982) where the Supreme Court held unconstitutional a Minnesota statute, enforced against the Unification Church, that imposed special registration and reporting requirements upon religious groups that received more than half of their income from nonmembers, a provision the Court found to have been aimed at unpopular cults. This provision, the Court said, constituted precisely the sort of official denominational preference and discrimination forbidden by the establishment clause in the absence of a compelling interest not otherwise amenable to protection. Moreover, the statute also violated the clause by authorizing excessive governmental entanglement with and politicizing of religion.

Compelling registration is only one comparatively mild sanction imposed by government upon religious cults. Although that term had not yet become popular in 1944, when *United States v. Ballard* was decided by the Supreme Court, that decision ruled unconstitutional a mail fraud conviction of "I Am" members who obtained donations by representing that their leader was divinely appointed with supernatural powers to heal the incurably ill. To allow a jury to determine the truth or falsity of religious doctrines, the Court said, would render vulnerable representations concerning the miracles of the New Testament, the divinity of Christ, life after death, and the power of prayer. The First Amendment permits only a determination whether the defendants themselves actually believed that what they recounted was true, not whether it was actually true.

Other devices applied against cults include denial of tax exemption, dissolution of the corporate structure and seizure of assets (as in CHURCH OF JESUS CHRIST OF LATTER DAY SAINTS v. UNITED STATES, 1890), and prosecution for disturbance of the peace (as in CANTWELL v. CONNECTICUT, 1940, involving Jehovah's Witnesses).

Whatever may have been the Court's response in earlier times, today it accords cults the same constitutional protection accorded to long-standing and commonly accepted faiths.

Bibliography

New York University Review of Law and Social Change   1979–1980   Volume 9, #1: *Proceedings of Conference on Alternative Religions, Government Control and the First Amendment.*